William Ernest Henley, Charles Whibley

A Book of English Prose, Character and Incident 1387-1649

William Ernest Henley, Charles Whibley

A Book of English Prose, Character and Incident 1387-1649

ISBN/EAN: 9783337075279

Printed in Europe, USA, Canada, Australia, Japan

Cover: Foto ©Thomas Meinert / pixelio.de

More available books at **www.hansebooks.com**

A BOOK OF
ENGLISH PROSE
CHARACTER AND
INCIDENT

By W. E. HENLEY

A BOOK OF VERSES. 5s. net.
LONDON VOLUNTARIES. 5s. net.
LYRA HEROICA. 3s. 6d.
VIEWS AND REVIEWS. 5s.

A BOOK OF ENGLISH PROSE

CHARACTER AND INCIDENT
1387-1649
SELECTED BY
WILLIAM ERNEST HENLEY
AND CHARLES WHIBLEY

METHUEN AND CO.
36 ESSEX STREET, W.C.
LONDON
1894

Edinburgh: T. and A. CONSTABLE, Printers to Her Majesty

PREFACE

It is not the object of this Book of Prose to illustrate the history of the English language, or to trace the development of the English sentence. Still less has it been our purpose to collect within two covers any such purple patches of diction as the taste and fashion of the past have marked out for admiration. Our bias is neither philological nor fantastical. Beyond the essential resolve to maintain a scrupulous standard of style, we have been guided in our selection by two definite principles: (1) that each passage should be complete in itself; (2) that each should relate a single incident or unfold a single character. It seemed that these principles, liberally interpreted, would at once give the book a concordant character, and ensure for every extract a separate and individual interest. Moreover, since our anthology is for young as well as for old, we have preferred before the prose of reflection and analysis the prose of adventure and romance—surely the best motives for sound and spirited English?

PREFACE

In the matter of length, we have permitted ourselves the widest latitude, and this for an obvious reason. The limits of a poem are generally set by its maker. A passage of prose cannot always be disengaged, and even where disengagement is possible, you must follow the episode to its legitimate conclusion. Also, if some writers are absent whose presence was anticipated, it is not that they have been overlooked, but that they were found inadmissable. On the other hand, many are present whose names are not familiar to the readers of anthologies; and it is believed that the consideration of these will strengthen an opinion that the level of prose our distant fathers held is far higher than our own.

It remains to add that the passages are quoted verbally; that the spelling has been modernised or Anglicised; and that the very few places where editing was found necessary are distinguished by dots of omission.

W. E. H.
C. W.

CONTENTS

	PAGE
JOHN TREVISA (1387).	
A Character of Irishmen	1
SIR JOHN MAUNDEVILLE (1410).	
The Court of the Great Chan	3
THE PASTON LETTERS (1455)	
The Battle of St. Albans	14
WILLIAM CAXTON (1474)	
The Dolorous Shirt	19
WILLIAM DE MACHLINIA (1482).	
How the Monk saw Heaven	26
SIR THOMAS MALORY (1485).	
The Adventure of the Chariot	30
JOHN FISHER (1505).	
A Mourning Remembrance	36
THE PASTON LETTERS (1506).	
A Pageant	42
SIR THOMAS MORE (1513).	
The Killing of Lord Hastings	44
LORD BERNERS (1523).	
Wat Tyler's Ending	47

CONTENTS

JOHN TIPTOFT, EARL OF WORCESTER (1530).
    The Conquest of Britain 52

SIR THOMAS ELYOT (1531).
    The Image of Detraction 58

THOMAS CRANMER (1533).
    The Crowning of Ann Boleyn 61

JOHN BELLENDEN (1536).
    A Roman Victory 63

ROGER ASCHAM (1545).
    Seeing the Wind 68

HUGH LATIMER (1548).
    A Character of London 70

RALPH ROBINSON (1551).
    Ralph Hythlodaye 72

GEORGE CAVENDISH (1557).
    Wolsey's Arrest 76

JOHN FOXE (1563).
    Two Bishops:—
        I. Nicholas Ridley 83
        II. Stephen Gardiner 88

WILLIAM ADLINGTON (1566).
    A Pretty Theft 91

THOMAS HARMAN (1567).
    An Old Man's Misadventure 95

LINDSAY OF PITSCOTTIE (1570).
    An Escape 97

CONTENTS

	PAGE
JOHN KNOX (1572).	
The Killing of David Beaton	101
JAMES MELVILL (1574).	
A Scot Abroad	107
RAPHAEL HOLINSHED (1577).	
Agincourt	113
SIR THOMAS NORTH (1579).	
The Young Alexander	127
SIR THOMAS NORTH (1579).	
The Banishing of Coriolanus	132
JOHN LYLY (1579).	
England	136
JOHN FLORIO (1580).	
How we came to the Town of Hochelaga	145
HAKLUYT: NAVIGATIONS (1584).	
A Coronation	149
REGINALD SCOT (1584).	
A False Witch	154
HAKLUYT: NAVIGATIONS (1584)	
The First Landing in Virginia	158
SIR FULK GREVILLE (1586).	
An Affair of Honour	166
SIR WALTER RALEIGH (1591).	
The Last Fight of the *Revenge*	169
SIR JAMES MELVILLE (1593).	
Gloriana	176

HAKLUYT: **NAVIGATIONS** (1593).
    John Davys the Navigator 182

THOMAS NASH (1594).
    The Divine Aretine **198**

SIR WALTER RALEIGH (1596).
    Discovering Guiana 199

WILLIAM SHAKESPEARE (1598).
    The Men in Buckram **204**

SIR JOHN HAYWARD (1599).
    A Plot against the Throne 208

PHILEMON HOLLAND (1600).
    The Passage of the Alps 216

THOMAS DANETT (1601).
    The Most Christian King **224**

JOHN FLORIO (1603).
    Julius Caesar 235

RICHARD KNOLLES (1603).
    Tamerlane **239**

JOSEPH HALL (1608)
    Two Characters :—
        I. The Patient Man 249
        II. The Slothful Man 250

THOMAS DEKKER (1609).
    Character of a Gallant 252

CONTENTS

SIR THOMAS OVERBURY (1616).
Three Characters:—
    I. A Worthy Commander in the Wars . . 257
    II. A Tinker 258
    III. A Fair and Happy Milk-maid . . . 259

THOMAS SHELTON (1620).
The Delightful Passage of the Puppet-play . . 261

SIR TOBIE MATHEW (1620).
The Proving of Alipius 269

FRANCIS BACON, VISCOUNT ST. ALBANS (1622).
A Wonder for Wise Men 273

JOHN DONNE (1624).
Steps in his Sickness:—
    Meditation I. 282
    Meditation II. 283
    Meditation III. 284
    Meditation IV. 286

PURCHAS HIS PILGRIMS (1625).
Two Pilgrims:—
    I. The Death of John Davys 288
    II. An Ordeal by Fire 291

JOHN EARLE (1628).
Some University Characters:—
    I. An Old College Butler 293
    II. A Downright Scholar 294
    III. A Mere Young Gentleman of the University 296
    IV. An University Dun 297

CONTENTS

SIR KENELM DIGBY (1629).
    An Unequal Combat 298

WILLIAM HABINGTON (1635).
    Three Characters :—
        I. A Mistress 303
        II. A Wife 305
        III. A Friend 306

REV. ROBERT BLAIR (1636).
    A Bout with the Adversary 308

SIR WILLIAM MONSON (1636).
    A Stratagem 311

REV. PRINCIPAL BAILLIE (1639).
    A Covenanting Army 319

ROBERT CAREY, EARL OF MONMOUTH (1639).
    Carey's Raid 326

JAMES MABBE (1640).
    A Night's Adventures 331

SIR ROBERT NAUNTON (1641).
    Two Favourites :—
        I. Leicester 336
        II. Raleigh 339

BEN JONSON (1641).
    Discoveries :—
        I. De Shakespeare Nostrat. . . . 342
        II. Dominus Verulamius 343
        III. The True Artificer 346

CONTENTS

REV. THOMAS FULLER (1642).
    Sir Francis Drake 347

REV. THOMAS FULLER (1642).
    The True Gentleman 355

JOHN MILTON (1644).
    A Vision of England 358

JAMES HOWEL (1645).
    A King of France 362

CAPTAIN HENRY BELL (1646).
    Luther at Worms 366

LORD HERBERT OF CHERBURY (1648).
    A Private Brawl 370

WILLIAM DRUMMOND OF HAWTHORNDEN (1649).
    Flodden Field 374

BIBLIOGRAPHY 385

ENGLISH PROSE
1387-1649

ENGLISH PROSE

A CHARACTER OF IRISHMEN

SOLINUS saith that men of this land be strange of nation, houseless, and great fighters, and account right and wrong all for one, and be single of clothing, scarce of meat, cruel of heart, and angry of speech, and drink first blood of dead men that be slain, and then wash their face therewith; and hold them appeased with flesh and fruit instead of meat, and with milk instead of drink, and they use much plays and idleness and hunting, and travail full little. In their childhood they be hard nourished and hard fed, and they be unseemly of manners and of clothing, and have breeches and hosen all one of wool, and straight hoods that stretch a cubit over the shoulders behind, and black faldings instead of mantles and cloaks. Also saddles, boots, and spurs they use none when they ride; but they drive their horses with a chambered yard [1] in the over end, instead of barnacles and of britels of reest [2]; and they use bridles that let not their horses of their meat. They fight unarmed, naked in body; nevertheless with two darts and spears and with broad sparths.[3] They fight with one hand, and when other weapons fail, they have good pebble stones ready at hand. These men forsake tilling of land and keep pasture for beasts: they use long beards and long locks hanging down behind their nolls. They use no craft of flax and wool, of metal, neither of merchandise; but give them all to idleness and to sloth, and count rest for liking and freedom for riches. And though Scotland, the daughter of Ireland, use harp, timbre, and

Trevisa
1387

---

[1] Bent rod.   [2] Bits of arrest.   [3] Axes.

A CHARACTER OF IRISHMEN

Trevisa
1387

tabor (and Wales uses harp and pipe and tabor), nevertheless Irishmen be cunning in two manner of instruments of music, in the harp and timbre that is armed with wire and with strings of brass. In the which instruments they play hastily and swiftly; they make well merry harmony and melody with well thick tunes, warbles, and notes; and they begin from B moll, and play privily under the deep sound of the great strings, and turn again into the same, so that the greatest part of the craft hide the craft; as it would seem as though the craft so hidden should be ashamed, an it were i-take. These men be of evil manners and of living; they pay no tithings, they wed lawfully no wives, they spare not their allies,[1] but the brother weds his brother's wife. They be busy for to betray their neighbours and others. They bear sparths in their hands instead of staves, and fight therewith against them that trust to them best. The men be variable and unsteadfast, treacherous and guileful. Who that deals with them needs more to beware of guile than of craft, of peace than of burning brands, of honey than of gall, of malice than of knighthood. They have such manners that they be not strong in war and battle, neither true in peace. They become gossips to them that they would falsely betray in gosibrede [2] and holy kindred; each drinketh the other's blood when it is shed. They love somdel [3] their nurses and their playing feres,[4] which that suck the same milk that they suck while they be children. And they pursue their brethren, their cousins, and their other kin; and despise their kin, while they be alive, and wreak their death, an they be slain. Among them long usage and evil custom hath so long endured, that it hath made the mastery, and turneth among themselves treason into kynd [5] so far forth, that as they be traitors by kynd, so aliens and men of strange lands that wone long among them draw after the manner of their company, and scape well

[1] Relations. [2] Fellowship. [3] Sometimes.
[4] Companions. [5] Nature.

unnethe,[1] but they be besmutted with the shrewdness and become traitors also. . . . There be many men in this land wonderful and evil shaped in limbs and in body. For in their limbs lacketh the benefice of kynd, so that nowhere be none better shaped, than they that be here well shaped, and nowhere none worse shaped, than they that be here evil shaped. And skilfully kynd, hurt and defouled by wickedness of living, bringeth forth such foul grooms and evil shaped of them that with unlawful wedding, with foul manners and evil living, so wickedly defoul kynd. In this land and in Wales, old wives and women were wont, and be yet (as me pleyneth) oft for to shape themselves in likeness to hares, for to milk their neighbour's kine, and so steal their milk, and oft greyhounds run after them and pursue them, and ween that they be hares. Also some by craft of necromancy make fat swine (that be red of colour) and none other, and sell them in cheping and in fairs; but anon as these swine pass any water they turn again into their own kynd, where it be straw, hay, grass, other turves. But these swine may not be kept by no manner of craft for to dure in likeness of swine over three days. Among these wonders and others take heed that in the uttermost ends of the world full oft new marvels and wonders, as though kynd played with larger leave privily and far in the ends than openly and nigh in the middle. Therefore in this island be many grisly marvels and wonders.

Trevisa
1387

John Trevisa.

[1] Hardly.

THE COURT OF THE GREAT CHAN

NOW shall I tell you the governance of the Court of the Great Chan, when he maketh solemn feasts, which is principally four times in the year. The first feast is of his

Maundeville
1410

THE COURT OF THE GREAT CHAN

Maunde-
ville
1410

birth; the second is of his presentation in their temple, such as they clepe here Moseache, where they make a manner of circumcision; and the other two feasts are of his idols. The first feast of the idol **is,** when he is first put into their temple and throned. The other feast is, when the idol beginneth first to speak **or** work miracles. More there are not of solemn feasts, but if he marry any of his children. Now understand, that at each of these feasts, **he** hath great multitude of people, well ordained and well arrayed, by thousands by hundreds, and by tens. And every man knoweth well what service **he** shall do; and every man giveth so good **heed** and so good attendance to his service, that no man findeth any default.

And there be first ordained four thousand Barons, mighty and rich, for to govern and make ordinance for the feast, and for to serve the Emperor. And these solemn feasts are made without, in halls and tents made of cloths of gold and of tartaries,[1] full nobly. And all the Barons have crowns of gold upon their heads, full noble and rich, full of precious stones and great pearls orient. And they are all clothed in clothes of gold, or of tartaries, or of camokas,[2] so richly and perfectly, that no man in the world can amend it, nor better devise it. And all these robes are orfrayed[3] all about, and dubbed full of precious stones and of great orient pearls, full richly. And they may well do so, for cloths of gold and of silk **are** cheaper there by much than are cloths of wool.

And these four thousand barons are divided in four companies: and every thousand **is** clothed in **cloths** all of one colour, **and** so well arrayed and so richly, **that it is** marvel to behold. The first thousand, that is **of** Dukes, of Earls, **of** Marquises, and of Admirals, all clothed **in** cloths of gold, with tissues **of** green silk, and bordered with gold, full of precious stones, **in** manner as I have said before. The

[1] Eastern fabrics.   [2] A silk fabric.
[3] Embroidered with gold.

second thousand is all in cloths diapered of red silk, all
wrought with gold, and the orfrayes set full of great pearls
and precious stones, full nobly wrought. The third thousand
is clothed in cloths of silk, of purple, or of Inde. And the
fourth thousand is in clothes of yellow. And all their
clothes are so nobly and richly wrought with gold and
precious stones and rich pearls, that if a man of this country
had but only one of their robes, he might well say that he
should never be poor. For the gold and the precious stones,
and the great orient pearls are of greater value on this half
the sea than they are beyond the sea in those countries.

And when they are thus apparelled, they go two and two
together, full ordinately, before the Emperor, without speech
of any word, save only inclining to him. And every one of them
beareth a tablet of jasper, or of ivory, or of crystal; and the
minstrels go before them, sounding their instruments of
divers melody. And when the first thousand is thus passed,
and hath made its muster, it withdraws it on that one side;
and then entereth that other second thousand, and doth right
so, in the same manner of array and countenance as did the
first; and after the third, and then the fourth, and none of
them saith not one word.

And at one side of the Emperor's table sit many Philosophers, who are proved for wise men in many divers sciences;
as of astronomy, necromancy, geomancy, pyromancy, hydro-
mancy, of augury, and of many other sciences. And every
one of them hath before him astrolabes of gold, some spheres,
some the brain-pan of a dead man, some vessels of gold full
of gravel or sand, some vessels of gold full of coals burning,
some vessels of gold full of water and of wine and of oil, and
some horologes of gold, made full nobly and richly wrought,
and many other manner of instruments after their sciences.
And at certain hours, when they think time, they say to
certain Officers who stand before them, ordained for the time
to fulfil their commandments: 'Make peace.' And then say

Maunde-
ville
1410

Maundeville 1410 — the Officers: 'Now peace, listen.' And after **that,** saitn another of the Philosophers: 'Every man do reverence, and incline to the Emperor, who is God'**s son and** Sovereign Lord of all the **World**; for now is time.' And then **every** man boweth his head towards the earth. And then commandeth the same Philosopher again: 'Stand up.' And they do so. And at another hour saith another Philosopher: 'Put your little finger in your ears.' And anon they do so. And at another hour saith **another Philosopher:** 'Put your hand before your mouth.' **And anon** they do **so.** And at another hour saith another Philosopher: 'Put your hand upon your head.' And after **that** he biddeth them to do their hand away; and they do so.

And so, from hour to hour, they command certain things. And they say that those things have divers significations. And I asked them privily what those things betokened. And one of the Masters told me that the bowing of the head at that hour betokened this, that all those that bowed their heads should evermore after be obeissant and true to the Emperor, and never for gifts, nor for promise in no kind be false nor traitor unto him for good nor evil. And the putting of the little finger in the ear betokeneth, as they say, that none of them shall not hear spoken no contrarious thing to the Emperor, but that he shall tell it anon to his council, or discover it to some men that will make relation to the Emperor, though he were his father or brother or son. And so forth of all other things that are done by the Philosophers, they told me the causes of many divers things. And trust right well in certain that no man doth no thing to the Emperor that **belongeth to** him, neither clothing, nor bread, nor wine, nor bath, nor other thing that belongeth to him, but at certain hours, **as** his Philosophers will devise.

And if there fall war in any side to the Emperor, anon the Philosophers come and say their advice after their calculations, and counsel the Emperor of their advice by their **sciences;** so that the Emperor doth nothing without their counsel. And when the Philosophers have done and performed their commandments, then the Minstrels begin to do their minstrelsy, every one on their instruments, each after the other, with all the melody that they can devise. And when they have done a good while, one of the Officers of the Emperor goeth up on a high stage, wrought full curiously, and crieth and saith with a loud voice: 'Make peace.' And then every man is still. And then, anon after, all the Lords that are of the Emperor's lineage, nobly arrayed in rich clothes of gold, and royally apparelled on white steeds, as many as may well suc[1] him at that time, are ready to make their presents to the Emperor. And then saith the steward of the court to the Lords, by name, 'N. of N.,' and nameth first the most noble and the worthiest by name, and saith: 'Be ye ready with such a number of white horses for to serve the Emperor your Sovereign Lord.' And, to another lord, he saith: 'N. of N., be ye ready with such a number to serve your Sovereign Lord.' And to another, right so. And to all the Lords of the Emperor's lineage, one after the other, as they are of estate.

And when they are all cleped, they enter each after the other, and present the white horses to the Emperor, and then go their way. And then after, all the other Barons, every one of them, give him presents, or jewels, or some other thing, after that they are of estate. And then, after them, all the Prelates of their law, and religious men and others; and every man giveth him something. And when all men have thus presented the Emperor, the greatest of dignity of the Prelates giveth him a blessing, saying an orison of their law. And then begin the Minstrels to make their minstrelsy on divers instruments, with all the melody that they can devise.

And when they have done their craft, then they bring before the Emperor lions, leopards, and other divers beasts,

Maundeville
1410

---

[1] Follow.

THE COURT OF THE GREAT CHAN

Maunde-
ville
1410

and eagles, and vultures, and other divers fowls, and fishes, and serpents, for to do him reverence. And then come jugglers and enchanters that do many marvels; for they make to come in the air the sun and the moon, beseeming, to every man's sight. And after they make the night so dark that no man may see no thing. And after they **make** the day **to come** again, fair and pleasant, with bright sun, to every **man's** sight. And then they bring in dances **of the** fairest **damsels** of the world, and richest arrayed.

And after they make to come in other damsels bringing cups of gold, full of milk **of** divers beasts, and give drink to **Lords and to** Ladies. **And then they make** knights to joust in arms full lustily; and they run together a great random and frush[1] together full fiercely; and they break their spears so rudely that the tronchouns[2] fly in sprotes[3] and pieces **all** about the hall. **And** then they make to come in hunting, for the hart and for the boar, with hounds running with open mouth. And many other things they do by craft of their enchantments, that it is marvel for **to see.** And such **plays of** disport they **make, until** the taking up of the **boards.**

This Great Chan hath full great people for to serve him, as I have told you before. For he hath of Minstrels the number of thirteen cumants,[4] but they abide not always with him. For all the Minstrels that come before him, of what nation they be of, they be witholden with him, as of his household, and entered **in his** books, **as** for his own men. And after that, **where that ever** they go, evermore they claim for Minstrels of the Great Chan; and, under that title, all Kings **and** Lords cherish them the more with gifts and all things. **And** therefore he hath so great multitude of them. And he **hath of** certain **men, as** though they were yeomen, that **keep** birds, as ostriches, gerfaucons, sparrow-hawks, falcons,

---

[1] Crash.　　　[2] Staves.　　　[3] Splinters.
[4] Ten-thousands.

gentles, lanyers,¹ sacres,² sacrettes,³ popinjays well speaking, and birds singing. And also of wild beasts, as of elephants, tame and other, baboons, apes, **marmozets**, and other divers beasts; the mountance⁴ of fifteen cumants of Yeomen.

Maundeville 1410

And of Physicians Christian he hath two hundred. **And of** Leeches that are Christians he hath two hundred and ten. **And** of Leeches and Physicians that are Saracens, twenty; but he trusteth more in the Christian Leeches than in the Saracens. And his other common household is without number; and they all **have all** necessaries and all that they need of the Emperor's court. And he **has in his** court many Barons, as servitors, that **are** Christians and converted to good faith by the preaching **of** religious Christian men that dwell with him, but there be many more that will not have it known that they are Christians.

This Emperor may dispend as much as he will, **without** estimation. For he dispendeth not nor maketh any money but of leather imprinted, or of paper. And of that money is some of greater price and some of less price, after the diversity of his statutes. **And** when that money has run so long that it beginneth to waste, then men bear it to the Emperor's treasury, and then they take **new** money for the old. **And** that money goeth throughout all the country and throughout all his provinces. For there, and beyond them, they make no money neither of gold nor of silver. And therefore, he may dispend enough, and outrageously. **And of gold and** silver that **men bear** in his country, he maketh ceilings, pillars and pavements in his palace, and other divers things that he liketh. This Emperor hath in his chamber, in one of the pillars of gold, **a ruby and a** carbuncle of half a foot long, which in the **night** giveth so great clearness and shining, that it is as light as day. And he hath many other precious stones, and many other **rubies and** carbuncles, but those are the greatest and the most precious.

¹ Hawks.　² A falcon (female).　³ A falcon (male).　⁴ Amount.

Maundeville 1410

This Emperor dwelleth **in summer in a** city that is toward the north, **that is called Saduz, and there** is cold enough. And in winter he dwelleth in a city **that** is called Camaaleche, and that is **a** hot country. But the country where he dwelleth in **most** commonly is in Gaydo, or in Jong, **that** is a good country **and a** temperate, after that the country is there; but to men of this country, it were passing hot. And when this Emperor will ride from one country to another, he ordaineth four hosts of his folk, of the which the first host goeth before him a day's journey. For that host shall be lodged **the** night where the emperor shall lie upon the morrow. And there shall every man have all manner of victuals and necessaries that are needful at the Emperor's costages.

And in this first host is the number of people fifty cumants; **what** of horse, what of foot, of the which every cumant amounteth to ten thousand, as I have told you before. And another host goeth on the right side of the Emperor, nigh half a journey from him. And another goeth on the left side of him in the same wise. And in every host is as much multitude of people as in the first host. And then after cometh the fourth host, that is much more than any of the other, and that goeth behind him, the mountance of a bow's draught. And every host hath its day's journey ordained in certain places, **where** they shall be lodged at night, and there they **shall have** all that they need. And if it befall that one of the **host** die, anon they put another in his place, so that the number shall ever be whole.

And you shall understand that the Emperor, in his proper person, rideth not **as** other great lords do beyond, but if he list to go privily **with** few men, for to be unknown. And else he rideth in a chariot with four wheels, upon the which is made a fair chamber; and it is made of a certain wood that comes out of Paradise Terrestrial, which they call *lignum aloes*, that the floods of Paradise bring out at diverse seasons, **as I have** told you here before. And this chamber is full well smelling, because of the wood that it is made of. And all this chamber is covered within of plates of fine gold, dubbed with precious stones and great pearls. And four elephants and four great destreres,[1] all white and covered with rich covertures, leading the chariot. And four, or five, or six of the greatest Lords ride about this chariot, full richly arrayed and full nobly, so that no man shall nigh the chariot but only those lords, but if the Emperor call any man to him that he lists to speak withal. And above the chamber of this chariot the Emperor sitteth in, are set upon a perch four, five, or six gerfaucons, to that intent, that when the Emperor seeth any wild fowl, he may take it at his own list, and have the disport and the play of the flight, first with one and after with another; and so he taketh his sport passing by the country.

Maundeville
1410

And no man rideth before him of his company, but all after him. And no man dare not come nigh the chariot by a bow-draught, but those Lords only that are about him; and all the host come fairly after him, in great multitude. And also such another chariot, with such hosts, ordained and arrayed, go with the Empress upon another side, each by itself, with four hosts, right as the Emperor did, but not with so great multitude of people. And his eldest son goeth by another way in another chariot, in the same manner. So that there is between them so great multitude of folk, that it is marvel to tell it. And no man should trow the number, but he had seen it. And sometimes it happens that when he will not go far, and that it liketh him to have the Empress and his children with him, then they go all together; and here folk are meddled[2] in one company, and divided in four parts only.

And you shall understand that the empire of this Great Chan is divided into twelve provinces; and every province hath more than two thousand cities, and towns without number. This country is full great. For it hath twelve

---

[1] Horses.   [2] Mixed.

THE COURT OF THE GREAT CHAN

Maundeville 1410

principal Kings in twelve provinces; and each of those Kings hath many Kings under him; and all they are obeissant to the Great Chan. And his land and his lordship dureth so far that a man may **not** go from ahead, neither by sea nor land, the space of seven years. And through the deserts of his lordship, there, as men may find no towns, there are inns ordained at every journey, to receive both man and horse, in the which they shall find plenty of victuals and of all things that they need for to go by the country.

And there is a marvellous custom in that country (but **is** profitable), that if there happen any contrarious thing that should be prejudice or grievance to the Emperor, in any kind, **anon** the Emperor hath tidings thereof and full knowledge in **a** day, though it be three or four journeys from him or more. For his ambassadors take their dromedaries, or their horses, and they prick in all that ever they may toward one of the inns; and when they come there, anon they blow a horn, and anon they of the inn know well enough that there are tidings to warn the Emperor of some rebellion against him. And then anon they make other men ready, in all haste that they may, to bear letters, and prick in all that ever they may, till they come to the other inns with their letters; and then they make fresh men ready, to prick forth with the letters towards the Emperor, while the last bringer resteth him, and baiteth his dromedary or his horse; and so from inn to inn, till it come to the Emperor. And thus anon he hath hasty tidings of anything that beareth charge by his couriers, that run so hastily throughout all the country.

And, also, **when** the Emperor sendeth his couriers hastily throughout his **land,** each of them hath a large thong full of small **bells**; and when they nigh near the inns of other couriers that are also ordained by the journeys, they ring their bells; and anon the other couriers make them ready, and run their way unto another inn; and thus runneth one to another, **full** speedily **and** swiftly, till the Emperor's intent be served, in all haste. And these couriers are called *Chydydo*, after their language, that is to say, a messenger.

Maundeville 1410

Also when the Emperor goeth from one country to another, as I have told you here before, and he passeth through cities and towns, every man makes a fire before his door, and putteth therein powder of good gums, that are sweet smelling, for to make good savour to the Emperor. And all the people kneel down against him, and do him great reverence. And there, where religious Christian men dwell, as they do in many cities in the land, they go before him with procession, with cross and holy water; and they sing, *Veni Creator, Spiritus*, with a high voice, and go towards him. And when he heareth them, he commandeth to his lords to ride beside him, that the religious men may come to him.

And when they are nigh him with the cross, then he doth adown his galiot, which sitteth upon his head in the manner of a chaplet, that is made of gold, and precious stones, and great pearls. And it is so rich that men prize it to the value of a realm, in that country. And then he kneeleth to the cross. And then the Prelate of the religious men saith before him certain orisons, and giveth him a blessing with the cross; and he inclineth to the blessing full devoutly. And then the Prelate giveth him some manner of fruit, to the number of nine, in a platter of silver, with pears or apples or other manner fruit. And he taketh one; and then men give to the other lords that are about him. For the custom is such that no stranger shall come before him but if he give him some manner thing, after the old law, that says, *Nemo accedat in conspectu meo vacuus*. And then the Emperor saith to the religious men that they withdraw them again, that they be not hurt nor harmed of the great multitude of horse that come behind him. And also in the same manner do the monks that dwell there to the Empresses that pass by them, and to his eldest son; and to every one of them they present fruit.

THE BATTLE OF ST. ALBANS

Maunde-
ville
1410

And you shall understand that **the people** that he hath so many hosts of **about** him, and about his wives and his sons, they dwell not continually with him, but always, when it liketh him, they are sent for; and after, when they **have** done, they return to their own households, save only those that are dwelling with him in household for **to** serve him, and his wives, and sons for **to govern** his household. And albeit, that **the** others are departed from him after they **have** performed **their service,** yet there abideth continually **with** him in court fifty thousand men at horse, and twenty thousand men a foot, without Minstrels **and those** that keep wild beasts and diverse birds, of the which I have told you the number before. **Under** the firmament, is not so great a lord, nor so mighty, nor so rich, **as the Great** Chan; neither Prester John, that is Emperor of the High **Inde, nor the Sultan of** Babylon, nor the Emperor of Persia.

All these **are not** in comparison to the Great Chan, neither of might, nor of nobleness, nor of royalty, nor of riches; for in all these he passeth all earthly princes. Wherefore it is great harm that he believeth not faithfully in God. And, nevertheless, he will gladly hear speak of God; and he suffereth well that Christian men dwell in his lordship, and that men of his faith **be** made Christian men, if they will, throughout all his country. **For** he defendeth no man to hold any law **other** than he liketh.

Sir John Maundeville.

THE BATTLE OF ST. ALBANS

Paston
1455

BE it known and had in mind that the 21st day of May the 33rd year **of** the reign of King Henry the Sixth, our sovereign Lord King took his journey from Westminster toward St. Albans, and rested at Watford all night; and on the morrow betimes he came to St. Albans, and with him on his party assembled under his banner the Duke of Buckingham, the Duke of Somerset, the Earl of Penbroke, the Earl of Northumberland, the Earl of Devonshire, the Earl of Stafford, the Earl of Dorset, the Earl of Wiltshire, the Lord Clifford, the Lord Dudley, the Lord Burnys, the Lord Rose, with other divers knights, squires, and other gentlemen and yeomen to the number of 2000 and more. And upon the 22d day of the said month above rehearsed assembled the Duke of York, and with him came in company the Earl of Salisbury, the Earl of Warwick, with divers knights and squires unto their party into the field, called the Key Field, beside St. Albans. Furthermore, our said sovereign Lord the King, hearing and knowing of the said Duke's coming with other Lords aforesaid, pitcheth his banner at the place called Boslaw in St. Petrus Street, which place was called aforetime past Sandeford, and commandeth the ward and barriers to be kept in strong wise; for the said Duke of York abiding in the field aforesaid from seven of the clock in the morn till it was almost ten, without any stroke smitten on either party.

The said Duke sent to the King our sovereign Lord, by the advice of his council, praying and beseeching him to take him as his true man and humble subject; and to consider and to tender at the reverence of Almighty God, and in way of charity the true intent of his coming —to be good and gracious sovereign Lord to his liegemen, which, with all their power and might, will be ready at all times to live and die with him in his right. And to what thing it should like his Majesty Royal to command him, if it be his worship, keeping right of the Crown and welfare of the land: 'Moreover, gracious Lord, please it your Majesty Royal of your great goodness and righteousness to incline your will to hear and feel the righteous part of us your subjects and liegemen; first, praying and beseeching to our Lord Jesus of His high and mighty power to give unto you virtue and prudence, and

Paston 1455

that through the mediation of the glorious martyr St. Alban to give you very knowledge to know the intent of our assembling at this time; for God that is in heaven knoweth that our intent is rightful and true. **And** therefore we pray unto Almighty Lord Jesus these words—*Domine sis clipeus defensionis nostrae.* Wherefore, gracious Lord, please it your high Majesty to deliver such as we will **accuse,** and they to have like, as they have deserved and done, **and** ye to be honourabled and worshipped as most rightful King **and** our governor. For and **we** shall now at this time be promised, as afore this time is **not** unknown, of promise broken which full faith fully hath **been** promised, and thereupon great **oaths made,** we will **not now cease for** none such promise, surety, nor other, till **we have him** which have deserved death, or else we to die therefore.'

And to that answered the King our sovereign Lord, and said: 'I, King Henry, charge and command that **no** manner person, of what degree, or state, or condition that ever he be, abide not, but void the field, and not be so hardy to make any resistance against me in mine own realm; for I shall know what traitor dare be so bold to raise a people in mine own land, wherethrough I am in great disease and heaviness. And by the faith that I owe to St. Edward and to the Crown of England, I shall destroy them every mother son, and they be hanged, and drawn, and quartered, that may be taken afterward, of them to have ensample to all such traitors to beware to make any such rising of people within my land, and so traitorly to abide her King and governor. **And,** for a conclusion, rather than they shall have any Lord here with me at this time, I shall this day, for her sake, and **in** this quarrel myself live or die.'

Which answer came to the Duke of York, the which Duke, by the advice of the Lords of his Council, said unto him these words: 'The King our sovereign Lord will not be reformed at our beseeching nor prayer, nor will not under-

THE BATTLE OF ST. ALBANS

stand the intent that we be come hither and assembled for and gathered at this time; but only is full purpose, and there none other way but that he will with all his power pursue us, and if we be taken, to give us a shameful death, losing our liveload[1] and goods, and our hairs shamed for ever. And therefore, sith it will be none otherwise but that we shall utterly die, better it is for us to die in the field than cowardly to be put to a great rebuke and a shameful death; moreover, considering in what peril England stands in at this hour, therefore every man help to help power for the right thereof, to redress the mischief that now reigneth, and to quit us like men in this quarrel; praying to that Lord that is King of Glory, that reigneth in the kingdom celestial, to keep us and save us this day in our right, and through the help of His holy grace we may be made strong to withstand the great abominable and cruel malice of them that purpose fully to destroy us with shameful death. We therefore, Lord, pray to Thee to be our comfort and defender, saying the words aforesaid, *Domine sis clipeus defensionis nostrae.*'

And when this was said, the said Duke of York, and the said Earl of Salisbury, and the Earl of Warwick, between eleven and twelve of the clock at noon, they broke into the town in three divers places and several places of the foresaid street. The King being then in the place of Edmond Westley, hunderdere[2] of the said town of St. Albans, commandeth to slay all manner men of lords, knights, and squires, and yeomen that might be taken of the foresaid Duke's of York. This done, the foresaid Lord Clifford kept strongly the barriers that the said Duke of York might not in any wise, with all the power that he had, enter nor break into the town. The Earl of Warwick, knowing thereof, took and gathered his men together, and furiously brake in by the

Paston 1455

---

[1] Lands from which an income was derived.
[2] Headman of an hundred.

Paston 1455

garden sides between the sign of the Key and the sign of the Chequer in Holwell **Street**; and anon **as** they were within **the** town, suddenly they blew up trumpets, and set a cry with a shout **and a great voice,** ' A Warwick ! A Warwick ! A Warwick **!' and into** that time the Duke of York might never have entry into the town; and they with strong hand kept it, and mightily fought together, and anon, forthwith after the breaking **in,** they set **on them** manfully. And as of Lords of name were slain the **Lord** Clifford, the **Duke of Somerset, the Earl** of Northumberland, Sir Bertram Entuwysselle, Knight; **and of men of court,** William Zouch, **John** Batryaux, Raaff **of Bapthorp, and his** son, William **Corbyn, squires;** William Cotton, receiver **of** the Duchy of Lancaster; Gilbert Starbrok, squire; Malmer Pagentoun, William Botelore, yeomen; Roger **Mercroft,** the King's messenger; Halyn, the King's porter; Raufe Wyllerby; and 25 more, which their names be not **yet known.** And of them that be slain **be** buried in **St. Albans 48.** And at **this** same time **were hurt Lords of** name—the King, our **sovereign** Lord, in the **neck with an arrow;** the Duke of Buckingham, with an arrow in the visage; the Lord of Stafford in the hand, with **an arrow; the** Lord of Dorset, **sore** hurt that he might not **go, but he was** carried home in a cart; and Wenlok, knight, in likewise in a cart sore hurt; and other divers knights and squires sore hurt. The Earl **of** Wiltshire, Thorp, and many others fled, and left their harness behind them cowardly, and the substance of the King's party were despoiled of horse and harness. This done, the said Lords, that is to wot, the Duke of York, the Earl of Salisbury, **the Earl** of Warwick, came to the King, **our** sovereign Lord, and on their knees besought him of grace and forgiveness of that they had done in his presence, **and** besought him of his highness to take them as his true liegemen, saying that **they** never intended hurt to his own **person,** and therefore **the** King our sovereign Lord took them to grace, and so desired them to cease their people, and that there should no more harm be done; and they obeyed his commandment, and let make a cry on the King's name that all manner of people should cease and not so hardy to strike any stroke more after the proclamation of the cry; and so ceased the said battle, *Deo gratias.*

And on the morrow the King and the said Duke, with other certain Lords, came in to the Bishop's of London, and there kept residence with joy and solemnity, concluding to hold the Parliament at London, the 9th day of July next coming.

The Paston Letters.

Paston
1455

THE DOLOROUS SHIRT

WHEN Hercules had read this letter, he understood well what it contained, and was smitten with remorse of conscience. By this remorse he understood that virtue was fouled in him; he was then all pensive, and so much prived from pleasance that none durst come to him in a great while and space, save only they that brought to him meat and drink; neither Yole durst not go to him. Lycas that had brought this letter was there awaiting and attending the answer long; no man could know whereof proceeded the solitude of Hercules, nor the cause why he withdrew him from the people. In the end, when Hercules had been long pensive, and had thought upon all his affairs, and that he had to do for to withdraw him and to eslonge[1] him from Yole, he departed from his chamber on a day, saying that he would go and make sacrifice to the god Apollo upon the mount named Oethea, and commanded and defended upon pain of death that no man should follow him, reserved Philotes. Of adventure as he issued out of his palace,

Caxton
1474

[1] Estrange.

accompanied only of **Philotes, for to go upon** the mount, he met Lycas. Lycas made to him reverence and demanded him if it pleased him anything to **send** to Deyanira. Hercules answered to Lycas that **he would** go make his sacrifice to the god Apollo, and that **at** his return and coming again he would go unto her **or else he** would send unto her.

With this word Hercules and Philotes **passed** forth and went on their pilgrimage, and Lycas returned unto Deyanira and told **to her the joyous** tidings that he had received of Hercules, **and also what life** that Hercules had led since the **day and the hour** that **he** had presented to him her letter. **Deyanira, all comforted** of these good **tidings,** went into her chamber **and** thanked **the** gods **and fortune.** Anon, after she began to think **on** her estate, **and thus** thinking she remembered her on the poison that Nessus had given her in the article of his death, and how she had shut it in one of her coffers, and forthwith incontinent she opened the coffer and took the cursed poison **and** one of the shirts of Hercules, and as she that imagined by the virtue of the poison to draw again to her the love **of** Hercules, like as Nessus had said unto her, she made **the** shirt to be boiled with the poison, and gave the charge thereof to one of her women. When the shirt was boiled enough the woman took off the vessel and set **it** to cool; after she took out the shirt appertly[1] and wrung it, **but she** could not so soon have wrung it but the fire sprang **in her** hands so anguishously, that as she cast it upon a perch **to dry** she fell down dead.

In process **of time** Deyanira desiring to have the shirt, and seeing that the woman that had charge thereof brought it not, she went into the chamber where the shirt had been boiled and found the woman dead, whereof she had great marvel. Nevertheless, she passed the death lightly, and by **one of** her damoiselles she made take the shirt that hung on

[1] Briskly.

THE DOLOROUS SHIRT

the perch and was dry, and commanded her that she should
fold it and wind it in a kerchief. At the commandment of
Deyanira the damoiselle folded and enveloped the shirt, but
so doing she was served of the poison in such wise that she
lost her speech and died anon after. This notwithstanding,
Deyanira that thought on nothing but for to come to her
intention, took the shirt and delivered it to Lycas and
charged him that he should bear it to Hercules, praying him
in her name that he would wear it. Lycas, that was ready
to accomplish the will of his mistress, took the charge of the
dolorous shirt and departed from thence and went unto the
mountain whereas Hercules was, and there he found him in
a forest whereas was the temple of Diana. Hercules had no
man with him but Philotes, which made ready for him a
great fire for to sacrifice an hart that Hercules had taken
running at a course. Lycas then finding Hercules in the
temple, he kneeled down low to him and said: 'Sire, here is
a shirt that your ancille[1] and servant Deyanira sendeth unto
you, she recommendeth her humbly unto your good grace,
and prayeth you that ye will receive this present in gree[2] as
from your wife.' Hercules was joyous of these words, and
anon unclothed him for to do on this cursed shirt, saying
that verily she was his wife and that he would for her sake
wear this shirt. In doing on this shirt, he felt a right great
dolour and pain in his body; this notwithstanding, he did
on his other clothes above as he that thought none evil.
When he was clothed and the shirt was chauffed,[3] his pain
and sorrow grew more and more. Then he began to think,
and knew anon that his malady came off his shirt; and feeling the pricking of the venom, without long tarrying he took
off his robe, and supposed to have taken off his shirt from his
back, and to have rent it and diffete it.[4] But he was not strong
enough for to do so, for the shirt held so sore and cleaved so
fast and terribly to his flesh, and was so fasted to his skin

Caxton
1474

[1] Handmaiden.   [2] Grace.   [3] Warmed.   [4] Undone.

Caxton
1474

by the vigour of the **aspre** poison, in **such** wise that he tare out his flesh and bare away certain pieces thereof when he would have taken off his shirt.

Hercules knew then that he was hurt and wounded to the **death**; the death began to fight against **him**. He began to resist by drawing off his shirt from his body by pieces of his flesh and of his blood. All might not **avail**; **he** all to-rent **and** dischaired [1] his **back, his** thighs, his body unto his entrails **and guts, his arms,** his shoulders unto the bones; his dolour **and** pain **grew and** enlarged to the utterance. Thus as he returned **by the force of** his great dolorous pain, he beheld **Lycas and** another fellow that he had brought with him that **were all abashed** of this adventure; **then** he went to them and said unto Lycas: 'Thou cursed and unhappy man! what thing has moved thee to come hither under the privy habitude of Deyanira to bring me into **the** chance of fortune? What weenest thou that thou hast done? Thou hast served me with a shirt intoxicate of mortal **venom; who** hath introduced thee **to do this?** Thou must needs receive thy desert.' And saying these words, Hercules caught by the **head poor** Lycas, that wist never what to say, and threw him against a rock so fiercely that he to-frushed [2] and to-brake his **bones** and so slew **him.** The fellow of Lycas fled and hid **him** in a bush; Philotes was so afraid that he wist not what **to do.** At the hour that Hercules was in this point, much people came **into** the temple. The entrails of Hercules broiled, his **blood** boiled in all his veins, the poison pierced unto his heart, his sinews shrunk and withdrew them; when he felt him **in this** misery, and that the death hasted him **by** terrible battle**, as** he that could not take away the repugnance of his virtuous force striving against the malice of venom, he began to run over hill and over valley, up and down in the forest, and pulled up the great trees and overthrew them. After he began to rend off his shirt with the

---

[1] Disfleshed.   [2] Crushed.

THE DOLOROUS SHIRT

flesh then sodden and broiled. When he had long led this life he returned into the temple all ascertained of the death, and lifted up his hands and his eyes unto the heaven and said :

'Alas! alas! must it be that fortune laugh at me for this miserable destiny, coming of the accusation of wood[1] jealousy and sorcery of that woman that in the world I held and reputed most wise and most virtuous. O Deyanira, disnatural woman, without wit, without shame, and without honour, with an heart of a tyrant, all affamed[2] of jealousy! How hast thou might to contrive against me this furor and treason envenomed, false feminine will disnatural, out of rule and out of order. Thou haddest never so much honour and worship as thou now hast deserved blame, not only for thee alone but for all the women that be or shall be ever in the world; for if it happen that the kings or princes acquaint them with ladies or damoiselles for the human multipliance, they shall never have credence nor affiance in their proper wives. O Deyanira, what hast thou done? The women present and they that be in the wombs of their mothers, all shall crach[3] thee in the face, and shall curse thee without end, for the reproach by the turning upon them is infinite, and the men shall have dread for to be served of the shirt. Alas! Deyanira, what shall Calcedonie now do that glorified her in thy glory, and put and set thee in the front of their honour as a carbuncle for the parement[4] of her precious things? Instead to set thee in the front, they shall cast thee under feet; and instead to have glory of, they shall have shame. Hereof they may not fail, for by impiety and diverse engines and by conspired and swollen cruelty, thou hast conspired my death, and hast desloyed[5] and unbounden one not recoverable infortune for thee and me and for our friends and kinsmen. O Deyanira, right remaudit,[6] unhappy, and most cursed serpent, too malicious and reproachable

Caxton
1474

[1] Mad.   [2] An-hungered.   [3] Spit.
[4] Adornment.   [5] Set loose.   [6] Accursed.

murderer, thy false jealousy **hath** more power to extermine my life than have had all the monsters of the world; by thine offence and by thy machination hid and covert, wherefrom I could not keep me, I must die and pass out of this world. Since it is so, I thank fortune, and ask of the gods no vengeance of thee; but certes, **to the** end that it be not said that the vanquisher of men be vanquished by a woman, I shall not pass the bitter passage **of** death by thy **mortal** sorceries full of abomination, but by the fire that is neat and clear, and the most excellent of the elements.'

These dolorous and sorrowful words accomplished, Hercules took his club and cast it in the fire that was made ready **for to** make his sacrifice; after he gave to Philotes his bow **and his** arrows, and **sin he** prayed him that he would recommend him to Yole and his friends. And then, feeling that his life had no more for to sojourn, he took leave of Philotes and then as all burnt and sodden he laid him down in the fire, lifting his hands and his eyes unto the heaven, and there consumed the course of his glorious life. When Philotes saw the end of his master Hercules, he burnt his body into ashes and kept these ashes in intention to bear them to the **temple** that the King Evander had to make. After he departed from thence, and returned into Lycye greatly discomforted, and with great source of tears he recounted to Yole and to his friends the piteous death of Hercules. No man could recount the great sorrow that Yole made and they of Lycye, **as** well the students as the rural people; all the world fell in tears, in sighs, and in bewailings for his death. So much abounded Yole in tears and weepings that her heart was drowned and departed her soul from the body by the bitter water of her weeping.

Each body cursed and spake shame of Deyanira; finably Deyanira, advertised by the fellow of Lycas of the mischief **that was** come by the shirt, she fell in despair and made **many piteous** bewailings, and among all other she said:

'What have I done, alas, what have I done? The most solemn man of men, shining among the clerks, he that traversed the strong marches, the fundaments terrestrial, that bodily conversed among the men, and spiritually among the sun, the moon, and the stars, and that sustained the circumference of the heavens, is dead by my cause and by my culpe and without my culpe! He is dead by my culpe, for I have sent to him the shirt that gave to him the bite of death; but this is without my culpe, for I knew nothing of the poison. O mortal poison! By me is he prived of his life, of whom I loved the life as much as I did mine own; he that bodily dwelled among the men here in earth, and spiritually above with the sun, the moon, and celestial secrets; he that was fountain of science, by whom the Athenians aroused and bedewed their wits and engines; he that made the monsters of the sea to tremble in their abysms and swallows, and destroyed the monsters of Hell. He confounded the monsters of the earth; the tyrants he corrected; the orguillous and proud he humbled and meaked, the humble and meak he enhanced and exalted; he that made no treasure but of virtue; he that all the nations of the world subjuged and subdued with his club; and he that if he had willed by ambition of seignourie, might have attained to be King of the East, of the West, of the South, and of the North, of the Seas and of the Mountains, of all these he might have named him King and Lord by good right, if he had willed. Alas, alas! what am I, born in an unhappy time, when so high and so mighty a Prince is dead by my simplesse? He was the glory of the men; there was never to him none like, nor never shall be. Ought I to live after him? Nay, certes that shall I never do; for to the end that among the ladies I be not showed nor pointed with the finger, and that I fall not into strange hand for to be punished as much as I have of culpe and blame in this death, I shall do the vengeance to myself.' And with that she took a knife, and saying: 'I feel myself and

Caxton
1474

Caxton 1474

know that I am innocent of the death of my lord Hercules!" And with the point of the knife she ended her despaired life. Whereof Philotes was all abashed, and so were all they of Greece that long bewept and bewailed Hercules and his death; and they of Athens bewailed him strongly, some for his science, and other for his virtues.

William Caxton.

HOW THE MONK SAW HEAVEN

De Machlinia 1482

NOW when we were past all these places and sights aforesaid, and had gone a good space more inward, and ever grew to us more and more joy and fairness of places: also at the last we saw afar a full glorious wall of crystal, whose height no man might see, and length no man might consider: and when we came thither I saw withinforth a full fair bright shining gate, and stood open, save it was signed and laid over with a cross. Truly thither came flockmeal the multitude of those blessed souls that were next to it, and would come in at that fair gate. The cross was set in the midst of that gate, and now she was lift up on high, and so gave to them that came thither an open and a free entering, and afterward she was let down again, and so sparred[1] other out that would have come in. But how joyful they were that went in, and how reverently they tarried that stood without, abiding the lifting up of the cross again, I cannot tell by no words.

Soothly here Saint Nicholas and I stood still together, and the liftings up of the cross and the lettings down again, whereby some went in and some tarried without, I beheld long time with great wonder. And at the last Saint Nicholas and I came thither to the same gate hand in hand. And when we came thither the cross was lift up. And so they that were

[1] Barred, staked.

there went in. Soothly then my fellow, Saint Nicholas, freely went in and I followed, but suddenly and unavised[1] the cross of the gate came down upon our hands and departed me from my fellow Saint Nicholas, and when I saw this full sore afraid I was. Then said Saint Nicholas to me: 'Be not afraid, but have only full certain faith in our Lord Jesus Christ, and doubtless thou shalt come in.' And after this my hope and trust came again, and the cross was lift up, and so I came in; but what brightness and clearness of light was there withinforth all about no man ask nor seek of me, for I can not only [not] tell it by word, but also I cannot remember it in mind. That glorious shining light was bright and smooth, and so ravished a man that beheld it, that it bare a man above himself by the great brightness of light, in so mickle that whatsoever I saw before, it was as nothing, methought, in comparison of it. That brightness, though it were inestimable, nevertheless it dulled not a man's sight; it rather sharpened it. Soothly it shone full marvellously, but more inestimably it delighted a man that beheld it, and wonderfully coupled a man's sight to see it. And withinforth nothing I might see but light and the wall of crystal through the which we came in. And also from the ground up to top of that wall were gryces[2] ordained and disposed fair and marvellously, by the which the joyful company that was come in at the foresaid gate gladly ascended up. There was no labour, there was no difficulty, there was no tarrying in their ascending, and the higher they went the gladder they were.

Soothly I stood beneath on the ground, and long time I saw and beheld how they that came in at the gate ascended up by the same gryces. And at the last, as I looked up higher, I saw in a throne of joy sitting our blessed Lord and Saviour Jesus Christ, in likeness of man; and about Him, as it seemed to me, were a five hundred souls, the which late had stied[3] up to that glorious throne; and so they came to our Lord and

De Machlinia
1482

[1] Without warning.   [2] Steps.   [3] Gone.

worshipped Him, and thanked Him for His great mercy and grace showed and done to them: and some were seen on the upper parts of the wall as they had walked hither and thither. Truly I knew for certain that this place, where I saw our Lord sitting in a throne, was not the high Heaven of Heavens where the blessed spirits of angels and the holy souls of righteous men joy in the sight of God, seeing Him in His majesty as He is: where also innumerable thousands of holy spirits and angels serve him and assist him But then from thence, without any hardness or tarrying, they ascend up to the high heaven, the which is blessed of the sight of the everlasting Godhead, whereas only the holy angels, and the souls of righteous men that be of angels' perfection, see the invisible and immortal King of all worlds face to face, **the** which hath only immortality and dwelleth in light that is inaccessible: for no man may come to it, the which no mortal man seeth, neither may see. Soothly He is seen only of holy spirits that be pure and clean, the which be not grieved by no corruption of body, neither of soul. And in this vision that I saw, so mickle I conceived in my soul of joy and gladness, that whatsoever may be said of it by man's mouth, full little **it** is, and insufficient to express the joy of my heart that I had there.

Therefore **when I** had seen all these sights above said, and many other innumerable, my lord Saint Nicholas, that held me by the hand, said shortly this to me: 'Lo, son,' he said, 'now a part after thy petition and great desire thou hast seen and beholden the state of the world that is to come as it might be to possible. Also the perils of them that offend and err, the pains of sinners, the rest also of them that have done their purgation, the desires of them that be going to heavenward, and the joys of them that now be come to the Court of Heaven, and also the joy of Christ's reigning. And now thou must go again to thyself and to thine [own], and to the world's fighting. Truly thou shalt have and perceive the joys that thou hast seen, and mickle more, if thou continue and persevere in the dread of God.' And when he had said this to me he brought me forth through the same gate that we came in: wherefore full heavy and sorry was I, and more than a man may suppose: for well I knew that I must turn again from that heavenly bliss to this world's wretchedness. And greatly he exhorted me how I should dispose me to abide the day of my calling out of my body in cleanness of heart and of body and meekness of spirit, with diligent keeping of my religion. 'Diligently,' he said to me, 'keep the commandments of God, and dispose thy living after the example of righteous men. And truly so it shall be, that after the term of thy bodily living thou shalt be admitted blessedly to their fellowship everlastingly.'

And while the holy confessor, Saint Nicholas, this wise spake yet with me, suddenly I heard there a solemn peal and a ringing of a marvellous sweetness, and as all the bells in the world, or whatsoever is of sounding, had been rung together at once. Truly in this peal and ringing brake out also a marvellous sweetness, and a variant meddling of melody sounded withal. And I wot not whether the greatness of melody or the sweetness of sounding of bells was more to be wondered [at]. And to so great a noise I took good heed, and full greatly my mind was suspended to hear it. Soothly, anon as that great and marvellous sounding and noise was ceased, suddenly I saw myself departed from the sweet fellowship of my duke and leader, Saint Nicholas. Then was I returned to myself again, and anon I heard the voices of my brethren that stood about our bed.

William De Machlinia.

De Machlinia 1482

THE ADVENTURE OF THE CHARIOT

Malory
1485

THEN by the Queen's commandment they left battle, and dressed the wounded knights on horseback, some sitting, some overthwart their horses, that it was pity to behold them. And then Sir Meliagrance charged the Queen and all her knights that none of all her fellowship should depart **from** her; for full sore he drad Sir Launcelot du Lake, lest he should have any knowledging. All this espied the Queen, **and** privily she called unto her a child of her chamber, **that** was swiftly horsed, to whom she said: 'Go thou, **when** thou seest thy time, and bear this ring unto Sir Launcelot du Lake, **and** pray him as **he** loveth me, that he will see me, and rescue me if ever he will have joy of me; and spare thou not thy horse,' (said the Queen), 'neither for water, neither for land.' So the child espied his time, and **lightly he** took his horse with the spurs, and departed as fast **as he** might. And when Sir Meliagrance saw him so flee, **he** understood that it was by the Queen's commandment for **to** warn Sir Launcelot. Then they that were best horsed chased him, and shot at him, but from them all the child went suddenly; and then Sir Meliagrance said unto the Queen: 'Madam, ye are about to betray me, but I shall ordain for Sir Launcelot that he shall not come lightly at you.' And then he **rode** with her and they all to his castle in all the haste that he might. And by the way Sir Meliagrance laid in an enbushment the best archers that he might get in **his** country, to the number of a thirty, to await upon Sir Launcelot, charging them that if they saw such a manner of knight come by the way upon a white horse, that in any **wise** they slay his horse, but in no manner of wise have not ado with him bodily, for he is over hard to be overcome. So this **was** done, and they were come to his castle, but in no wise the Queen would never let none of the ten knights and her ladies out of her sight, but always they were in her presence, for the book saith Sir Meliagrance durst make no masteries for dread of Sir Launcelot, in so much he deemed that he had warning.

Malory 1485

So when the child was departed from the fellowship of Sir Meliagrance, within a while he came to Westminster. And anon he found Sir Launcelot. And when he had told his message, and delivered him the Queen's ring, 'Alas,' said Sir Launcelot, 'now am I shamed for ever, unless that I may rescue that noble lady from dishonour.' Then eagerly he asked his armour, and ever the child told Sir Launcelot how the ten knights fought marvellously, and how Sir Pelleas, and Sir Ironside, and Sir Brandiles, and Sir Persant of Inde, fought strongly, but namely Sir Pelleas, there might none withstand him, and how they all fought till at the last they were laid to the earth, and then the Queen made appointment for to save their lives, and go with Sir Meliagrance. 'Alas,' said Sir Launcelot, 'that most noble lady, that she should be so destroyed! I had lever (said Sir Launcelot) than all France that I had been there well armed.' So when Sir Launcelot was armed and upon his horse, he prayed the child of the Queen's chamber to warn Sir Lavaine how suddenly he was departed, and for what cause: 'And pray him, as he loveth me, that he will hie him after me, and that he stint not until he come to the castle where Sir Meliagrance abideth,' or dwelleth, for there (said Sir Launcelot) 'shall he hear of me and I am a man living, and rescue the Queen and the ten knights the which he traitorously hath taken, and that shall I prove upon his head, and all them that hold with him.'

Then Sir Launcelot rode as fast as he might, and the book saith he took the water at Westminster Bridge, and made his horse to swim over Thames to Lambeth. And then within a while he came to the place there as the ten knights had fought with Sir Meliagrance, and then Sir

THE ADVENTURE OF THE CHARIOT

Malory
1485

Launcelot followed that **track** until that he came to a wood, and there was a strait way, and **there the** thirty archers bade Sir Launcelot **turn** again, and **follow** no longer that track. '**What** commandment have **ye** thereto,' said Sir Launcelot, 'to cause me, that am a knight of the Round Table, to leave my right way?' 'This way shalt thou leave, or else thou shalt go **it** on thy foot, for wit thou well thy horse shall **be** slain.' 'That is little mastery,' said Sir Launcelot, '**to** slay my horse: but as for myself, when my horse is **slain, I** give right nought for you, not and ye were five **hundred more.**' So **then** they shot Sir Launcelot's **horse, and smote him** with many arrows. And then Sir Launcelot avoided his horse, and went on foot: but there were so many ditches **and** hedges betwixt them and him, that he might not meddle with none of them. 'Alas, for shame,' said Launcelot, 'that ever one knight should betray another knight, but it is an old saw, "A good man is never in danger but when he is in the danger of a coward."'

Then Sir Launcelot went a while, and then he was foul cumbered of his armour, his shield, and his spear, and all that longed unto him. Wit ye well he was full sore annoyed, and full loth he was to leave anything that longed unto him, for he dreaded sore the treason of Sir Meliagrance. And then **by** fortune there came by a chariot, that came thither for to fetch **wood.** 'Say me, carter,' said Sir Launcelot, 'what shall I **give thee** for to suffer **me** to leap into thy chariot, and that thou bring me unto **a** castle within this two mile?' 'Thou shalt not come within my chariot,' said the carter, 'for I am sent for to fetch wood for my lord Sir Meliagrance.'— 'With him would I speak.' 'Thou shalt not go with me,' said the carter. Then Sir Launcelot leapt to him, and gave him such a buffet that he fell to the earth stark dead. Then the other carter, his fellow, was afraid, and weened to have gone the same way, and then he cried, ' Fair lord, save my life, and I shall bring you where you will.' 'Then I charge thee,' said Sir Launcelot, 'that thou drive me and this chariot, even unto Sir Meliagrance's gate.' 'Leap up into the chariot,' said the carter, 'and ye shall be there anon.'

So the carter drove on a great wallop,[1] and Sir Launcelot's horse followed the chariot, with more than a forty arrows broad and rough in him: and more than an hour and an half Dame Guenever was in a bay window with her ladies, and espied an armed knight standing in a chariot. 'See, madam,' said a lady, 'where rideth in a chariot a goodly armed knight: I suppose he rideth unto hanging.' 'Where?' said the Queen. Then she espied by his shield that he was there himself Sir Launcelot du Lake. And then she was ware where came his horse ever after that chariot, and ever he trod his entrails and his paunch under his feet. 'Alas,' said the Queen, 'now I see well and prove that well is him that hath a trusty friend. Ha, hey, most noble knight! I see well thou art hard bested when thou ridest in a chariot.' Then she rebuked that lady that likened Sir Launcelot to ride in a chariot to hanging. 'It was foul-mouthed,' said the Queen, 'and evil likened, so for to liken the most noble knight of the world unto such a shameful death. O Jesu, defend him and keep him,' said the Queen, 'from all mischievous end!'

By this was Sir Launcelot come to the gates of that castle, and there he descended down, and cried, that all the castle rang of it: 'Where art thou, false traitor Sir Meliagrance, and knight of the Table Round? Now come forth here, thou traitor knight, thou and thy fellowship with thee: for here I am, Sir Launcelot du Lake, that shall fight with you.' And therewithal he bare the gate wide open upon the porter, and smote him under his ear with his gauntlet that his neck burst in sunder. When Sir Meliagrance heard that Sir Launcelot was there, he ran unto Queen Guenever, and fell upon his knee, and said, 'Mercy, madam, now I put me

Malory
1485

---

[1] Gallop.

wholly into your **grace**. 'What aileth you now?' said Queen Guenever. '**Forsooth** I might well **wit some** good knight would revenge **me**, though **my lord Arthur** wist not of this your work.' 'Madam,' said Sir Meliagrance, 'all this that **is amiss on my** part **shall** be amended right as yourself will devise, **and** wholly **I put** me in your **grace**.' 'What would ye that **I** did?' said the Queen. 'I would **no** more,' said Meliagrance, 'but that ye would take all in your own hands, and that ye will rule my lord Sir Launcelot: and such cheer **as may be made him in** this poor castle ye and he shall **have** until to-morn, and **then** may ye and all they return **unto** Westminster, **and** my body and all that I have I shall put in your rule.' '**Ye** say well,' said the Queen, 'and better **is** peace than ever war, and the less noise the more is my worship.'

Then the Queen and **her ladies** went **down** unto the knight Sir Launcelot, that stood wroth **out of** measure in the inner court, to abide battle; **and** ever he bade 'Thou traitor knight, come forth!' **Then the** Queen came to him and said, 'Sir Launcelot, why **be ye** so moved?' 'Ha, madam,' said Sir Launcelot, 'why ask ye **me** that question? Meseemeth' (said Sir Launcelot) 'ye ought to be more wroth than I am, for ye have the **hurt and** the dishonour. For wit ye well, madam, my hurt is but little, for the killing of a mare's son; but the despite grieveth me much more than all my hurt.' '**Truly**,' said the Queen, 'ye say truth, but heartily I thank you' **(said** the Queen) 'but ye must come in with me peaceably, for **all** thing is put in my hand, and all that is evil **shall be for** the best, for the knight full sore repenteth him of the misadventure that is befallen him.' 'Madam,' said **Sir Launcelot,** 'sith it is so that ye are accorded with him, as for **me I may** not be against it, howbeit Sir Meliagrance hath done **full** shamefully to me, and cowardly. Ah, madam, and **I had wist** ye would have been so soon accorded with him, **I would not** have made **such** haste unto

THE ADVENTURE OF THE CHARIOT

you.' 'Why say ye so?' said the Queen, 'do ye forthink[1] yourself of your good deeds? Wit you well' (said the Queen), 'I accorded never unto him for favour nor love that I had unto him, but for to lay down every shameful noise.' 'Madam,' said Sir Launcelot, 'ye understand full well I was never willing nor glad of shameful slander, nor noise; and there is neither king, queen, nor knight, that beareth the life, except my lord King Arthur, and you, madam, that should let me, but I should make Sir Meliagrance's heart full cold or ever I departed from hence.' 'That I wot well,' said the Queen, 'but what will ye more? ye shall have all thing ruled as ye list to have it.' 'Madam,' said Sir Launcelot, 'so ye be pleased I care not, as for my part ye shall soon please.'

Right so the Queen took Sir Launcelot by the bare hand, for he had put off his gauntlet, and so she went with him till her chamber; and then she commanded him to be unarmed, and then Sir Launcelot asked where the ten knights were that were wounded sore. So she showed them unto Sir Launcelot, and there they made great joy of the coming of him, and Sir Launcelot made great dole[2] of their hurts, and bewailed them greatly; and there Sir Launcelot told them how cowardly and traitorly Meliagrance set archers to slay his horse, and how he was fain to put himself in a chariot. Thus they complained every each to other, and full fain they would have been revenged, but they peaced themselves because of the Queen. Then, as the French book saith, Sir Launcelot was called many a day after, Le Chevaler du Chariot, and did many deeds, and great adventures he had.

Sir Thomas Malory.

Malory 1485

[1] Repent.   [2] Sorrow.

A MOURNING REMEMBRANCE

Fisher
1505

SHE came of noble blood, lineally descending of King Edward the Third, within the fourth degree of the same. Her father was John, Duke of Somerset; her mother was called Margaret, right noble as well in manners as in blood, to whom she **was** a very daughter in all noble **manners,** for she was bounteous and liberal to every person **of her knowledge** or acquaintance. Avarice and covetousness **she most hated, and** sorrowed it full much in all **persons, but** specially **in any** that belonged unto her. **She** was also of singular easiness **to be** spoken unto, and full courteous answer she **would make to** all that came unto her. Of marvellous gentleness **she was** unto all folks, but specially unto her own, whom she trusted and loved right tenderly. Unkind she would **not** be unto no creature, nor forgetful of any kindness **or** service done to her before, which **is no** little part of **very** nobleness. She **was** not vengeable, nor cruel, but ready anon to forget **and** to forgive injuries done unto her at the least desire or motion made unto her for the same. Merciful also and piteous she was unto such as were grieved and **wrongfully** troubled, and to them that **were** in poverty or sickness or any **other** misery.

To **God** and **to the** Church full obedient and tractable, searching His honour and pleasure full busily. A wariness of herself she had **alway to** eschew everything that might dishonest any noble **woman,** or distain her honour in any condition. Frivolous things, that were little to be regarded, **she** would let pass by, but the other, that were of weight **and** substance, wherein **she** might profit, she would not **let** for any pain **or** labour **to** take upon hand. These and **many** other such noble conditions, left unto her by her ancestors, she **kept and increased therein with a great diligence.** . . .

Also she wanted not **the nobleness of Nature. She had in manner all that** was praiseable in a woman, either in **soul** or in body. First, she was of singular **wisdom,** far passing the common rate of women. She was **good in** remembrance, and of holding memory; a ready **wit she** had also to conceive all things, albeit they were right dark. Right studious she was in books, which she had in great number, both in English and in French, **and for her** exercise **and** for the **profits of others,** she did translate divers matters of devotion out of the French into English. Full often she complained that **in her** youth she **had not given her** to the understanding **of Latin, wherein she had a little** perceiving, specially of the rubric of **the ordinal, for the** saying of her service, which she did well understand. Hereunto in favour, in words, in gesture, in every **demeanour of herself, so great nobleness did appear, that what she spake** or did it marvellously became her. . . .

A nobleness gotten or increased, she had also. **For** albeit she **of her** lineage was right **noble,** yet, nevertheless, by **marriage** and adjoining of other blood, it took some increasement. For in her tender age, she being endued with so great towardness of **nature,** and likelihood of inheritance, many sued to have **had her** to marriage. The Duke of Suffolk, which then **was** a **man of** great experience, most diligently procured to have had her **for** his son and heir. Of the contrary part, King Henry the Sixth did make means for Edmond, his brother, then the Earl of Richmond. She, which as then was not fully nine **years old, doubtful in** her mind, what she were best to do, asked counsel **of an old** gentlewoman, whom she much loved **and trusted, which did** advise her to commend herself to St. Nicholas, **the** patron and helper of all true maidens; **and** to beseech him to put in **her** mind what **she** were best to do. This counsel she

Fisher
1505

<small>Fisher
1505</small>

followed, **and made her** prayer so full often, but specially **that** night, when **she should the morrow after** make answer of her mind determinately. A marvellous thing! the same night, as I have heard her tell many a time, as she lay in prayer, calling upon St. Nicholas, whether sleeping or waking she could not assure, but about four of the clock in the morning, one appeared unto her arrayed like a bishop, and naming unto **her** Edmond, bade take **him** unto her husband. And so by this mean she did incline **her** mind unto Edmond, **the** King's brother, and Earl of Richmond, by whom she was made mother of the King that dead is (whose soul God pardon) **and** grandam to our sovereign lord, **King** Henry the Eighth; which now, by the grace of God, governeth the realm. So, what by lineage, what by affinity, she had thirty Kings and Queens within the fourth degree of marriage unto her, beside Earls, Marquises, Dukes, **and** Princes. And thus much we **have spoken** of her nobleness. . . .

Her sober temperance in meats and drinks was known to all them that were conversant with her, wherein she lay in as great weight of **herself as** any person might, keeping alway her straight measure, and offending as little as any creature might: eschewing banquets, rere-suppers,[1] joucries[2] betwixt meals. As for fasting, for age and feebleness, albeit she were not bound, yet those days, that by the Church were appointed, she kept them diligently and seriously, and in especial the holy Lent, throughout that she restrained her appetite till one meal and till one fish on the day; besides her other peculiar fasts of devotion, as St. Anthony, St. Mary Magdalene, St. Catherine, with other; and throughout all the year, the Friday and Saturday she full truly observed. **As to** hard clothes' wearing, she had her shirts and girdles of hair, which, when she was in health, every week she failed **not** certain days **to** wear, sometime the one, sometime the

---

[1] Late suppers.   [2] Sweetmeats.

other, that full often her skin, as I heard her say, was pierced therewith. . . .

Her own household, with marvellous diligence and wisdom, this noble Princess ordered, providing reasonable statutes and ordinances for them, which by her officers she commanded to be read four times a year. And oftentimes by herself she would so lovingly courage every of them to do well, and sometime by other mean persons.[1] If any factions or bonds were made secretly amongst her head officers, she with great policy did bolt it out, and likewise if any strife or controversy, she would with great discretion study the reformation thereof. For the strangers, O marvellous God! what pain, what labour she of her very gentleness would take with them, to bear them manner and company and entreat every person, and entertain them, according to their degree and honour, and provide by her own commandment, that nothing should lack that might be convenient for them, wherein she had a wonderful ready remembrance and perfect knowledge.

For the suitors, it is not unknown how studiously she procured justice to be administered by a long season, so long as she was suffered, and of her own charges provided men learned for the same purpose, evenly and indifferently to hear all causes, and administer right and justice to every party, which was in no small number; and yet meat and drink was denied to none of them. . . .

But specially, when they saw the death so haste upon her, and that she must needs depart from them, and that they should forego so gentle a mistress, so tender a lady; then wept they marvellously, wept her ladies and kinswomen, to whom she was full kind; wept her poor gentlewomen, whom she had loved so tenderly before; wept her chamberers,[2] to whom she was full dear; wept her chaplains and priests, wept her true and faithful servants. And who would not have

Fisher
1505

---

[1] Go-betweens.   [2] Gentlemen of the Household.

Fisher
1505

wept that there had **been present.** All England for her death had cause **of weeping.** The poor creatures that were wont to receive her **alms, to whom** she was alway piteous and merciful; the students of both the universities, **to** whom she was a mother; all the **learned** men of England, to whom she was a very patroness; **all the** virtuous and devout persons, to whom she was as a loving sister; all the good religious men and women, whom she so often was wont to visit and comfort; all good priests and clerks to whom **she was a true** defendress; all the noblemen and women, **to whom she was** a mirror and exemplar of honour; all the **common people of this** realm, for whom she was in their **causes a** common mediatress, and took right great displeasure for them, and generally the whole realm hath cause to complain and to mourn her death. **And all we,** considering her gracious and charitable mind, so universally, and considering the readiness of mercy and pity in our **Saviour Jesus,** may say, by lamentable **complaint** of our **unwisdom unto** Him: *Ah, domine, si fuisses hic*—Ah, my Lord! **if thou** had been present and had heard these sorrowful **cries** of her thy Servant, with the other lamentable mournings of her friends and servants, thou, **for thy** goodness would not have suffered her **to die:** but thou wouldst have taken pity and compassion upon **her.** . . .

Dare **I** say of her, she never yet was in that prosperity, but the greater **it was,** the more alway she dreaded the adversity. For when **the** King, her son, was crowned, in all that great triumph **and** glory, she wept marvellously; and likewise at the great triumph of the marriage of Prince Arthur, and **at** the last coronation, wherein she had full great joy, she **let** not to say **that** some adversity would follow; so that either she was **in** sorrow by reason of the present adversities, **or** else when she was in prosperity, she was in dread of the adversity for to come. I pass over the perils and dangers innumerable, which daily and hourly might have happed unto her, whereof this life is full, and therefore St. Gregory saith: *Vita haec terrena, aeternae vitae comparata, mors est potius dicenda, quam vita,* and for that cause, who that once hath tasted the pleasures of that life, this is unto them a very death for ever after. . . . Now, therefore, would I ask you this one question: Were it, suppose ye, at this considered, a meetly thing for us to desire, to have this noble princess here amongst us again? To forego the joyous life above, to want the presence of the glorious Trinity whom she so long hath sought and honoured, to leave that most noble kingdom, to be absent from the most blessed company of Saints and Saintesses, and hither to come again to be wrapped and endangered with the miseries of this wretched world, with the painful diseases of her age, with the other encumbrances that daily happeth in this miserable life. Were this a reasonable request of our party?[1] Were this a kind desire? Were this a gentle wish? that where she hath been so kind and loving a mistress unto us, all we should more regard our own profits than her more singular weal and comfort? The mother that hath so great affection unto her son, that she will not suffer him to depart from her to his promotion and furtherance, but alway keep him at home, more regarding her own pleasure than his weal, were not she an unkind and ungentle mother? Yes, verily. Let us, therefore, think our most loving mistress is gone hence for her promotion, for her great furtherance, for her most weal and profit, and herein comfort us, herein rejoice ourself, and thank Almighty God, which of His infinite mercy so graciously hath disposed for her.

Fisher
1505

John Fisher, *Bishop of Rochester.*

[1] On our part.

A PAGEANT

Makefyrr
1506

RIGHT worshipful masters, I recommend me unto you, certifying you that the King's Grace and the King of Castile met this day at three of the clock, upon Cleworth Green, two mile out of Windsor, and there the King received him in the goodliest manner that ever I saw, and each of them embraced other in arms.

To show you the King's apparel of England, thus it was: his horse of bay, trapped with needlework; a gown of purple velvet, a chain with a George[1] of diamonds, and a hood of purple velvet, which he put not off at the meeting of the said King of Castile; his hat and his bonnet he availed,[2] and the King of Castile in case like. And the King of Castile rode upon a sorrelled hobby, which the King gave unto him; his apparel was all black, a gown of black velvet, a black hood, a black hat, and his horse's harness of black velvet.

To show you of the King's company: my Lord Harry of Stafford rode in a gown of cloth of tusser,[3] tucked, furred with sables, a hat of goldsmith work, and full of stones, diamonds, and rubies, riding upon a sorrelled courser barded with a bard[4] of goldsmith's work, with roses and dragons red.

And my Lord Marquis riding upon a bald sorrelled horse, with a deep trapper full of long tassels of gold of Venice, and upon the crupper of his horse a white feather, with a coat upon his back, the body goldsmith's work, the sleeves of crimson velvet, with letters of gold.

My Lord of Kent upon a sorrelled horse, bald, the harness of Venice gold, with a deep fringe of half yard of length. My Lord of Kent's coat was one bar of cloth of gold, another

---

[1] Ensign of the Garter.   [2] Took off.   [3] Silk.
[4] Caparisoned with a horse-armour.

of crimson velvet, pyrled[1] with a demy manche[2] cut off by the elbow. These be the lords that bear the bruit.

Makefyrr 1506

Sir Hew Waghan upon a bay horse trapped with crimson velvet full of gilt bells, a gown of black velvet, and a chain of gold, baldric-wise, worth five hundred pound.

These be the spears: Master St. John upon a black horse, with harness of cloth of gold with tassels of plunket[3] and white, a coat of plunket and white, the body of goldsmith's work; the sleeves full of spangles.

John Carr and William Parr coats like, the horses grey, of Parr trapped with crimson velvet with tassels of gold, and bells gilt. Carr, horse bay, with an Almain harness of silver, an inch broad of beaten silver, both the coats of goldsmith's work the bodies, the sleeves one strip of silver, the other gilt.

Edward Neville upon a gray horse trapped with black velvet full of small bells, his coat the one half of green velvet, the other of white cloth of gold; these to the rutters[4] of the spears, with other divers well appointed.

On the King of Castile's party: the Lord Chamberlain chief, I cannot tell his name as yet; his apparel was sad, and so was all the residue of his company, with cloaks of sad tawny black, guarded, some with velvet, and some with sarcenet, not passing a dozen in number. It is said there is many behind, which comes with the Queen of Castile, which shall come upon Tuesday.

When the King rode forth from Windsor Castle, the King rode upon the right hand the King's of Castile; howbeit, the King's Grace offered him to take him upon the right hand, the which he refused. And at the alighting the King of Castile was off his horse a good space or our King was alight; and then the King's Grace offered to take him by the arm, the which he would not, but took the King by the

---

[1] Fringed.   [2] Sleeve.   [3] Light blue.
[4] Troopers.

Makefyrr 1506 — the arm, and so went **to the** King of Castile's chamber, which **is** the richestly hanged that ever I **saw**; seven chambers together hanged with cloth of arras, wrought with gold as thick as could be; and as for three beds of state, no King christened can show such three.

This is as far as I can show you of this **day**, and when I can know more, ye shall have knowledge.

The Paston Letters.

THE KILLING OF LORD HASTINGS

More 1513 — WHEREUPON soon after, that is to wit, on the Friday the — day of — many Lords assembled in the Tower, and there sat in council, devising the honourable solemnity of the King's coronation, of which the time appointed then so near approached, that the pageants and subtleties were in making day and night at Westminster, and much victual killed therefore, that afterwards **was** cast away. These Lords so sitting together **commoning of** this matter, the Protector came in among them, **first** about nine of the clock, saluting them courteously, **and** excusing himself that he had been from them **so** long, saying merely that he had been asleep **that day.** And after a little talking with them, he **said** unto **the Bishop of** Ely: 'My lord, you have very good strawberries **at your garden** in Holborn, I require you let us have **a** mess **of them.**' 'Gladly, my lord,' quoth he, 'would God I had **some** better thing as ready to your pleasure as that.' **And** therewith in all the haste he sent his servant for **a** mess of strawberries. The Protector set the Lords fast **in** commoning, and thereupon praying them to spare him for **a** little while, departed thence. And soon, after one hour, between **ten** and eleven he returned into **the** chamber among them, all changed, **with a** wonderful sour

THE KILLING OF LORD HASTINGS

More 1513

angry countenance, knitting the brows, frowning and frothing and knawing on his lips, and so sat him down in his place; all the Lords much dismayed and sore marvelling of this manner of sudden change, and what thing should him ail. Then when he had sitten still a while, thus he began: 'What were they worthy to have, that compass and imagine the destruction of me, being so near of blood unto the King and Protector of his royal person and his realm?' At this question, all the Lords sat sore astonished, musing much by whom this question should be meant, of which every man wist himself clear. Then the Lord Chamberlain, as he that for the love between them thought he might be boldest with him, answered and said, that they were worthy to be punished as heinous traitors, whatsoever they were. And all the other affirmed the same. 'That is' (quoth he) 'yonder sorceress, my brother's wife and other with her,' meaning the Queen. At these words many of the other Lords were greatly abashed that favoured her. But the Lord Hastings was in his mind better content, that it was moved by her, than by any other whom he loved better. Albeit his heart somewhat grudged, that he was not afore made of counsel in this matter, as he was of the taking of her kindred, and of their putting to death, which were by his assent before devised to be beheaded at Pomfret, this self same day, in which he was not ware that it was by other devised, that himself should the same day be beheaded at London. Then said the Protector: 'Ye shall all see in what wise that sorceress and that other witch of her counsel, Shore's wife, with their affinity, have by their sorcery and witchcraft wasted my body.' And therewith he plucked up his doublet sleeve to his elbow upon his left arm, where he shewed a werish[1] withered arm and small, as it was never other. And thereupon every man's mind sore misgave them, well perceiving that this matter was but a quarrel. For well they wist, that the Queen

---

[1] Ill-shapen.

THE KILLING OF LORD HASTINGS

More
1513

was too wise to go about any such folly. And also if she would, yet would **she of** all folk **least** make Shore's wife of counsel, whom of all women she most hated, as that concu**bine** whom the King her **husband had** most loved. And also no man was there present, but well **knew that** his arm was ever such since his birth. Natheles the **Lord** Chamberlain answered and said: 'Certainly, my Lord, **if** they have so heinously done, they be worthy heinous punishment.' 'What,' quoth the Protector, 'thou servest **me, I** wene, with ifs **and** with ands, **I** tell thee they have so done, and that I will make good on thy body, traitor.' **And,** therewith, as in **great** anger, he clapped his fist upon the board a great rap. **At** which token given, **one** cried treason without the chamber. Therewith **a** door clapped, and in come there rushing men in harness, as many as the chamber might hold. And anon the Protector said to the Lord Hastings: 'I arrest thee, traitor.' 'What, me, my Lord?' quoth he. 'Yea thee, traitor,' quoth the Protector. **And another let fly at** the Lord Stanley, which shrank at the stroke and fell under the **table,** or else his head had been cleft to the teeth: for as **shortly as** he shrank, yet ran the blood about his ears. Then were they all quickly bestowed in diverse chambers, except the Lord Chamberlain, whom the Protector bade speed **and** shrive him apace, 'for by Saint Paul' (quoth he) 'I will not to dinner till I see thy **head off.'** It boded him not to ask why, but heavily he took a priest at adventure, and made a short shrift, for a longer would not be suffered, the Protector made so much haste to dinner; which he might not go to till this were done for saving of his oath. So was he brought forth into the green beside the chapel within the Tower, and his head laid down upon a long log of timber, and there stricken off, and afterward his body with the head interred at Windsor beside the body of King Edward, whose both souls our Lord pardon.

Sir Thomas More.

WAT TYLER'S ENDING

THE Saturday the King departed from the Wardrobe in Bourchier the Royal, and went to Westminster and heard mass in the church there, and all his lords with him; and beside the church there was a little chapel, with an image of Our Lady, which did great miracles, and in whom the Kings of England had ever great trust and confidence. The King made his orisons before this image, and did there his offering; and then he leapt on his horse, and all his lords, and so the King rode toward London; and when he had ridden a little way on the left hand, there was a way to pass without London.

1523

The same proper morning, Wat Tyler, Jack Straw, and John Ball had assembled their company to common together, in a place called Smithfield, whereas every Friday there is a market of horses; and there were together all of affinity more than twenty thousand, and yet there were many still in the town, drinking and making merry in the taverns, and paid nothing, for they were happy that made them best cheer. And these people in Smithfield had with them the King's banners, the which were delivered them the day before; and all these gluttons were in mind to overrun and to rob London the same day, for their captains said how they had done nothing as yet: 'These liberties that the King hath given us is to us but a small profit; therefore let us be all of one accord, and let us overrun this rich and puissant city, or they of Essex, of Sussex, of Cambridge, of Bedford, of Arundel, of Warwick, of Reading, of Oxford, of Guildford, of Linne, of Stafford, of Germany, of Lincoln, of York, and of Durham do come hither; for all these will come hither. Wallyor and Lyster will bring them hither; and if we be first lords of London, and have the possession of the riches that is therein

Bourchier we shall **not repent us; for if we leave it, they that** come
1523 after will **have it** from us.' To this **counsel** they all agreed.
And therewith **the** King came the **same** way unaware of
them, **for** he had thought to have **passed** that way without
London, and with him a forty horse; and when he came
before the abbey of St. Bartilmeus, and beheld all these
people, then the King rested and said how **he** would go no
farther till he knew what these people ailed, saying, if they
were in any trouble, how he would repease¹ **them again.** The
lords **that were** with him tarried also, as reason **was** when
they saw the King **tarry.** And when Wat Tyler saw the
King **tarry, he** said **to his** people : 'Sirs, yonder is the King,
I will go and speak **with** him; stir **not** from hence without I
make you a sign, and **when I make you** that sign, come **on**,
and slay all them, except the King; **but do** the King no
hurt; he is young, we shall do with **him as we** list, and
shall lead him with **us all** about England, **and so** shall **we** be
lords of all the realm without doubt.'

And there was a doublet maker **of** London **called** John
Tycle, and he had brought to these gluttons **a** sixty doublets,
the which they wore; then he demanded of these captains who
should pay him for his doublets; he demanded thirty marks.
Wat Tyler answered him and said : 'Friend, appease yourself,
thou shalt be well payed ere this day be ended; keep thee
near me, I shall be thy creditor.' And therewith he spurred
his **horse** and departed from his company, and came to the
King, so near him that **his** horse's head touched the croup
of the King's horse. **And** the first word **that** he said was
this : 'Sir King, seest **thou** all yonder people?' 'Yea, truly,'
said the King; 'wherefore sayest thou?' 'Because,' said
he, 'they be all at my commandment, and have sworn to me
faith and truth to do **all** that I will have them.' 'In a good
time,' said the King, 'I will well it be so.' Then Wat Tyler
said, as he that nothing demanded but riot : 'What, believest

¹ Appease.

thou, King, that these people, and as many more as be in London at my commandment, that they will depart from thee thus, without having thy letters?' 'No,' said the King; 'ye shall have them, they be ordained for you, and shall be delivered every one each after other; wherefore, good fellows, withdraw fair and easily to your people, and cause them to depart out of London, for it is our intent that each of you by villages and townships shall have letters patent, as I have promised you.'

<small>Bourchier 1523</small>

With those words Wat Tyler cast his eyes on a squire that was there with the King, bearing the King's sword. And Wat Tyler hated greatly the same squire, for the same squire had displeased him before for words between them. 'What,' said Tyler, 'art thou there? Give me thy dagger.' 'Nay,' said the squire, 'that will I not do. Wherefore should I give it thee?' The King beheld the squire, and said: 'Give it him, let him have it.' And so the squire took it him sore against his will. And when this Wat Tyler had it he began to play therewith, and turned it in his hand, and said again to the squire: 'Give me also that sword.' 'Nay,' said the squire, 'it is the King's sword; thou art not worthy to have it, for thou art but a knave; and if there were no more here but thou and I, thou durst not speak those words for as much gold in quantity as all yonder Abbey.' 'By my faith,' said Wat Tyler, 'I shall never eat meat till I have thy head.' And with those words the Mayor of London came to the King with a twelve horses, well armed under their coats, and so he brake the press, and saw and heard how Wat Tyler demeaned himself, and said to him: 'Ha! thou knave, how art thou so hardy in the King's presence to speak such words? It is too much for thee so to do.' Then the King began to chafe, and said to the Mayor: 'Set hands on him.' And while the King said so, Tyler said to the Mayor: 'A God's name, what have I said to displease thee?' 'Yes, truly,' quoth the Mayor, 'thou false stinking knave, shalt thou speak thus in the presence

Bourchier of the King, my natural lord? I commit[1] never to live
1523 without **thou shalt dearly abye**[2] **it.'** And with those words
the Mayor drew out **his** sword and struck Tyler so great a
stroke on the head, that he fell down at the feet of his horse;
and as soon as he was fallen, they **environed** him all about,
whereby he was not seen of his **company.** Then a squire
of the King's alighted, called John **Standish,** and he drew
out his sword and put it into Wat Tyler's **belly,** and so he
died.

Then the ungracious people there assembled, perceiving
their captain **slain, began to** murmur among themselves and
said : ' Ah ! **our captain is slain ;** let us go and slay them all ;'
and therewith they arranged themselves on the place in
manner of battle, and their **bows before** them. Thus the
King began a great outrage; howbeit, all turned to the
best, for as soon as Tyler was on the earth the **King** departed
from all his company, and all alone he rode to these people,
and said to his own men : ' Sirs, none **of you follow me ;** let
me alone.' And so when **he came before these** ungracious
people, who put themselves in ordinance to revenge their
captain, **then** the King said to **them : ' Sirs, what** aileth you?
ye shall have no captain but me: I am your King ; be all in
rest and peace.' And **so the most** part of the people that
heard the King **speak and** saw him among them were
shamefast, and began to wax peaceable and to depart ; but
some, such as were malicious and evil, would not depart, but
made semblant[3] as though they would do somewhat. Then
the King returned **to his** own company and demanded of
them what was best to be done. Then he was counselled to
draw into the field, for **to fly away was** no boot. Then said
the Mayor : ' It is good that we do so, for I think surely we
shall have shortly some comfort of them of London, and of
such good men as be of our part, who are purveyed,[4] and
have their friends and **men** ready armed in their houses.'

[1] Promise. [2] Repay. [3] Made as they would. [4] Provided.

WAT TYLER'S ENDING

And in this meantime voice and bruit ran through London, how these unhappy people were likely to slay the King and the Mayor in Smithfield; through the which noise all manner of good men of the King's party issued out of their houses and lodgings, well armed, and so came all to Smithfield and to the field where the King was; and they were anon to the number of seven or eight thousand men well armed. And first thither came Sir Robert Knolles and Sir Perducas Dalbret, well accompanied, and divers of the Aldermen of London, and with them a six hundred men in harness, and a puissant man of the city, who was the King's draper, called Nicholas Bramber, and he brought with him a great company; and ever as they came they ranged them afoot in order of battle. And on the other part these unhappy people were ready ranged, making semblance to give battle; and they had with them divers of the King's banners. There the King made three knights: the one the Mayor of London, Sir Nicholas Walworth, Sir John Standish, and Sir Nicholas Braule.

Bourchier 1523

Then the lords said among themselves: 'What shall we do? We see here our enemies, who would gladly slay us, if they might have the better hand of us.' Sir Robert Knolles counselled to go and fight with them and slay them all; yet the King would not consent thereto, but said: 'Nay, I will not so; I will send to them, commanding them to send me again my banners, and thereby we shall see what they will do; howbeit, either by fairness or otherwise, I will have them.' 'That is well said, sir,' quoth the Earl of Salisbury. Then these new knights were sent to them, and these knights made token to them not to shoot at them. And when they came so near them that their speech might be heard, they said: 'Sirs, the King commandeth you to send to him again his banners, and we think he will have mercy of you.' And incontinent they delivered again the banners, and sent them to the King: also they were com-

Bourchier manded, on pain of their heads, **that** all such as had letters
1523 of the King to bring them forth, and to send them again to
the King. And so, many of them delivered their letters, but
not all: then the King made them to be all torn in their
presence. And as soon as the King's banners were delivered
again, these unhappy people kept none array, but the most
part of them did cast down their bows, and **so** break their
array, and returned into London. Sir **Robert** Knolles was
sore displeased in that he might not go to slay them all; but
the King would not consent thereto, but said he would be
revenged of them well enough, and so he was after.

John Bourchier, Lord Berners.

THE CONQUEST OF **BRITAIN**

Tiptoft THE horsemen of the Britons and their essedaries fought
1530 sharply with the horsemen of the Romans as they were
on their journey: but the Romans were victors, and chased
them into the woods and mountains. But after that the
Romans had slain many **of** their enemies, and followed them
farther for covetousness, they lost many of their men. And
after that a little time, **the** Romans, being negligent and
nothing doubting, were about to fortify their camp, the
Britons suddenly leapt out of the wood, and began to assail
fiercely, and set on them which kept the watch of the
camp, the which withstood them strongly. Then Caesar
sent for succours, two companies, and with them the first
legion of the two next legions, between which legions and
their first fighters was a little space. But the Romans were
abashed because of the new manner and fashion that they
of Britain used in fighting, the which struck courageously
in the midst of the Romans and departed again at their
pleasure, without **any** hurt or wounds. That same day was

Quintus Laberius Durus, captain of the horsemen, slain. But after that Caesar had sent in aid certain company with all things necessary, the Britons were soon discomfited. Now, for so much as this was open in the sight of all men, because it was fought before the camp where the whole host lay, it was well perceived that the Romans, for weight of their heavy armour, were not able to follow quickly, nor chase their enemies, nor also they durst not depart from their standards. Wherefore they were not meet to fight with their enemies, which used such manner of battle. They perceived also the horsemen could not fight without great peril, because their enemies would oftentimes flee for the nonce. And when they had moved by fraud the Romans a good distance from the legions, then they leapt out of their chariots and began a new battle on foot, after another fashion than the Romans used. And the manner of fight of the horsemen was very perilous, whether they assailed their enemies or whether they followed them. Their enemies also fought not all together, but some here and some there, and great spaces between them when they fought. And some stood still to see the array kept, and to furnish the field ever with fresh men when the other were weary or hurt.

The next day after this battle the Britons were lodged on the mountains not far from the host of the Romans, and showed themselves in a small company, and began to assail the horsemen of the Romans, but not so fiercely as they had done the day before. But about the hour of noon, when Caesar had sent on foraging three legions and all his horsemen, under the conduct of Caius Trebonius, his lieutenant, their enemies leapt suddenly out of all parts on them that went a-foraging, insomuch as they came and assailed them that bare the banners and the legions. But after that the Romans had made a strong assault against them, they put them to flight, and ceased

Tiptoft
1530

Tiptoft
1530

not to follow them : for the horsemen had much confidence to have succours, **because they** perceived the legions following after them : they **chased** their enemies, and slew a great number of them, and followed them so near that they had neither space to gather themselves together in array, nor to arrest themselves, nor yet to leap out of their chariots. After this flight, all the aliens which were come out of all parts to succour the Britons departed, and after this time never made any plain field with their power against the Romans. When this battle was **thus** finished, **Caesar** having knowledge of the counsel of all **his enemies,** caused his **host to** march toward the country of Cassevelan by the **river of the** Thames, over which flood a man can pass afoot, **and that very** hardily, **but** at one **place.** And when he **came thither, he perceived** on the other side of the river **a great army of enemies** ready in good ordinance.

Now, the side of the river where his enemies stood was pitched full of sharp piles : and beside it, at the brink of the river, were other piles which were covered with water. Of the which things, when Caesar was advertised by the **report of** the prisoners, **and** by them which had left the **Britons and** were come to Caesar, he sent first his men of arms, **and** commanded the legions should follow them immediately without delay. And the army went so hastily and with such great violence together, notwithstanding that they had their heads **all** only above the water, that the Britons, which were not able to resist the strength of the legions and of the horsemen, were compelled to leave the banks and to flee away. Then Cassevelanus, as before, showed when he had lost all his hope that he had to make war, and also had put from him his great army, and kept all only with him four thousand essedaries: he espied all that he might what way the Romans held, and ever kept himself aloof a little out of the way, and lurked in woods and other

places that were not easy to journey in. And in all Tiptoft
countries where he knew the Romans should come, he 1530
caused both the people and the beasts out of the towns and
fields to be chased into the forests. And when the horsemen of the Romans would boldly go into the fields on
foraging, or else in destroying the country, he would send
his essedaries by privy ways and by-paths that he knew
out of the woods against the Romans to fight with them, to
the great hurt and damage of the horsemen. And by reason
of the fear that they put the Romans in, they letted them
to stray any more abroad, wherefore it came to this point,
that Caesar would suffer his people to go no further on
foraging than the host of the legions extended, and ordained
that in burning of houses and destroying the land of their
enemies, there should be done as much hurt as the men of
arms of the legions with all their power might do in riding
by the way. In this season the Trinobantes (which men
suppose to be them of London), the which is almost the
strongest and surest city of all the country of Britain, sent
ambassadors to Caesar, and offered themselves to be at his
commandment. Of which city a certain young man called
Mandubracius, taking part with Caesar, came to him into the
stablished land, whose father, Imanuencius, before that time
had borne great rule and authority in the said city, and was
slain by Cassevelan ; and his son, fearing death, fled out of the
city. Which ambassadors required Caesar that he would defend
and help Mandubracius to avenge the wrongs that Cassevelan
did to him, and that he would send to them Mandubracius
to have the rule and governing of the city. Then Caesar
commanded to the ambassadors that they should send him
eleven hostages and corn sufficient for his host, and so he
sent to them Mandubracius. When the ambassadors were
returned, the Trinobantes with all diligence did that which
Caesar had commanded, and sent to him the number of
hostages and the corn which he did command. When the

Tiptoft
1530

Trinobantes **were** thus assured because that Caesar had commanded that no **man of** war should do them any hurt or damage, the Cenimagnies, the Segontiaces, the Ancalytes, the Bibroces and Cassiens (which be inhabiting near the **sea), sent** their ambassadors to Caesar, and yielded them to him. Of them Caesar had perfect knowledge that the fortress where Cassevelan held himself was not far from thence. The which fortress was fortified with forests and marshes, and there was assembled together a great number of men and also of beasts. Note that the Britons call a fortress **or a** walled town when they have fortified a strong wood with ditches and pales, there where they may assemble together to eschew **the** danger of their **enemies.** Then Caesar marched **toward** this fortress, and found the place marvellous strong, **both by** situation of nature and by labour of men's hands. Yet notwithstanding he enforced to assault it at two sides. The enemies after that they had tarried a little, perceiving that they **were** not able to resist the assault, fled out by another part. When the fortress was taken, there was found a **great** number of bestial, and many men were slain and taken in the flight. While these things were adoing in these parts, Cassevelan sent his messengers into the country of Kent, the which country, as is showed before, doth stand on the sea coast.

In the which country were four Kings reigning, that is to say, Cingetorix, Carvilius, Taximagulus, and Segonax, whom he commanded to assemble together all their armies and suddenly to assail and destroy all the navy (which Caesar had left at the sea coast). When those four Kings were arrived where the navy was, the Romans made out and **slew** many of them, and took prisoner the noble captain Cingetorix, and brought home all their people safe unhurt. After that the losing of this battle was showed to Cassevelan, and **that** he considered the great misfortunes and damages that he had sustained, and perceived his country so robbed, pilled,¹ and exiled, and the most of all troubled him that so many cities and towns had forsaken him and were yielded to Caesar: he therefore sent ambassadors to Caesar, which, by the means of Attributus Comius, should intreat that he might yield him to ransom. Now, because Caesar before intended to lie the winter time in continent land, because of the sudden movings in France, and because that little of the summer remained, and the rest would be soon spent, he commanded Cassevelan to send him hostages, and ordained what tribute Britain should pay yearly to the Romans. He also forbade and commanded Cassevelan that he should do no prejudice neither to Mandubracius nor to the Trinobantes. And when he had received the hostages, he drew with his host toward the seaside, where he found his navy repaired. And insomuch as Caesar had great number of prisoners, and because one part of his navy was perished by the tempest, he purposed to make his navy to repass at two several times. But it happened so that of all the number of ships, and for all the passages that were made, neither this year nor the last year, yet there lacked no ships to recarry over the host. But as for all the ships that should have been sent from the other part, and the ships in which the first men of war passed and should have come again, and also such ships as Labienus had in charge to see made to the number of forty, few or none of them came to the even port. Wherefore it was necessary to make again the remnant which were broken. The which navy, when Caesar had long tarried for in vain, lest he should be hindered or let to pass because of the late season that the nights and days were of one length; he was compelled by necessity to shift his men together more straightly in such ships as he had. And as soon as the weather was fair and convenient to sail, he parted about the second hour

Tiptoft
1530

¹ Pillaged.

Tiptoft
1530

of the night, and at the point of day he took land, and all his navy safe and sound, which he caused to be drawn up on land.

John Tiptoft, Earl of Worcester.

THE IMAGE OF DETRACTION

Elyot
1531

THERE is much conversant among men in authority a vice very ugly and monstruous, who under the pleasant habit of friendship and good counsel with a breath pestilential infecteth the wits of them that nothing mistrusteth. This monster is called in English Detraction, in Latin *Calumnia*, whose property I will now declare. If a man, being determined to equity, having the eyes and ears of his mind set only on the truth and the public weal of his country, will have no regard to any request or desire, but proceedeth directly in the administration of justice, then either he which by justice is offended, or some his fautours, abettors, or adherents, if he himself or any of them be in service or familiarity with him that is in authority, as soon as by any occasion mention happeneth to be made of him who hath executed justice exactly, forthwith they imagine some vice or default, be it never so little, whereby they may minish his credence, and craftly omitting to speak anything of his rigour in justice, they will note and touch something of his manners, wherein shall either seem to be lightness or lack of gravity, or too much sourness, or lack of civility, or that he is not benevolent to him in authority, or that he is not sufficient to receive any dignity, or to dispatch matters of weighty importance, or that he is superfluous in words, or else too scarce. Also if he live temperately and delighteth much in study, they embraid[1] him with nigardship, or in

[1] Upbraid.

THE IMAGE OF DETRACTION

derision do call him a clerk or a poet, unmete for any other purpose. And this do they covertly and with a more gravity than any other thing that they enterprise.

Elyot
1531

This evil report is called Detraction, who was wonderfully well expressed in figures by the most noble painter Apelles, after that he was discharged of the crime whereof he was falsely accused to Ptholomee, King of Egypt, having for his amends of the said king twelve thousand pounds sterling and his accuser to his bondman perpetually. The table wherein Detraction was expressed was painted in this form: at the right hand was made sitting a man having long ears, putting forth his hand to Detraction, who far off came towards him; about this man stood two women, that is to say, Ignorance and Suspicion. On the other side came Detraction, a woman above measure well trimmed, all chafed and angry, having her aspect or look like to the fire, in showing a manner of rage or fury. In her left hand she held a burning torch or brand, and with her other hand she drew by the hair of his head a young man who held up his hands toward heaven, calling God and the Saints for witness. With her came a man, pale and evil favoured, beholding the young man intentively, like unto one that had been with long sickness consumed, whom ye might lightly conject to be Envy. Also there followed two other women, that trimmed and apparelled Detraction; the one was Treason, the other Fraud. After followed a woman in a mourning weed, black and ragged, and she was called Repentance, who turning her back weeping and sore ashamed beheld Verity, who then approached. In this wise Apelles described Detraction, by whom he himself was in peril. Which, in mine opinion, is a right necessary matter to be in tables or hangings set in every man's house that is in authority, considering what damage and loss hath ensued, and may hereafter ensue, by this horrible pestilence, false Detraction.

To the avoiding whereof, Luciane, who writeth of this

Elyot
1531

picture, giveth **a** notable **counsel,** saying, that a wise man, when he doubteth of the honesty and virtue of the person accused, **he** should keep close his **ears** and not open them hastily to them which be with this sickness infected, and put reason for a diligent porter and watch, which ought to examine and let in the reports that be good, and exclude and prohibit them that be contrary. For it is a thing to laugh at and very unfitting to ordain for thy house a keeper or porter, and thine ears and mind to leave to all men wide open. Wherefore, when any person cometh to us to tell **us** any report or complaint, first, it shall behove us throughly and evenly to consider the thing, not having respect to the ears of him that reporteth, or to his form of living or wisdom **in** speaking. For the more vehement the reporter is in persuading, so much more diligent and exact trial and examination ought to be used. Therefore trust is not to be given **to** another man's judgment, much less to the malice of an accuser. But every man shall retain to himself the power to ensearch out the truth, and leaving the envy or displeasure to the detractor, he shall ponder or weigh the matter indifferently, that everything in such wise being curiously ensearched and proved, he may at his pleasure either love or hate him whom he hath so substantially tried. For in good faith to give place **to** Detraction at the beginning, it is a thing childish and base, and to be esteemed among the most great inconveniences and mischiefs. These be well nigh the words **of** Luciane; whether the counsel be good I remit it to the wise readers. Of one thing am I sure, that by Detraction as well many good wits have been drowned, as also virtue, and painful study have been unrewarded, and many zelatours or favourers **of** the public **weal** have been discouraged.

Sir *Thomas Elyot.*

THE CROWNING OF ANN BOLEYN

THE Thursday next before the feast of Pentecost, the King and the Queen being at Greenwich, all the crafts of London thereunto well appointed, in several barges decked after the most gorgeous and sumptuous manner, with divers pageants thereunto belonging, repaired and waited all together upon the Mayor of London; and so well furnished came all unto Greenwich, where they tarried and waited for the Queen's coming to her barge: which so done, they brought her unto the Tower, trumpets, shawms, and other divers instruments all the ways playing and making great melody, which, as is reported, was so comely done as never was like in any time nigh to our remembrance.

Cranmer
1533

And so her Grace came to the Tower on Thursday at night, about five of the clock, where also was such a peal of guns as hath not been heard like a great while before. And the same night, and Friday all day, the King and Queen tarried there; and on Friday at night the King's Grace made eighteen Knights of the Bath, whose creation was not alonely so strange to hear of, as also their garments stranger to behold or look on; which said Knights the next day, which was Saturday, rid before the Queen's Grace throughout the city of London towards Westminster Palace, over and besides the most part of the nobles of the realm, which like accompanied her Grace throughout the said City; she sitting in her hair upon a horse litter, richly apparelled, and four Knights of the five ports bearing a canopy over her head. And after her came four rich chariots, one of them empty, and three other furnished with divers ancient old ladies; and after them came a great train of other ladies and gentlewomen; which said progress, from the beginning to the ending, extended half a mile in length by estimation, or thereabout. To whom also, as she came along the City,

Cranmer was shewed **many costly pageants,** with **divers other** 1533 encomies spoken of children to her. Wine also running **at** certain conduits plentifully. **And so** proceeding throughout the streets, [she] passed forth unto Westminster Hall, where was a certain banquet prepared for **her; which** done, she was conveyed out of the backside of the palace into a barge, and so unto York Place, where the **King's Grace was** before her coming: for this you must ever presuppose, that his Grace came always before her secretly in a barge, **as well** from Greenwich to the Tower as from the Tower to York Place.

Now, then, **on Sunday** was the Coronation, which also **was of** such **a** manner. In **the** morning **there** assembled with me at Westminster Church the Bishop of York, the Bishop **of** London, the Bishop of Winchester, the Bishop of Lincoln, **the** Bishop of Bath, and **the Bishop of St. Asse,** the Abbot of Westminster, with ten **or twelve** more abbots, which all revestred ourselves in our pontificalibus, and so furnished, with our crosses and crosiers, proceeded out of the abbey in a procession unto Westminster Hall, where we received the Queen apparelled in a robe of purple velvet, and all the ladies and gentlewomen in robes and gowns of scarlet, according to the manner used before time in such business: and so her Grace, sustained of each side with two Bishops, the Bishop of London and the Bishop of Winchester, came forth in procession unto the Church of Westminster, she in her hair, my Lord of Suffolk bearing before her the Crown, and two other lords bearing also before her a Sceptre and a white rod, and so entered up into the high altar, where divers ceremonies used about her, I did set the Crown on her head, and then was sung *Te Deum,* etc. And after that **was** sung a solemn mass: all which while her Grace sat **crowned** upon a scaffold, which was made between the high altar and the choir in Westminster Church; which mass and ceremonies done and finished, all the assembly of noblemen brought her into Westminster Hall again, where was kept a great solemn feast all that day; the good order thereof were too long to write at this time to you. But now, Sir, you may not imagine that this Coronation was before her marriage; for she was married much about St. Paul's day last, as the condition thereof doth well appear, by reason she is now somewhat big with child. Notwithstanding it hath been reported throughout a great part of the realm that I married her; which was plainly false, for I myself knew not thereof a fortnight after it was done. And many other things be also reported of me which be mere lies and tales.

Cranmer 1533

Thomas Cranmer, Archbishop of Canterbury.

A ROMAN VICTORY

MAXIMUS, in the year following, was so ithandly[1] occupied with this trouble of Britain's, afore rehearsed, that he might not return to the wars of Scots. Nevertheless, many frequent incursions continued all the said time betwixt his wageours[2] and the Scots. At last, when the Scots had assayed long time, howbeit it was in vain, to recover the strengths of Galloway, they passed through Menteith, Stirling, and Fife, and sundry other bounds of Picts, invading the same with such cruelty, that they were left desert. Maximus appeared right heavy at their offences; howbeit nothing was more pleasing to him than to hear the Scots and Picts invading other, to both their mischiefs. Finally, he came in Galloway, with purpose to pass through all the remanent bounds of Scots.

Bellenden 1536

Then was Eugenius not far from the Romans, abiding the coming of his people: to whom compeared great confluence of fencible[3] men and women, to the number of fifty thousand

[1] Continually.   [2] Mercenaries.   [3] Able-bodied.

Bellenden people, right desirous to fight, and crying at once with huge
1536 noise, either to die, or else **to** have victory; for they were
cruelly slain in all parts where they might be apprehended
by Romans, but[1] any mercy or ransom. And, notwithstanding
their great courage, they **were** some part astonist,
hearing the Romans coming in their lands, with more multitude
and puissance of people than ever was seen in any of
their bounds afore. Yet others, having the Roman **tyranny**
at despite, were raised in most fury, regarding nothing **their**
life in defence of their liberty. Then Eugenius, with great
courage, dissimuled his countenance, as he were affrighted of
nothing less than of the Romans; and divided his army in three
battles: **the right wing** was given to his brother Ethodius;
the left **wing to Doalus, captain of** Argyll; **and in** the middleward
was himself. **These battles were arrayed in such** craft,
that in the place where the battle was set, he believed not
only to have **the river of** Munda, **deep but**[1] **any ford,** on the
backs of his army, that they should fight but refuge, but
also to have the sun going to suchlike on their backs, that
their enemies might **not hold** up their een for reflection of
contrary beams in their sight.

Such things done, Eugenius went to a high mound, **and**
called his army to the standard, and said in this manner:
'Our elders that began this realm with continual labour,
and **brought** the same with honour to our days, forcy[2]
champions, commanded their posterity to defend their realm
and liberty, which is most dulce and heavenly treasure in
the earth, against all invaders; having esperance of victory,
when time was to fight against their enemies, in nothing
more than in their hands: and to be obedient to the
wise and noble captains of this realm; whose authority
and prudence be sicker targe,[3] both to their goods, lands,
and lives, against all press and danger of enemies. All our
elders, that are passed afore us, were aye obedient to the

[1] Without.   [2] Strong.   [3] A sure shield.

A ROMAN VICTORY

command of their nobles; and though they have fought oftimes, with sundry chances of battle, against the dantours[1] of the world, yet they were finally victors. Now maun we fight, most valiant champions, with such manhood and courage as our elders fought afore us; or else maun we tine[2] our realm and liberty, and be thirled[3] to most vile servitude, at the will of our enemies. Now approaches Maximus, our cruel and unmerciful enemy, to reif[4] both our lands and goods, if we support not ourself by grace of God and our manhood. He is so full of false ingine[5] and slights, that he is now confederate with Picts, as well in perdition of them as of us; intending therethrough to bring the whole empire of Albion, howbeit the same was never heard afore, under Roman obedience. The Picts, by mischant[6] folly, pass to battle in support of their professed enemies, which are right desirous to reif from them their kingdom and honours. They come against us, which were aye their protectors, since first their realm began. It is uncertain by what mischief these Picts be abused, not knowing the irrecoverable damage that is to fall on them, in eversion of their common weal and liberty: and though they know the same, they give no attendance thereto. Yet, so far as pertains to our action, consider that our enemies are to fight against us, whom we never offended with injuries: through which, their works shall be the more unchancy, and more odious to God. By contrary, remember ye are to resist their invasion, and in your pure defence, are to fight for your realm and liberty: and are the posterity of those forcy champions that sometime most gloriously chased the Romans out of these bounds. Now it is come to such point, that we maun either be vanquished, and suffer extreme misery and servitude, or else to be victors, and stable[7] our lands to us with glory, honour, and permanent ease. I beseech you, my good companions, for the unvincible manhood, faith,

Bellenden 1536

---

[1] Tamers. [2] Lose. [3] Bound. [4] Take by violence.
[5] Cunning (*ingenium*). [6] Wicked. [7] Stablish.

Bellenden and virtue of your elders, and **for** their pale ghosts, which
1536 defended this your realm **in liberty** to these days; to suffer
not you, their sons, **to be reft and** spoilt of your realm,
liberties, and goods; nor yet **to be** taken, as caitiffs, to
underlie their tyrannies. And if it happens you by adverse
chance, which God defend, to die, then do, so far as in you,
to acquit your death; and think, better **is** to die honestly,
than to live in shame. Know yourself dotat[1] with incredible
manhood and virtue; and heritors, by ancient lineage, **as**
well to your noble fathers in wisdom and chivalry as in their
lands; not gathered of divers nations, but of one people
under one mind: and servants to the eternal God, that
gives victory **to** just **people in reward** of their virtue; and
to false and wrongous **people shame,** discomfiture, and
slaughter. **Belt** you, therefore, **lusty gallants,** with manhood and wisdom, to **have victory: which shall not** fail to
succeed,[2] if ye, with constant courage, **have** nothing but
shameful fleeing in dread; and invade your enemies with
suchlike cruelty as they intend to invade you.'

Scarcely had Eugenius raised the spright of his army by
this hortation, when Maximus appeared in sight, with all his
army, and came forthward with more diligence than was
believed: for he came soon after the sun rising. The Scots
were astonished by huge multitude of enemies: nonetheless,
seeing no refuge, they determined to assay the extreme
jeopardy of arms. Soon after, they arrayed them, with
their backs to the sun, that the glance and beams thereof
should not be impediment to their fighting: and scarcely
were they well arrayed, when they rushed forward on their
enemies. This fierce running was impediment to Maximus to
do his devoir; nonetheless, seeing the time so short, he exhorted his army to remember the Roman virtue, and to be
not afraid of barbarous people, whom they recently discomfist.
Incontinent, both the armies, by sound of trumpet, joined,

[1] Endowed.   [2] Follow.

A ROMAN VICTORY

with huge noise and clamour on all sides. At the first coun- Bellenden
tering, it was so cruelly fought, that it was uncertain to what 1536
party most danger succeeded: then followed sundry chances
of fortune. For the Scots that fought in the right wing under
Ethodius, to win no less honour than glory, set on the Picts
forenence[1] them, and chased them through the water of Dune;
where many of them, overset with slik and glar[2] thereof,
were slain: then, by proud and insolent glory, as they had
been sicker of victory, they straggled from their fellows,
cassin[3] to spoil; through which many of them were slain after,
by a Roman legion that was sent by Maximus in support
of the said Picts. In the last wing, where Doalus fought,
the Scots met with Frenchmen, Britons, and Almains:
where they were slain, fighting with persevering manhood to
the death, for defence of their realm. Then all the Roman
army, by command of Maximus, rushed on the middle ward,
where Eugenius fought with his nobles, weary, and near
vanquished by multitude of their enemies: howbeit, many of
them, fiercely repugnant while they might, failed nothing
that pertained to forcy champions. The nobles that fought
in Eugenius's army, seeing the victory incline to Romans,
desired Eugenius to save him by flight to better fortune;
and incontinent they raif[4] off his coat armour perforce, to
make him unknown: nonetheless, he abode, fighting with
persevering malice against the Romans; and was slain the
third year of his reign.

While such terrible murder was made in the army of
Scots, all their carriage men, that were left to keep their
bestial and victuals, having no armour but swords to defend
them, and seeing so many noblemen slain; by piteous com-
miseration rushed on their enemies, and were all slain,
fighting to the death.

While the Romans were following in the chase, by great
ire and hatred, on this manner, they fell in an uncouth

[1] In front of. [2] Slime and mud. [3] Broken up. [4] Tore.

Bellenden
1536

manner of berganc[1]**; for the** aged and feeble persons, **that were** left at home as unfencible bodies, right desirous to hear what chance was fallen **to** their **sons,** came to the place where the battle was: but when **they saw** so piteous and lamentable slaughter made on their sons and friends, they rushed on their enemies like furious **creatures,** regarding neither life, reason, nor age. The women came after, with terrible noise, rummishing[2] as wood,[3] raging beasts, and set on the **Romans.** Nonetheless, both the aged men **and** women were finally slain. The Romans passed the night following with so huge fear and dread, that no trenches nor watching might be sufficient munition to their army; for the hills, valleys, and lesures[4] resounded all the night with most terrible spraichs[5] of yammering[6] people in the deaththrow: for nought was heard but horrible mourning **of sobbing** and dying people, crying a vengeance **on Romans and** Picts, by whose treasonable slights this **huge** murder was **made on** them. On the morrow, Maximus parted the spoil of the field among his army, and made the dead bodies to be buried: and to show him nothing degenerate from Roman mercy, he made them that were left on life, and sore wounded, to be cured with **most** crafty surgeons: among whom was Ethodius, brother to Eugenius, taken, and cured, by ruth of Maximus, of all his wounds.

John Bellenden, Archdean of Moray.

SEEING THE WIND

Ascham
1545

TO see the wind, with **a** man his eyes, it is unpossible, the nature of it is **so** fine, and subtile; yet this experience of the wind had **I** once myself, and that was in the great snow that fell four years ago: I rode in the highway

[1] Skirmish. [2] Roaring. [3] Mad.
[4] Meadow-lands. [5] Shrieks. [6] Lamenting.

betwixt Topcliff-upon-Swale, and Borowe Bridge, the way Ascham being somewhat trodden afore, by wayfaring men. The 1545 fields on both sides were plain and lay almost yard deep with snow, the night afore had been a little frost, so that the snow was hard and crusted above. That morning the sun shone bright and clear, the wind was whistling aloft, and sharp according to the time of the year. The snow in the highway lay loose and trodden with horse feet: so as the wind blew, it took the loose snow with it, and made it so slide upon the snow in the field which was hard and crusted by reason of the frost overnight, that thereby I might see very well the whole nature of the wind as it blew that day. And I had a great delight and pleasure to mark it, which maketh me now far better to remember it. Sometime the wind would be not past two yards broad, and so it would carry the snow as far as I could see. Another time the snow would blow over half the field at once. Sometime the snow would tumble softly, by and by it would fly wonderful fast. And this I perceived also, that the wind goeth by streams and not whole together. For I should see one stream within a score on me, then the space of two score no snow would stir, but after so much quantity of ground, another stream of snow at the same very time should be carried likewise, but not equally. For the one would stand still when the other flew apace, and so continue sometime swiftlier, sometime slowlier, sometime broader, sometime narrower, as far as I could see. Nor it flew not straight, but sometime it crooked this way, sometime that way, and sometime it ran round about in a compass. And sometime the snow would be lift clean from the ground up into the air, and by and by it would be all clapped to the ground as though there had been no wind at all, straightway it would rise and fly again.

And that which was the most marvel of all, at one time two drifts of snow flew, the one out of the West into the East,

Ascham
1545

the other out of the North into the East: and I saw two winds by reason of the snow the one cross over the other, as it had been two highways. And again I should hear the wind blow in the air, when nothing was stirred at the ground. And when all was still where I rode, not very far from me the snow should be lifted wonderfully. This experience made me more marvel at the nature of the wind, than it made me cunning in the knowledge of the wind: but yet thereby I learned perfectly that it is no marvel at all though men in a wind lease their length in shooting, seeing so many ways the wind is so variable in blowing.

Roger Ascham.

A CHARACTER OF LONDON

Latimer
1548

NOW what shall we say of these rich citizens of London? What shall I say of them? Shall I call them proud men of London, malicious men of London, merciless men of London? No, no, I may not say so; they will be offended with me then. Yet must I speak. For is there not reigning in London as much pride, as much covetousness, as much cruelty, as much oppression, and as much superstition, as was in Nebo? Yes, I think, and much more too. Therefore I say, repent, O London; repent, repent. Thou hearest thy faults told thee, amend them, amend them. I think, if Nebo had had the preaching that thou hast, they would have converted. And, you rulers and officers, be wise and circumspect, look to your charge, and see you do your duties; and rather be glad to amend your ill living than to be angry when you are warned or told of your fault. What ado was there made in London at a certain man, because he said

A CHARACTER OF LONDON

(and indeed at that time on a just cause), 'Burgesses!' quoth he, 'nay, Butterflies.' Lord, what ado there was for that word. And yet would God they were no worse than butterflies! Butterflies do but their nature; the butterfly is not covetous, is not greedy of other men's goods; is not full of envy and hatred, is not malicious, is not cruel, is not merciless. The butterfly glorieth not in her own deeds, nor preferreth the traditions of men before God's word; it committeth not idolotry, nor worshippeth false gods. But London cannot abide to be rebuked; such is the nature of man. If they be pricked, they will kick; if they be rubbed on the gall, they will wince; but yet they will not amend their faults, they will not be ill spoken of. But how shall I speak well of them? If you could be content to receive and follow the word of God, and favour good preachers, if you could bear to be told of your faults, if you could amend when you hear of them, if you would be glad to reform that is amiss: If I might see any such inclination in you, that you would leave to be merciless, and begin to be charitable, I would then hope well of you, I would then speak well of you. But London was never so ill as it is now. In times past men were full of pity and compassion, but now there is no pity; for in London their brother shall die in the streets for cold, he shall lie sick at the door between stock and stock, I cannot tell what to call it, and perish there for hunger: Was there ever more unmercifulness in Nebo? I think not. In times past, when any rich man died in London, they were wont to help the poor scholars of the Universities with exhibition. When any man died, they would bequeath great sums of money towards the relief of the poor. When I was a scholar in Cambridge myself, I heard very good report of London, and knew many that had relief of the rich men of London; but now I can hear no such good report, and yet I inquire of it, and hearken for it; but now charity is waxen cold, none helpeth the scholar,

Latimer
1548

Latimer 1548

nor yet the **poor**. And in **those days, what** did they when they helped **the** scholars? **Marry,** they maintained and gave them livings that **were** very papists, and professed the Pope**'s** doctrine: and now **that the** knowledge of God's word is brought to light, and many earnestly study and labour **to set it** forth, now almost no man helpeth to maintain them.

O London, London! repent, repent; for I think **God is** more displeased with London than ever he was with the city of Nebo. **Repent** therefore, repent, London, and remember that **the** same God liveth now that punished Nebo, even the same God, and none other; and he will punish sin **as** well now as he did then: **and he** will punish the iniquity **of** London, as well as he did **then of Nebo.** Amend therefore.
Hugh Latimer.

RALPH HYTHLODAYE

Robinson 1551

WHILE I was there abiding, oftentimes among other, **but** which to me was more welcome than any other, did visit me one Peter Giles, a citizen of Antwerp, a man there in his country of honest reputation, and also preferred to **high** promotions, worthy truly of the highest. For it is hard **to say** whether the young man be in learning or in honesty **more** excellent. For he is both of wonderful virtuous conditions, and also singularly well learned, and towards all sorts of people exceeding gentle: but towards **his** friends so kind-hearted, so loving, so faithful, so trusty, and **of** so earnest affection, that **it** were very hard in any place **to find a** man, that with **him in** all points of friendship may be compared. No man **can be** more lowly or courteous. No man useth less simulation or dissimulation, in no man is more prudent simplicity. Besides this, he is in his talk and

communication so merry and pleasant, yea and that without
harm, that through his gentle entertainment, and his sweet
and delectable communication, in me was greatly abated
and diminished the fervent desire that I had to see my
native country, my wife, and my children, whom then I did
much long and covet to see, because that at that time I had
been more than four months from them. Upon a certain
day when I had heard the divine service in our Lady's
Church, which is the fairest, the most gorgeous and curious
Church of building in all the city, and also most frequented
of people, and the service being done, was ready to go home
to my lodging, I chanced to espy this foresaid Peter talking
with a certain stranger, a man well stricken in age, with a
black sunburned face, a long beard, and a cloak cast homely
about his shoulders, whom, by his favour and apparel forthwith I judged to be a mariner. But the said Peter seeing
me, came unto me and saluted me.

And as I was about to answer him: 'See you this man,'
saith he (and therewith he pointed to the man, that I saw
him talking with before), 'I was minded,' quoth he, 'to bring
him straight home to you.' 'He should have been very
welcome to me,' said I, 'for your sake.' 'Nay' (quoth he)
'for his own sake, if you knew him: for there is no man this
day living that can tell you of so many strange and unknown
peoples, and countries, as this man can. And I know well
that you be very desirous to hear of such news.'

'Then I conjectured not far amiss' (quoth I), 'for even at
the first sight I judged him to be a mariner.'

'Nay' (quoth he), 'there ye were greatly deceived: he hath
sailed indeed, not as the mariner Palinure, but as the expert and prudent prince Ulysses: Yea, rather as the ancient
and sage philosopher Plato. For this same Raphael Hythlodaye (for this is his name) is very well learned in the Latin
tongue, but profound and excellent in the Greek language.
Wherein he ever bestowed more study than in the Latin,

Robinson
1551

Robinson 1551 — because he had given himself wholly to the study of Philosophy. Whereof, **he knew that there** is nothing extant in Latin, that is to any purpose, saving **a** few of Seneca's and Cicero's doings. His patrimony that he was born unto, he left **to** his brethren (for he is a Portugal born), and for the **desire** that he had to see and know the far countries of the **world, he joined** himself in company with **Amerike** Vespuce, and **in the** three last voyages of those four that **be now in print** and abroad in every man's hands, he continued still in his company, saving that in the last voyage he came **not home** again with **him.** For he made such means and shift, what by intreatance, and what **by** importune suit, that he got licence of Master Amerike (though it were sore against **his** will) to be one of **the twenty-four, which in the** end of the last voyage **were left in the country of** Gulike. He **was** therefore left behind **for his mind** sake, **as** one that **took more** thought **and care for** travelling than dying: **having** customably in **his mouth** these sayings: He that **hath no** grave is covered **with** the sky; and, The way to heaven **out** of all places is **of** like length and distance. Which fantasy of his (if God had not been his better friend) he had surely bought full **dear.** But after the departing of of Master Vespuce, when he had travelled through and about many countries with five of his companions, Gulikians, at the last by marvellous chance **he** arrived in Taprobane, from whence **he went to Caliquit,** where he chanced to find certain of **his** country ships, wherein he returned again into his country, nothing less than looked for.'

All this when Peter had told me, I thanked him for his gentle kindness, that he had vouchsafed to bring me to the **speech** of that man, whose communication he thought should **be to** me pleasant and acceptable. And therewith I turned **me to** Raphael. **And when** we had halsed [1] each other, and **had** spoken these common words that be customably

---

[1] Embraced.

spoken at the first meeting and acquaintance of strangers, we went thence to my house, and there in my garden, upon a bench covered with green turves, we sat down talking together. There he told us, how that after the departing of Vespuce, he and his fellows, that tarried behind in Gulike, began by little and little, through fair and gentle speech, to win the love and favour of the people of that country, insomuch that within short space they did dwell amongst them, not only harmless, but also occupying with them very familiarly. He told us also, that they were in high reputation and favour with a certain great man (whose name and country is now quite out of my remembrance), which of his mere liberality did bear the costs and charges of him and his five companions. And besides that gave them a trusty guide to conduct them in their journey (which by water was in boats, and by land in wagons) and to bring them to other princes with very friendly commendations. Thus after many days' journeys, he said, they found towns, and cities, and weal publics, full of people, governed by good and wholesome laws. For under the line equinoctial, and on both sides of the same, as far as the sun doth extend his course, lieth (quoth he) great and wide deserts and wildernesses, parched, burned, and dried up with continual and intolerable heat. All things be hideous, terrible, loathsome, and unpleasant to behold: all things out of fashion and comeliness, inhabited with wild beasts and serpents, or at the leastwise, with people that be no less savage, wild, and noisome than the very beasts themselves be. But a little farther beyond that, all things begin by little and little to wax pleasant. The air soft, temperate, and gentle. The ground covered with green grass. Less wildness in the beasts. 'At the last shall ye come again to people, cities, and towns, wherein is continual intercourse and occupying of merchandise and chaffer, not only among themselves and with their borderers, but also with merchants of far countries, both by land

Robinson
1551

Robinson 1551

and water. **There** I had **occasion**' (said he) 'to go to many countries on every side. **For there was no** ship ready to any voyage or journey but **I** and my fellows were into it very gladly received.' The ships **that** they found first were made plain, flat, and broad in the bottom, troughwise. The sails were made of great rushes, or of wickers, and in some places of leather. Afterward they found ships **with** ridged keels, and sails of canvas: 'yea, and shortly after having all things like **ours**. The shipmen also very expert and cunning both in the sea and in the weather.' But he said, that **he found** great favour and friendship among them, for teaching **them** the feat and the use of the loadstone, which to them **before** that time was **unknown. And** therefore they were wont to be very **timorous and fearful upon the sea,** nor to venture **upon** it but only in the summer **time.** But now they have such **a** confidence **in** that stone, **that** they fear not stormy winter: in **so** doing farther from care than danger, insomuch that it is greatly to be doubted, lest that thing, through their own foolish hardiness, shall turn them to evil and harm, which at the first was supposed should be to them good and commodious.

Ralph Robinson.

WOLSEY'S ARREST

Cavendish 1557

MY lord sitting at dinner upon All-Halloween day in Cawood Castle, having at his board's end divers of his most worthiest chaplains sitting at dinner to keep him company, for lack of strangers, ye shall understand that my lord's great cross of silver accustomably stood in the corner, at the table's end, leaning against the tappet or hanging of the chamber. And when the table's end was taken up, and a convenient time for them to arise; in arising from the table, one Doctor Augustine, physician, being a Venetian born, having a boisterous gown of black velvet upon him; as he would have come out at the table's end, his gown overthrew the cross that stood there in the corner, and the cross trailing down along the tappet, it chanced to fall upon Doctor Bonner's head, who stood among others by the tappet, making of curtsy to my lord, and with one of the points of the cross razed his head a little, that the blood ran down. The company standing there were greatly astonished with the chance. My lord sitting in his chair, looking upon them, perceived the chance, demanded of me, being next him, what the matter meant of their sudden abashment. I showed him how the cross fell upon Doctor Bonner's head. 'Hath it,' quoth he, 'drawn any blood?' 'Yea, forsooth, my lord,' quoth I, 'as it seemeth me.' With that he cast down his head, looking very soberly upon me a good while without any word speaking; at the last, quoth he, shaking of his head: '*Malum omen*'; and therewith said grace, and rose from the table, and went into his bedchamber, there lamenting, making his prayers. Now mark the signification, how my lord expounded this matter unto me afterward at Pomfret Abbey. First, ye shall understand, that the cross, which belonged to the dignity of York, he understood to be himself; and Augustine, he understood, that overthrew the cross, to be he that should accuse him, by means whereof he should be overthrown. The falling upon Master Bonner's head, who was master of my lord's faculties and spiritual jurisdictions, which was damnified by the overthrowing of the cross by the physician, and the drawing of blood betokened death, which shortly after came to pass. About the very same time of the day of this mischance, Master Walshe took his horse at the Court Gate, as nigh as it could be judged. And thus my lord took it for a very sign or token of that which after ensued, if the circumstance be equally considered and noted, although no man was there

Cavendish
1557

present at that time that had any knowledge of Master Walshe's coming down, or what should follow. Wherefore, as it was supposed that God showed him more secret knowledge of his latter days and end of his trouble than all men supposed; which appeared right well by divers talks that he had with me at divers times, of his last end. And now that I have declared unto you the effect of this prodigy and sign, I will return again to my matter.

The time drawing nigh of his stallation; sitting at dinner, upon the Friday next before Monday on the which he intended to be stalled at York, the Earl of Northumberland and Master Walshe, with a great company of gentlemen, as well of the Earl's servants as of the country, which he had gathered together to accompany him in the King's name, not knowing to what purpose or to what intent, came into the hall at Cawood, the officers sitting at dinner, and my lord not fully dined, but being at his fruits, nothing knowing of the Earl's being in his hall. The first thing that the Earl did, after he came into the castle, commanded the porter to deliver him the keys of the gates, who would in no wise deliver him the keys, although he were very roughly commanded in the King's name to deliver them to one of the Earl's servants; saying unto the Earl: 'Sir, ye do intend to deliver them to one of your servants to keep them and the gates, and to plant another in my room; I know no cause why ye should so do, and this I assure you, that you have no one servant, but that I am as able to keep them as he, to what purpose soever it be; and also, the keys were delivered me by my lord, my master, with a charge both by oath and by other precepts and commandments; therefore I beseech your lordship to pardon me, though I refuse your commandment. For whatsoever ye shall command me to do that belongeth to my office, I shall do it with a right good will, as justly as any other of your servants.' With that quoth the gentlemen there present unto the Earl, hearing him speak so stoutly, like a man, and with so good reason: 'Sir,' quoth they, 'he is a good fellow, and speaketh like a faithful servant to his master; and like an honest man: therefore give him your charge, and let him keep still the gates; who, we doubt not, will be obedient to your lordship's commandment.' 'Well then,' quoth the Earl, 'hold him a book,' and commanded him to lay his hand upon the book, whereat the porter made some doubt, but being persuaded by the gentlemen there present, was contented, and laid his hand upon the book, to whom, quoth the Earl: 'Thou shalt swear, to keep well and truly these gates to the king our sovereign lord's use, and to do all such things as we shall command thee in the king's name, being his highness's commissioners, and as it shall seem to us at all times good, as long as we shall be here in this castle; and that ye shall not let in nor out at these gates, but such as ye shall be commanded by us, from time to time.' And upon this oath he received the keys at the Earl's and Master Walshe's hands.

Of all these doings knew my lord nothing; for they stopped the stairs that went up into my lord's chamber where he sat, so that no man could pass up again that was come down. At the last, one of my lord's servants chanced to look down into the hall at a loop that was upon the stairs, and returned to my lord, and showed him that my Lord of Northumberland was in the hall; whereat my lord marvelled, and would not believe him at the first; but commanded a gentleman, being his gentleman-usher, to go down and bring him perfect word. Who going down the stairs, looking down at the loop, where he saw the Earl, who then returned to my lord, and showed him that it was very he. 'Then,' quoth my lord, 'I am sorry that we have dined, for I fear that our officers be not stored of any plenty of good fish, to make him such honourable cheer as to his estate is convenient. Notwithstanding, he shall have such as we have, with a right good will, and loving heart. Let the table be standing still, and we will go down and meet him, and bring him up; and then he shall see how far forth we be at our dinner.' With that he put the table from him and rose up; going down, he encountered the Earl upon the midst of the stairs, coming up, with all his men about him. **nd** as soon as my lord espied **the** Earl, he put off his cap, and **said to** him : 'My lord, ye be most heartily welcome,' and therewith **they** embraced **each** other. 'Although, my lord,' quoth he, 'that I have often desired and wished in my heart to see you in **my house, yet** if ye had loved me as I do you, ye would have sent me **word** before **of your** coming, to the intent that I might have received **you according** to your honour and mine. Notwithstanding, ye shall have such cheer **as I** am able to make you, with a right **good will; trusting that** ye will accept the same of me as **of your very old** and loving friend, hoping hereafter to see you oftener, when I shall be more able, and better provided to receive you **with** better fare.' And **then** my lord took the Earl of Northumberland by the **hand, and** led him up into the chamber; whom followed all **the Earl's** servants; where the table stood in the state that **my lord left** it when he rose, saying unto the Earl : 'Sir, now ye may perceive how far forth we were at our dinner.' Then my lord led the Earl to the fire, saying : 'My lord, ye shall go into my bedchamber, where is a good fire made for you, and there ye may shift your apparel until your chamber be made ready. Therefore, let your male be brought up: and or ever I go, I pray you give me leave to take these gentlemen, your servants, by the hands.' And when he had taken them all by the hands, he returned to the Earl, and said : '**Ah**! my lord, I perceive well that ye have observed my old precepts and instructions which I gave you, when you were abiding with me in your youth, which was, to cherish your **father's** old servants, whereof I see here present with you a great number. Surely, my lord, ye do therein very well and nobly, and like a wise gentleman; for these be they that will not only serve and love you, but they will also live and die with you, and be true and faithful servants to you, and glad to see you prosper in honour; the which I beseech God to send you, with long life.' This said, he took the Earl by the hand, and led him into his bedchamber. And they being there all alone, save only I, that kept the door, according to my duty, being gentleman usher, these two lords standing at a window by the chimney, in my lord's bedchamber, the Earl trembling said, with a very faint and soft voice, unto my lord (laying his hand upon his arm): 'My lord, I arrest you of high treason.' With which words my lord was marvellously astonied, standing both still a long space without any further words. But at the last, quoth my lord: 'What moveth you, or by what authority do you this?' 'Forsooth, my lord,' quoth the Earl, 'I have a commission to warrant me and my doings.' 'Where is your commission?' quoth my lord, 'let me see it.' 'Nay, sir, that you may not,' quoth the Earl. 'Well, then,' quoth my lord, 'I will not obey your arrest; for there hath been between some of your predecessors and mine great contentions and debate grown upon an ancient grudge, which may succeed in you, with like inconvenience, as it hath done heretofore. Therefore, unless I see your authority and commission, I will not obey you.' Even as they were debating this matter between them in the chamber, so busily was Master Walshe arresting of Doctor Augustine, the physician, at the door within the portal, whom I heard say unto him: 'Go in then, traitor, or I shall make thee'; and with that, I opened the portal door, and the same being opened, Master Walshe thrust Doctor Augustine in before him with violence. These matters on both the sides astonied me very sore, musing what all this should mean; until at the last, Master Walshe, being entered the chamber, began to pluck off his hood, the which he had made him with a coat of the same

Cavendish
1557

Cavendish cloth, of cotton, to the intent he would not be known. And
1557 after he had plucked **it off, he kneeled** down to my lord, to whom he spake first, commanding him to stand up, saying thus: 'Sir, here my Lord of Northumberland hath arrested me of treason, but by what authority **or** commission he showeth me not; but saith he hath **one.** If ye be privy thereto, or be joined with him therein, I pray you show me.' 'Indeed, my lord,' quoth Master Walshe, 'if it please your **Grace, it is** true that he hath one.' 'Well, then,' said my **lord, 'I pray you** let me see it.' 'Sir, I beseech your Grace **hold us** excused,' quoth Master Walshe, 'there is annexed **unto** our commission a schedule with certain instructions which **ye** may in **no wise be privy unto.**' 'Why,' quoth my lord, **'be** your instructions such that **I** may not see them? Peradventure, if I might be privy to them, I could the better help you **to** perform them. It **is not** unknown unto you both, I am assured, but **I** have been privy and **of** counsel in **as** weighty matters **as this** is, for **I** doubt not for my part **but I** shall prove and clear myself to be a true man against **the** expectation of all my cruel enemies. I have an understanding whereupon all this matter groweth. Well, there is no more **to** do. I trow, gentlemen, ye be one of the King's Privy Chamber; your name, I suppose, is Walshe; I am content to yield unto you, but not to my Lord of Northumberland, without I see his commission. And also you are a sufficient commissioner yourself in that behalf, inasmuch as ye be one of the King's Privy Chamber; for the worst person there is a sufficient warrant to arrest the greatest peer of this realm, by the King's only commandment, without any commission. Therefore I am ready to be ordered and disposed at your will. Put therefore the King's commission and **your** authority in execution, a' God's name, and spare not, **and I** will obey the King's will and pleasure; for I fear **more** the cruelty of my unnatural enemies than I do my **truth and** allegiance; wherein, I take God to witness, I

never offended the King's Majesty in word or deed; and Cavendish therein I dare stand face to face with any man alive, having 1557 indifferency without partiality.'

Then came my Lord of Northumberland unto me, standing at the portal door, and commanded me to avoid the chamber: and being loth to depart from my master, I stood still, and would not remove; to whom he spake again, and said: 'There is no remedy, ye must needs depart.' With that I looked upon my lord, as who sayeth, shall I go? Upon whom my lord looked very heavily, and shook at me his head. Perceiving by his countenance it booted me not to abide, and so I departed the chamber, and went into the next chamber, where abode many gentlemen of my fellows and other, to learn of me some news of the matter within; to whom I made report what I saw and heard; which was to them great heaviness to hear.

George Cavendish.

TWO BISHOPS

1

AMONG many other worthy and sundry histories and Foxe notable acts of such as of late days have been tur- 1563 moiled, murdered, and martyred for the true gospel of Christ in Queen Mary's reign, the tragical story and life of Dr. Ridley I thought good to commend to chronicle and leave to perpetual memory; beseeching thee (gentle reader) with care and study well to peruse, diligently to consider, and deeply to print the same in thy breast, seeing him to be a man beautified with such excellent qualities, so ghostly inspired and godly learned, and now written doubtless in the book of life, with the blessed saints of the Almighty, crowned and throned amongst the glorious company of martyrs. First, descending of a stock right worshipful, he was born in

Foxe
1563

Northumberlandshire, **who, being** a child, learned his grammar with great dexterity in Newcastle, and was removed from thence to the University of Cambridge, where he **in** short time became so famous, that **for** his singular aptness, he was called to higher functions and offices of the University, by degree attaining thereunto, and was **called to be** head of Pembroke Hall, and there made doctor of divinity. **After** this, departing from thence, he travelled to Paris, **who, at his return, was** made chaplain to King Henry the Eighth, **and promoted** afterwards by him to the bishopric **of** Rochester; and so from thence translated to the see **and** bishopric of London in **King** Edward's **days.**

In which calling and offices **he so** travailed and occupied himself by preaching and **teaching the true** and wholesome doctrine of Christ, that never **good** child was more singularly loved of his dear parents **than he of his flock** and diocese. Every holiday and Sunday **he** lightly **preached in** some one place **or** other, except he **were otherwise** letted by weighty affairs **and** business, to whose **sermons the** people resorted, swarming **about** him like bees, **and** coveting the sweet flowers **and** wholesome juice of the fruitful doctrine, which he did **not** only preach, but showed the same by **his** life, **as a** glittering lanthorn to **the** eyes and senses of the blind, in such **pure order** and chastity of life (declining from all evil desires **and** concupiscences) that even his very enemies could not reprove him in any one jot thereof.

Besides this, he was passingly well learned, his memory was great, and he of such reading withal, that of right he deserved to be comparable to the best of this our age, as can testify as well divers his notable works, pithy sermons, and sundry his disputations in both the Universities, as also his very adversaries, all which will say no less themselves.

Besides all this, wise he **was** of counsel, deep of wit, and **very** politic in all his doings. How merciful and careful he **was** to reduce the obstinate papists from their erroneous opinions, and by gentleness to win them to the truth, his gentle ordering and courteous handling of Dr. Heath, late Archbishop of York, being prisoner with him in King Edward's time in his house one year, sufficiently declareth. In fine, he was such a prelate, and in all points so good, godly, and ghostly a man, that England may justly rue the loss of so worthy a treasure. And thus hitherto concerning these public matters.

Foxe
1563

Now will I speak something further, particularly of his person and conditions. He was a man right comely and well proportioned in all points, both in complexion and lineaments of the body. He took all things in good part, bearing no malice nor rancour in his heart, but straightways forgetting all injuries and offences done against him. He was very kind and natural to his kinsfolk, and yet not bearing with them anything otherwise than right would require, giving them always for a general rule, yea to his own brother and sister, that they, doing evil, should seek or look for nothing at his hand, but should be as strangers and aliens unto him; and they to be his brother and sister, which used honesty and a godly trade of life.

He, using all kinds of ways to mortify himself, was given to much prayer and contemplation; for duly every morning, so soon as his apparel was done upon him, he went forthwith to his bedchamber, and there upon his knees prayed the space of half an hour; which being done, immediately he went to his study, if there came no other business to interrupt him, where he continued till ten of the clock, and then came to the common prayer, daily used in his house. The prayers being done, he went to dinner, where he used little talk, except otherwise occasion by some had been ministered, and then was it sober, discreet, and wise, and sometimes merry, as cause required.

The dinner done, which was not very long, he used to sit an hour or thereabouts, talking, or playing at the chess: that

Foxe
1563

done, he returned **to his** study, **and** there would continue, except suitors **or business abroad** were occasion of the contrary, until five of the **clock at** night, and then would come to common prayer, as in the forenoon : which being finished, he went to supper, behaving himself there as at his dinner before. After supper recreating himself in playing **at** chess **the** space of an hour, he would then return again to his **study,** continuing there till eleven of the clock **at** night, which was **his** common hour to go to bed, then saying **his** prayers upon **his** knees, as **in** the morning when he rose. Being at his manor of Fulham, as divers times he used to be, he read daily **a** lecture **to his** family **at the** common prayer, beginning at the Acts **of the Apostles, and so** going through all the Epistles of **St. Paul, giving, to** every **man** that could **read,** a New Testament, hiring **them** besides **with** money to **learn** by heart certain principal chapters, but especially Acts xiii., reading also unto his household oftentimes Psalm ci., **being** marvellous careful over his family**, that** they might be **a spectacle** of all virtue and honesty to others. To be short, **as he** was godly and virtuous himself, so nothing but virtue **and** godliness reigned in his house, feeding them with the food of our Saviour Jesus Christ.

Now **remaineth** a word **or** two to be declared of his gentle nature **and kindly** pity in **the** usage of an old woman called Mrs. **Bonner,** mother to Dr. Bonner, sometime Bishop of London, **which** I thought good to touch, as well for the rare clemency **of** Dr. Ridley, **as** the unworthy inhumanity and ungrateful disposition again of Dr. Bonner. Bishop Ridley, being at his manor of Fulham, always sent for this said Mrs. Bonner, dwelling in a house adjoining to his house, to dinner **and** supper, with one Mrs. Mungey, Bonner's sister, saying, '**Go for** my mother Bonner'; who, coming, was ever placed **in the** chair at the table's end, being so gently entreated, **welcomed,** and taken, **as** though he had been born of her **own body,** being never displaced of her seat, although the

King's Council had been present; saying, when any of them were there, as divers times they were: 'By your Lordship's favour, this place of right and custom is for my mother Bonner.' But how well he was recompensed for this his singular gentleness and pitiful piety after, at the hands of the said Dr. Bonner, almost the least child that goeth by the ground can declare. For who afterward was more enemy to Ridley than Bonner and his? Who more went about to seek his destruction than he? Recompensing this his gentleness with his extreme cruelty; as well appeared by the strait handling of Ridley's own natural sister, and George Shipside her husband, from time to time: whereas the gentleness of the other did suffer Bonner's mother, sister, and other of his kindred, not only quietly to enjoy all that which they had of Bonner, but also entertained them in his house, showing much courtesy and friendship daily unto them: whereas on the other side, Bishop Bonner, being restored again, would not suffer the brother and natural sister of Bishop Ridley, and other his friends, not only not to enjoy that which they had by the said their brother Bishop Ridley, but also currishly, without all order of law or honesty, by extort power wrested from them all the livings they had.

And yet, being not therewith satisfied, he sought all the means he could to work the death of the foresaid Shipside, saying, that he would make twelve godfathers to go upon him; which had been brought to pass indeed, at what time he was prisoner at Oxford, had not God otherwise wrought his deliverance by means of Dr. Heath, then the Bishop of Worcester.

Hereby all good indifferent readers notoriously have to understand what great diversity was in the disposition of these two natures, whereof as the one excelled in mercy and pity, so the other again as much or more excelled in churlish ingratitude and despiteful disdain. But of this matter enough.

Foxe
1563

II

Foxe
1563

THE next month after the burning of Dr. Ridley and Master Latimer, which was the month of November, Stephen Gardiner, Bishop and Chancellor, a man hated of God and all good men, ended his wretched life: concerning the qualities, nature, and disposition of which man, forsomuch as somewhat hath been declared before in the story of King Edward's reign, I shall need therefore the less now to stand greatly upon the same. First, this viper's bird, crept out of the town of Bury in Suffolk, was brought up most part of his youth in Cambridge; his wit, capacity, memory, and other endowments of nature were not to be complained of, if he had well used and rightly applied the same; wherein there was no great want of God's part in him, if he had not rather himself wanted to the goodness of his gifts. Through this promptness, activity, and towardness of his, he profited not a little in such studies as he gave his head unto, as first in the civil law, then in languages and such other like, especially in those arts and faculties which had any prospect to dignity and preferment to be hoped for. Besides other ornaments or helps of nature, memory chiefly seemed in him very beneficial, rather than diligence of study.

To these gifts and qualities were joined again as great or greater vices, which not so much followed him, as overtook him; not so much burdened him, as made him burdenous to the whole realm. He was of a proud stomach and high-minded, in his own opinion and conceit flattering himself too much; in wit, crafty and subtle; towards his superiors flattering and fair spoken; to his inferiors fierce; against his equal stout and envious, namely, if in judgment and sentence he anything withstood him, as appeared between the good Lord Cromwell and him in the reign of King Henry, being of like haughtiness of stomach as the poets write of Pelides, *cedere nescius*: who, although he would give no place to men, yet notwithstanding I wish he would have given place to truth, according as he seemed not altogether ignorant of that truth. What his knowledge was therein, it is evidently partly to understand as well by his book *De Verâ Obedientiâ*, as also by his sermon before King Edward. Also by his answers to the council the same time, and moreover by his own words it may be gathered in sundry places, as more plainly may appear by that which hereafter followeth.

Foxe
1563

Upon his estimation and fame he stood too much, more than was meet for a man of his coat and calling, whose profession was to be crucified unto the world, which thing made him so stiff in maintaining that he had once begun to take upon him. I will not here speak of that which hath been constantly reported to me touching the monstrous making and misshaped fashion of his feet and toes, the nails whereof were said not to be like to other men's, but to crook downward, and to be sharp like the claws of ravening beasts. What his learning was in the civil and canon law I have not to say. What it was in other liberal sciences and arts, this I suppose, that neither his continuance in study, nor diligence of reading was such (by reason of his too mnch intermeddling in prince's matters) as could truly well merit unto him the title of a deep learned man. But what learning or cunning soever it was he had, so it fared in him, as it doth in butchers, which used to blow up their flesh: even so he with boldness and stoutness, and specially with authority, made those gifts that he had to appear much greater than they were in very deed. Whereunto, peradventure, use also, and experience abroad, brought no little helps, rather than either quickness of wit or happiness of education.

And as touching divinity, he was so variable, wavering with time, that no constant censure can be given what to make of him. If his doings and writings were according to his conscience, no man can rightly say whether he was a right protestant or papist. If he wrote otherwise than he thought, for fear or to bear with time, then was he a double deep dissembler before God and man, to say and unsay, to write and unwrite, to swear and forswear, so as he did. For first in the beginning of Queen Anne's time, who was so forward or so busy in the matter of the King's divorce as Stephen Gardiner, who was first sent to Rome, and then to the Emperor with Edmund Foxe, as chief agent in the behalf of the Lady Anne? by whom also he was preferred to the bishopric of Winchester, as Edward Bonner was preferred to the bishopric of London. Again, at the abolishing of the Pope, who so ready to swear or so vehement to write against the Pope as he, as not only by his sermons, but also by his book *De Obedientiâ* may appear? in which book *De Obedientiâ*, lest any should think him drawn thereunto otherwise than by his own consent, he plainly declareth how, not rashly nor upon a sudden, but upon a long deliberation and advertisement in himself about the matter, he at length uttered his judgment; whereof read before. And moreover, so he uttered his judgment in writing against the usurped supremacy of the Pope, that, coming to Louvain afterward, he was there accounted for a person excommunicate and a schismatic, insomuch that he was not permitted in their church to say mass; and moreover in their public sermons they openly cried out against him. Whereof read hereafter following.

And thus long continued he firm and forward, so that who but Winchester, during all the time and reign of Queen Anne? After her decease that time by little and little carried him away, till at length the emulation of Cromwell's estate, and especially (as it seemeth) for his so much favouring of Bonner, whom Winchester at that time in no case could abide, made him an utter enemy both against him, and also his religion: till again, in King Edward's days, he began a little to rebate from certain points of popery, and somewhat to smell of the gospel, as both by his sermon before King Edward, as also by his subscribing to certain articles, may appear. And this was a half turn of Stephen Gardiner from popery again to the gospel, and, no doubt, he would have further turned, had not the unlucky decay of the Duke of Somerset clean turned him away from true divinity to plain popery, wherein he continued a cruel persecutor to his dying day.

Foxe
1563

And thus much concerning the trade and profession of Stephen Gardiner's popish divinity. In which his popish trade, whether he followed more true judgment, or else time, or rather the spirit of ambition and vainglory, it is doubtful to say; and so much the more doubtful, because in his doings and writings a man may see him not only contrary to himself, but also in some points contrary to other papists. And furthermore, where he agreeth with them, he seemeth therein not so much to follow his own sense, as the mind and meaning of Pereseus; out of whose book the greatest part of Winchester's divinity seemeth to be borrowed.

And therefore as in the true knowledge of God's holy word and scripture he appeareth nobody; so in his pen and style of writing no less far is he from commendation, than he is from all plainness and perspicuity: in whose obscure and perplex kind of writing, although peradventure some sense may be found with some searching, yet shall no reader find any sweetness in his reading.

John Foxe.

A PRETTY THEFT

THEN by and by Babulus and I devised a pretty sport: we drew one of the greatest of the bears to our lodging, as though we would prepare to eat thereof, where we

Adlington
1566

Adlington 1566

flayed off his skin, and kept his ungles[1] whole, but we meddled not with the head, **but cut it off by** the neck, and so let **it** hang to the skin. Then **we rased off the** flesh from the neck, and cast dust thereon, and set it **in** the sun to dry.

When the skin was a drying we **made** merry with the flesh, and then we devised with ourselves, **that one** of us being more valiant than the rest both in **body and** courage (so that he would consent thereto) should put **on the skin**, and feigning that he were a bear, should be led **to Demo**chares' house in the night, by which means we thought **to be received and let in.** Many were desirous to play the bear, but especially one **Thrasileon of** a courageous mind would take this enterprise **in hand. Then we** put him into **the bear's** skin, which fitted **him finely in** every point, we buckled **it** fast under his belly**, and covered** the seam with the hair, that it might **not be seen. After** this **we** made little holes through the bear's head, **and** through his nostrils and eyes, for Thrasileon to see out and take wind at, in such sort **that he** seemed a very lively and natural beast: when this was done we went into a cave which we hired **for the** purpose, and he crept **in** after like a bear with a good courage. Thus we began our subtilty, and then **we** imagined thus : **we** feigned letters as though they came from one Nicanor, which dwelt in the country of Thracia, which was of great acquaintance with this Demochares, wherein we wrote, that **he** had sent **him** being his friend, the first fruits of his coursing and hunting. When night was come, which was **a** meet time for our purpose, we brought Thrasileon and **our** forged letters and presented them to Demochares. **When** Demochares beheld this mighty bear, and saw the liberality of Nicanor his friend, he commanded his servants to deliver unto us ten crowns, having great store in his coffers. Then (as the novelty of a thing doth accustom to stir men's **minds to** behold the **same**) many persons came on every side

---
[1] Claws.

to see this bear: but Thrasileon, lest they should by curious viewing and prying perceive the truth, ran upon them to put them in fear that they durst not come nigh. The people said: 'Verily Demochares is right happy, in that after the death of so many beasts, he hath gotten, maugre fortune's head, so goodly a bear.' Then Demochares commanded him with all care to be put into the park among the other beasts: but immediately I spake unto him and said: 'Sir, I pray you take heed how you put a beast tired with the heat of the sun and with long travel among others which, as I hear say, have divers maladies and diseases; let him rather lie in some open place of your house nigh some water, where he may take air and ease himself, for do not you know that such kind of beasts do greatly delight to couch under the shadow of trees and hillocks near pleasant wells and waters?' Hereby Demochares admonished, and remembering how many he had before that perished, was contented we should put the bear where we would. Moreover we said unto him, that we ourselves were determined to lie all night near the bear, to look unto him, and to give him meat and drink at his due hour.

Then he answered: 'Verily, masters, you need not put yourselves to such pains, for I have men that serve for nothing but for that purpose.' So we took leave of him and departed: and when we were come without the gates of the town, we perceived before us a great sepulchre standing out of the highway in a privy and secret place, and thither we went and opened the mouth thereof, whereas we found the sides covered with the corruption of man, and the ashes and dust of his long-buried body, wherein we got ourselves to bring our purpose to pass, and having respect to the dark time of night, according to our custom, when we thought that every one was asleep, we went with our weapons and besieged the house of Demochares round about. Then Thrasileon was ready at hand, and leaped out of the cavern,

Adlington 1566

and went to kill all such as he found asleep: but when he came to the porter, he opened the gates and let us all in, and then he showed us a large counter, wherein we saw put the night before a great abundance of treasure: which when by violence we had broken open, I bade every one of my fellows take as much gold and silver as they could carry away, and bear it to the sepulchre, and still as they carried I stood at the gate, watching diligently when they should return. The bear runned about the house, to make such of the family afeared as fortuned to wake and come out. For who is he that is so puissant and courageous, that at the ugly sight of so great a monster will not quail and keep his chamber, especially in the night? But when we had brought this matter to so good a point, there chanced a pitiful case, for as I looked for my companions that should come from the sepulchre, behold there was a boy of the house that fortuned to look out of a window, and espied the bear running about, and he went and told all the servants of the house. Whereupon incontinently they came forth with torches, lanthorns, and other lights, that they might see all the yard over: they came with clubs, spears, naked swords, greyhounds, and mastiffs to slay the poor beast. Then I during this broyle thought to run away, but because I would see Thrasileon fight with the dogs, I lay behind the gate to behold him. And although I might perceive that he was well nigh dead, yet remembered he his own faithfulness and ours, and valiantly resisted the gaping and ravenous mouths of the hell hounds, so took he in gree the pageant which willingly he took in hand himself, and with much ado tumbled at length out of the house: but when he was at liberty abroad yet could he not save himself, for all the dogs of the street joined themselves to the greyhounds and mastiffs of the house, and came upon him.

Alas, what a pitiful sight it was to see our poor Thrasileon thus environed and compassed with so many dogs that tare and rent him miserably. Then I, impatient of so great a misery, ran in amongst the press of the people, and aiding him with my words as much as I might, exhorted them all in this manner: 'O great and extreme mischance, what a precious and excellent beast have we lost.' But my words did nothing prevail, for there came out a tall man with a spear in his hand, that thrust him clean through, and afterwards many that stood by drew out their swords, and so they killed him. But verily our good Captain Thrasileon, the honour of our comfort, received his death so patiently, that he would not betray the league between us, either by crying, howling, or any other means, but being torn with dogs and wounded with weapons, did yield forth a doleful cry, more like unto a beast than a man. And taking his present fortune in good part, with courage and glory enough did finish his life, with such a terror unto the assembly, that no person was so hardy until it was day, as to touch him, though he were stark dead: but at last there came a butcher more valiant than the rest, who, opening the paunch of the beast, slit out an hardy and venturous thief.

In this manner we lost our Captain Thrasileon, but he lost not his fame and honour.

Adlington 1566

William Adlington.

AN OLD MAN'S MISADVENTURE

I HAD of late years an old man to my tenant, who customably a great time went twice in the week to London, either with fruit or with peascods, when time served therefor. And as he was coming homeward on Blackheath, at the end thereof next to Shooters' Hill, he overtook two rufflers,[1] the one mannerly waiting on the other, as one had been the master, and the other the man or servant,

Harman 1567

[1] Part foot-pad, part cheat, part beggar.

carrying his **master's cloak**. **This** old man was **very** glad that he might have their company over the Hill, because that day he had made a good **market; for** he had seven shillings in his purse, and an old angel, **which** this poor man had thought had **not** been in his purse, for **he** willed his wife over night to take out the same angel, **and lay it up** until his coming home again. And he verily thought **that** his wife had **so** done, which indeed forgot to do **it**. **Thus** after salutations had, this master ruffler entered **into communication** with this simple old man, who, riding softly beside them, **communed of many** matters. Thus feeding this old **man** with pleasant talk, until **they were on** the top of the Hill, where these rufflers might well **behold** the coast about them clear, quickly steps **unto this poor man, and** taketh hold of **his** horse-bridle, **and** leadeth **him** into **the wood,** and demandeth of him what **and** how **much money he** had in his purse. 'Now, by my troth,' **quoth** this old man; 'you are a merry gentleman. I know you **mean not to** take away anything from me, but rather to give me some if I should ask it **of you.' By** and by, this servant thief casteth the cloak **that he** carried on his arm about this poor man's face, that he should not mark or view them, with sharp words to deliver quickly that he **had, and to** confess truly what was in his purse. **This** poor man, **then** all abashed, yielded, and confessed **that he** had but just seven shillings in his purse; and the truth is he knew of no more. This old angel was fallen out of a little purse into the bottom of a great purse. **Now**, this seven shillings in **white** money they quickly found, thinking indeed that there had been no more; yet farther groping and searching, found this old angel. And with great admiration this gentleman thief began to bless him, saying: 'Good Lord, what a world is this! How may' (quoth he) 'a man believe or trust **in** the same? See you not' (quoth he) 'this old knave told me that he had but seven shillings, and here is more by an angel: what an old knave and a false knave have we here!' quoth this ruffler; 'Our Lord have mercy on us, will this world never be better?'—and therewith went their way. And left the old man in the wood, doing him no more harm. But sorrowfully sighing, this old man, returning home, declared his misadventure, with all the words and circumstances above showed. Whereat for the time was great laughing, and this poor man for his losses among his loving neighbours well considered in the end.

Harman 1567

Thomas Harman.

AN ESCAPE

AFTER this a long time there was peace and rest in the realm, and that through the court and counsel of the Duke of Albany, who soon thereafter married the Earl of Orkney's daughter, and begat upon her a son, called Alexander, who was thereafter Bishop of Moray, but not long after he parted with her, and passed in France, and was married upon the Duchess of Boulogne. But this Alexander, Duke of Albany, had the great indignation of many of the nobles in Scotland, for fortifying and maintaining the King in his private affairs, and gave him the wyte that so many Lords were in captivity at that time, and for rendering of Berwick, according to the King's promise, who gave him commission to render the same for his relief. And the Lords could not be content therewith, but alleged it to be treason; and were very desirous to have had some crime to accuse the Duke of Albany, and to have put a new suspicion betwixt him and his brother the King, thinking well they could [not] anyways get their will of the King except they had his brother cut off. And for that effect they caused certain flatterers and evil speakers show the King that the Duke of Albany

Lindsay 1570

Lindsay
1570

intended to have the Crown, **for he was** likelier **to be** king nor the King himself **as he proceeded;** for he disponed all things pertaining to the liberty **of** the Crown, and caused the King to understand that he would fulfil the prophecy of the witch who prophesied to the King that the nearest of his kin should destroy him. These words, and sic like other feigned tales, made the King so afeard of the Duke of Albany, that he could have been content to have been quit of him, notwithstanding **of** all the travails he had made for **the** King's weal, and **for the** delivering of him out of captivity. All his **good service was forgot** with this flattery, and the **fear** that **the** King **took of** him by the persuasion of wicked counsellors **caused him to summon** his brother before the Council for such points of **treason as after** follows. That is **to say: for** rendering the **town of Berwick** in Englishmen's **hands** but counsel or commission of **the** Lords of Scotland. So the Duke of Albany compeared pertly [1] before the **King** and Council, and produced the King's commission, under his Great Seal, to render the same, to the effect that support might come to the King for his deliverance. But the Lords alleged that commission was of no effect at that time, because he was in captivity, and did the same without the advice of the Lords and Council. Wherefore the Lords of Council for the time convicted the said Duke, and sent him to the Castle to be imprisoned.

In this meantime, the Earl of Angus got the whole lords that was in ward relieved,[2] upon caution to enter again when the King pleased, under the pain of ten thousand pounds each man, etc. Soon after this they counselled the King to justify[3] his brother, the Duke of Albany, thinking if they **were quit** of him they **should** do with the King what they **pleased.** For they stood in sic awe of the Duke that they **durst** never meddle **with** the King, nor put hands on him, **he being** alive. Wherefore these conspirators insisted and

[1] Readily.   [2] Released.   [3] Execute.

were very desirous to have this noble and famous man put to death, and continued in this ungodly and unleisum[1] suit, till it was known in France by sic as favoured the Duke of Albany; and therefore there came a French ship out of France hastily in Scotland, with secret writings to the Duke of Albany, who was then in prison in the Castle of Edinburgh, to advertise him that it was concluded by the King and Council that he should be justified upon a certain day, which was the day after the ship came to the town of Leith, beside Newhaven, and gave herself forth as a passenger with wine. When he had heard of these news, he desired leave of the Captain to send for two bottles of wine, who gave him leave gladly, and provided the bosses[2] himself: and then the Duke of Albany sent one of his familiar servants to the Frenchman, and desired him to bring him of the finest and starkest wine, who was obeyed thankfully, and sent him two bosses of Malvesie; and in the one end of the bottle put a roll of wax, wherein was enclosed a secret writing, which showed the Duke of Albany sic news as he was not content therewith; and in the other boss there was a long tow[3] to support him in his need. So the messenger hasted him back to the Castle, and showed his master certain things by tongue which the Frenchman had told him; and that night the Duke called the Captain to supper, and promised him a drink of good wine. So the Captain came to him gladly, and supped with him. The Duke gave his chamber-child command that he should drink no wine that night, but hold himself temperate, for he knew not what he would have to do, and if there arose any dissention betwixt him and the Captain, he prayed him to stand by him, as he should be a good master to him thereafter. When the supper was done, the Captain passed to the King's chamber to see what was doing, who was then lodged in the Castle: and when he had visited all, he caused them close the gates and set the watch-

Lindsay
1570

---

[1] Hateful.   [2] Bottles.   [3] Rope.

Lindsay 1570

men; and thereafter **came** to the Duke's chamber to the collation. And after they had drunken their collation, and all men in their beds, the Duke **and the** Captain passed to the tables and played for the wine. The fire was hot and the wine was strong, and the Captain and his men became merry, till at the last the Duke perceived his time, and saw them merry, and made a sign to his chamber-child to be ready as he had instructed him, for the Duke was fully resolved either to do or to die; for he was surely informed by the French ship that he was to be beheaded on the **morrow.** So he thought best to preveine[1] the time, and leaped from the board and struck the Captain with a whinger and **slew him, and** also sticked other **two** with his own hand. **And in** the meantime **his chamber-child was very** busy; **and so** they two overthrew **five: that is, the** Captain and **four of** his men: and when they had done, cast them in the fire; and afterwards took out their **tows and passed** to the wall-head, at a quiet place **where** the watchmen might have **no** sight of them, and then stretched their cords over the wall-head, and the chamber-boy passed first; but the tows were short, and he fell and broke his thigh-bone. Then he cried to his master to make the tow longer, for he was gone. Then the Duke rived the sheets off his bed and lengthened the tow, **and** passed safely himself. And when he was come down and perceived his servant in point of death, he took him upon his back and carried him away as far as he might, and left him **in a** quiet place where he trowed he might be safe, and syne went to the Newhaven beside Leith, and made him a sign to the ship, who sent a boat to the land and received him in. But no man knew whether his servant went with him or not; but surely many gentlemen of Scotland wished themselves to have been with him, and, amongst the rest, Sir Alexander Jardine of Applegarth, knight, passed with him, and sundry other gentlemen.

[1] Anticipate.

But on the morn, when the watchmen perceived that the tows were hanging over the walls, then ran they to seek the Captain to show him the matter and manner, but he was not in his own chamber. Then they passed to the Duke's chamber and found the door open, and a dead man lying in the chamber door, and the Captain and the rest burning in the fire, which was very dolorous to them; and when they missed the Duke of Albany and his chamber-child, they ran speedily and showed the King how the matter had happened. But he would not give it credence till he passed himself and saw the matter. Then he considered the whole cause how it stood, and caused the gates to be holden close, that no word should pass to the town, till he had searched all the place, to see whether the Duke of Albany was within or not. But when he could not find him, he caused horsemen to be sent forth in all parts to see if they could apprehend him in any place, and bring him to him again, and they should have great rewards therefor. But yet they could get no kind of trial[1] of him, until at the last there came a man out of Leith and showed the King that there came a boat from the French ship and took in certain men, and thereafter pulled up her sails, and travished[2] up and down the Firth, whom they judged to be the Duke of Albany, as it was true; for he passed to France incontinent, and got in marriage the Duchess of Boulogne. *Robert Lindsay of Pitscottie.*

Lindsay
1570

THE KILLING OF DAVID BEATON

AFTER the death of this blessed martyr of God [George Wishart] began the people, in plain speaking, to damn and detest the cruelty that was used. Yea, men of great birth, estimation, and honour, at open tables avowed, that the blood of the said Master George should be revenged, or else they

Knox
1572

---

[1] Sign, news.   [2] Sailed back and forward.

should cost life for life. Amongst whom John Lesley, brother to the Earl of Rothes, was the chief; for he, in all companies, spared not to say, 'That same whinger (showing forth his dagger), and that same hand, should be priests to the Cardinal.' These bruits came to the Cardinal's ears; but he thought himself stout enough for all Scotland; for in Babylon, that is, in his new block-house, he was sure, as he thought; and upon the fields he was able to match all his enemies. And to write the truth, the most part of the nobility of Scotland had either given unto him their bonds of manrent,[1] or else were in confederacy and promised amity with him. He only feared them in whose hands God did deliver him, and for them had he laid his nets so secretly (as that he made a full compt), that their feet could not escape, as we shall after hear; and something of his former practices we maun reaccompt.

After the Pasche he came to Edinburgh to hold the seinzie[2] (as the Papists term their unhappy assembly of Baal's shaven sort). It was bruited that something was purposed against him at that time by the Earl of Angus and his friends, whom he mortally hated, and whose destruction he sought. But it failed, and so returned he to his strength[3]; yea, to his God and only comfort, as well in heaven as in earth. And there he remained without all fear of death, promising unto himself no less pleasure nor did the rich man, of whom mention is made by our Master in the Evangel; for he did not only rejoice and say, 'Eat and be glad, my soul, for thou hast great riches laid up in store for many days;' but also he said: 'Tush, a fig for the fead,[4] and a button for the bragging of all the heretics and their assistance in Scotland! Is not my Lord Governor mine? Witness his eldest son, their pledge at my table? Have I not the Queen at my own devotion? (He meant of the mother to Mary that now mischievously reigns.) Is not France my friend, and I friend to France? What danger should I fear?'

[1] Allegiance.   [2] Synod.   [3] Stronghold.   [4] Feud. (?)

THE KILLING OF DAVID BEATON

And thus in vanity the carnal Cardinal delighted himself a little before his death. But yet he had devised to have cut off such as he thought might cumber him; for he had appointed the whole gentlemen of Fife to have met him at Falkland the Monday after that he was slain upon the Saturday. His treasonable purpose was not understood but by his secret Council; and it was this: That Norman Lesley, Sheriff of Fife, and appearing heir to his father, the Earl of Rothes; the said John Lesley, father-brother to Norman; the Lairds of Grange, elder and younger; Sir James Leirmonth of Dairsye, and Provost of St. Andrews; and the faithful Laird of Raith; should either have been slain, or else taken, and after to have been used at his pleasure. This enterprise was disclosed after his slaughter, partly by letters and memorials found in his chamber, but plainly affirmed by such as were of the Council. Many purposes were devised how that wicked man might have been taken away. But all failed till Friday, the 28th of May, Anno 1546, when the foresaid Norman came at night to St. Andrews; William Kirkcaldy of Grange, younger, was in the town before, awaiting upon the purpose; last came John Lesley foresaid, who was most suspected. What conclusion they took that night it was not known but by the issue which followed.

But early upon the Saturday, in the morning, the 29th of May, were they in sundry companies in the Abbey kirkyard, not far distant from the Castle. First, the gates being open, and the drawbridge letten down, for receiving of lime and stones, and other things necessary for building (for Babylon was almost finished)—first, we say, assayed William Kirkcaldy of Grange, younger, and with him six persons, and getting entrance, held purpose with the porter: 'If my Lord was waking?' who answered, 'No.' (And so it was indeed; for he had been busy at his compts with Mistress Marion Ogilvy that night, who was espyed to depart from him by the privy postern that morning; and therefore quietness,

Knox
1572

Knox
1572

after the rules of physic, and a morning sleep was requisite for My Lord.) While the said William and the porter talked, and his servants made them to look the work and the workmen, approached Norman Lesley with his company; and because they were in no great number, they easily got entrance. They address them to the midst of the close, and immediately came John Lesley, somewhat rudely, and four persons with him. The porter, fearing, would have drawn the bridge; but the said John, being entered thereon, stayed, and leapt in. And while the porter made him for defence, his head was broken, the keys taken from him, and he castin in the fosse; and so the place was seized. The shout arises: the workmen, to the number of more than a hundred, ran off the walls, and were without hurt put forth at the wicket gate. The first thing that ever was done, William Kirkcaldy took the guard of the privy postern, fearing that the fox should have escaped. Then go the rest to the gentlemen's chambers, and without violence done to any man, they put more than fifty persons to the gate. The number that enterprised and did this was but sixteen persons. The Cardinal, awakened with the shouts, asked from his window, What meant that noise? It was answered that Norman Lesley had taken his Castle. Which understand, he ran to the postern; but perceiving the passage to be kept without, he returned quickly to his chamber, took his two-handed sword, and gart[1] his chamber-child cast chests and other impediments to the door. In this meantime came John Lesley unto it and bids open. The cardinal asking, 'Who calls?' he answers, 'My name is Lesley.' He redemands, 'Is that Norman?' The other says, 'Nay; my name is John.' 'I will have Norman,' says the cardinal; 'for he is my friend.' 'Content yourself with such as are here; for other shall ye get none.' There were with the said John, James Melvin, a man familiarly acquainted with Master

---
[1] Made.

George Wishart, and Peter Carmichael, a stout gentleman. In this meantime, while they force at the door, the Cardinal hides a box of gold under coals that were laid in a secret corner. At length he asked: 'Will ye save my life?' The said John answered: 'It may be that we will.' 'Nay,' says the Cardinal; 'swear unto me by God's wounds, and I will open unto you.' Then answered the said John: 'It that was said is unsaid;' and so cried, 'Fire, fire' (for the door was very stark); and so was brought a chimleyful of burning coals. Which perceived, the Cardinal or his chamber-child (it is uncertain) opened the door, and the Cardinal sat down in a chair, and cried: 'I am a priest; I am a priest: ye will not slay me.' The said John Lesley (according to his former vows) struck him first once or twice, and so did the said Peter. But James Melvin (a man of nature most gentle and most modest) perceiving them both in choler, withdrew them, and said: 'This work and judgment of God (although it be secret) ought to be done with greater gravity;' and presenting unto him the point of the sword, said: 'Repent thee of thy former wicked life, but especially of the shedding of the blood of that notable instrument of God, Master George Wishart, which albeit the flame of fire consumed before men, yet cries it a vengeance upon thee, and we from God are sent to revenge it. For here, before my God, I protest that neither the hetterent[1] of thy person, the love of thy riches, nor the fear of any trouble thou could have done to me in particular, moved, nor moves me to strike thee; but only because thou hast been, and remains, an obstinate enemy against Christ Jesus and his holy Evangel.' And so he struck him twice or thrice through with a stog[2] sword; and so he fell, never word heard out of his mouth, but 'I am a priest, I am a priest: fie, fie: all is gone.'

While they were thus occupied with the Cardinal, the fray[3] rises in the town. The Provost assembles the community,

Knox 1572

[1] Hatred (?) [2] Stabbing. [3] Panic.

and comes to the **fosse's** side, **crying**: 'What have **ye** done with my Lord Cardinal? Where **is** my Lord Cardinal? **Have ye** slain my **Lord Cardinal?** Let us see **my** Lord Cardinal!' They that were within answered gently: 'Best it **were** unto you to return to your own **houses**; for the man ye call the Cardinal has received his **reward, and** in his own person will trouble the world no more.' But then, more enragedly, they cry: 'We shall never depart till **that we** see him.' And so was he brought to the east blockhouse **head, and shown** dead over the wall to the faithless multitude, **which would** not believe before it saw how miserably lay David Beaton, careful **Cardinal.** And so they departed, without *Requiem æternam,* **and** *Requiescat in pace,* sung for his soul. Now, because the weather **was hot** (for it was in **May, as** ye have heard), and **his funerals could** not suddenly be prepared, it was thought best, to keep him from stinking, to give him great salt enough, a cope of lead, **and** a nook in the bottom of the Sea-Tower (a place where many of God's children had been imprisoned before) to await what exequies his brethren **the** bishops would prepare for him.

These things we write merrily. But we would that the reader should observe God's just judgments, and how that he **can** deprehend the worldly **wise** in their own wisdom, make **their** table to **be a** snare to trap their own feet, and their own presupposed strength to be their own destruction. These are the works of our God, whereby He would admonish the tyrants **of** this earth, **that** in the end He will be revenged of their cruelty, what **strength** soever they make in the contrary. But such is the blindness of man (as David speaks), 'That **the** posterity **does ever** follow **the** footsteps of their wicked fathers, and principally in their impiety.' For how little differs the cruelty **of** that bastard, that yet is called Bishop of St. Andrews, **from** the cruelty of the former, we will after hear. *John Knox.*

A SCOT ABROAD

BECAUSE I said before that Scotland received never a greater benefit at the hands of God nor this man, I will shortly set down, first, a little discourse of his life before his coming home, and syne what he brought with him. He was born in Baldowy, a place pleasant, fertile, and well aired, lying within a mile to the town of Montrose, upon the southwest, hard by the *Æstuarium fluminis Æskae meridionalis*, in the year of Christ's birth 1545, the first day of the month August, begotten of gentle and honest parents, Richard Melvill of Baldowy, brother-german of John Melvill of Dysart, and Gills Abercrombie, daughter to Thomas Abercrombie, burgess of Montrose, of the house of Murthley. He was the youngest of nine brothers, all left alive when their father was slain with the greatest part of the gentlemen of Angus, in the vanguard of the field of Pinkie. His mother lived an honourable widow till he was twelve years of age, trained up in letters in the school of Montrose, under Mr. Thomas Anderson, esteemed the best master in his time, howbeit not the most learned. She left six of her sons in honest rooms; all, even then or shortly thereafter, bearing office in Kirk or commonweal, and with the best esteemed in their rank and above. They were, Richard Melvill of Baldowy, and minister of Christ's Evangel soon after, the eldest: Mr. Thomas, a fine scholar, well travelled in France and Italy, Secretary-Depute of Scotland: Walter, burgess, and oft bailie of Montrose, a wise and stout man: Roger, burgess of Dundee, a man of singular gifts of nature and God's grace, but was not trained up in letters (I heard that faithful pastor of Dundee, William Christison, a little after his death, with tears say, 'Alas! when God took this Roger Melvill, he took from me my father, and the care-

Melvill
1574

Melvill fullest father **that ever Dundee had.** His **name** will **be**
1574 remembered so long **as Dundee is a** town'): Mr. James, minister of Christ's Evangel: John, **then** guidman **and** ruler of his mother's affairs, and after **a** minister in the Kirk: the rest were Robert, David, and Andrew; whereof the first two **were** kept at the school till they tired, and were put to crafts; the last was a sickly, tender boy, **and** took pleasure in nothing so mickle as his book. So, with the portion that was left him, he spent a year or two in Montrose, namely, hiring a France man, called Petrus de Marsiliers, teach the Greek grammar, and something of that language, honestly conduced to the same as a rare thing in the country, not heard of before, by that notable instrument in the Kirk, John Erskine of Done, of most honourable and happy memory; wherein he profited so, that, entering thereafter in the course of Philosophy within the University of St. Andrews, all that was teached of Aristotle he learned and studied it out of the Greek text, which his masters understood not. He passed **his** course in the New College, tenderly beloved of Mr. John Douglas, Provost of that College and Rector of the University; who would take him betwixt his legs at the **fire in** winter, and warm his hands and cheeks, and, blessing him, **say,** 'My silly fatherless and motherless child, it's ill to wit what God may make of thee yet!'

So, ending his course of philosophy, he left the University of St. Andrews with the commendation of the best philosopher, poet, and Grecian of any young master in the land; and with all possible diligence made his preparation and past to France. By the way he was extremely tormented with sea-sickness and storm of weather, so that ofttimes, whiles by danger of shipwreck, whiles by infirmity and sickness, he looked for death. He arrived first in England, and again embarking came to Bordeaux, where he tarried not long, but embarking from that came to Dieppe; from **that to** Paris, where **he** remained in the University two years at his own studies, hearing the lights of the most shining age in all good letters, the king's public professors, Andreas Tornebus in Greek and Latin Humanity; Petrus Ramus in Philosophy and Eloquence; Johannes Mercerus in the Hebrew language, whereupon he was specially set. In the last year of they two, he grew so expert in the Greek, that he declaimed and teached lessons, uttering never a word but Greek, with such readiness and plenty, as was marvellous to the hearers. From Paris he passed to Poitiers, where he regented[1] in the College of St. Marcian three years. There he had the best lawyers, and studied so mickle thereof as might serve for his purpose, which was Theology, whereto he was dedicate from his mother's womb. And when the Colleges were given up, because of the siege laid to the town, which was long and fearful, he was employed by an honourable Councillor to instruct his only son. The bairn profited exceeding well, and was of a sweet inclination, taken away from him and his parents by a shot out of the camp, which parted the wall of his chamber, and wounded him deadly in the thigh. He called incontinent for his master, whom how soon he saw, he caught him in his arms, and uttered the words of the apostle in Greek, διδάσκαλε, τὸν δρόμον μοῦ τετέληκα, 'Master, I have perfected my course!' and so, with many other godly and sweet words, he died. That bairn gaed never out of his heart; but in teaching of me, he often remembered him with tender compassion of mind. He tarried in that house, which was well furnished, during the time of the siege. There was a corporal with a few suddarts[2] put to keep the house, who espied him in his prayers and speeches to be holy and devout; and one day (being a Papist and man of war), with a great oath he challenged Mr. Andrew that he was a Huguenot, and would help to betray the town; therefore, because the alarm was stricken, he could not trust him in

Melvill 1574

---

[1] Acted as regent or professor.   [2] Soldiers.

*Melvill
1574*

that house. Mr. Andrew answers incontinent, 'I am as honest a man to my God, and magistrate, and estate of the town, and master of this family, as thou art; and so shall prove this day—do thy best!' And with that starts to the next armour, and on with it; and all in arms to the stable, and takes the best horse by the head. This when the corporal saw, he comes with felon fair [1] terms, and intreats him to leave off and forgive him. 'O no, no!' says he, 'I shall prove as honest and stout as thyself.' 'O Monsieur,' says the other, 'my captain and the master of this house will rebuke me and put me from it, if ye be thus troubled; therefore, I pray you, take me oblesit [2] to my uttermost, and tarry and forgive me.' So he took ease in good part, and was never troubled thereafter. If it had come to the worst, he was resolved, being well horsed, to have gotten him to the camp of the Admiral, who was in person besieging the town.

The siege of the town being raised, he left Poitiers, and accompanied with a Frenchman, he took journey to Geneva, leaving books and all there, and carried nothing with him but a little Hebrew Bible in his belt. So he came to Geneva all upon his feet, as he had done before from Dieppe to Paris, and from that to Poitiers; for he was small and light of body, but full of sprights, vigorous and courageous. His companions of the way, when they came to the inn, would lie down like tired tykes, but he would out and sight the towns and villages whithersoever they came. The ports of Geneva were tentily [3] kept, because of the troubles of France, and multitude of strangers that came. Being therefore inquired what they were, the Frenchman, his companion, answered, 'We are poor scholars.' But Mr. Andrew, perceiving that they had no will of poor folks, being already overlaid therewith, said, 'No, no, we are not poor! We have as mickle as will pay for all we take, so

[1] Very smooth.   [2] Bound.   [3] Carefully.

long as we tarry. We have letters from his acquaintance to Monsieur de Beza; let us deliver those, we crave no farther.' And so, being convoyed to Beza, and then to their lodging, Beza, perceiving him a scholar, and they having need of a Professor of Humanity in the College, put him within a two or three days to trial in Virgil and Homer; which he could acquit so well, that but farther[1] he is placed in that room of profession; and at his first entry, a quarter's fee paid him in hand. So that, howbeit there was but a crown to the fore betwixt them both, and the Frenchman weak-spirited, and wist not what to do, yet he found God's providence to relieve both himself and help his marrow[2] till he was provided.

Melvill
1574

In Geneva he abode five years; during the which time his chief study was Divinity, whereanent he heard Beza his daily lessons and preachings; Cornelius Bonaventura, Professor of the Hebrew, Chaldaic, and Syriac languages; Portus, a Greek born, Professor of the Greek tongue, with whom he would reason about the right pronunciation thereof; for the Greek pronounced it after the common form, keeping the accents; the which Mr. Andrew controlled by precepts and reason, till the Greek would grow angry, and cry out: *Vos Scoti, vos barbari! docebitis nos Graecos pronunciationem linguae nostrae, scilicet?* He heard there also Francis Ottoman, the renowndest lawyer in his time. There he was well acquainted with my eame,[3] Mr. Henry Scrymgeour, who, by his learning in the laws and policy and service of many noble princes, had attained to great riches, conquaced[4] a pretty room within a league to Geneva, and biggit[5] thereon a trim house called 'The Vilet,' and a fair lodging within the town, which all, with a daughter, his only bairn, he left to the Syndiques of the town.

About the end of five years, the Bishop of Brechin, and Mr. Andrew Polwart with him, came there; and, tarrying a

[1] Without more ado. [2] Companion. [3] Uncle. [4] Purchased. [5] Builded.

Melvill
1574

while, purposed **homeward**; with **whom** Mr. Andrew Melvill, after the receiving of letters from his brethren and me, with great difficulty purchased leave of **the** Kirk and Magistrates of Geneva (who would **on no ways have** contented to part with him, if his conscience had suffered him to reserve his gifts any longer unoffered to his country, **and** employed for the benefit of his friends. Beza, in his letter to the General Kirk of Scotland, alleges, that as the **greatest token** of affection the Kirk of Geneva could show to Scotland, that they had suffered themselves to be spoiled of Mr. Andrew Melvill, whereby **the** Kirk of Scotland might be enriched, **and** taking journey came homeward. From Lyons they traversed **the Franche-Compté to the** head of the river of Loire, and **came down the same** by water to Orleans, having in company, seven or eight days, a captain, a mediciner, and a priest, superstitious papists at their meeting, kythed[1] in their speech and meats, **but** by merry **and** solid reasoning withal, became flesh-eaters **on** Friday, and **the** captain not **far from** the kingdom **of** heaven or they parted. The **ports of** Orleans were strait kept (being but a year and half after the horrible massacres). Brechin and **Mr.** Andrew Polwart was on foot, and Mr. Andrew well mounted on horse, because he had wrested his leg, they past **the** two footmen, **and,** detaining the horseman, the soldiers inquires what he **was**. He answered, 'A Scotsman.' 'O! ye Scotsmen **are** all Huguenots,' says the guard. 'Huguenots!' says he, 'what's that? we ken none such.' 'O!' says the soldier, 'ye have not **mess?**' 'Forsooth,' says he merrily, 'our bairns in Scotland **go** daily to mess!' 'Good companion,' says the other, laughing, 'go thy way.' Coming to their lodging, he tells **his** neighbours, and gars them laugh: '**But** surely,' say they, '**we** were very fleyed[2] our passport **should** have been loked,[3] and finding us come from Geneva, should have been troubled.' 'Yea,' says their host, 'take

[1] Open, *i.e.* conforming. [2] Frightened. [3] Inspected.

it for a special providence of God, for within this twelve month many thousands for less have lost their lives.' Going out of the town again, at the turn of a rew,[1] they met the procession; Brechin and his pedagogue were before, Mr. Andrew a little after. Brechin turns back and says, 'What shall I do?' 'Forward!' quoth he, and so he does. Mr. Andrew holds out his side cloak with his arms as though he had been bearing something under his oxters, and so passes by. But his heart beat him thereafter oft and sore, that he should have so stoutly counselled the other, and used a piece of dissimulation himself. Coming to Paris, there they remained divers days; where Mr. Andrew, meeting with the Lord Ogilvy, his countryman, is requested by him to go to the Jesuits' College, where he reasoned with Father Tyrie sundry days; but the time being so dangerous, and [because] of some menacing speeches of the Bishop of Glasgow, he was counselled to haste [out] of the town. So they came from Dieppe over to Rye in England, from thence to London, where they remained a space; and buying horses, came home Loudon-way, by Berwick, to Edinburgh. And this for a short recital of his life till his coming home.

Rev. James Melvill.

Melvill
1574

AGINCOURT

THE King the same day found a shallow, between Corbie and Peron, which never was espied before, at which he with his army and carriages the night ensuing passed the water of Some without let or danger, and therewith determined to make haste towards Calis, and not to seek for battle, except he were thereto constrained, because that his army by sickness was sore diminished, insomuch that he had but only two thousand horsemen and thirteen thousand archers, billmen, and of all sorts of other footmen.

Holinshed
1577

[1] Street.

Holinshed 1577

The Englishmen were brought into some distress in this journey, by reason of their **victuals in** manner spent, and no hope to get more; for the **enemies** had destroyed all the corn before they came. Rest **could they** none take, for their enemies with alarms did ever so infest them; daily it rained and nightly it freezed; of fuel there was great scarcity, of fluxes plenty; money enough, but wares for their relief **to** bestow it on had they none. Yet in this great **necessity, the** poor people of the country were not spoiled, nor anything taken of them without payment, nor any outrage or offence **done by the** Englishmen, except one, which was, that **a** soldier **took a** pyx **out** of a church, for which he was apprehended, and the King not once removed till the box was restored and the offender strangled. **The** people of the countries thereabout, hearing **of** such zeal in him to the maintenance of justice, ministered **to his** army victuals and **other** necessaries, although **by open** proclamation **so** to do they were prohibited.

The French King being **at Rone, and** hearing that King **Henry was** passed the river of Some, was much displeased therewith, and assembling his Council to the number of five and thirty, asked their advice what was to be done. There were amongst these five and thirty his son the Dolphin, calling himself King of Sicille; the Dukes of Berre and Brittaine, the Earl **of** Pontieu, the King's youngest son, and other high estates. At length thirty of them agreed that the Englishmen should not depart unfought withal, and five were of a contrary opinion, but the greater number ruled the matter: and so Montjoy, King-at-Arms, **was** sent to the King of England to defy him as the enemy **of** France, and to tell him that he should shortly have battle. King Henry advisedly answered: 'Mine intent is to do **as it** pleaseth God, I will not seek your master **at** this time; but **if** he or his seek me, I will meet with them, God willing. **If** any of your nation attempt once **to stop me** in my journey **now** towards Calis, at their jeopardy be it; and yet I wish not any of you so unadvised as to be the occasion that I dye your tawny ground with your red blood.'

When he had thus answered the herald, he gave him a princely reward, and licence to depart. Upon whose return, with this answer, it was incontinently on the French side proclaimed, that all men of war should resort to the Constable to fight with the King of England. Whereupon, all men apt for armour and desirous of honour drew them toward the field. The Dolphin sore desired to have been at the battle, but he was prohibited by his father: likewise Philip, Earl of Charolois, would gladly have been there, if his father the Duke of Burgognie would have suffered him: many of his men stole away, and went to the Frenchmen. The King of England hearing that the Frenchmen approached, and that there was another river for him to pass with his army by a bridge, and doubting lest if the same bridge should be broken it would be greatly to his hindrance, appointed certain captains with their bands to go thither with all speed before him, and to take possession thereof, and so to keep it till his coming thither.

Those that were sent, finding the Frenchmen busy to break down their bridge, assailed them so vigourously, that they discomfited them, and took and slew them; and so the bridge was preserved till the King came, and passed the river by the same with his whole army. This was on the two and twentieth day of October. The Duke of York that led the vanguard (after the army was passed the river) mounted up to the height of an hill with his people, and sent out scouts to discover the country, the which upon their return advertised him that a great army of Frenchmen was at hand, approaching towards them. The Duke declared to the King what he had heard, and the King thereupon, without all fear or trouble of mind, caused the battle which he led himself to stay, and incontinently rode forth to view his adversaries, and that done, returned to his people, and with cheerful countenance

Holinsl
1577

Holinshed caused them to be **put in order of battle,** assigning to every
1577 captain such room and **place as he** thought convenient, and
so kept them still **in that order till** night was come, and then
determined to seek **a place to encamp and lodge his** army in
for that night.

There was not **one** amongst them **that knew any** certain
place whither to go, **in** that unknown country: **but by chance
they happened upon a** beaten way, white in **sight; by the
which they were brought** unto a little village, **where they
were refreshed with meat** and drink somewhat **more plenteously than they had been divers** days before. Order **was
taken by commandment from the** King after the **army** was
first set in battle array, that no noise or clamour should **be
made in the host; so that in marching forth to** this village
every man kept himself **quiet: but at their** coming into the
village, fires were made **to give light on every side, as** there
likewise were in the **French** host, which was encamped not
past two hundred and fifty **paces distant from the** English.
The chief leaders of the French **host were these:** the Constable of France, the Marshal, the Admiral, the Lord **Rambures, Master** of the Crossbows, and other of the **French**
nobility, which came and pitched down their standards and
banners in **the** county **of St. Paul,** within the territory of
Agincourt, having in their army (as some write) to the number
of threescore thousand horsemen, besides footmen, waggoners,
and other.

They **were lodged even in** the way by which the
Englishmen must **needs pass** towards Calis, and all that night
after their coming thither, made great cheer, and were very
merry, pleasant, and full **of** game. The Englishmen also for
their parts were of good comfort and nothing abashed of the
matter, and yet they were both hungry, weary, sore travelled,
and vexed with many **cold** diseases. Howbeit reconciling
themselves with God by housel[1] and shrift, requiring assis-

[1] Confession.

tance at His hands that is the only giver of victory, they determined rather to die than to yield or flee. The day following was the five and twentieth of October in the year 1415, being then Friday, and the feast of Crispin and Crispinian, a day fair and fortunate to the English, but most sorrowful and unlucky to the French.

In the morning, the French captains made three battles, in the vaward were eight thousand helmes of knights and esquires, four thousand archers, and fifteen hundred crossbows, which were guided by the Lord de la Breth, Constable of France, having with him the Dukes of Orleance and Burbon, the Earls of Ewe and Richmond, the Marshal Bouciquault, and the Master of the Crossbows, the Lord Dampier, Admiral of France, and other captains. The Earl of Vandosme, with sixteen hundred men of arms, were ordered for a wing to that battle; and the other wing was guided by Sir Guichard Dolphine, Sir Clugnet of Brabant, and Sir Lewis Bourdon, with eight hundred men of arms, of elect chosen persons. And to break the shot of the Englishmen were appointed Sir Guilliam de Saveuses, with Hector and Philip, his brethren, Ferrie de Maillie, and Allen de Gaspanes, with other eight hundred of arms.

In the middle ward were assigned as many persons, or more, as were in the foremost battle, and the charge thereof was committed to the Dukes of Barr and Alanson, the Earls of Nevers, Vaudemont, Blamont, Salinges, Grant Prée, and of Russie. And in the rearward were all the other men of arms guided by the Earls of Marle, Dampmartine, Fauconberg, and the Lord of Lourreie, Captain of Arde, who had with him the men of the frontiers of Bolonois. Thus the Frenchmen, being ordered under their standards and banners, made a great show: for surely they were esteemed in number six times as many or more than was the whole company of the Englishmen, with waggoners, pages, and all. They rested themselves, waiting for the bloody blast of the terrible

Holinsl
1577

trumpet, till the hour between nine and ten of the clock of the same day, during which season the Constable made unto the captains and other men of war a pithy oration, exhorting and encouraging them to do valiantly, with many comfortable words and sensible reasons. King Henry also like a leader and not as one led, like a sovereign and not an inferior, perceiving a plot of ground very strong and meet for his purpose, which on the back half was fenced with the village, wherein he had lodged the night before, and on both sides defended with hedges and bushes, thought good there to embattle his host, and so ordered his men in the same place, as he saw occasion, and as stood for his most advantage.

First he sent privily two hundred archers into a low meadow, which was near to the vanguard of his enemies, but separated with a great ditch; commanding them there to keep themselves close till they had a token to them given, to let drive at their adversaries: beside this, he appointed a vaward, of the which he made captain Edward, Duke of York, who of an haughty courage had desired that office, and with him were the Lords Beaumont, Willoughby, and Fanhope, and this battle was all of archers. The middle ward was governed by the King himself, with his brother the Duke of Glocester, and the Earls of Marshall, Oxenford, and Suffolk, in the which were all the strong billmen. The Duke of Excester, uncle to the King, led the rearward, which was mixed both with billmen and archers. The horsemen like wings went on every side of the battle.

Thus the King, having ordered his battles, feared not the puissance of his enemies, but yet to provide that they should not with the multitude of horsemen break the order of his archers, in whom the force of his army consisted (for in those days the yeomen had their limbs at liberty, sith their hosen were then fastened with one point, and their jacks long and easy to shoot in; so that they might draw bows of great strength, and shoot arrows of a yard long, beside the head), he caused stakes bound with iron, sharp at both ends, of the length of five or six feet to be pitched before the archers, and of each side the footmen like an hedge, to the intent that if the barded horses ran rashly upon them, they might shortly be gored and destroyed. Certain persons also were appointed to remove the stakes, as by the moving of the archers occasion and time should require, so that the footmen were hedged about with stakes, and the horsemen stood like a bulwark between them and their enemies, without the stakes. This device of fortifying an army was at this time first invented; but since that time they have devised caltrops, harrows, and other new engines against the force of horsemen; so that if the enemies run hastily upon the same, either ere their horses wounded with the stakes, or their feet hurt with the other engines, so as thereby the beasts are gored, or else made unable to maintain their course. *Holinshed 1577*

King Henry, by reason of his small number of people to fill up his battles, placed his vanguard so on the right hand of the main battle, which himself led, that the distance betwixt them might scarce be perceived, and so in like case was the rearward joined on the left hand, that the one might the more readily succour another in time of need. When he had thus ordered his battles, he left a small company to keep his camp and carriage, which remained still in the village, and then calling his captains and soldiers about him, he made to them a right grave oration, moving them to play the men, whereby to obtain a glorious victory, as there was hope certain they should, the rather if they would but remember the just cause for which they fought, and whom they should encounter, such faint-hearted people as their ancestors had so often overcome. To conclude, many words of courage he uttered, to stir them to do manfully, assuring them that England should never be charged with his ransom, nor any Frenchman triumph over him as a captive; for either by famous death or glorious victory **would** he (by God's grace) win honour and fame.

It is said that as he heard one of **the host** utter his wish to another thus: 'I would to God **there** were with us now so many good soldiers as are at this hour within England!' the King answered: 'I would not wish a man more here than I have: we are indeed in comparison to the enemies but a few, but, if God of His clemency do favour us and **our just cause** (as I trust He will), we shall speed well enough. **But let no man** ascribe victory to our own strength and might, but only to God's assistance, **to** whom I have no doubt we shall worthily have cause to **give** thanks therefor. And if so be that for our offences' sakes we shall be delivered into the hands of our enemies, the less number we be, the less damage shall **the** realm of England sustain; **but if we should** fight in trust of multitude of men, and so **get** the victory (our **minds** being prone to pride), we should thereupon peradventure ascribe the victory not so much to the gift of God **as to** our **own** puissance, **and** thereby provoke his high indignation and displeasure against us: and if **the** enemy get the upper hand, then should our realm and country suffer more damage and stand in further danger. But be you of good comfort, and **show** yourselves valiant, God and our just quarrel shall defend **us, and** deliver these our proud adversaries with **all the** multitude of them which you see (or at the least the most of them) into our hands.' Whilst the King was yet **thus in** speech, either army so maligned the other, being as then in open sight, that every man cried, 'Forward, forward.' **The** Dukes of Clarence, Glocester, and York were of the **same** opinion, yet the King stayed a while, lest any jeopardy were not foreseen, or any hazard **not** prevented. The Frenchmen in the meanwhile, as **though** they had been sure of victory, made great triumph, for the captains had determined before **how** to divide the spoil, and the soldiers the night before had played the Englishmen **at** dice. The noblemen had devised

a chariot, wherein they might triumphantly convey the King Holinshed
captive to the city of Paris, crying to their soldiers: 'Haste   1577
you to the spoil, glory, and honour'; little weening (God
wot) how soon their brags should be blown away.

Here we may not forget how the French thus in their
jollity sent an herald to King Henry, to inquire what ransom
he would offer. Whereunto he answered, that within two or
three hours he hoped it would so happen that the Frenchmen should be glad to commune rather with the Englishmen
for their ransoms, than the English to take thought for their
deliverance, promising, for his own part, that his dead carcass
should rather be a prize to the Frenchmen, than that his
living body should pay any ransom. When the messenger
was come back to the French host, the men of war put on
their helmets and caused their trumpets to blow to the
battle. They thought themselves so sure of victory, that
divers of the noblemen made such haste towards the battle,
that they left many of their servants and men of war behind
them, and some of them would not once stay for their standards: as amongst other the Duke of Brabant, when his
standard was not come, caused a banner to be taken from a
trumpet and fastened to a spear, the which he commanded
to be borne before him instead of his standard.

But when both these armies coming within danger either
of other, set in full order of battle on both sides, they stood
still at the first, beholding either other's demeanour, being
not distant in sunder past three bow shoots. And when they
had on both parts thus stayed a good while without doing anything (except that certain of the French horsemen advancing
forwards, betwixt both the hosts, were by the English archers
constrained to return back) advice was taken amongst the
Englishmen what was best for them to do. Thereupon all
things considered, it was determined, that sith the Frenchmen would not come forward, the King with his army em-
battled (as ye have heard) should march towards them, and

Holinshed 1577 so leaving their truss and baggage in the village where they lodged the night before, only with their weapons, armour, and stakes prepared for the purpose, as ye have **heard.**

These made somewhat forward, before whom there went **an old** knight, Sir Thomas Erpingham (a man of great experience in the war) with a warder in his hand; and when he cast up his warder, all the army shouted, but that was a sign to the archers in the meadow, which therewith **shot** wholly altogether at the vaward of the Frenchmen, who when they perceived **the** archers in the meadow, and saw they could not **come at them for** a ditch that was betwixt them, with all haste set upon the fore ward of King Henry; **but ere** they could join, **the** archers in the forefront and the archers on that side which stood in the meadow so wounded the footmen, galled the horses, and cumbered the men of arms, that the footmen durst not go forward, the horsemen ran together upon plumps without order, some overthrew such as were next them, and the horses overthrew their masters, and so at the first joining, the Frenchmen were foully discomforted and the Englishmen highly encouraged.

When **the** French vaward was thus brought to confusion, the English archers cast away their bows, and took into their hands axes, malls,[1] swords, bills, and other hand-weapons, and with the same slew the Frenchmen, until they came to the middle ward. Then approached the King, and so encouraged his people, that shortly the second battle of the Frenchmen was overthrown and dispersed, not without great slaughter of men; howbeit, divers were relieved by their varlets and conveyed out of the field. The Englishmen **were so** busied in fighting, and taking of the prisoners at hand, that they followed not in chase of their enemies, **nor would** once break **out** of their array of battle. Yet

---

[1] Maces.

sundry of the Frenchmen strongly withstood the fierceness of the English, when they came to handy strokes, so that the fight sometime was doubtful and perilous. Yet as part of the French horsemen set their course to have entered upon the King's battle, with the stakes overthrown, they were either taken or slain. Thus this battle continued three long hours.

Holinshed
1577

The King that day showed himself a valiant knight, albeit almost felled by the Duke of Alanson; yet with plain strength he slew two of the Duke's company, and felled the Duke himself; whom when he would have yielded, the King's guard (contrary to his mind) slew out of hand. In conclusion, the King, minding to make an end of that day's journey, caused his horsemen to fetch a compass about, and to join with him against the rearward of the Frenchmen, in the which was the greatest number of people. When the Frenchmen perceived his intent, they were suddenly amazed and ran away like sheep, without order or array. Which when the King perceived, he encouraged his men, and followed so quickly upon the enemies, that they ran hither and thither, casting away their armour: many on their knees desired to have their lives saved.

In the mean season, while the battle thus continued, and that the Englishmen had taken a great number of prisoners, certain Frenchmen on horseback, whereof were Captains Robinet of Borneville, Rifflart of Clamas, Isambert of Agincourt, and other men of arms, to the number of six hundred horsemen, which were the first that fled, hearing that the English tents and pavilions were a good way distant from the army, without any sufficient guard to defend the same, either upon a covetous meaning to gain by the spoil, or upon a desire to be revenged, entered upon the King's camp, and there spoiled the hails,[1] robbed the tents, broke up chests, and carried away caskets, and slew such servants as

[1] Mails?

Holinshed they found to make any resistance. For which treason and
1577 haskardie[1] in thus leaving **their camp** at the very point of fight, for winning of spoil where none to defend it, very many were after committed to **prison,** and had lost their lives if the Dolphin had longer lived.

But when the outcry of the lackeys and **boys,** which ran **away for** fear of the Frenchmen thus **spoiling the** camp, came to the King's ears, he doubting lest his enemies should gather together again, and begin a new field, and mistrusting further that the prisoners would be an aid to his enemies, or the very enemies **to** their takers in deed if they were suffered to **live, contrary to** his accustomed gentleness, commanded, by sound **of trumpet,** that every man (upon pain of death) should incontinently slay his prisoner. When this dolorous decree and pitiful proclamation was pronounced, pity it was to see how some **Frenchmen were** suddenly sticked with daggers, some were brained with poleaxes, some **slain** with malls, other had their throats cut, and some their bellies panched,[2] so that in effect, having respect to the great number, few prisoners were saved.

When this lamentable slaughter was ended, the Englishmen disposed themselves in order of battle, ready to abide a new field, and also to invade, and newly set on their enemies. With great force they assailed the Earls of Marle and Fauconberg, and the Lords of Lourreie and of Thine, with six hundred men of arms, who had all that day kept together, but now slain and beaten down out of hand. Some write, that the King perceiving his enemies in one part to assemble together, as though they meant to give a new battle for preservation of the prisoners, sent to them an herald, commanding them either to depart out of his sight, **or else** to come forward at once and give battle: promising herewith, that if they **did** offer to fight again, not only those prisoners which his people already had taken, but also

[1] Savagery. [2] Ripped.

so many of them as in this new conflict which they thus
attempted should fall into his hands, should die the death
without redemption.

The Frenchmen fearing the sentence of so terrible a
decree, without further delay parted out of the field. And
so about four of the clock in the afternoon, the King, when
he saw no appearance of enemies, caused the retreat to be
blown; and gathering his army together, gave thanks to
Almighty God for so happy a victory, causing his prelates
and chaplains to sing this psalm: *In exitu Israel de Ægypto*,
and commanded every man to kneel down on the ground
at this verse: *Non nobis Domine, non nobis, sed nomini tuo da
gloriam.* Which done, he caused *Te Deum*, with certain
anthems, to be sung, giving laud and praise to God, without
boasting of his own force or any human power. That night
he and his people took rest, and refreshed themselves with
such victuals as they found in the French camp, but lodged
in the same village where he lay the night before.

In the morning, Montjoy King-at-Arms and four other
French heralds came to the King to know the number of
prisoners, and to desire burial for the dead. Before he
made them answer (to understand what they would say)
he demanded of them why they made to him that request,
considering that he knew not whether the victory was his
or theirs? When Montjoy by true and just confession had
cleared that doubt to the high praise of the King, he desired
of Montjoy to understand the name of the castle near
adjoining. When they had told him that it was called Agincourt, he said, 'Then shall this conflict be called the Battle of
Agincourt.' He feasted the French officers of arms that day
and granted them their request, which busily sought through
the field for such as were slain. But the Englishmen suffered
them not to go alone, for they searched with them, and found
many hurt, but not in jeopardy of their lives, whom they
took prisoners, and brought them to their tents. When the

Holinshed
1577

King of England **had well refreshed** himself and his soldiers, that had taken the spoil of such **as were** slain, he with his prisoners in good order returned **to** his town of Calis.

When tidings of this great victory was blown into England, solemn processions and other praisings **to** Almighty God, with bonfires and joyful triumphs, were ordained **in** every **town,** city, and burgh, and the mayor and citizens **of** London **went** the morrow after the day of St. Simon **and** Jude **from** the church of St. Paul to the church of **St. Peter** at Westminster in devout manner, rendering to God **hearty** thanks for such fortunate luck sent to the king and his army. The same Sunday that the King removed from the camp at Agincourt towards Calis, **divers** Frenchmen came to the field to view again the **dead bodies; and** the peasants of the country spoiled the **carcases of all such** apparel and other things as the Englishmen **had** left, **who** took nothing but gold and silver, jewels, rich apparel, and costly **armour.** But the ploughmen and peasants left nothing behind, neither shirt nor clout, so that the bodies lay stark naked until Wednesday. On the which day divers of the noblemen **were** conveyed into their countries, and the remnant were by Philip, Earl Charolois (sore lamenting the chance, and moved with pity) at his costs and charges buried in a square plot of ground of fifteen hundred yards; in the which he caused to be made three pits, wherein were buried by account five thousand and eight hundred persons, beside them that were carried away by their friends and servants, and others, which being wounded died in hospitals and other places.

Raphael Holinshed.

THE YOUNG ALEXANDER

THE ambition and desire he had of honour shewed a certain greatness of mind and noble courage, passing his years. For he was not (as his Father Philip) desirous of all kind of glory: who, like a rhetorician, had a delight to utter his eloquence, and stamped in his coins the victories he had won at the Olympian games, by the swift running of his horse and coaches. For when he was asked one day (because he was swift of foot) whether he would assay to run for victory at the Olympian games, 'I could be content' (said he) 'so I might run with Kings.' And yet, to speak generally, he misliked all such contention for games. For it seemeth that he utterly misliked all wrestling and other exercise for prize, where men did use all their strength: but otherwise, he himself made certain festival days and games of prize for common Stage-players, Musicians, and Singers, and for the very Poets also. He delighted also in hunting of divers kinds of beasts, and playing at the staff. Ambassadors being sent on a time from the King of Persia, whilst his Father was in some journey out of his realm, Alexander familiarly entertaining of them, so won them with his courteous entertainment (for that he used no childish questions unto them, nor asked them trifling matters, but what distance it was from one place to another, and which way they went into the high countries of Asia, and of the King of Persia himself, how he was towards his Enemies, and what power he had), that he did ravish them with delight to hear him, insomuch that they made no more account of Philip's eloquence and sharp wit, in respect of his Son's courage and noble mind to attempt great enterprises. For when they brought him news that his Father had taken some famous city, or had won some great battle, he was nothing glad to hear it, but would say to his playfellows: 'Sirs, my

North 1579

Father will have all, I shall have nothing left me to conquer with you that shall be ought worth.' For he delighting neither in pleasure nor riches, but only in valiantness and honour, thought that the greater conquests and realms his Father should leave him the less he should have to do for himself. And therefore, seeing that his Father's dominions and empire increased daily more and more, perceiving all occasion taken from him to do any great attempt, he desired no riches nor pleasure, but wars and battles, and aspired to a seigniory where he might win honour.

He had divers men appointed him (as it is to be supposed) to bring him up: as Schoolmasters, Governors, and Grooms of his chamber to attend upon him: and among those, Leonidas was the chiefest man that had the government and charge of him, a man of a severe disposition, and a kinsman, also, unto the Queen Olympias. He misliked to be called a Master or Tutor, though it be an office of good charge; whereupon others called him Alexander's Governor, because he was a Nobleman, and allied to the Prince. But he that bare the name of his Schoolmaster was Lysimachus, an Acarnanian born, who had no other manner of civility in him, saving that he called himself Phœnix, Alexander Achilles, and Philip Peleus: and therefore he was well thought of, and was the second person next unto Leonidas. At what time Philonicus, Thessalian, had brought Bucephall, the horse, to sell unto King Philip, asking thirteen talents, they went into the field to ride him. The horse was found so rough and churlish that the riders said he would never do service; for he would let no man get upon his back, nor abide any of the gentlemen's voices about King Philip, but would jerk out at them. Thereupon Philip, being afraid, commanded them to carry him away as a wild beast, and altogether unprofitable: the which they had done, had not Alexander that stood by said: 'O gods, what a horse do they turn away for lack of skill and heart to handle him?' Philip heard what he said, but held his peace. Alexander, oft repeating his words, seeming to be sorry that they should send the horse back again: 'Why,' said Philip, 'dost thou control them that have more experience than thou, and that know better than thou how to handle a horse?' Alexander answered, 'And yet methinks I should handle him better than all they have done.' 'But if thou canst not, no more than they,' replied Philip, 'what wilt thou forfeit for thy folly?' 'I am content,' quoth Alexander, 'to jeopard the price of the horse.' Every man laughed to hear his answer, and the wager was laid between them. Then ran Alexander to the horse, and took him by the bridle: and turned him towards the Sun. It seemed that he had marked (as I suppose) how mad the horse was to see his own shadow, which was ever before him in his eye, as he stirred too and fro. Then Alexander, speaking gently to the horse, and clapping him on the back with his hand, till he had left his fury and snorting, softly let fall his cloak from him, and lightly leaping on his back, got up without any danger, and holding the reins of the bridle hard, without striking or stirring the horse, made him to be gentle enough. Then when he saw that the fury of the horse was past, and that he began to gallop, he put him to his full career, and laid on spurs and voice a good. Philip at the first with fear beholding his Son's agility, lest he should take some hurt, said never a word: but when he saw him readily turn the horse at the end of his career, in a bravery for that he had done, all the lookers-on gave a shout for joy. The Father on the other side (as they say) fell a-weeping for joy. And when Alexander was lighted from the horse, he said unto him, kissing his head: 'O son, thou must needs have a realm that is meet for thee, for Macedon will not hold thee.' Furthermore, considering that of nature he was not to be won by extremity, and that by gentle means and persuasion he could make him do what he would, he ever sought

North
1579

rather to persuade than **command him** in anything he had to do.

Now Philip, putting no great **affiance** in his Schoolmasters of music and humanity, for the instruction and education of his Son, whom he had appointed to teach him, but thinking rather that he needed men of greater **learning** than their capacities would reach unto: and that, as **Sophocles** saith,

'**He** needed many reins and many bits at once,'

he sent for Aristotle (the greatest Philosopher in his time **and best learned) to** teach his Son, unto whom he gave honourable stipend. **For** Philip having won and taken before the City **of Stagira, where** Aristotle was born, for his sake he built it again, **and replenished it** with inhabitants which fled away, **or otherwise were in** bondage. He appointed them for a schoolhouse and dwelling-place the pleasant house that is by **the City of Mieza.** In that place are yet seen seats of stone **which** Aristotle caused to be made, and close walks to walk in the shadow. It is thought also, **that** Alexander did not only learn of Aristotle moral philosophy and humanity, but also he heard of him other more secret, hard, and grave doctrine, which Aristotle's Scholars do properly call Acroamata, or Epoptica, meaning things speculative, which requireth the master's teaching to understand them, or else are kept from common knowledge: which sciences they did not commonly teach. Alexander being passed into Asia, and hearing that Aristotle had put out certain books of that matter, for the honour's sake of philosophy, he wrote a letter unto him, somewhat too plain, and **of** this effect: 'Alexander unto Aristotle, greeting: Thou hast **not** done **well** to put forth the Acroamatical sciences. For wherein **shall** we excel other if those things which thou hast secretly taught us be made common to all? I do thee to understand that I had rather excel others in **excellency of knowledge** than in greatness **of** power.

THE YOUNG ALEXANDER

Farewell.' Aristotle, to pacify this his ambitious humour, wrote unto him again, that these books were published, and not published. For, to say truly, in all his treatises, which he called μετὰ τὰ φυσικὰ, there is no plain instruction profitable for any man, neither to pick out by himself, nor yet to be taught by any other than Aristotle himself, or his Scholars. So that it is written as a memorial for them that have been entered and brought up in the peripatetic sect and doctrine.

It seemeth, also, that it was Aristotle above all other that made Alexander take delight to study physic. For Alexander did not only like the knowledge of speculation, but would exercise practice also, and help his friends when they were sick: and made, besides, certain remedies and rules to live by: as appeareth by his letters he wrote, that of his own nature he was much given to his book and desired to read much. He learned, also, the *Iliads* of Homer of Aristotle's correction, which they call τὴν ἐκ τοῦ νάρθηκος, the corrected, as having passed under the rule: and laid it every night under his bed's head with his dagger, calling it (as Onesicritus writeth) the institution of martial discipline. And when he was in the high countries of Asia, where he could not readily come by other books, he wrote unto Harpalus to send them to him. Harpalus sent him the histories of Philistus, with divers tragedies of Euripides, Sophocles, and Æschylus, and certain hymns of Telestus and Philoxenus. Alexander did reverence Aristotle at the first as his Father, and so he termed him: because from his natural Father he had life, but from him the knowledge to live. But afterwards he suspected him somewhat; yet he did him no hurt, neither was he so friendly to him as he had been: whereby men perceived that he did not bear him the good-will he was wont to do. This notwithstanding, he left not that zeal and desire he had to the study of philosophy, which he had learned from his youth, and still continued with him. For

North
1579

he shewed divers testimonies thereof: as the honour he did unto Anaxarchus, the Philosopher; the fifty talents which he sent unto Xenocrates, Damdamis, and Calanus, of whom he made great account.

When King Philip made war with the Bizantines, Alexander, being but sixteen years old, **was left his** lieutenant in Macedon, with the custody and charge of **his** great seal: at what time he also subdued the Medarians which had **rebelled** against **him**: and having won their city by assault, he drave out the barbarous people, and made a colony of it **of** sundry nations, and called it Alexandropolis, to say, the City of Alexander. **He** was with his father at the battle of Chæronea against the Grecians, where it was reported that it was he that gave charge first of all upon the holy band of the Thebans. Furthermore, there **was an** old oak seen in my time, which the countrymen commonly **call** Alexander's Oak, because his tent or pavilion **was** fastened **to** it; and not far from thence is the charnel house where those Macedonians were buried that were slain at the battle. For these causes his Father Philip loved him very dearly, and was glad to hear the Macedonians call Alexander King and himself their Captain.

Sir Thomas North.

THE BANISHING OF CORIOLANUS

WHEN they came to tell the voices of the Tribes, there were three voices odd which condemned him to be banished for ever. After declaration of the sentence, the People made such joy, as they never rejoiced more for any battle they had won upon their enemies, they were so brave and lively, and went home so jocundly from the Assembly, for triumph of this sentence. The Senate again, in contrary manner, were as sad and heavy, repenting themselves beyond measure that they had not rather determined to have done and suffered anything whatsoever, before the common People should so arrogantly and outrageously have abused their authority. There needed no difference of garments, I warrant you, nor outward shows to know a Plebeian from a Patrician, for they were easily discerned by their looks. For he that was on the People's side looked cheerfully on the matter: but he that was sad, and hung down his head, he was sure of the Noblemen's side. Saving Martius alone, who neither in his countenance nor in his gait did ever show himself abashed, or once let fall his great courage: but he only of all other Gentlemen that were angry at his fortune, did outwardly show no manner of passion, nor care at all of himself. Not that he did patiently bear and temper his evil hap, in respect of any reason he had, or by his quiet condition: but because he was so carried away with the vehemency of anger and desire of revenge, that he had no sense nor feeling of the hard state he was in, which the common People judge not to be sorrow, although indeed it be the very same. For when sorrow (as you would say) is set on fire, then it is converted into spite and malice, and driveth away for that time all faintness of heart and natural fear. And this is the cause why the choleric man is so altered and mad in his actions, as a man set on fire with a burning ague: for when a man's heart is troubled within, his pulse will beat marvellous strongly.

Now that Martius was even in that taking, it appeared true soon after by his doings. For when he was come home to his house again, and had taken his leave of his mother and wife, finding them weeping and shrieking out for sorrow, and had also comforted and persuaded them to be content with his chance: he went immediately to the gate of the city, accompanied with a great number of Patricians, that brought him thither, from whence he went on his way with three or four of his friends

North
1579

only, taking nothing **with** him, **nor** requesting anything **of** any man. **So he** remained **a** few days in the country at his houses, turmoiled with **sundry** sorts and kinds of thoughts, such as the fire of **his choler** did stir up. In the end, seeing he could resolve **no way to take a** profitable or honourable course, but only was pricked **forward** still to be revenged of the Romans: he thought to **raise up some** great wars against them **by** their nearest neighbours. Whereupon he thought it his best way first to stir up the Volsces against them, knowing they were yet able enough in strength **and** riches to encounter them, notwithstanding their former losses they had received not long before, and that their power was not so much impaired as **their** malice and desire was increased to be revenged **of the Romans. Now** in the City of **Antium** there **was one called** Tullus Aufidius, who for his riches, as also for his nobility and **valiantness was** honoured among the Volsces as a King. Martius knew very well that Tullus did more malice **and envy him than** he did all the Romans besides: because that many times in battles where they met, they were ever at the encounter one against another, like lusty courageous youths, striving in all emulation of honour, and had encountered many times together. In**somuch** as besides the common quarrel between them, there **was bred a** marvellous private hate one against another. Yet notwithstanding, considering that Tullus Aufidius was a man **of a** great mind, and that **he** above all other of the Volsces most desired revenge of the Romans, for the injuries they had done unto them, **he** did an act that confirmed the words of an ancient Poet **to be** true, who said:

> It is a thing full hard, man's anger to withstand,
> If it be stiffly bent to take an enterprise in hand.
> For then most men will have the thing that they desire,
> Although it cost **their** lives therefor, such force hath wicked ire.

And so did he. For he disguised himself in such array and

THE BANISHING OF CORIOLANUS 135

attire as he thought no man could ever have known him for the person he was, seeing him in that apparel he had upon his back : and as Homer said of Ulysses :

> So did he enter into the enemies' town.

It was even twilight when he entered the city of Antium, and many people met him in the streets, but no man knew him. So he went directly to Tullus Aufidius house, and when he came thither, he got him up straight to the chimney hearth, and sate him down, and spake not a word to any man, his face all muffled over. They of the house spying him, wondered what he should be, and yet they durst not bid him rise. For ill-favouredly muffled and disguised as he was, yet there appeared a certain majesty in his countenance and in his silence : whereupon they went to Tullus, who was at supper, to tell him of the strange disguising of this man. Tullus rose presently from the board, and coming towards him, asked him what he was, and wherefore he came. Then Martius unmuffled himself, and after he had paused awhile, making no answer, he said unto him : ' If thou knowest me not yet, Tullus, and seeing me, dost not perhaps believe me to be the man I am indeed, I must of necessity bewray myself to be that I am. I am Caius Martius, who hath done to thyself particularly, and to all the Volsces generally, great hurt and mischief, which I cannot deny for my surname of Coriolanus that I bare. For I never had other benefit nor recompence of the true and painful service I have done, and the extreme dangers I have been in, but this only surname : a good memory and witness of the malice and displeasure thou shouldest bear me. Indeed the name only remaineth with me ; for the rest, the envy and cruelty of the People of Rome have taken from me, by the sufferance of the dastardly Nobility and Magistrates, who have forsaken me, and let me be banished by the People. This extremity hath now driven me to come as a poor suitor, to take thy chimney hearth, not of any **hope I** have to save my life thereby. For if I had feared **death, I would not** have come hither to have put myself in hazard : but pricked forward with desire to be revenged of them that **thus have** banished me, which **now** I do begin, in putting my person **into the** hands of their enemies. Wherefore, if thou hast any **heart to** be recked of the injuries thy Enemies have done thee, speed thee now, and let my misery serve thy turn, and so use it, as my service may be **a** benefit to the Volsces: promising thee that I will fight with better good will for all you than I did when I **was** against you, knowing **that** they fight more valiantly who know the force of the Enemy than such as have never proved **it.** And if it **be so** that thou **dare** not, and that thou art **weary to prove fortune any more, then am I** also weary to **live** any longer. And **it were** no wisdom in thee to save the life of him who hath **been** heretofore **thy mortal** Enemy, and whose service now can nothing help nor pleasure thee.' Tullus hearing what he said**, was a marvellous** glad man, and taking him by the **hand, he said unto** him: 'Stand up, O Martius, and be of good cheer, for in proffering thyself unto **us,** thou dost us great honour: and by this means thou mayest hope also of greater things at all the Volsces' hands.' **So** he feasted him for that time, and entertained him **in the** honourablest manner he could, talking with him of no other matter at that present.

Sir Thomas North.

ENGLAND

THERE is an Isle lying in the Ocean Sea, directly against that part of France which containeth Picardy and Normandy, called now England, heretofore named Britain. It hath Ireland upon the West side, on the North the main sea, on the East side, the Germany Ocean. This island is in circuit 1720 miles, in form like unto a triangle, being broadest in the South part, and gathering narrower and narrower till it come to the farthest point of Caithness, Northward, where it is narrowest, and there endeth in manner of a promontory. To repeat the ancient manner of this island, or what sundry nations have inhabited there, to set down the Giants, which in bigness of bone have passed the common size, and almost common credit, to rehearse what diversities of languages have been used, into how many kingdoms it hath been divided, what religions have been followed before the coming of Christ, although it would breed great delight to your eyes, yet might it happily seem tedious: for that honey taken excessively cloyeth the stomach though it be honey.

Lyly
1579

But my mind is briefly to touch such things as at my being there I gathered by mine own study and enquiry, not meaning to write a Chronicle, but to set down in a word what I heard by conference.

It hath in it twenty and six cities, of the which the chiefest is named London, a place both for the beauty of building, infinite riches, variety of all things, that excelleth all the cities in the world: insomuch that it may be called the storehouse and mart of all Europe. Close by this city runneth the famous river called the Thames, which from the head where it riseth, named Isis, unto the full midway, it is thought to be an hundred and fourscore miles. What can there be in any place under the heavens that is not in this noble city either to be bought or borrowed?

It hath divers Hospitals for the relieving of the poor, six-score fair Churches for divine service, a glorious Burse which they call the Royal Exchange, for the meeting of merchants of all countries where any traffic is to be had. And among all the strange and beautiful shows, methinketh there is none so notable as the Bridge which crosseth the Thames, which

Lyly
1579

is in manner of a continual street, well replenished with large and stately houses on both sides, and situate upon twenty arches, whereof each one is made of excellent freestone squared, every one of them being threescore foot in height, and full twenty in distance one from another.

To this place the whole Realm hath his recourse, whereby it seemeth so populous, that one would scarce think so many people to be in the whole island, as he shall see sometimes in London.

This maketh Gentlemen brave, and Merchants rich, Citizens to purchase, and sojourners to mortgage, so that it is to be thought, that the greatest wealth and substance of the whole realm is couched within the walls of London, where they that be rich keep it from those that be riotous, not detaining it from the lusty youths of England by rigour, but increasing it until young men shall savour of reason, wherein they show themselves treasurers for others, not hoarders for themselves: yet although it be sure enough, would they had it [not]: in my opinion, it were better to be in the Gentleman's purse than in the Merchant's hands.

There are in this Isle two and twenty Bishops, which are as it were superintendents over the Church, men of great zeal and deep knowledge, diligent preachers of the word, earnest followers of their doctrine, careful watchmen that the Wolf devour not the Sheep, in civil government politic, in ruling the spiritual sword (as far as in them under their Prince appertaineth) just, cutting off those members from the Church by rigour that are obstinate in their heresies, and instructing those that are ignorant, appointing godly and learned Ministers in every of their sees, that in their absence may be lights to such as are in darkness, salt to those that are unsavoury, leaven to such as are not seasoned.

Visitations are holden oftentimes, whereby abuses and disorders, either in the laity for negligence, or in the clergy for superstition, or in all for wicked living, there are punishments, by due execution whereof the divine service of God is honoured with more purity, and followed with greater sincerity.

Lyly 1579

There are also in this Island two famous **Universities**, the one Oxford, the other Cambridge, both for the profession of all sciences, for Divinity, Physic, Law, and all kind of learning, excelling all the Universities in Christendom.

I was myself in either of them, and like them both so well, that I mean not in the way of controversy to prefer any for the better in England, but both for the best in the world: saving this, that colleges in Oxford are much more stately for the building, and Cambridge much more sumptuous for the houses in the town; but the learning neither lieth in the freestones of the one, nor the fine streets of the other, for out of them both do daily proceed men of great wisdom, to rule in the commonwealth, of learning to instruct the common people, of all singular kind of professions to do good to all. And let this suffice, not to enquire which of them is the superior, but that neither of them have their equal; neither to ask which of them is the most ancient, but whether any other be so famous.

But to proceed: in England their buildings are not very stately, unless it be the houses of noble men, and here and there the place of a Gentleman, but much amended, as they report that have told me. For their munition they have not only great store, but also great cunning to use them, and courage to practise them: their armour is not unlike unto that which in other countries they use, as corselets, Almain rivets, shirts of mail, jacks quilted and covered over with leather, fustian, or canvas, over thick plates of iron that are sowed into the same.

The Ordnance they have is great, and thereof great store. Their Navy is divided as it were into three sorts, of the which the one serveth for wars, the other for burthen, the third for fishermen. And some vessels there be (I know not

Lyly
1579

by experience, and yet **I believe by** circumstance) that will sail nine hundred miles in a week, when I should scarce think that a bird could fly **four hundred.**

Touching other commodities, they have four baths, the first called St. Vincent's; the second, Holywell; the third, Buxton; the fourth (as in old time they read) Cair Bledud, but **now** taking his name of a town near adjoining, it is called the Bath.

Besides this many wonders there are to be found in this Island, which I will not repeat, because I myself never saw **them,** and you have heard of greater.

Concerning their diet, in number of dishes and change of meat, the Nobility of England **do exceed** most, having all **things that** either **may be bought for** money or gotten for the season. Gentlemen and Merchants feed very finely, and a poor man it is that dineth with one dish, and yet so content with a little, that having half dined, they say as it were in a proverb, that they are as well satisfied as the Lord Mayor of London, whom they think to fare best, though he eat not most.

In **their** meals there is great silence and gravity, using wine **rather to** ease the stomach than to load it; not like unto other nations, who never think that they have dined till they be drunken.

The attire they use is rather led by the imitation of others than their own invention, so that there is nothing in England more constant than the inconstancy of attire: now using the French fashion, now the Spanish, then the Morisco gowns, then one thing, then another: insomuch that in drawing of an Englishman the painter setteth him down naked, having in the one hand a pair of shears, in the other a piece of cloth, who having cut his collar after the French guise is ready to make his sleeve after the Barbarian manner. And although this were the greatest enormity that I could see in England, yet is **it to** be excused, for they that cannot

maintain this pride must leave of necessity, and they that be Lyly
able will leave when they see the vanity. 1579

The laws they use are different from ours, for although the Common and Civil Law be not abolished, yet are they not had in so great reputation as their own common laws, which they term the laws of the Crown.

The regiment that they have dependeth upon statute law, and that is by Parliament which is the highest court, consisting of three several sorts of people, the Nobility, Clergy, and Commons of the Realm, so as whatsoever be among them enacted, the Queen striketh the stroke, allowing such things as to Her Majesty seemeth best. Then upon Common Law, which standeth upon maxims and principles, years and terms; the cases in this law are called pleas or actions, and they are either criminal or civil; the mean to determine are writs, some original, some judicial. Their trials and recoveries are either by verdict or demur, confession or default, wherein if any fault have been committed, either in process or form, matter or judgment, the party grieved may have a writ of error.

Then upon Customable Law, which consisteth upon laudable customs used in some private country.

Last of all upon Prescription, which is a certain custom continued time out of mind, but it is more particular than their Customary Law.

Murtherers and thieves are hanged, witches burnt, all other villainies that deserve death punished with death, insomuch that there are very few heinous offences practised in respect of those that in other countries are commonly used.

Of savage beasts and vermin they have no great store, nor any that are noisome. The cattle they keep for profit are oxen, horses, sheep, goats, and swine, and such like, whereof they have abundance; wildfowl and fish they want none, nor anything that either may serve for pleasure or profit.

They have more store of pasture than tillage, their

Lyly
1579

meadows better **than their** corn fields, which maketh more graziers than cornmongers, **yet sufficient** store of both.

They excel for one thing, **their dogs of** all sorts: spaniels, hounds, mastiffs, and divers **such: the** one they keep for hunting and hawking, the other **for** necessary **uses** about their houses, **as to** draw water, **to** watch thieves, **etc.**, and **thereof** they derive the word mastiff of *Mase* **and** *Thief*.

There is in that **Isle** salt made, and saffron; **there are** great quarries **of** stones for building, sundry minerals of quicksilver, antimony, sulphur, black-lead, and orpiment red **and yellow.** Also there groweth the finest alum that is, vermilion, bittament, **chrisocolla,** coperus, the mineral stone whereof petroleum is **made, and that which** is most strange, the mineral pearl, which **as they are** for greatness **and colour most** excellent, so **are they digged out of the** mainland, in places far distant from the **shore.**

Besides **these,** though **not strange, yet** necessary, they **have coal** mines, saltpetre for **Ordnance,** salt sode **for** glass. **They want no tin nor** lead, there groweth **iron,** steel, **and** copper, and **what not: so hath God** blessed that country, as it should seem not only to have sufficient to serve their own turns, **but also others'** necessities; whereof there **was an old** saying, all countries stand in need of Britain, and Britain of **none.**

Their **air is** very wholesome and pleasant, their civility not **inferior to those** that deserve best, their wits very sharp and **quick,** although I have heard that the Italian and the Frenchman **have** accompted them but gross and dull-pated, which **I think came not to** pass by the proof they made of their wits, **but** by the Englishman's report.

For this is strange (and **yet how true it is, there is none** that ever travelled thither **but** can report) **that it** is always incident to an Englishman to think worst of his own nation, **either** in learning, experience, common reason, or wit, preferring always **a stranger** rather for **the** name than **the wisdom.** I for mine own part think, that in all Europe there are not Lawyers more learned, Divines more profound, Physicians more expert, than are in England.

Lyly
1579

But that which most allureth a stranger is their courtesy, their civility, and good entertainment. I speak this by experience, that I found more courtesy in England among those I never knew, in one year, than I have done in Athens or Italy among those I ever loved, in twenty.

But having entreated sufficiently of the country and their conditions, let me come to the Glass I promised, being the Court, where although I should as order requireth begin with the chiefest, yet I am enforced with the painter to reserve my best colours to end Venus, and to lay the ground with the basest.

First then I must tell you of the grave and wise Councillors, whose foresight in peace warranteth safety in war, whose provision in plenty maketh sufficient in dearth, whose care in health is as it were a preparative against sickness, how great their wisdom hath been in all things, the twenty-two years' peace doth both show and prove. For what subtilty hath there been wrought so closely, what privy attempts so craftily, what rebellions stirred up so disorderly, but they have by policy bewrayed, prevented by wisdom, repressed by justice? What conspiracies abroad, what confederacies at home, what injuries in any place hath there been contrived, the which they have not either foreseen before they could kindle, or quenched before they could flame?

If any wily Ulysses should feign madness, there was among them always some Palamedes to reveal him: if any Thetis went about to keep her son from the doing of his country service, there was also a wise Ulysses in the court to bewray it: if Sinon came with a smooth tale to bring in the horse into Troy, there hath been always some courageous Lacaon to throw his spear against the bowels, which being not bewitched with Lacaon, has unfolded that which Lacaon suspected.

Lyly
1579

If Argus with his hundred eyes went prying to undermine Jupiter, yet met he with **Mercury**, who whistled all **his** eyes out; insomuch as there **could never** yet any craft prevail against their policy, or any challenge against their courage. There hath always been Achilles **at home to** buckle with Hector abroad, Nestor's gravity **to countervail** Priam's counsel, Ulysses' subtilties to match with **Antenor's** policies. England hath all those that can and have wrestled with **all** others, **whereof we** can require no greater proof than **experience.**

Besides **they have all a** zealous care for the increasing of **true** religion, **whose faiths** for the most part hath been tried through the fire, which **they had felt** had not they fled over the water. Moreover the **great** study they bend towards schools of learning, doth sufficiently declare that they are not only furtherers of learning, **but** fathers of the learned. O thrice happy England where such counsellors **are,** where **such** people live, where such **virtue** springeth!

Among these shall you find Zopirus that will mangle himself **to do** his country good, Achates that will never start an **inch** from his Prince Æneas, Nausicla that never wanted a shift **in** extremity, Cato **that** ever counselled to the best, Ptolomeus Philadelphus **that** always maintained learning. Among **the** number of all which noble and wise Councillors (I cann**ot but for** his honour's sake remember) the most prudent **and** right honourable the Lord Burleigh, High Treasurer **of** that realm, **no** less reverenced for his wisdom than renowned for his office, more loved at home than feared abroad, and yet more feared for his counsel among other nations than sword or fire, in whom the saying of Agamemnon may be verified: who rather wished for one such as Nestor, than many such as Ajax.

This noble man I found so ready, being but a stranger, to do me good, that neither I ought to forget him, neither **cease** to pray for him, that as he hath the wisdom of Nestor, so he may have the age; that having the policies of Ulysses, he may have his honour; worthy to live long, by whom so many live in quiet, and not unworthy to be advanced, by whose care so many have been preferred.

Lyly
1579

Is not this a Glass, fair Ladies, for all other countries to behold, where there is not only an agreement in faith, religion, and counsel, but in friendship, brotherhood, and living? By whose good endeavours vice is punished, virtue rewarded, peace established, foreign broils repressed, domestical cares appeased? What nation can of councillors desire more? what dominion, that excepted, hath so much? when neither courage can prevail against their chivalry, nor craft take place against their counsel, nor both joined in one be of force to undermine their country. When you have dazzled your eyes with this Glass, behold here another. It was my fortune to be acquainted with certain English gentlemen, which brought me to the Court, where when I came I was driven into a maze to behold the lusty and brave gallants, the beautiful and chaste ladies, the rare and godly orders, so as I could not tell whether I should most commend virtue or bravery.

John Lyly.

HOW WE CAME TO THE TOWN OF HOCHELAGA

SO soon as we were come near the town, a great number of the inhabitors thereof came to present themselves before us after their fashion, making very much of us: we were by our guides brought into the midst of the town. They have in the middlemost part of their houses a large square place, being from side to side a good stone's cast, where we were brought, and there with signs were commanded to stay. Then suddenly all the women and maidens of the town gathered themselves together, part of which had their arms full of young children, and as many as could

Florio
1580

146 HOW WE CAME TO THE TOWN OF HOCHELAGA

Florio
1580

came to rub our faces, our arms, and what part of the body soever they could touch, weeping for very joy that they saw us, showing us the best countenance that possible was, desiring us with their signs that it would please us to touch their children. That done, the men caused the women to withdraw themselves back, then they every one sate down on the ground round about us, as if they would have shown and rehearsed some comedy or other show.

Then presently came the women again, every one bringing a four-square mat in manner of carpets, and spreading them abroad on the ground in that place; then they caused us to sit upon them. That done, the Lord and King of the country was brought upon nine or ten men's shoulders (whom in their tongue they call Agouhanna), sitting upon a great stag's skin, and they laid him down upon the foresaid mats near to our Captain, every one beckoning unto us that he was their Lord and King. This Agouhanna was a man about fifty years old; he was no whit better apparelled than any of the rest, only excepted, that he had a certain thing made of beasts' skins (called *Ricci*) like a red towel, and that was instead of his crown. He was full of the palsy, and his members shrunk together. After he had with certain signs and becks saluted our Captain and all his company, and by manifest tokens bid us all welcome, he showed his legs and arms to our Captain, and with signs desired him to touch them, and so he did, rubbing them with his own hands. Then did Agouhanna take the wreath or crown he had about his head, and gave it unto our Captain.

That done, they brought before him divers diseased men, some blind, some cripple, some lame and impotent, and some so old that the hair of their eyelids came down and covered their cheeks, and laid them all along before our Captain, to the end they might of him be touched, for it seemed unto them that God had been descended

HOW WE CAME TO THE TOWN OF HOCHELAGA

and come down from heaven to heal them. Our Captain, seeing the misery and devotion of this poor people, recited the Gospel of St. John, that is to say, In the beginning was the word: touching every one that was diseased, praying to God that it would please Him to open the hearts of this poor people, and to make them know His holy Word, and that they might receive baptism and Christendom. That done, he took a book in his hand, and with a loud voice read all the Passion of Christ, word by word, that all the bystanders might hear him, all which while this poor people kept silence, and were marvellously attentive, looking up to heaven, and imitating us in gestures.

Florio 1580

Then he caused the men all orderly to be set on one side, the women on another, and likewise the children on another, and to the chiefest of them he gave hatchets, to the other knives, and to the women beads, and such other small trifles. Then where the children were, he cast rings, counters, and branches made of tin, whereat they seemed to be very glad. That done, our Captain commanded shawms and other musical instruments to be sounded, which, when they heard, they were very merry. Then we took our leave and went to our boat. The women seeing that, put themselves before to stay us, and brought us out of their meats that they had made ready for us, as fish, pottage, beans, and such other things, thinking to make us eat and dine in that place; but because the meats had no savour at all of salt, we liked them not, but thanked them, and with signs gave them to understand that we had no need to eat. When we were out of the town, divers of the men and women followed us, and brought us to the top of the foresaid mountain, which we named Mount Royal: it is about a league from the town. When as we were on the top of it, we might discern and plainly see thirty leagues off.

On the north side of it there are many hills to be seen, running west and east, and as many more on the south, amongst and between the which the country is as fair and as pleasant as possibly can be seen, being level, smooth, and very plain, fit to be husbanded and tilled: and in the midst of those fields we might see further a great way than where we had left our boats, where was the greatest and the swiftest fall of water that anywhere hath been seen, as great, wide, and large as our sight might discern, going south-west along three fair and round mountains that we saw, as we judged about fifteen leagues from us. Those which brought us thither told and showed us, that in the said river there were three such falls of water more, as it was where we had left our boats, but because we could not understand their language, we could not know how far they were from another. Moreover, they showed us with signs, that the said three falls being past, a man might sail the space of three months more alongst that river, and that along the hills that are on the north side, there is a great river, which, even as the other cometh from the east, we thought it to be the river that runneth through the country of Saguenay; and without any sign or question moved or asked of them, they took the chain of our Captain's whistle, which was of silver, and the dagger haft of one of our fellow mariners, hanging on his side, being of yellow copper gilt, and showed us that such stuff came from the said river, and that there be *Agouionda*, that is as much as to say, as evil people, who go all armed, even to their finger ends.

Also, they showed us the manner and making of their armour: they are made of cords and wood, finely and cunningly wrought together. They gave us also to understand that those *Agouionda* do continually war against them: but because we did not understand them well, we could not perceive how far it was to that country. Our Captain showed them red copper, which in their language they call *Caignetadze*, and, looking toward that country with signs, asked them if any came from thence, they, shaking their heads, answered no: but they showed us that it came from **Saguenay**, and that lieth clean contrary to the other. After we had heard and seen these things of them, we drew to our boats, accompanied with great multitude of those people. Some of them, whenas they saw any of our fellows weary, they would take them upon their shoulders, and carry them as on horseback. So soon as we came to our boats, we hoisted sail to go toward our galleon, doubting of some mischance. Our departure grieved and displeased them very much, for they followed us along the river as far as they could. We went so fast that on Monday, being the fourth of October, we came where our galleon was. The Tuesday following, being the fifth of the month, we hoisted sail, and with our galleon and boats, departed from thence toward the province of Canada, to the port of the Holy Cross, where we had left our ships. The seventh day we came against a river that cometh from the north, and entered into that river, at the entrance whereof are four little islands, full of fair and goodly trees. We named that river the River of Fouetz. But because one of those islands stretcheth himself a great way into the river, our Captain at the point of it caused a goodly great cross to be set up, and commanded the boats to be made ready, that with the next tide he might go up to the said river, and consider the quality of it, which we did, and that day went up as far as we could; but because we found it to be of no importance, and that we could sound no bottom, we returned down and back again.

John Florio.

A CORONATION

THE time of mourning after their use being expired, called Sorachyn, or forty orderly days, the day of the solemnising of this coronation, with great preparations, was come, being upon the 10th day of June 1584; and that day then Sunday, he being of the age of twenty-five years, at which time, Master **Jerome Horsey** was orderly sent for, and placed in **a** fit room to see all **the solemnity.** The Emperor coming out of his Palace, there **went before** him the Metropolitan, Archbishops, Bishops, **and** chiefest **Monks,** and Clergymen, with very rich copes and priests' **garments upon them,** carrying pictures of our Lady, etc., with **the Emperor's angel, banners,** censers, **and** many other **such ceremonious things,** singing all the way. The Emperor with **his nobility in order entered** the church named Blaueshina, or Blessedness, **where** prayers and service were used, according **to** the **manner of their Church:** that done, they went thence **to the Church** called Michael **the Archangel, and there** also **used the like** prayers **and service: and from thence** to our **Lady Church,** Prechista, being **their Cathedral Church. In the** midst **thereof was a chair** of **majesty placed,** wherein his **Ancestors** used to sit at **such extraordinary times: his** robes **were then** changed, and **most rich and** invaluable garments put on him. Being placed in this princely seat, his Nobility standing **round about** him in their degrees, **his imperial crown** was set upon **his head** by the Metropolitan, **his** sceptre **globe in his** right hand, **his sword of justice in his** left of great **riches; his six crowns** also, **by which he holdeth his kingdoms, were set before him, and the Lord Boris Pheodorowich was placed at his right hand.** Then the Metropolitan **read** openly **a** book of **a small** volume, with exhortations **to the** Emperor **to** minister **true** justice, **to enjoy with tranquillity the** crown of his **Ancestors,** which God **had given** him, and used **these words** following:

'Through the will of **the** Almighty and **without** beginning **God, Which was** before **this world, Whom we** glorify in the **Trinity,** one only **God, the Father, the Son,** and the Holy Ghost, maker of all things, worker of all in **all** everywhere, fulfiller of all things, by which will and working He both liveth **and giveth** life to man: **that** our only God Which inspireth every one of us, His only children, with His word to discern God through our Lord Jesus Christ, and the holy quickening spirit of life, now in these perilous times establish us to keep the right sceptre, and suffer us to reign of ourselves to the good profit of the land, to the subduing of the people, together with the enemies, and the maintenance of virtue.' And so the Metropolitan blessed and laid his cross upon him. After this, he was taken out of his chair of majesty, having upon him an upper robe adorned with precious stones of all sorts, orient pearls of great quantity, but always augmented in riches: it was in weight two hundred pounds, the train and parts thereof borne up by six Dukes, his chief imperial crown upon his head very precious: his staff imperial in his right hand of an unicorn's horn of three foot and a half in length, beset with rich stones, bought of merchants of Augsburg by the old Emperor in Anno 1581, and cost him 7000 marks sterling. This jewel Master Horsey kept sometimes, before the Emperor had it. His sceptre globe was carried before him by the Prince Boris Pheodorowich, his rich cap, beset with rich stones and pearls, was carried before him by a Duke: his six crowns also were carried by Demetrius Ivanowich Godonova, the Emperor's uncle, Mekita Romanowich, the Emperor's uncle, Stephan Vasiliwich, Gregory Vasiliwich, Ivan Vasiliwich, brothers of the blood royal. Thus at last the Emperor came to the great Church door, and the people cried: 'God save our Emperor Pheodor Ivanowich of all Russia.' His horse was there ready most richly adorned, with a covering of embroidered pearl and precious stones, saddle, and all furniture agreeable to it, reported to be worth 300,000 marks sterling.

There was a bridge made of 150 fathom in length, three manner of ways, three foot above ground and two fathom broad, for him to go from one Church to the other with his princes and nobles from the press of the people, which were in number infinite, and some at that time pressed to death with

Horsey
1584

the throng. As the Emperor returned out of the Churches, they were spread under foot with cloth of gold, the porches of the Churches with red velvet, the bridges with scarlet, and stammell cloth[1] from one church to another: and as soon as the Emperor was passed by, the cloth of gold, velvet, and scarlet was cut, and taken of those that could come by it, every man desirous to have a piece, to reserve it for a monument: silver and gold coin, then minted of purpose, was cast among the people in great quantity. The Lord Boris Pheodorowich was sumptuously and richly attired, with his garments decked with great orient pearl, beset with all sorts of precious stones. In like rich manner were apparelled all the family of the Godonovaes in their degrees, with the rest of the princes and nobility, whereof one named Knez Ivan Michalowich Glynsky, whose robe, horse, and furniture was in register found worth 100,000 marks sterling, being of great antiquity. The Empress being in her palace, was placed in her chair of Majesty also before a great open window: most precious and rich were her robes, and shining to behold, with rich stones and orient pearl beset; her crown was placed upon her head, accompanied with her Princesses and Ladies of Estate. Then cried out the people: 'God preserve our noble Empress Irenia.' After all this the Emperor came into the Parliament House, which was richly decked: there he was placed in his royal seat adorned as before: his six crowns were set before him upon a table: the basin and ewer royal of gold held by his Knight of Guard with his men standing two on each side in white apparel of cloth of silver, called Kindry, with sceptres and battleaxes of gold in their hands: the princes and nobility were all placed according to their degrees all in their rich robes.

The Emperor after a short oration permitted every man in order to kiss his hand, which being done, he removed to a princely seat prepared for him at the table: where he was

[1] A coarse woollen.

A CORONATION

served by his nobles in very princely order. The three out-rooms being very great and large, were beset with plate of gold and silver round, from the ground up to the vaults one upon the other: among which plate were many barrels of silver and gold. This solemnity and triumph lasted a whole week, wherein many royal pastimes were showed and used, after which the chiefest men of the nobility were elected to their places of office and dignity, as the Prince Boris Pheodorowich was made Chief Counsellor to the Emperor, Master of the Horse, had the charge of his person, Lieutenant of the Empire and warlike engines, Governor or Lieutenant of the Empire of Cazan and Astrakan and others. To this dignity were by Parliament and gift of the Emperor given him many revenues and rich lands, as there was given him and his for ever to inherit a province called Vaga, of 300 English miles in length and 250 in breadth, with many towns and great villages populous and wealthy: his yearly revenue out of that province is 35,000 marks sterling, being not the fifth part of his yearly revenue. Further, he and his house be of such authority and power, that in forty days' warning they are able to bring into the field 100,000 soldiers well furnished.

The conclusion of the Emperor's Coronation was a peal of ordnance, called a peal royal, two miles without the city, being 170 great pieces of brass of all sorts, as fair as any can be made. These pieces were all discharged with shot against bulwarks made of purpose: 20,000 harquebusers standing in eight ranks two miles in length, apparelled all in velvet, coloured silk, and stammels, discharged their shot also twice over in good order: and so the Emperor, accompanied with all his Princes and Nobles, at the least 50,000 horse, departed through the city to his palace. This royal coronation would ask much time, and many leaves of paper to be described particularly as it was performed: it shall suffice to understand that the like magnificence was never seen in Russia.

Hakluyt: Navigations.

Horsey
1584

A FALSE WITCH

Scot 1584

MILDRED, the base daughter of Alice Norrington, and now servant to William Sponer of Westwell in the county of Kent, being of the age of seventeen years, was possessed with Satan in the night and day aforesaid. About two of the clock in the afternoon of the same day, there came to the same Sponer's house, Roger Newman, minister of Westwell, John Brainford, minister of Kenington, with others whose names are underwritten, who made their prayers unto God, to assist them in that needful case; and then commanded Satan in the name of the eternal God, and of His Son Jesus Christ, to speak with such a voice as they might understand, and to declare from whence he came. But he would not speak, but roared and cried mightily. And though we did command him many times in the name of God, and of His Son Jesus Christ, and in His mighty power to speak, yet he would not: until he had gone through all his delays, as roaring, crying, striving, and gnashing of teeth; and otherwhile with mowing, and other terrible countenances, and was so strong in the maid, that four men could scarce hold her down. And this continued by the space almost of two hours. So sometimes we charged him earnestly to speak, and again praying unto God that He would assist us. At the last he spake, but very strangely, and that was thus: 'He comes, He comes;' and that oftimes he repeated; and, 'He goes, He goes.' And then we charged him to tell us who sent him. And he said: 'I lay in her way like a log, and I made her run like fire, but I could not hurt her.' 'And why so?' said we. 'Because God kept her,' said he. 'When camest thou to her?' said we. 'To-night in her bed,' said he. Then we charged him, as before, to tell what he was, and who sent him, and what his name was. At first he said, 'The devil,

A FALSE WITCH

the devil.' Then we charged him as before. Then he roared and cried as before, and spake terrible words: 'I will kill her, I will kill her, I will tear her in pieces, I will tear her in pieces.' We said, 'Thou shalt not hurt her.' He said, 'I will kill you all.' We said, 'Thou shalt hurt none of us all.' Then we charged him as before. Then he said, 'You will give me no rest.' We said, 'Thou shalt have none here, for thou must have no rest within the servants of God: but tell us in the name of God what thou art, and who sent thee.' Then he said, he would tear her in pieces. We said, 'Thou shalt not hurt her.' Then he said again, he would kill us all. We said again, 'Thou shalt hurt none of us all, for we are the servants of God.' And we charged him as before. And he said again, 'Will you give me no rest?' We said, 'Thou shalt have none here, neither shalt thou rest in her, for thou hast no right in her, since Jesus Christ hath redeemed her with His blood, and she belongeth to Him, and therefore tell us thy name, and who sent thee?' He said his name was Satan. We said, 'Who sent thee?' He said, 'Old Alice, Old Alice.' 'Which Old Alice?' said we. 'Old Alice,' said he. 'Where dwelleth she?' said we. 'In Westwell Street,' said he. We said, 'How long hast thou been with her?' 'These twenty years,' said he. We asked him where she did keep him? 'In two bottles,' said he. 'Where be they?' said we. 'In the backside of her house,' said he. 'In what place?' said we. 'Under the wall,' said he. 'Where is the other?' 'In Kenington.' 'In what place?' said we. 'In the ground,' said he. Then we asked him, what she did give him. He said, 'Her will, her will.' 'What did she bid thee do?' said we. He said, 'Kill her maid.' 'Wherefore did she bid thee kill her?' said we. 'Because she did not love her,' said he. We said, 'How long is it ago since she sent thee to her?' 'More than a year,' said he. 'Where was that?' said we. 'At her master's,' said he. 'Which master's?' said we. 'At

Scot 1584

Scot
1584

her Master Brainford's, at Kenington,' said he. 'How oft wert thou there?' said we. 'Many times,' said he. 'Where first?' said we. 'In the garden,' said he. 'Where the second time?' 'In the hall.' 'Where the third time?' 'In her bed.' 'Where the fourth time?' 'In the field.' 'Where the fifth time?' 'In the court.' 'Where the sixth time?' 'In the water, where I cast her into the moat.' 'Where the seventh time?' 'In her bed.' We asked him again, 'Where else?' He said, 'In Westwell.' 'Where there?' said we. 'In the Vicarage,' said he. 'Where there?' 'In the loft.' 'How camest thou to her?' said we. 'In the likeness of two birds,' said he. 'Who sent thee to that place?' said we. 'Old Alice,' said he. 'What other spirits were with thee there?' said we. 'My servant,' said he. 'What is his name?' said we. He said 'Little Devil.' 'What is thy name?' said we. 'Satan,' said he. 'What doth Old Alice call thee?' said we. 'Partner,' said he. 'What doth she give thee?' said we. 'Her will,' said he. 'How many hast thou killed for her?' said we. 'Three,' said he. 'Who are they?' said we. 'A man and his child,' said he. 'What were their names?' said we. 'The child's name was Edward,' said he. 'What more than Edward?' said we. 'Edward Ager,' said he. 'What was the man's name?' said we. 'Richard,' said he. 'What more?' said we. 'Richard Ager,' said he. 'Where dwelt the man and the child?' said we. 'At Dig, at Dig,' said he. This Richard Ager of Dig was a gentleman of forty pounds land by the year, a very honest man, but would often say he was bewitched, and languished long before he died. 'Whom else hast thou killed for her?' said we. 'Wolton's wife,' said he. 'Where did she dwell?' 'In Westwell,' said he. 'What else hast thou done for her?' said we. 'What she would have me,' said he. 'What is that?' said we. 'To fetch her meat, drink, and corn,' said he. 'Where hadst thou it?' said we. 'In every house,' said he. 'Name the houses,' said we.

'At Petman's, at Farme's, at Millen's, at Fuller's, and in every house.' After this, we commanded Satan in the name of Jesus Christ to depart from her, and never to trouble her any more, nor any man else. Then he said, he would go, he would go: but he went not. Then we commanded him as before, with some more words. Then he said, 'I go, I go;' and so he departed. Then said the maid: 'He is gone, Lord have mercy upon me, for he would have killed me.' Then we kneeled down and gave God thanks, with the maiden, praying that God would keep her from Satan's power, and assist her with His grace. And noting this in a piece of paper, we departed. Satan's voice did differ much from the maid's voice, and all that he spake was in his own name. . . .

But to make short work with the confutation of this bastardly quean's enterprise and cosenage; you shall understand that upon the bruit of her divinity and miraculous trances, she was convented before Master Thomas Wotton of Bocton Malherbe, a man of great worship and wisdom, and for deciding and ordering of matters in this commonwealth of rare and singular dexterity; through whose discreet handling of the matter, with the assistance and aid of Master George Darrel, Esq.; being also a right good and discreet Justice of the same limit, the fraud was found, and the cosenage confessed, and she received condign punishment. Neither was her confession won according to the form of the Spanish Inquisition, to wit, through extremity of tortures, nor yet by guile or flattery, nor by presumptions; but through wise and perfect trial of every circumstance the illusion was manifestly disclosed. Not so (I say) as witches are commonly convinced and condemned; to wit, through malicious accusations, by guesses, presumptions, and extorted confessions contrary to sense and possibility, and for such actions as they can show no trial nor example before the wise, either by direct or indirect means; but after due trial she showed her

Scot
1584

Scot
1584

feats, illusions, and trances, with the residue of all her miraculous works, in the presence of divers gentlemen and gentlewomen of great worship and credit, at Bocton Malherbe, in the house of the said Mr. Wotton. Now compare this wench with the Witch of Endor, and you shall see that both the cosenages may be done by one art.

Reginald Scot.

THE FIRST LANDING IN VIRGINIA

Barlow
1584

THE second of July we found shoal water, where we smelt so sweet and so strong a smell, as if we had been in the midst of some delicate garden abounding with all kind of odoriferous flowers, by which we were assured that the land could not be far distant; and keeping good watch, and bearing but slack sail, the fourth of the same month we arrived upon the coast, which we supposed to be a continent and firm land, and we sailed along the same 120 English miles before we could find any entrance, or river issuing into the sea. The first that appeared unto us we entered, though not without some difficulty, and cast anchor about three harquebus-shot within the haven's mouth, on the left hand of the same; and after thanks given to God for our safe arrival thither, we manned our boats and went to view the land next adjoining, and 'to take possession of the same, in the right of the Queen's most excellent Majesty, as rightful Queen and Princess of the same, and after delivered the same over to your use, according to her Majesty's grant and letters patent, under her Highness's great seal.' Which being performed, according to the ceremonies used in such enterprises, we viewed the land about us, being, whereas we first landed, very sandy and low towards the water's side, but so full of grapes, as the very beating and surge of the sea overflowed them, of which we found such plenty, as well there as in all places else, both on the sand and on the green soil on the hills, as in the plains, as well on every little shrub, as also climbing towards the tops of high cedars, that I think in all the world the like abundance is not to be found: and myself having seen those parts of Europe that most abound, find such difference as were incredible to be written.

Barlow
1584

We passed from the sea side towards the tops of those hills next adjoining, being but of mean height, and from thence we beheld the sea on both sides to the North and to the South, finding no end any of both ways. This land lay stretching itself to the West, which after we found to be but an island of twenty miles long, and not above six miles broad. Under the bank or hill whereon we stood, we beheld the valleys replenished with goodly cedar trees, and having discharged our harquebus-shot, such a flock of cranes (the most part white) arose under us, with such a cry redoubled by many echoes, as if an army of men had shouted all together.

This island had many goodly woods full of deer, conies, hares, and fowl, even in the midst of summer in incredible abundance. The woods are not such as you find in Bohemia, Moscovia, or Hercynia, barren and fruitless, but the highest and reddest cedars of the world, far bettering the cedars of the Açores, of the Indies, or Lybanus, pines, cypresses, sassafras, the lentisk, or the tree that beareth the mastic, the tree that beareth the rine of black cinnamon, of which Mr. Winter brought from the Straits of Magellan, and many other of excellent smell and quality. We remained by the side of this island two whole days before we saw any people of the country: the third day we espied one small boat rowing towards us having in it three persons: this boat came to the island side, four harquebus-shot from our ships, and there two of the people remaining, the third came along the shoreside towards us, and we being then all within board, he walked up and down upon the point of the land

Barlow 1584

next unto us. Then the Master and the Pilot of the admiral, Simon Ferdinando, and the Captain Philip Amadas, myself, and others rowed to the land, whose coming this fellow attended, never making any show of fear or doubt. And after he had spoken of many things not understood by us, we brought him with his own good liking aboard the ships, and gave him a shirt, a hat, and some other things, and made him taste of our wine and our meat, which he liked very well: and after having viewed both barques, he departed and went to his own boat again, which he had left in a little cove or creek adjoining: as soon as he was two bow-shoot into the water, he fell to fishing, and in less than half-an-hour he had laden his boat as deep as it could swim, with which he came again to the point of the land, and there he divided his fish into two parts, pointing one part to the ship, and the other to the pinnace; which, after he had (as much as he might) requited the former benefits received, departed out of our sight.

The next day there came unto us divers boats, and in one of them the King's brother, accompanied with forty or fifty men, very handsome and goodly people, and in their behaviour as mannerly and civil as any of Europe. His name was Granganimeo, and the King is called Wingina, the country Wingandacoa, and now by her Majesty Virginia. The manner of his coming was in this sort: he left his boats altogether as the first man did a little from the ships by the shore, and came along to the place over against the ships, followed with forty men. When he came to the place, his servants spread a long mat upon the ground, on which he sate down, and at the other end of the mat four others of his company did the like, the rest of his men stood round about him, somewhat afar off: when we came to the shore to him with our weapons, he never moved from his place, nor any of the other four, nor never mistrusted any harm to be offered from us, but sitting still he beckoned us to come and sit by him, which we performed: and being set, he made all signs of joy and welcome, striking on his head and his breast and afterwards on ours, to show we were all one, smiling and making show the best he could of all love and familiarity. After he had made a long speech unto us, we presented him with divers things, which he received very joyfully and thankfully. None of the company durst speak one word all the time: only the four which were at the other end spake one in the other's ears very softly.

Barlow 1584

The King is greatly obeyed, and his brothers and children reverenced: the King himself in person was at our being there sore wounded in a fight which he had with the King of the next country, called Wingina, and was shot in two places through the body, and once clean through the thigh, but yet he recovered: by reason whereof and for that he lay at the chief town of the country, being six days' journey off, we saw him not at all.

After we had presented this his brother with such things as we thought he liked, we likewise gave somewhat to the other that sat with him on the mat: but presently he arose and took all from them and put it into his own basket, making signs and tokens that all things ought to be delivered unto him, and the rest were but his servants and followers. A day or two after this, we fell to trading with them, exchanging some things that we had for chamois, buff, and deer skins: when we showed him all our packet of merchandise, of all things that he saw, a bright tin dish most pleased him, which he presently took up and clapt it before his breast, and after made a hole in the brim thereof and hung it about his neck, making signs that it would defend him against his enemies' arrows: for those people maintain a deadly and terrible war with the people and King adjoining. We exchanged our tin dish for twenty skins, worth twenty crowns, or twenty nobles: and a copper kettle for fifty skins worth fifty crowns. They offered us

Barlow
.1584

good exchange for our hatchets and axes, and for knives, and would have given anything for swords: but we would not depart with any. After two or three days the King's brother came aboard the ships, and drank wine, and ate of our meat and of our bread, and liked exceedingly thereof: and after a few days overpassed, he brought his wife with him to the ships, his daughter and two or three children: his wife was very well favoured, of mean stature, and very bashful: she had on her back a long cloak of leather, with the fur side next to her body, and before her a piece of the same: about her forehead she had a band of white coral, and so had her husband many times: in her ears she had bracelets of pearls hanging down to her middle (whereof we delivered your worship a little bracelet), and those were of the bigness of good peas. The rest of her women of the better sort had pendants of copper hanging in either ear, and some of the children of the King's brother and other noblemen have five or six in either ear: he himself had upon his head a broad plate of gold or copper, for being unpolished we knew not what metal it should be, neither would he by any means suffer us to take it off his head, but feeling it, it would bow very easily. His apparel was as his wife's, only the women wear their hair long on both sides, and the men but on one. They are of colour yellowish, and their hair black for the most part, and yet we saw children that had very fine auburn and chestnut-coloured hair.

After that these women had been there, there came down from all parts great store of people, bringing with them leather, coral, divers kinds of dyes, very excellent, and exchanged with us; but when Granganimeo, the King's brother, was present, none durst trade but himself, except such as wear red pieces of copper on their heads like himself: for that is the difference between the noblemen and the governors of countries, and the meaner sort. And we both noted there, and you have understood since by

these men, which we brought home, that no people in the
world carry more respect to their King, Nobility, and
Governors, than these do. The King's brother's wife, when
she came to us (as she did many times), was followed with
forty or fifty women always; and when she came into the
ship, she left them all on land, saving her two daughters,
her nurse, and one or two more. The King's brother always
kept this order: as many boats as he would come withal to
the ships, so many fires would he make on the shore afar
off, to the end we might understand with what strength and
company he approached. Their boats are made of one tree,
either of pine or of pitch trees: a wood not commonly known
to our people, nor found growing in England. They have
no edge-tools to make them withal: if they have any they
are very few, and those it seems they had twenty years
since, which, as those two men declared, was out of a wreck
which happened upon their coast of some Christian ship
being beaten that way by some storm and outrageous
weather, whereof none of the people were saved, but only
the ship, or some part of her being cast upon the sand, out
of whose sides they drew the nails and the spikes, and with
those they made their best instruments. The manner of
making their boats is thus: they burn down some great tree,
or take such as are windfallen, and putting gum and rosin
upon one side thereof, they set fire into it, and when it
hath burnt it hollow, they cut out the coal with their shells,
and ever where they would burn it deeper or wider they
lay on gums, which burn away the timber, and by this
means they fashion very fine boats, and such as will transport
twenty men. Their oars are like scoops, and many times
they set with long poles, as the depth serveth.

   The King's brother had great liking of our armour, a
sword, and divers other things which we had, and offered to
lay a great box of pearl in gage for them, but we refused it
for this time, because we would not make them know that

Barlow
1584

we esteemed thereof, until **we** had understood in what places of the country the pearl **grew**: which now your worship doth very well understand.

He was very just of his promise: for many times we delivered him merchandise upon **his** word, but ever he came within the day and performed his **promise. He** sent us every day a brace or two of fat bucks, conies, **hares,** fish, the best of the world. He sent us divers kinds **of fruits,** melons, walnuts, cucumbers, gourds, peas, and divers roots, and fruits very excellent good, and of their country corn, which is very white, fair and well tasted, and groweth three times in five months: in May they sow, in July they reap: in June they sow, in August they reap: in July they sow, in September they reap; **only they cast the** corn into the ground, breaking **a** little of **the soft turf** with a wooden mattock or pickaxe: ourselves **proved the** soil, and put some of our peas in the ground, and **in ten** days they were of fourteen inches high: they **have also beans** very fair of divers colours and wonderful plenty: some growing naturally and some in their gardens, and so have they both wheat and oats.

The soil is the most plentiful, sweet, fruitful, and wholesome of all the world: there are above fourteen several sweet-smelling timber trees, and the most part of their underwoods are bays and such like: they have those oaks that we have, but far greater and better. After they had been divers times aboard our ships, myself, with seven more, went twenty mile into the river that runneth toward the City of Skicoak, which river they call Occam, and the evening following we came to an island which they call Raonoak, distant from the harbour by which we entered seven leagues: and at the North end thereof was a village of nine houses, built of cedar, and fortified round about with sharp trees, to keep out their enemies, and the entrance into it made like a turnpike very artificially; when we

THE FIRST LANDING IN VIRGINIA

came towards it, standing near unto the water's side, the wife of Granganimeo, the King's brother, came running out to meet us very cheerfully and friendly, her husband was not then in the village; some of her people she commanded to draw our boat on shore for the beating of the billow: others she appointed to carry us on their backs to the dry ground, and others to bring our oars into the house for fear of stealing. When we were come into the outer room, having five rooms in her house, she caused us to sit down by a great fire, and after took off our clothes and washed them, and dried them again: some of the women plucked off our stockings and washed them, some washed our feet in warm water, and she herself took great pains to see all things ordered in the best manner she could, making great haste to dress some meat for us to eat.

After we had thus dried ourselves, she brought us into the inner room, where she set on the board standing along the house some wheat like furmenty, sodden venison and roasted, fish sodden, boiled, and roasted, melons raw and sodden, roots of divers kinds and divers fruits: their drink is commonly water, but while the grape lasteth, they drink wine, and for want of casks to keep it all the year after they drink water, but it is sodden with ginger in it, and black cinnamon, and sometimes sassafras, and divers other wholesome and medicinable herbs and trees. We were entertained with all love and kindness, and with as much bounty (after their manner) as they could possibly devise. We found the people most gentle, loving, and faithful, void of all guile and treason, and such as live after the manner of the golden age. The people only care how to defend themselves from the cold in their short winter, and to feed themselves with such meat as the soil affordeth: their meat is very well sodden, and they make broth very sweet and savoury: their vessels are earthen pots, very large, white, and sweet; their dishes are wooden platters of

Barlow
1584

Barlow
1584

sweet timber: within the **place** where they feed was their lodging, and within that their Idol, which they worship, of whom they speak incredible **things**. While we were at meat, there came in at the gates **two** or three men with their bows and arrows from hunting, **whom** when we espied, we began to look one towards another, **and offered** to reach our weapons, but as soon as she espied our mistrust, she **was** very much moved, and caused some of her **men** to run out, and take away their bows and arrows and break them, **and** withal beat the poor fellows out of the gate again. **When** we departed in the evening and would not tarry all night **she was** very sorry, and gave us into our boat our **supper** half dressed, pots **and** all, **and** brought us to our boat side, **in** which we lay **all** night, removing the same a pretty distance **from** the shore : **she** perceiving our jealousy, was much grieved, and sent **divers men and** thirty women to sit all night on the bank side **by** us, and sent us **into** our boats five mats to cover us from **the rain**, using very many words to intreat us to rest in their houses : but because **we** were few men, and if we had miscarried, the voyage had been in very great danger, **we** durst not adventure anything, although there was no cause of doubt, for a more kind and loving people there cannot be found in the world, as far as we have hitherto had trial.

Hakluyt : Navigations.

AN AFFAIR OF HONOUR

Greville
1586

AND in this freedom of heart being one **day** at tennis, a Peer of this Realm, born great, greater by alliance, and superlatively in the Prince's favour, abruptly came into the tennis-court ; and speaking out of these three paramount authorities, he forgot to entreat that which he could not

AN AFFAIR OF HONOUR

legally command. When by the encounter of a steady object, finding unrespectiveness in himself (though a great Lord) not respected by this princely spirit, he grew to expostulate more roughly. The returns of which style coming still from an understanding heart, that knew what was due to itself, and what it ought to others, seemed (through the mists of my Lord's passions, swollen with the wind of his faction then reigning) to provoke in yielding. Whereby, the less amazement or confusion of thoughts he stirred up in Sir Philip, the more shadows this great Lord's own mind was possessed with: till at last with rage (which is ever ill-disciplined) he commands them to depart the court. To this Sir Philip temperately answers: that if his Lordship had been pleased to express desire in milder characters, perchance he might have led out those, that he should now find would not be driven out with any scourge of fury. This answer (like a bellows) blowing up the sparks of excess already kindled, made my Lord scornfully call Sir Philip by the name of Puppy. In which progress of heat, as the tempest grew more and more vehement within, so did their hearts breathe out their perturbations in a more loud and shrill accent. The French Commissioners unfortunately had that day audience in those private galleries whose windows look into the tennis-court. They instantly drew all to this tumult: every sort of quarrels sorting well with their humours, especially this. Which Sir Philip perceiving, and rising with inward strength, by the prospect of a mighty faction against him, asked my Lord, with a loud voice, that which he heard clearly enough before. Who (like an echo, that still multiplies by reflections) repeated this epithet of Puppy the second time. Sir Philip, resolving in one answer to conclude both the attentive hearers and passionate actor, gave my Lord a lie, impossible (as he averred) to be retorted; in respect all the world knows puppies are gotten by dogs, and children by men.

Greville
1586

Hereupon those glorious inequalities of Fortune in his Lordship were put to a kind of pause, by a precious inequality of nature in this gentleman. So that they both stood silent a while, like a dumb show in a tragedy; till Sir Philip, sensible of his own wrong, the foreign and factious spirits that attended, and yet, even in this question between him and his superior, tender to his country's honour, with some words of sharp accent, led the way abruptly out of the tennis-court, as if so unexpected an accident were not fit to be decided any farther in that place. Whereof the great Lord making another sense, continues his play, without any advantage of reputation, as by the standard of humours in those times it was conceived.

A day Sir Philip remains in suspense, when hearing nothing of or from the Lord, he sends a Gentleman of worth to awake him out of his trance; wherein the French would assuredly think any pause, if not death, yet a lethargy of true honour in both. This stirred a resolution in his Lordship to send Sir Philip a challenge. Notwithstanding, these thoughts in the great Lord wandered so long between glory, anger, and inequality of state, as the Lords of her Majesty's Council took notice of the differences, commanded peace, and laboured a reconciliation between them. But needlessly in one respect, and bootlessly in another. The great Lord being (as it should seem) either not hasty to adventure many inequalities against one, or inwardly satisfied with the progress of his own acts: Sir Philip, on the other side, confident he neither had nor would lose, or let fall anything of his right. Which her Majesty's Council quickly perceiving, recommended this work to herself.

The Queen, who saw that by the loss or disgrace of either she would gain nothing, presently undertakes Sir Philip; and (like an excellent Monarch) lays before him the difference in degrees between Earls and Gentlemen; the respect inferiors ought to their superiors, and the necessity in

Princes to maintain their own creations, as degrees descend- — Greville
ing between the people's licentiousness and the anointed   1586
sovereignty of Crowns; how the Gentleman's neglect of the
Nobility taught the Peasant to insult upon both.

Whereunto Sir Philip, with such reverence as became
him, replied: First, that place was never intended for privilege to wrong: witness herself, who how sovereign soever
she were by Throne, Birth, Education, and Nature, yet
was she content to cast her own affections into the same
moulds her subjects did, and govern all her rights by their
laws. Again, he besought her Majesty to consider, that
although he were a great Lord by birth, alliance, and grace,
yet he was no lord over him; and therefore the difference
of degrees between free men could not challenge any other
homage than precedency. And by her father's act (to make
a princely wisdom become the more familiar) he did instance
the government of King Henry the Eighth, who gave the
gentry free and safe appeal to his feet, against the oppression of the grandees; and found it wisdom, by the stronger
corporation in number, to keep down the greater in power:
inferring else, that if they should unite, the overgrown
might be tempted, by still coveting more, to fall (as the
Angels did) by affecting equality with their Maker.

Sir Fulk Greville, Lord Brooke.

THE LAST FIGHT OF THE *REVENGE*

THE Lord Thomas Howard, with six of Her Majesty's — Raleigh
ships, six victuallers of London, the barque *Ralegh*,   1591
and two or three pinnaces riding at anchor near unto
Flores, one of the westerly islands of the Azores, the
last of August in the afternoon, had intelligence by one
Captain Midleton, of the approach of the Spanish Armada.

Raleigh 1591

Which Midleton being in a very good sailer, had kept **them** company three days before, **of good** purpose, both **to** discover their forces the more, as **also to** give advice to my Lord Thomas of their approach. He had no sooner delivered the news but the fleet was in sight: **many of our** ships' companies were on shore in the island; some providing ballast for their ships; others filling of water and refreshing themselves from the land with such things as they could either for money or by force recover. By reason whereof our ships being all pestered and rummaging everything out **of** order, [were] very light for want of ballast. And that which was most to our disadvantage, the one half part of the men of **every** ship sick, and utterly unserviceable. **For** in the *Revenge* there were ninety diseased: in the *Bonaventure* not so many in health as could handle her mainsail. For had not twenty men been taken out of a barque of Sir George Cary's, his being commanded to be sunk, and those appointed to her, she had hardly ever recovered England. The rest for the most part were in little better state. The names of Her Majesty's ships were these as followeth: the *Defiance*, which was admiral; the *Revenge*, vice-admiral; the *Bonaventure*, commanded by Captain Cross; the *Lion*, by George Fenner; the *Foresight*, by Master Thomas Vavisour; and the *Crane*, by Duffeild. The *Foresight* and the *Crane* being but small ships; only the other were of the middle size; the rest, besides the barque *Ralegh*, commanded by Captain Thin, were victuallers, and of small force or none. The Spanish fleet having shrouded their approach by reason of the island, were now so soon at hand as our ships had scarce time to weigh their anchors, but some of them were driven to let slip their cables, and set sail. Sir Richard Grinvile was the last weighed, to recover the men that were upon the island, which otherwise had been lost. The Lord Thomas with the **rest** very hardly recovered the wind, which Sir Richard Grinvile not being able to do, was persuaded by the Master

and others to cut his mainsail and cast about, and to trust Raleigh
to the sailing of his ship: for the squadron of Sivil were on 1591
his weather-bow. But Sir Richard utterly refused to turn
from the enemy, alleging that he would rather choose to die
than to dishonour himself, his country, and her Majesty's
ship, persuading his company that he would pass through the
two squadrons, in despite of them, and enforce those of
Sivil to give him way. Which he performed upon divers of
the foremost, who, as the mariners term it, sprang their luff,
and fell under the lee of the *Revenge*. But the other course
had been the better, and might right well have been answered
in so great an impossibility of prevailing. Notwithstanding,
out of the greatness of his mind, he could not be persuaded.
In the meanwhile as he attended those which were nearest
him, the great *San Philip* being in the wind of him, and
coming towards him, becalmed his sails in such sort, as the
ship could neither weigh nor feel the helm: so huge and
high cargued was the Spanish ship, being of a thousand and
five hundred tons. Who after laid the *Revenge* aboard. When
he was thus bereft of his sails, the ships that were under his
lee luffing up, also laid him aboard: of which the next was
the Admiral of the *Biscaines*, a very mighty and puissant ship
commanded by Brittan Dona. The said *Philip* carried three
tier of ordnance on a side, and eleven pieces in every tier.
She shot eight forth right out of her chase, besides those of
her stern ports.

After the *Revenge* was intangled with this *Philip*, four
other boarded her: two on her larboard, and two on her
starboard. The fight, thus beginning at three of the clock in
the afternoon, continued very terrible all that evening. But
the great *San Philip* having received the lower tier of the
Revenge, discharged with crossbarshot, shifted herself with all
diligence from her sides, utterly misliking her first entertainment. Some say that the ship foundered, but we cannot
report it for truth, unless we were assured. The Spanish

ships were filled with **companies** of soldiers, in some **two** hundred besides the mariners; **in** some five, in others eight hundred. In ours there were none at all, beside the mariners, but the servants of the **commanders** and some few voluntary gentlemen only. After **many** interchanged volleys of great ordnance and small shot, the Spaniards deliberated to enter the *Revenge,* and made divers attempts, hoping to force her by the multitudes of their armed soldiers and musketeers, but were still repulsed again and again, and **at** all times beaten back, into their own ships, or into the seas. In the beginning of the fight, the *George Noble* of London, having received some shot through her by the Armadoes, fell under the lee of the *Revenge,* and asked Sir Richard what he would command him, being but one of the victuallers and of small force : Sir Richard bid him save himself, and leave him to his fortune. After the fight had thus without intermission continued while the day lasted and some hours **of** the night, many of our men were slain and hurt, and one of the great galleons of the Armada, and the admiral of the Hulks both sunk, and in many other of the Spanish ships great slaughter was made. Some write that Sir Richard was very dangerously hurt almost in the beginning of the fight, and lay speechless for a time ere he recovered. But two of the *Revenge's* own company brought home in a ship of Lime from the Islands, examined by some of the Lords and others, affirmed that he was never so wounded as that he forsook the upper deck, till an hour before midnight ; and then being shot into the body with a musket as he was a-dressing, was again shot into the head, and withal his Chirurgeon wounded to death. This agreeth also with an examination taken by Sir Frances Godolphin, of four other mariners of the same ship being returned, which examination the said Sir Frances sent unto Mr. William Killigrue, of her Majesty's Privy Chamber.

But to return to the fight : the Spanish ships which attempted to board the *Revenge,* as they were wounded and

THE LAST FIGHT OF THE *REVENGE*

beaten off, so always others came in their places, she having never less than two mighty galleons by her sides, and aboard her. So that ere the morning from three of the clock the day before, there had fifteen several Armadoes assailed her; and all so ill approved their entertainment, as they were by the break of day far more willing to hearken to a composition than hastily to make any more assaults or entries. But as the day increased, so our men decreased: and as the light grew more and more, by so much more grew our discomforts. For none appeared in sight but enemies, saving one small ship called the *Pilgrim*, commanded by Jacob Whiddon, who hovered all night to see the success: but, in the morning bearing with the *Revenge*, was hunted like a hare amongst many ravenous hounds, but escaped.

All the powder of the *Revenge* to the last barrel was now spent, all her pikes broken, forty of her best men slain, and the most part of the rest hurt. In the beginning of the fight she had but one hundred free from sickness, and fourscore and ten sick, laid in hold upon the ballast. A small troop to man such a ship, and a weak garrison to resist so mighty an army. By those hundred all was sustained, the volleys, boardings, and enterings of fifteen ships of war, besides those which beat her at large. On the contrary, the Spanish were always supplied with soldiers brought from every squadron: all manner of arms and powder at will. Unto ours there remained no comfort at all, no hope, no supply either of ships, men, or weapons; the masts all beaten overboard, all her tackle cut asunder, her upper work altogether rased, and in effect evened she was with the water, but the very foundation or bottom of a ship, nothing being left overhead either for flight or defence. Sir Richard finding himself in this distress, and unable any longer to make resistance, having endured in this fifteen hours' fight the assault of fifteen several Armadoes, all by turns aboard him, and by estimation eight hundred shot of great artillery,

Raleigh
1591

besides many assaults **and entries;** and that himself and the ship must needs be possessed by the enemy, who were now all cast in a ring round about him; **the** *Revenge* not able to move one way or other, but as she was moved with the waves and billow of the sea: commanded the Master-Gunner, whom he knew **to** be a most resolute man, to split **and sink** the ship; that **thereby** nothing might remain of glory **or** victory to the Spaniards, seeing in so many hours' fight, and with so great a navy they were not able to take her, having had fifteen hours' **time,** fifteen thousand men, and fifty and three **sail** of **men-of-war** to perform it withal: and persuaded the company, or **as** many as he could induce, to yield themselves unto God, and to the mercy **of** none else; but as they had **like valiant resolute men** repulsed **so many** enemies, they should not now shorten **the** honour of their nation, by prolonging their own lives for a few hours, or a few days. The Master-Gunner readily condescended, and divers others; but the Captain and the Master were of another opinion, and besought **Sir** Richard to have care of them: alleging that the Spaniard would be as **ready to** entertain **a** composition as they were willing to offer the same: **and** that there being divers sufficient and valiant men yet living, and whose wounds were not mortal, they might do their country and prince acceptable service hereafter. And (that where Sir Richard had alleged that the Spaniards should never glory to have **taken** one ship of **Her** Majesty's, seeing that they had so long and so notably defended themselves) they answered, **that** the ship had six foot water in hold, three shot under water, which were so weakly stopped as with the first working of the sea she must need sink, and was besides so crushed and bruised as **she** could **never be** removed out of the place.

And **as** the matter was thus in dispute, and Sir Richard refusing to hearken to any of those reasons, the Master of the *Revenge* (while the Captain wan unto him the greater party) was convoyed aboard the General, Don Alonso Bassan. Who finding none over hasty to enter the *Revenge* again, doubting lest Sir Richard would have blown them up and himself, and perceiving by the report of the Master of the *Revenge* his dangerous disposition: yielded that all their lives should be saved, the company sent for England, and the better sort to pay such reasonable ransom as their estate would bear, and in the mean season to be free from galley or imprisonment. To this he so much the rather condescended as well, as I have said, for fear of further loss and mischief to themselves, as also for the desire he had to recover Sir Richard Grinvile; whom for his notable valour he seemed greatly to honour and admire.

Raleigh
1591

When this answer was returned, and that safety of life was promised, the common sort being now at the end of their peril, the most drew back from Sir Richard and the Master-Gunner, being no hard matter to dissuade men from death to life. The Master-Gunner finding himself and Sir Richard thus prevented and mastered by the greater number, would have slain himself with a sword, had he not been by force withheld and locked into his cabin. Then the General sent many boats aboard the *Revenge*, and divers of our men fearing Sir Richard's disposition, stole away aboard the general and other ships. Sir Richard, thus overmatched, was sent unto by Alonso Bassan to remove out of the *Revenge*, the ship being marvellous unsavoury, filled with blood and bodies of dead and wounded men like a slaughter house. Sir Richard answered that he might do with his body what he list, for he esteemed it not, and as he was carried out of the ship he swooned, and reviving again desired the company to pray for him. The General used Sir Richard with all humanity, and left nothing unattempted that tended to his recovery, highly commending his valour and worthiness, and greatly bewailed the danger wherein he was, being unto them a rare spectacle, and a resolution seldom approved, to

Raleigh
1591

see one ship turn towards so many enemies, to endure the charge and boarding of so many huge Armadoes, and to resist and repel the assaults **and entries** of so many soldiers. All which, and more, is confirmed **by a** Spanish Captain, of the same Armada, and a present actor in the fight, who being severed from the rest in a storm, **was by the** *Lyon* of London, a small ship, taken, and is now prisoner in **London.**

The general commander of the Armada was Don Alonso Bassan, brother to the Marquess of Santa Cruce. **The** Admiral of the *Biscaine* squadron was Brittan Dona. Of the squadron of Sivil, Marquess of Arumburch. The Hulks and Flyboats were commanded by Luis Cutino. There were slain and drowned in this fight, well near two thousand of the enemies, and two especial commanders **Don** Luis de Sant John, and Don George de Prunaria de Mallaga, as the Spanish Captain confesses, besides divers others of special account, whereof as yet report is not made.

The admiral of the Hulks and the *Ascention* of Sivil were both sunk by the side of the *Revenge*; one other recovered the road of Saint Michels, and sunk also there ; a fourth ran herself with the shore to save her men. Sir Richard died, as **it is** said, the second or third day aboard the general, and was by them greatly bewailed. What became of his body, whether it were buried in the sea or on the land we know not : the comfort that remaineth to his friends is, that he hath ended his life honourably in respect of the reputation won to his nation and country, and of the same to his posterity, and that being dead, he hath not outlived his own honour.

Sir Walter Raleigh.

GLORIANA

Melville
1593

IN the meantime I was favourably and familiarly used, for during nine days that I remained at that Court, her Majesty pleased to confer with me every day, and sometimes

thrice upon a day, to wit a forenoon, afternoon, and after Melville
supper. Sometimes she would say, that since she could not 1593
meet with the Queen, her good sister, herself, to confer familiarly with her, that she should open a good part of her inward mind unto me, that I might show it again unto the
Queen; and said that she was not so offended at the Queen's
angry letter, as for that she seemed to disdain so far the
marriage with my Lord of Leicester; which she had caused
Mr. Randolph propone unto her. I said that it might be he
had touched something thereof to my Lords of Murray and
Lethington, but that he had not proponed the matter directly
unto herself; and that as well her Majesty, as they that
were her most familiar counsellors, could conjecture nothing
thereupon but delays and drifting of time, anent the declaring of her to be second person; which would try at the
meeting of the Commissioners above specified. She said
again, that the trial and declaration thereof would be hasted
forward, according to the Queen's good behaviour, and apply-
ing to her pleasure and advice in her marriage; and seeing
the matter concerning the said declaration was so weighty,
she had ordained some of the best lawyers in England
diligently to search out who had the best right; which she
would wish should be her dear sister rather than any other.
I said I was assured that her Majesty was both out of doubt
thereof, and would rather she should be declared than any
other; but I lamented that even the wisest princes will
not skance[1] sufficiently upon the partialities and pretences of
some of their familiar counsellors and servants; except it
were such a notable and rare prince as King Harry the
Eighth, her Majesty's father, of good memory, who of his
own head was determined to declare his sister's son, King
James the Fifth (at what time her Majesty was not yet born,
but only her sister, Queen Mary), heir-apparent to the crown
of England, failing the heirs gotten of his own body, for the

[1] Consider with suspicion.

Melville
1593

earnest desire he had **to unite** this whole island. She said she was glad he did **it not**. **I said** that then he had but a daughter, and was in doubt to have any more children, and yet had not so many suspicions **in** his head; and that her Majesty was out of all doubt ever to have any children, as being deliberate to die a virgin. She said that she was never minded to marry, except she were compelled by the Queen her sister's hard behaviour towards her, **in** doing by her **counsel** as said **is**. I said: 'Madam, ye need not to tell me **that;** I know your stately stomach: ye think if ye were married, ye would be but Queen of England, and now ye **are** King and Queen both; ye may not suffer a commander.'

She appeared to be so affectionate to the Queen, her good sister, that she had a great desire to see her; and because their **desired** meeting could not be so hastily brought to **pass**, she delighted oft to look upon her picture, and took me into her bedchamber, and opened **a** little lettroun[1] wherein were divers little pictures wrapped within paper, and written upon the paper their names with her own hand. Upon the first that she took up was written, 'My lord's **picture.**' I held the candle and pressed to see my lord's picture. Albeit she was loath to let me see it, at length I by importunity obtained the sight thereof, and asked the same to carry home with me unto the Queen; which she refused, alleging she had but that one of his. I said again that she had the principal; for he was at the farthest part of the chamber speaking with **the** Secretary Cecil. Then she took out the **Queen's** picture **and** kissed it; and I kissed her hand, for the great love I saw she bore to the Queen. She showed me also a fair ruby, great like a racket ball. Then I desired that she would either send it as a token unto the Queen, or else my Lord of Leicester's picture. **She** said, gin the Queen would follow her counsel, that she would get them both with time, and all **that** she had; but should send her a diamond for a token

[1] Lectern, desk: also work-table.

with me. Now it was late after supper; she appointed me
to be at her the next morning by eight hours, at which time
she used to walk in her garden; and inquired sundry things
at me of this country, or other countries wherein I had
lately travelled; and caused me to eat with her dame of
honour, my **Lady Stafford**, an honourable and godly lady,
who had been at Geneva, banished during the reign of
Queen Mary, that I might be always near her Majesty, that
she might confer with me; and my Lady Stafford's daughter
was my mistress, for I was of their acquaintance when they
passed through France, and had good intelligence by her
and by my Lady Throgmorton.

At divers meetings there would be divers purposes; and
the Queen, my sovereign, had instructed me sometimes
to leave matters of gravity and cast in some purposes of
merriness, or else I would be tired upon, as being well informed of her sister's naturelle.[1] Therefore, in declaring the
customs of Dutchland, Polle, and Italy, the busking and
clothing of the dames and women was not forgot, and what
country weed was best setten[2] for gentlewomen to wear. The
Queen of England said she had of divers sorts; which
every day so long as I was there she changed; one day the
English weed, one the French, and one the Italian, and so of
others; asking at me which of them set her best. I said
the Italian weed; which pleased her well, for she delighted
to show her golden-coloured hair, wearing a kell[3] and bonnet
as they do in Italy. Her hair was redder than yellow, curled
apparently of nature. Then she entered to discern what
kind of colour of hair was reputed best; and inquired whether
the queen's or hers was best, and which of them two was
fairest. I said the fairness of them both was not their worst
faults. But she was earnest with me to declare which of
them I thought fairest. I said she was the fairest Queen in
England, and ours the fairest Queen in Scotland. Yet she

Melville
1593

---

[1] Disposition.   [2] Suited.   [3] Caul.

Melville 1593

was earnest. **I said they were both** the fairest ladies of their **Courts, and that** the Queen of England was whiter, **but** our Queen was very lusome.[1] **She** inquired which of them was of highest stature. I said, our Queen. Then she said the Queen was over high, and that herself **was** neither over high nor over **low.** Then she asked what kind of exercises she used. I said that I was dispatched out of Scotland, that the Queen **was but new come** back from the Highland hunting; and **when she had** leisure from the affairs of her country, she read **upon good books** the histories of divers countries, and some- **times would play upon lute** and virginals. She speered **gin she played well.** I said, reasonably for a queen.

That same day, after dinner, my Lord of Hunsdon drew me up **to a** quiet gallery, **that** I might hear some music, but **he** said he **durst not avow it,** where I might hear the Queen play upon the virginals. **But after I had** hearkened a while, I took by the tapestry that hung before the **door** of the **chamber,** and seeing **her** back **was toward the** door, I entered within the chamber and stood still at the door-cheek, and heard her play excellently well; but she left off so soon **as she** turned her about and saw me, and came forwards, **seeming** to strike me with her left hand, and to think shame; alleging that she used not to play before men, **but** when she was solitary **her** allane,[2] to eschew melancholy; and asked how I came **there.** I said, as I was walking with my Lord of Hunsdon, as we passed by the chamber door I heard such melody, which roused and drew me within the chamber I wist not how; excusing my fault of homeliness as being brought up in the Court of France, and was **now** willing to suffer what kind of punishment would please her lay upon me for my offence. Then she sat down low upon a cushion, **and** I upon my knee **beside** her; but she gave me a cushion with her own hand to lay under my knee, which I refused, but she compelled me; and called for my Lady Stafford out

[1] Loveable.   [2] By herself.

of the next chamber, for she was her allane there. Then she asked whether the Queen or she played best. In that I gave her the praise. She said my French was good; and speired if I could speak Italian, which she spake reasonably well. I said I tarried not above two months in Italy, and had brought with me some books to read upon; but had no leisure to learn the language perfectly. Then she spake to me in Dutch, but it was not good; and would wit what kind of books I liked best, whether of theology, history, or love matters. I said I liked well of all the sorts.

Melville 1593

I was earnest to be dispatched; but she said that I tired sooner of her company nor she did of mine. I said, albeit I had no occasion to tire, that it was time to return; but I was stayed two days longer till I might see her dance, as I was informed; which being done, she inquired at me whether she or the Queen danced best. I said the Queen danced not so high and disposedly as she did. Then again she wished that she might see the Queen at some convenient place of meeting. I offered to convoy her secretly to Scotland by post, clothed like a page disguised, that she might see the Queen; as King James the Fifth passed in France disguised, with his own ambassador, to see the Duke of Vendome's sister that should have been his wife; and how that her chamber should be kept as though she were sick, in the meantime, and none to be privy thereto but my Lady Stafford and one of the grooms of her chamber. She said, Alas! gin she might do it; and seemed to like well of such kind of language, and used all the means she could to cause me persuade the Queen of the great love that she bore unto her, and was minded to put away all jealousies and suspicions, and in times coming a straiter friendship to stand between them than ever had been of before; and promised that my dispatch should be delivered unto me very shortly by Mr. Cecil at London.

Sir James Melville.

JOHN DAVYS THE NAVIGATOR

June
1593

THE sixth of August **we set sail and** went to Penguin Isle, **and the** next day **we** salted twenty hogsheads of seals, which was as much as our salt could possibly do, and **so we** departed for The Straits [of Magellan] **the** poorest **wretches** that **ever** were created. The seventh **of** August, **toward** night, we departed from Penguin Isles, **shaping our course for The** Straits, **where** we had full confidence **to meet with our** General **[Cavendish].** The **ninth we** had a **sore** storm, **so that we were constrained to** hull, for our **sails were not to endure any force. The** fourteenth we **were driven in among certain Isles, never** before discovered by any known relation, lying **fifty leagues or better** from the shore, East and Northerly **from The Straits**: in which place, unless **it** had pleased God of **his** wonderful **mercy** to have ceased the wind, **we must** of necessity have **perished.** But the wind shifting **to the** East, **we** directed **our course** for **The** Straits, and the eighteenth **of** August **we fell** with the **Cape in a** very thick fog; **and** the **same** night we anchored **ten** leagues **within** the Cape. The nineteenth day **we** passed the first **and the second** Straits. The twenty-first we doubled Cape **Froward.** The twenty-second we **anchored in** Savage Cove, **so** named because **we** found many savages there. Notwithstanding the extreme cold of this place, **yet do all these** wild people go naked, **and** live in the woods **like** satyrs, painted and disguised, **and** fly from you like wild deer. They are very strong, **and** threw stones at us of three **or** four **pound** weight an incredible distance. The twenty-fourth, **in the** morning, we departed from this cove, and the same day we came into the North-West reach, which is the last reach of The Straits. **The** twenty-fifth we anchored in a **good cove,** within **fourteen** leagues of the South Sea: in **this place we** purposed **to** stay **for the**

General, for the strait in this place is scarce three miles broad, so that he could not pass but we must see him. After we had stayed here a fortnight in the deep of winter, our victuals consuming (for our seals stunk most vilely, and our men died pitifully through cold and famine, for the greatest part of them had not clothes to defend the extremity of the winter's cold), being in this heavy distress, our Captain [John Davys] and Master thought it the best course to depart from The Straits into the South Sea, and to go for the Isle of Santa Maria, which is to the Northward of Baldivia in thirty-seven degrees and a quarter, where we might have relief, and be in a temperate clime, and there stay for the General, for of necessity he must come by that Isle.

Jane 1593

So we departed the thirteenth of September, and came in sight of the South Sea. The fourteenth we were forced back again, and recovered a cove three leagues within The Straits from the South Sea. Again we put forth, and being eight or ten leagues free of the land, the wind rising furiously at West-North-West, we were enforced again into The Straits only for want of sails; for we never durst bear sail in any stress of weather, they were so weak. So again we recovered the cove three leagues within The Straits, where we endured most furious weather, so that one of our two cables brake, whereby we were hopeless of life. Yet it pleased God to calm the storm, and we unrived our sheets, tacks, halliers, and other ropes, and moored our ship to the trees close by the rocks. We laboured to recover our anchor again, but could not by any means, it lay so deep in the water, and, as we think, clean covered with ooze. Now had we but one anchor, which had but one whole fluke, a cable spliced in two places, and a piece of an old cable. In the midst of these our troubles it pleased God that the wind came fair the first of October; whereupon with all expedition we loosed our moorings and weighed our

Jane
1593

anchor, and so towed off into the channel; for we had mended our boat in Port Desire, and had five oars of the pinnace. When we had weighed our anchor, we found our cable broken, only one strand held: then we praised God, for we saw apparently His mercies in preserving us. Being in the channel, we rived our ropes, and again rigged our ship; no man's hand was idle, but all laboured even for the last gasp of life. Here our company was divided; some desired to go again for Port Desire, and there to be set on shore, where they might travel for their lives, and some stood with the Captain and Master to proceed.

Whereupon the Captain said to the Master: 'Master, you see the wonderful extremity of our estate, and the great doubts among our company of the truth of your reports, as touching relief to be had in the South Sea. Some say in secret, as I am informed, that we undertake these desperate attempts through blind affection that we bear to the General. For mine own part, I plainly make known unto you that the love which I bare to the General caused me first to enter into this action, whereby I have not only heaped upon my head this bitter calamity now present, but also have in some sort procured the dislike of my best friends in England, as it is not unknown to some in this company. But now, being thus entangled by the providence of God for my former offences (no doubt), I desire that it may please His Divine Majesty to show us such merciful favour, that we may rather proceed than otherwise: or if it be His will that our mortal being shall now take an end, I rather desire that it may be in proceeding than in returning. And because I see in reason that the limits of our time are now drawing to an end, I do in Christian charity entreat you all, first to forgive me in whatsoever I have been grievous unto you; secondly, that you will rather pray for our General than use hard speeches of him; and let us be fully persuaded that not for his cause and negligence, but for our own offences against the Divine Majesty, we are presently punished; lastly, let us forgive one another and be reconciled as children in love and charity, and not think upon the vanities of this life: so shall we in leaving this life live with our glorious Redeemer, or abiding in this life find favour with God. And now (good Master), forasmuch as you have been in this voyage once before with your master the General, satisfy the company of such truths as are to you best known; and you the rest of the General's men, which likewise have been with him in his first voyage, if you hear anything contrary to the truth, spare not to reprove it, I pray you. And so I beseech the Lord to bestow his mercy upon us.'

<small>Jane 1593</small>

Then the Master began in these speeches: 'Captain, your request is very reasonable, and I refer to your judgment my honest care and great pains taken in the General's service, my love towards him, and in what sort I have discharged my duty, from the first day to this hour. I was commanded by the General to follow your directions, which hitherto I have performed. You all know that when I was extremely sick the General was lost in my mate's watch, as you have well examined: sithens which time, in what anguish and grief of mind I have lived, God only knoweth, and you are in some part a witness. And now, if you think good to return, I will not gainsay it: but this I assure you, if life may be preserved by any means, it is in proceeding. For at the Isle of Santa Maria I do assure you of wheat, pork, and roots enough. Also I will bring you to an Isle where pelicans be in great abundance, and at Santos we shall have meal in great plenty, besides all our possibility of intercepting some ships upon the coast of Chili and Peru. But if we return there is nothing but death to be hoped for: therefore do as you like, I am ready, but my desire is to proceed.' These his speeches being confirmed by others that were in the former voyage, there was a general consent of proceeding; and so the second of October

Jane 1593

we put into the South Sea, **and were** free of all land. This night the wind began to blow **very** much at West-North-West, and still increased in fury, so **that** we were in great doubt what course to take; to put **into the** straits we durst not for lack **of** ground tackle; to bear sail we doubted, the tempest was so furious, and our sails so bad. The pinnace came room with us, and told us that she had received **many** grievous seas, **and** that her ropes did every hour fail her, **so as** they could **not tell** what shift to make: we, being unable in any sort **to** help them, stood under our courses in view of the **lee-shore,** still expecting our ruinous end.

The fourth of October the storm growing beyond all **reason furious, the pinnace being in the wind of** us, struck suddenly ahull, so **that we thought she** had received some grievous sea, or sprung **a leak, or that** her sails failed her, because she came not with us; but we durst not hull in that unmerciful storm, but sometimes tried under our main course, sometime with **a** haddock off our sail, for **our** ship was very leeward and most laboursome in the sea. This night we lost the pinnace **and** never saw her again.

The **fifth** our foresail **was** split and all to torn; then our Master **took** the mizzen and brought it to the foremast, to make **our ship** work, and with our spritsail **we** mended our foresail, the **storm** continuing without all reason in fury, with hail, snow, rain, **and** wind such and so mighty as that in nature it could **not** possibly be more: the seas such and so lofty with continual breach, that many times we were doubtful whether our ship did **sink** or swim.

The tenth of October, being by the accompt of our Captain and Master very near the shore, the weather dark, the storm furious, and most of our men having given over to travail, we yielded ourselves to death, without further hope of succour. Our Captain sitting in the gallery very pensive, I came and brought him some rosa solis to comfort him; for he was so **cold that** he was scarce able to move a joint. After he had drunk, and was comforted in heart, he began for the ease of his conscience to make a large repetition of his forepassed time, and with many grievous sighs he concluded in these words: 'O most glorious God, with Whose power the mightiest things among men are matters of no moment, I most humbly beseech Thee that the intolerable burthen of my sins may through the blood of Jesus Christ be taken from me: and end our days with speed, or show us some merciful sign of Thy love and our preservation.' Having thus ended, he desired me not to make known to any of the company his intolerable grief and anguish of mind, because they should not thereby be dismayed. And so suddenly, before I went from him, the sun shined clear; so that he and the Master both observed the true elevation of the Pole, whereby they knew by what course to recover The Straits. Wherewithal our Captain and Master were so revived, and gave such comfortable speeches to the company, that every man rejoiced, as though we had received a present deliverance.

Jane 1593

The next day, being the eleventh of October, we saw Cabo Deseado, being the cape on the South shore (the North shore is nothing but a company of dangerous rocks, isles, and shoals). This cape being within two leagues to leeward of us, our Master greatly doubted that we could not double the same. Whereupon the Captain told him: 'You see there is no remedy, either we must double it, or before noon we must die: therefore loose your sails, and let us put it to God's mercy.' The Master, being a man of good spirit, resolutely made quick dispatch and set sail. Our sails had not been half-an-hour aboard, but the foot-rope of our foresail broke, so that nothing held but the oylet holes. The seas continually broke over the ship's poop, and flew into the sails with such violence that we still expected the tearing of our sails or oversetting of the ship, and withal to our utter discomfort we perceived that we fell still more and more to leeward, so that we could not double the cape. We were

Jane 1593

now come within half **a mile of the** cape, and so **near** the shore that the counter-surf of the sea would rebound against the ship's side, so that we were much dismayed with the horror of our present end. Being **thus at** the very pinch of death, the wind and seas raging beyond measure, our Master veered some of the main sheet; and **whether it was** by that occasion, or by some current, or by the wonderful power of God, as we verily think it was, the ship quickened her **way**, and shot past that rock, where we thought she would have shored. Then between the cape and the point there was a little bay; **so** that **we were** somewhat farther from the shore. **And** when we were come so far as the cape, we yielded to death. Yet our good God, the Father of all mercies, de**livered us, and** we doubled **the cape about the** length of our ship, or very little more. Being shot past the cape, we presently took in our sails, which **only God had** preserved unto **us**: and when we were shot **in between the** high lands, the wind blowing trade, without **any** inch of sail, we spooned before **the** sea, three men being not able to guide the helm, and in six hours we were put five-and-twenty leagues within The Straits, where we found a sea answerable to the Ocean.

In this **time we** freed our ship from water, and after we had rested **a** little, our men were not able to move; their sinews were stiff, and their flesh dead, and many of them (which is most lamentable to be reported) were so eaten with lice, as that in their flesh did lie clusters of lice as big as peason, yea, and some as big as beans. Being in this misery, we were constrained to put into a cove for the refreshing our men. Our Master knowing the shore and every cove very perfectly, put in with the shore and moored to the trees, as beforetime we had done, laying our anchor to **the** seaward. Here we continued until the twentieth of **October**; but not being able any longer to stay through extremity of famine, the one-and-twentieth we put off into the channel, the weather being reasonable calm: but before night it blew most extremely at West-North-West. The storm growing outrageous, our men could scarcely stand by their labour; and The Straits being full of turning reaches, we were constrained by discretion of the Captain and Master in their accounts to guide the ship in the hell-dark night, when we could not see any shore, the channel being in some places scarce three miles broad. But our Captain, as we first passed through The Straits, drew such an exquisite plat[1] of the same, as I am assured it cannot in any sort be bettered; which plat he and the Master so often perused, and so carefully regarded, as that in memory they had every turning and creek, and in the deep dark night without any doubting they conveyed the ship through that crooked channel: so that I conclude the world hath not any so skilful pilots for that place as they are: for otherwise we could never have passed in such sort as we did.

The twenty-fifth we came to an Island in The Straits named Penguin Isle, whither we sent our boat to seek relief, for there were great abundance of birds, and the weather was very calm; so we came to an anchor by the Island in seven fathoms. While our boat was at shore, and we had great store of penguins, there arose a sudden storm, so that our ship did drive over a breach, and our boat sank at the shore. Captain Cotton and the Lieutenant, being on shore, leaped in the boat and freed the same, and threw away all the birds, and with great difficulty recovered the ship: myself also was in the boat the same time, where for my life I laboured to the best of my power. The ship all this while driving upon the lee shore, when we came aboard, we helped to set sail, and weighed the anchor; for before our coming they could scarce hoist up their yards, yet with much ado they set their fore-course. Thus in a mighty fret of weather the seven-and-twentieth day of October we were free of The Straits, and the thirtieth of October we came to Penguin Isle,

Jane
1593

[1] Chart.

Jane 1593

being three leagues from Port Desire, the place where we purposed to seek for our relief.

When we were come to this Isle, we sent our boat on shore, which returned laden with birds and eggs; and our men said that the penguins were so thick upon the Isle, that ships might be laden with them, for they could not go without treading upon the birds, whereat we greatly rejoiced. Then the Captain appointed Charles Parker and Edward Smith, with twenty others, to go on shore, and to stay upon the Isle for the killing and drying of those penguins, and promised after the ship was in harbour to send the rest, not only for expedition, but also to save the small store of victuals in the ship. But Parker, Smith, and the rest of their faction suspected that this was a device of the Captain to leave his men on shore, that by these means there might be victuals for the rest to recover their country; and when they remembered that this was the place where they would have slain their Captain and Master, surely (thought they) for revenge hereof will they leave us on shore. Which, when our Captain understood, he used these speeches unto them: ' I understand that you are doubtful of your security through the perverseness of your own guilty consciences: it is an extreme grief unto me that you should judge me bloodthirsty, in whom you have seen nothing but kind conversation: if you have found otherwise, speak boldly, and accuse me of the wrongs that I have done; if not, why do you then measure me by your own uncharitable consciences? All the company knoweth indeed that in this place you practised to the utmost of your powers to murther me and the Master, causeless, as God knoweth, which evil in this place we did remit you: and now I may conceive without doing you wrong, that you again purpose some evil in bringing these matters to repetition: but God hath so shortened your confederacy, as that I nothing doubt you: it is for your master's sake that I have forborne you in your unchristian practices:

and here I protest before God that for his sake alone I will
yet endure this injury, and you shall in no sort be prejudiced,
or in anything be by me commanded; but when we come
into England (if God so favour us), your master shall know
your honesties. In the mean space be void of these suspicions, for, God I call to witness, revenge is no part of my
thought.' They gave him thanks, desiring to go into the
harbour with the ship, which he granted. So there were
ten left upon the Isle, and the last of October we entered
the harbour. Our Master at our last being here having
taken careful notice of every creek in the river, in a very
convenient place, upon sandy ooze, ran the ship on ground,
laying our anchor to seaward, and with our running ropes
moored her to stakes upon the shore, which he had fastened
for that purpose; where the ship remained till our departure.

Jane
1593

The third of November our boat with water, wood, and as
many as she could carry, went for the Isle of Penguin; but
being deep, she durst not proceed, but returned again the
same night. Then Parker, Smith, Townsend, Purpet, with
five others, desired that they might go by land, and that the
boat might fetch them when they were against the Isle, it
being scarce a mile from the shore. The Captain bade them
do what they thought best, advising them to take weapons
with them: 'For,' said he, 'although we have not at any
time seen people in this place, yet in the country there may
be savages.' They answered that here were great store of
deer and ostriches; but if they were savages, they would
devour them. Notwithstanding, the Captain caused them
to carry weapons, calivers, swords, and targets: so the
sixth of November they departed by land, and the boat by
sea; but from that day to this day we never heard of our
men. The eleventh, while most of our men were at the
Isle, only the Captain and Master with six others being left
in the ship, there came a great multitude of savages to the

Jane
1593

ship, throwing dust in the air, leaping and running like brute beasts, having vizards on their faces like dogs' faces, or else their faces are dogs' faces indeed. We greatly feared lest they would set our ship on fire, for they would suddenly make fire, whereat we much marvelled: they came to windward of our ship, and set the bushes on fire, so that we were in a very stinking smoke: but as soon as they came within our shot, we shot at them, and striking one of them in the thigh, they all presently fled, so that we never heard nor saw more of them. Hereby we judged that these cannibals had slain our nine men. When we considered what they were that thus were slain, and found that they were the principal men that would have murdered our Captain and Master, with the rest of their friends, we saw the just judgment of God, and made supplication to His Divine Majesty to be merciful unto us. While we were in this harbour, our Captain and Master went with the boat, to discover how far this river did run, that if need should enforce us to leave our ship, we might know how far we might go by water. So they found that further than twenty miles they could not go with the boat. At their return they sent the boat to the Isle of Penguin; whereby we understood that the penguins dried to our heart's content, and that the multitude of them was infinite. This penguin hath the shape of a bird, but hath no wings, only two stumps in the place of wings, by which he swimmeth under water with as great swiftness as any fish. They live upon smelts, whereof there is great abundance upon this coast: in eating they be neither fish nor flesh: they lay great eggs, and the bird is of a reasonable bigness, very near twice so big as a duck. All the time that we were in this place we fared passing well with eggs, penguins, young seals, young gulls, besides other birds, such as I know not: of all which we had great abundance. In this place we found an herb called scurvy grass, which we fried with eggs, using train oil instead of butter. This herb did so purge the blood that it took away all kind of swellings, of which many died, and restored us to perfect health of body, so that we were in as good case as when we came first out of England. We stayed in this harbour until the twenty-second of December, in which time we had dried twenty thousand penguins; and the Captain, the Master, and myself had made some salt by laying salt water upon the rocks in holes, which in six days would be kerned.[1] Thus God did feed us even as it were with manna from heaven.

Jane 1593

The twenty-second of December we departed with our ship for the Isle, where with great difficulty, by the skilful industry of our Master, we got fourteen thousand of our birds, and had almost lost our Captain in labouring to bring the birds aboard. And had not our Master been very expert in the set of those wicked tides, which run after many fashions, we had also lost our ship in the same place. But God of His goodness hath in all our extremities been our protector. So the twenty-second, at night, we departed with fourteen thousand dried penguins, not being able to fetch the rest, and shaped our course for Brazil. Now our Captain rated our victuals, and brought us to such allowance as that our victuals might last six months; for our hope was that within six months we might recover our country, though our sails were very bad. So the allowance was two ounces and a half of meal for a man a day, and to have so twice a week, so that five ounces did serve for a week. Three days a week we had oil, three spoonfuls for a man a day; and two days in a week peason, a pint between four men a day; and every day five penguins for four men, and six quarts of water for four men a day. This was our allowance; wherewith (we praise God) we lived, though weakly, and very feeble.

The thirtieth of January we arrived at the Isle of Placencia, in Brazil, the first place that outward bound we were at; and having made the shold,[2] our ship lying off at sea, the Captain,

---

[1] Hardened into lumps.   [2] Shoal.

Jane 1593

with twenty-four of the company, went with the boat on shore, being a whole night before they could recover it. The last of January at sun-rising they suddenly landed, hoping to take the Portugals in their houses, and by that means to recover some Casavi-meal, or other victuals for our relief. But when they came to the houses they were all razed and burnt to the ground, so that we thought no man had remained on the Island. Then the Captain went to the gardens, and brought from thence fruits and roots for the company, and came aboard the ship, and brought her into a fine creek which he had found out, where we might moor her by the trees, and where there was water, and hoops to trim our cask. Our case being very desperate, we presently laboured for dispatch away; some cut hoops, which the coopers made, others laboured upon the sails and ship, every man travailing for his life, and still a guard was kept on shore to defend those that laboured, every man having his weapon likewise by him. The third of February our men, with twenty-three shot, went again to the gardens, being three miles from us upon the North shore, and fetched Casavi roots out of the ground, to relieve our company instead of bread; for we spent not of our meal while we stayed here. The fifth of February being Monday, our Captain and Master hasted the company to their labour; so some went with the coopers to gather hoops, and the rest laboured aboard. This night many of our men in the ship dreamed of murther and slaughter. In the morning they reported their dreams, one saying to another: 'This night I dreamt that thou wert slain'; another answered, 'And I dreamed that thou wert slain': and this was general through the ship. The Captain hearing this, who likewise had dreamed very strangely himself, gave very strict charge that those which went on shore should take weapons with them, and saw them himself delivered into the boat, and sent some of purpose to guard the labourers. All the forenoon they laboured in quietness, and when it was ten of the clock, the heat being extreme, they came to a rock near the wood side (for all this country is nothing but thick woods), and there they boiled Casavi roots and dined. After dinner some slept, some washed themselves in the sea, all being stripped to their shirts, and no man keeping watch, no match lighted, not a piece charged. Suddenly, as they were thus sleeping and sporting, having gotten themselves into a corner out of sight of the ship, there came a multitude of Indians and Portugals upon them, and slew them sleeping. Only two escaped, one very sore hurt, the other not touched, by whom we understood of this miserable massacre. With all speed we manned our boat, and landed to succour our men; but we found them slain, and laid naked on a rank, one by another, with their faces upward, and a cross set by them. And withal we saw two very great pinnaces come from the river of Jenero very full of men; whom we mistrusted came from thence to take us; because there came from Jenero soldiers to Santos when the General had taken the town, and was strong in it.

Of seventy-six persons which departed in our ship out of England, we were now left but twenty-seven, having lost thirteen in this place, with their chief furniture, as muskets, calivers, powder, and shot. Our cask was all in decay, so that we could not take in more water than was in our ship, for want of cask, and that which we had was marvellous ill-conditioned. And being there moored by trees for want of cables and anchors, we still expected the cutting of our moorings, to be beaten from our decks with our own furniture, and to be assailed by them of Jenero: what distress we were now driven into I am not able to express. To depart with eight tons of water in such bad cask was to starve at sea, and in staying our case was ruinous. These were hard choices; but being thus perplexed, we made choice rather to fall into the hands of the Lord than into the hands of men: for His exceeding mercies we had tasted, and

Jane
1593

Jane
1593

of the others' cruelty we were not ignorant. So concluding to depart, the sixth of February we were off in the channel, with our ordnance and small shot in a readiness for any assault that should come, and having a small gale of wind, we recovered the sea in most deep distress. Then bemoaning our estate one to another, and recounting over all our extremities, nothing grieved us more than the loss of our men twice, first by the slaughter of the cannibals at Port Desire, and at this Isle of Placencia by the Indians and Portugals. And considering what they were that were lost, we found that all those that conspired the murthering of our Captain and Master were now slain by savages, the Gunner only excepted. Being thus at sea, when we came to Cape Frio the wind was contrary; so that three weeks we were grievously vexed with cross winds, and our water consuming, our hope of life was very small. Some desired to go to Baya, and to submit themselves to the Portugals, rather than to die for thirst: but the Captain with fair persuasions altered their purpose of yielding to the Portugals.

In this distress it pleased God to send us rain in such plenty, as that we were well watered, and in good comfort to return. But after we came near unto the sun our dried penguins began to corrupt, and there bred in them a most loathsome and ugly worm of an inch long. This worm did so mightily increase, and devour our victuals, that there was in reason no hope how we should avoid famine, but be devoured of these wicked creatures. There was nothing that they did not devour, only iron excepted: our clothes, boots, shoes, hats, shirts, stockings: and for the ship, they did so eat the timbers, as that we greatly feared they would undo us by gnawing through the ship's side. Great was the care and diligence of our Captain, Master, and company to consume these vermin; but the more we laboured to kill them, the more they increased; so that at the last we could not sleep for them, but they would eat our flesh and bite like mosquitoes. In this woful case, after we had passed the equinoctial toward the North, our men began to fall sick of such a monstrous disease as I think the like was never heard of: for in their ankles it began to swell; from thence in two days it would be in their breasts, so that they could not draw their breath, and then . . . . so that they could neither stand, lie, nor go. Whereupon our men grew mad with grief. Our Captain, with extreme anguish of his soul, was in such woful case that he desired only a speedy end, and though he were scarce able to speak for sorrow, yet he persuaded them to patience, and to give God thanks, and like dutiful children to accept of His chastisement. For all this divers grew raging mad, and some died in most loathsome and furious pain. It were incredible to write our misery as it was: there was no man in perfect health but the Captain and one boy. The Master, being a man of good spirit, with extreme labour bore out his grief, so that it grew not upon him. To be short, all our men died except sixteen, of which there were but five able to move. The Captain was in good health, the Master indifferent, Captain Cotton and myself swollen and short winded, yet better than the rest that were sick, and one boy in health: upon us five only the labour of the ship did stand. The Captain and Master, as occasion served, would take in and heave out the topsails, the Master only attended on the spritsail, and all of us at the capstan without sheets and tacks. In fine our misery and weakness was so great that we could not take in nor heave out a sail: so our topsail and spritsails were torn all in pieces by the weather. The Master and Captain taking their turns at the helm, were mightily distressed and monstrously grieved with the most woful lamentation of our sick men. Thus, as lost wanderers upon the sea, the eleventh of June 1593, it pleased God that we arrived at Bearhaven in Ireland, and there ran the ship on shore; where the Irishmen

June 1593

Jane
1593

helped **us to take in our sails and to** moor our **ship for** floating: which slender pains of theirs cost the Captain some ten pounds before he could have the ship in safety. Thus without victuals, sails, men, **or any** furniture, God only guided us into Ireland, where **the Captain left** the Master and three or four of the company **to keep the** ship; and within five days after he and certain others **had** passage in **an** English fisher-boat to Padstow in Cornwall. In this **manner** our small remnant by God's only mercy **were** preserved and restored to our country, to whom be all **honour and glory, world without end.**

Hakluyt: Navigations.

THE DIVINE ARETINE

Nash
1594

BEFORE I go any further, **let me speak a word** or two of this Aretine. **It was one** of the wittiest knaves that ever God made. If out of **so base** a thing as ink there may be extracted a spirit, he writ with nought but the spirit **of** ink, and his style was the spirituality of art's, and nothing **else,** whereas all others **of his** age were but the **lay** temporality of inkhorn terms. For indeed they were mere temporisers, and no better. **His pen was** sharp pointed like [a] poniard. **No** leaf he wrote on but was like a burning glass to set on fire **all** his readers. With more than musket shot did he charge his quill, where he meant to inveigh. **No one** hour but he sent a whole legion of devils into some herd of swine or other. If Martiall had ten Muses (as he saith of himself) when he but tasted a cup of wine, he had ten score when he determined to tyrannise. Ne'er a line of his but was able to make a man drunken with admiration. His sight pierced like lightning into the entrails of all abuses. This I must needs say, that most **of** his learning he got by hearing the lectures **at** Florence. It is sufficient that learning he had, and a conceit exceeding all learning, to quintessence everything which he heard. He was no timorous servile flatterer of the commonwealth wherein he lived. His tongue and his invention were foreborne, what they thought they would confidently utter. Princes he spared not, that in the least point transgressed. His life he contemned in comparison of the liberty of speech.

Nash 1594

Thomas Nash.

DISCOVERING GUIANA

AFTER we departed from the port of these Ciawani, we passed up the river with the flood, and anchored the ebb, and in this sort we went onward. The third day that we entered the river our galley came on ground, and stuck so fast as we thought that even there our discovery had ended, and that we must have left sixty of our men to have inhabited like rooks upon trees with those nations: but the next morning, after we had cast out all her ballast, with tugging and hauling to and fro, we got her afloat, and went on. At four days' end we fell into as goodly a river as ever I beheld, which was called the great Amana, which ran more directly without windings and turnings than the other. But soon after the flood of the sea left us, and we enforced either by main strength to row against a violent current, or to return as wise as we went out; we had then no shift but to persuade the companies that it was but two or three days' work, and therefore desired them to take pains, every gentleman and others taking their turns to row, and to spell one the other at the hour's end. Every day we passed by goodly branches of rivers, some falling from the West, others from the East into Amana, but those I leave to the description in the chart of discovery, where every one shall be named, with

Raleigh 1596

his rising and descent. When three days more were overgone, our companies began to despair, the weather being extremely hot, the river bordered with very high trees that kept away the air, and the current against us every day stronger than other. But we evermore commanded our pilots to promise an end the next day, and used it so long as we were driven to assure them from four reaches of the river to three, and so to two, and so to the next reach; but so long we laboured as many days were spent, and so driven to draw ourselves to harder allowance, our bread even at the last, and no drink at all; and our men and ourselves so wearied and scorched, and doubtful withal whether we should ever perform it or no, the heat increasing as we drew towards the Line: for we were now in five degrees.

The farther we went on (our victual decreasing and the air breeding great faintness) we grew weaker and weaker when we had most need of strength and ability, for hourly the river ran more violently than other against us, and the barge, wherries, and ship's boat of Captain Gifford and Captain Calfield had spent all their provisions, so as we were brought into despair and discomfort, had we not persuaded all the company that it was but only one day's work more to attain the land, where we should be relieved of all we wanted, and if we returned that we were sure to starve by the way, and that the world would also laugh us to scorn. On the banks of these rivers were divers sorts of fruits good to eat, flowers and trees of that variety as were sufficient to make ten volumes of herbals; we relieved ourselves many times with the fruits of the country, and sometimes with fowl and fish: we saw birds of all colours, some carnation, some crimson, orange-tawny, purple, green, watchet, and of all other sorts both simple and mixed, as it was unto us a great good passing of the time to behold them, besides the relief we found by killing some store of them with our fowling-pieces, without which, having little or no bread and less drink, but only the thick and troubled water of the river, we had been in a very hard case.

Our old pilot of the Ciawani (whom, as I said before, we took to redeem Ferdinando) told us, that if we would enter a branch of a river on the right hand with our barge and wherries, and leave the galley at anchor the while in the great river, he would bring us to a town of the Arwacas where we should find store of bread, hens, fish, and of the country wine, and persuaded us that departing from the galley at noon, we might return ere night. I was very glad to hear this speech, and presently took my barge, with eight musketeers, Captain Gifford's wherry with himself and four musketeers, and Captain Calfield with his wherry and as many, and so we entered the mouth of this river, and because we were persuaded that it was so near, we took no victual with us at all. When we had rowed three hours we marvelled we saw no sign of any dwelling, and asked the pilot where the town was; he told us a little farther: after three hours more, the sun being almost set, we began to suspect that he led us that way to betray us, for he confessed that those Spaniards which fled from Trinidad, and also those that remained with Carapana in Emeria, were joined together in some village upon that river. But when it grew towards night, and we demanding where the place was, he told us but four reaches more; when we had rowed four and four, we saw no sign, and our poor watermen, even heartbroken and tired, were ready to give up the ghost; for we had now come from the galley near forty miles.

At the last we determined to hang the pilot, and if we had well known the way back again by night, he had surely gone, but our own necessities pleaded sufficiently for his safety; for it was as dark as pitch, and the river began so to narrow itself, and the trees to hang over from side to side, as we were driven with arming swords to cut a passage through those branches that covered the water. We were

Raleigh
1596

very desirous to find this **town,** hoping of a feast, because **we made but** a short breakfast aboard the galley **in** the morning, and it was now eight o'clock at night; and our stomachs began to gnaw apace; **but** whether it was best to return or go on, we began to doubt, suspecting treason in the pilot more and more: but the poor old Indian ever assured us that it was but a little farther, and but this one turning, and that turning, and at last about one o'clock after midnight **we** saw a light, and rowing towards it, **we** heard **the** dogs **of the** village. When we landed we found few people for the lord **of** that place was gone with divers canoas about 400 miles off, **upon** a journey towards the head **of** Orenoque to trade for **gold,** and to buy women of the **cannibals,** who afterwards **unfortunately passed** by us as we **rode at an anchor in the port of Morequito** in the dark of night, and yet came so **near us, as** his canoas grated against **our** barges: and [he] left one of his company at the port of Morequito, by whom we understood that he had brought thirty young women, divers plates of gold, and had **great store** of fine pieces of cotton cloth and cotten beds. In his house we had good store of bread, fish, hens, and Indian drink, and so rested that night; and in the morning, after we had traded with such of his people as came down, we returned **towards** our galley, and brought with us some quantity of bread, fish, and hens.

On both **sides** of this river we passed the most beautiful country that ever mine **eyes** beheld; and whereas all that we had seen before was nothing but woods, prickles, bushes, and thorns, here we beheld plains of twenty miles in length, the grass short and green, and in divers parts groves of trees **by** themselves, as if they had been by all the art and labour **in the** world so made of purpose: and still as we rowed, the deer came down feeding by the water-side, as if they had been used to a keeper's call. Upon this river there were great store of **fowl,** and of many sorts: we saw in it divers sorts of strange fishes, and of marvellous bigness; but for lagartos[1] it exceeded, for there were thousands of those ugly serpents, and the people call it, for the abundance of them, the River of Lagartos in their language. I had a negro, a very proper young fellow, who leaping out of the galley to swim in the mouth of this river, was in all our sights taken and devoured by one of those lagartos.

In the meanwhile our companies in the galley thought we had been all lost (for we promised to return before night), and sent the *Lion's Whelp's* ship-boat with Captain Whiddon to follow us up the river; but the next day after we had rowed up and down some fourscore miles, we returned, and went on our way up the great river: and when we were even at the last cast for want of victuals, Captain Gifford being before the galley and the rest of the boats, seeking out some place to land upon the banks to make fire, espied four canoas coming down the river, and with no small joy caused his men to try the uttermost of their strength, and after a while two of the four gave over, and ran themselves ashore, every man betaking himself to the fastness of the woods; the two other lesser got away, while he landed to lay hold of these, and so turned into some by-creek we knew not whither: those canoas that were taken were loaden with bread, and were bound for Marguerita in the West Indies, which those Indians (called Arwacas) proposed to carry thither for exchange. But in the lesser there were three Spaniards, who having heard of the defeat of their Governor in Trinidado, and that we purposed to enter Guiana, came away in those canoas: one of them was a Cavallero, as the Captain of the Arwacas after told us, another a Soldier, and the third a Refiner.

Sir Walter Raleigh.

[1] Alligators.

THE MEN IN BUCKRAM

Shake-
speare
1598

Poins. Welcome, Jack: where hast thou been?

Falstaff. A plague of all cowards, I say, and a vengeance too! marry, and amen! Give me a cup of sack, boy. Ere I lead this life long, I'll sew nether socks and mend them and foot them too. A plague of all cowards! Give me a cup of sack, rogue. Is there no virtue extant? [*He drinks.*

Prince. Didst thou never see Titan kiss a dish of butter? pitiful-hearted Titan, that melted at the sweet tale of the sun's! if thou didst, then behold that compound.

Fal. You rogue, here's lime in this sack too: there is nothing but roguery to be found in villainous man: yet a coward is worse than a cup of sack with lime in it. A villainous coward! Go thy ways, old Jack; die when thou wilt, if manhood, good manhood, be not forgot upon the face of the earth, then am I a shotten herring. There live not three good men unhanged in England; and one of them is fat, and grows old: God help the while! a bad world, I say. I would I were a weaver; I could sing psalms or anything. A plague of all cowards, I say still.

Prince. How now, wool-sack! what mutter you?

Fal. A king's son! If I do not beat thee out of thy kingdom with a dagger of lath, and drive all thy subjects afore thee like a flock of wild geese, I'll never wear hair on my face more. You Prince of Wales!

Prince. Why, you whoreson round man, what's the matter?

Fal. Are not you a coward? answer me to that: and Poins there?

Poins. 'Zounds, ye fat paunch, an ye call me coward, by the Lord, I'll stab thee.

Fal. I call thee coward! I'll see thee damned ere I call thee coward: but I would give a thousand pound I could

THE MEN IN BUCKRAM

run as fast as thou canst. You are straight enough in the shoulders, you care not who sees your back: call you that backing of your friends? A plague upon such backing! give me them that will face me. Give me a cup of sack: I am a rogue, if I drunk to-day.

Shakespeare 1598

PRINCE. O villain! thy lips are scarce wiped since thou drunkest last.

FAL. All's one for that. [*He drinks.*] A plague of all cowards, still say I.

PRINCE. What's the matter?

FAL. What's the matter! there be four of us here have ta'en a thousand pound this day morning.

PRINCE. Where is it, Jack? where is it?

FAL. Where is it! taken from us it is: a hundred upon poor four of us.

PRINCE. What, a hundred, man?

FAL. I am a rogue, if I were not at half-sword with a dozen of them two hours together. I have 'scaped by miracle. I am eight times thrust through the doublet, four through the hose; my buckler cut through and through; my sword hacked like a hand-saw—*ecce signum!* I never dealt better since I was a man: all would not do. A plague of all cowards! Let them speak: if they speak more or less than truth, they are villains and the sons of darkness.

PRINCE. Speak, sirs; how was it?

GADSHILL. We four set upon some dozen——

FAL. Sixteen at least, my lord.

GADS. And bound them.

PETO. No, no, they were not bound.

FAL. You rogue, they were bound, every man of them; or I am a Jew else, an Ebrew Jew.

GADS. As we were sharing, some six or seven fresh men set upon us——

FAL. And unbound the rest, and then come in the other.

PRINCE. What, fought you with them all?

Shake-
speare
1598

FAL. All! I know not what you call all: but if I fought not with fifty of them, I am a bunch of radish: if there were not two or three and fifty upon poor old Jack, then am I no two-legged creature.

PRINCE. Pray God you have not murdered some of them.

FAL. Nay, that's past praying for: I have peppered two of them; two I am sure I have paid, two rogues in buckram suits. I tell thee what, Hal, if I tell thee a lie, spit in my face, call me horse. Thou knowest my old ward; here I lay, and thus I bore my point. Four rogues in buckram let drive at me——

PRINCE. What, four? thou saidst but two even now.

FAL. Four, Hal: I told thee four.

POINS. Ay, ay, he said four.

FAL. These four came all a-front, and mainly thrust at me. I made me no more ado but took all their seven points in my target, thus.

PRINCE. Seven? why, there were but four even now.

FAL. In buckram?

POINS. Ay, four, in buckram suits.

FAL. Seven, by these hilts, or I am a villain else.

PRINCE. Prithee, let him alone; we shall have more anon.

FAL. Dost thou hear me, Hal?

PRINCE. Ay, and mark thee too, Jack.

FAL. Do so, for it is worth the listening to. These nine in buckram that I told thee of——

PRINCE. So, two more already.

FAL. Their points being broken——

POINS. Down fell their hose.

FAL. Began to give me ground: but I followed me close, came in foot and hand; and with a thought seven of the eleven I paid.

PRINCE. O monstrous! eleven buckram men grown out of two!

FAL. But, as the devil would have it, three misbegotten

knaves in Kendal green came at my back and let drive at me ; for it was so dark, Hal, that thou couldst not see thy hand.

PRINCE. These lies are like thy father that begets them ; gross as a mountain, open, palpable. Why, thou clay-brained guts, thou knotty-pated fool, thou whoreson, obscene, greasy tallow-catch——

FAL. What, art thou mad ? art thou mad ? is not the truth the truth ?

PRINCE. Why, how couldst thou know these men in Kendal green, when it was so dark thou couldst not see thy hand ? come, tell us your reason : what sayest thou to this ?

POINS. Come, your reason, Jack, your reason.

FAL. What, upon compulsion ? 'Zounds, an I were at the strappado, or all the racks in the world, I would not tell you on compulsion. Give you a reason on compulsion ! if reasons were as plentiful as blackberries, I would give no man a reason upon compulsion, I.

PRINCE. I 'll be no longer guilty of this sin ; this sanguine coward, this bed-presser, this horseback breaker, this huge hill of flesh,——

FAL. 'Sblood, you starveling, you elf-skin, you dried neat's tongue, you bull's pizzle, you stock-fish ! O for breath to utter what is like thee ! you tailor's-yard, you sheath, you bow-case, you vile standing-tuck,——

PRINCE. Well, breathe awhile, and then to it again : and when thou hast tired thyself in base comparisons, hear me speak but this.

POINS. Mark, Jack.

PRINCE. We two saw you four set on four and bound them, and were masters of their wealth. Mark now, how a plain tale shall put you down. Then did we two set on you four ; and, with a word, out-faced you from your prize, and have it ; yea, and can show it you here in the house : and, Falstaff, you carried your guts away as nimbly, with as quick dexterity,

Shakespeare 1598

Shakespeare 1598

and roared for mercy and still run and roared, as ever I heard bull-calf. What a slave art thou, to hack thy sword as thou hast done, and then say it was in fight! What trick, what device, what starting-hole, canst thou now find out to hide thee from this open and apparent shame?

POINS. Come, let's hear, Jack; what trick hast thou now?

FAL. By the Lord, I knew ye as well as he that made ye. Why, hear you, my masters: was it for me to kill the heir apparent? should I turn upon the true prince? why, thou knowest I am as valiant as Hercules: but beware instinct; the lion will not touch the true prince. Instinct is a great matter; I was now a coward on instinct. I shall think the better of myself and thee during my life; I for a valiant lion, and thou for a true prince. But, by the Lord, lads, I am glad you have the money. Hostess, clap to the doors: watch to-night, pray to-morrow. Gallants, lads, boys, hearts of gold, all the titles of good fellowship come to you! What, shall we be merry? shall we have a play extempore?

PRINCE. Content; and the argument shall be thy running away.

FAL. Ah, no more of that, Hal, an thou lovest me!

William Shakespeare.

A PLOT AGAINST THE THRONE

Hayward 1599

SO, partly upon love to King Richard, and partly upon fear lest King Henry would be as ready to invade as he was to inveigh against the riches of religious houses: this Abbot [of Westminster] was the first man that blew the coals, and put fuel to the fire of this confederacy. And first he observed afar off, then he searched more nearly and narrowly (and yet warely too) how the minds of certain Noblemen were affected, or, rather, infected against King Henry; tempering his speeches in such sort, that, if matters sorted to his mind, he might

A PLOT AGAINST THE THRONE

take them upon him; if his courses were crossed, he might clearly decline them. At last, he invited to his house, upon a day in Michaelmas term, those whom he had found to be most sound for his purpose: the chief of whom were such as in the Parliament before had in some sort been touched in reputation, although by pardon and reconcilement the harm did seem to be closed up. Their names were John Holland, Duke of Exeter, of whom mention hath been made before; Thomas Holland, his brother's son, Duke of Surrey; Edward, Duke of Aumerle; John Montacute, Earl of Salisbury; Hugh Spencer, Earl of Gloucester; John, Bishop of Carlisle; Sir Thomas Blunt, and Magdalen, one of King Richard's chapel, who, in all points, both of feature and favour, so nearly resembled King Richard, that the Lords dissembled afterwards that he was King Richard indeed.

Hayward
1599

These and some others were highly feasted by the Abbot; and after dinner they withdrew themselves into a secret chamber to counsel. Here the Duke of Exeter, who was most hotly bent either to restore or to revenge the cause of his deposed brother, declared unto the rest the allegiance that they had sworn unto King Richard; the honours and preferments whereunto they were by him advanced; that, therefore, they were bound, both in conscience by the one, and in kindness by the other, to take his part against all men; that King Henry, contrary to both, had dispoiled him of his royal dignity, and unjustly possessed himself thereof, whilst they stood looking on, and showed neither the obedience of subjects nor love of friends, as though they were men who knew to do anything better than to defend, and, if need were, to die for their lawful Prince and loving Patron; that King Henry, by violent invading or fraudulent insinuating himself into the kingdom of his natural and liege Prince, was but a tyrant and usurper, and such a one as it was lawful for any man by any means to throw down, without respect whether he were a good man or evil, for it

Hayward 1599 is lawful **for no man, upon pretence** and show of goodness, to draw sovereignty unto **himself; that** the laws and examples of best governed commonwealths did **not** only permit **this action, but** highly honoured **it with** statues and garlands, and titles of nobility, and **also rewarded** it with all **the wealth of** the suppressed tyrant; **that** this enterprise would **be very** profitable, **and** almost necessary **to the commonwealth,** by extinguishing those **wars which the Scots menaced, the** Frenchmen prepared, and **the Welshmen had already begun upon** this occasion and quarrel; **that he did not** distrust but **it might** be accomplished by open arms, **but** he thought **it more sure for them,** and for the commonwealth **more safe,** to put first **in proof some** secret policy; **and to that** purpose he **devised, that a solemn** joust should **be challenged, to be kept at Oxford in** Christmas holidays, between him and twenty **on his part, and the Earl** of Salisbury **and** twenty on his **part, to** which **King** Henry should be invited, and when **he was most intentive in regarding** their military disport, **he** should suddenly **be** surprised by men which without suspicion might at that time be assembled, both for number and preparation sufficient **for** the exploit, and thereby King Richard **presently be restored,** both to his **liberty,** and to his estate.

This device was no sooner uttered, then allowed and applauded **of** the rest of the confederates: and so resolving **upon the enterprise, they** took an oath upon the Evangelists, the one to be true and secret **to** the other, even to the hour **and** point **of** death; **the** Lords also made an indenture sextipartite, wherein **they** bound themselves to **do** their best assay, for the death **of one** King and **deliverance** of the other; this they sealed and subscribed, and delivered to every Lord a counterpane of the **same:** and, further, they concluded what forces should **be** gathered, by whom, how they should be ordered and **placed,** and to whose **trust** the execution should be committed.

A PLOT AGAINST THE THRONE

When all things were thus contrived, and their hungry, ambitious minds were well-filled with the vain winds of hope and desire, the Duke of Exeter came to the king at Windsor, and desired him, for the love that he bare to the noble feats of Chivalry, that he would vouchsafe to honour with his presence the martial exercise, that was appointed between him and the Earl of Salisbury, and to be the Judge of their performances if any controversy should arise.

Hayward 1599

The King supposing that to be intended in deed which was pretended in show, easily yielded to his request. The Duke, supposing his purpose now half performed, departed to his house, and so did the other confederates, where they busily bestirred themselves, in raising men, and preparing horse and armour for the accomplishment of this act.

When the Duchess of Exeter, King Henry's sister, perceived the drift of the device, and saw that the Duke was upon his journey: alas! good lady, how was she distracted in mind, with a sharp conflict of her conceits! One way she was moved with nature towards her brother; another way she was more strongly stirred, with love towards her Lord and husband; and both ways she was divided in duty. 'And what' (said she) 'is this love then against nature? or above it? shall I be undutiful to my Prince? or is no duty comparable to the duty of a wife? heigh ho: in what perplexities (wretched woman) am I plunged, to see my two dearest friends in this case of extremity, that (it is doubtful which) but certainly one must be ruined by the other!' Herewith, such a shower of tears streamed down her cheeks, that it drowned her speech, and stopped the passage of further complaint: which, when the Duke espied, he stepped unto her, and seizing softly upon her hand, used these words: 'What, Bess? is it kindness to me or kindred to your brother that thus hath set your eyes on float? Content yourself, woman, for whatsoever the event shall be, it cannot be evil to you, nor worse to me than now it is. For if my purpose prevail,

Hayward 1599

and my brother be restored again to his crown, both of us shall be sure never to decline; if it be prevented, and your brother continue still in his estate, no harm shall be done unto you, and I shall be then sure of that destruction which I do now continually dread; the fear whereof in expecting, is a greater torment than the pain in suffering.' When he had thus said, he kissed her, and so leaving her to the torture of a thousand thorny thoughts, he took his journey towards Oxford, with a great company, both of Archers and Horsemen. There he found all the rest of his complices, well armed and banded, except only the Duke of Aumerle. The King also hearing that both the Challengers and Defendants were in a readiness, determined the day following to ride to Oxford, according to his promise and appointment.

Now, the confederates much marvelled at the stay of the Duke of Aumerle; some only blamed his slackness, others began to suspect it; every man conjectured as he was diversly affected between confidence and fear: and in this confusion of opinions, they sent unto him in post, to know the certain truth. Before the messenger came to the Duke, he was departed from Westminster towards Oxford, not the direct way, but went first to see his Father the Duke of York, and carried with him his counterpane of the indenture of confederacy. As they sat at dinner, the Father espied it in his bosom, and demanded what it was? The Son humbly craved pardon, and said that it nothing touched him. ' By St. George ' (quoth the Father) ' but I will see it,' and so whether upon a precedent jealousy, or some present cause of suspicion, he took it away from him by force. When he perceived the contents, he suddenly arose from the table, and with great fierceness both of countenance and speech, uttered to his Son these words:

' I see, traitor, that idleness hath made thee so wanton and mutinous, that thou playest with thy faith as children do with sticks: thou hast been once already faithless to King

Richard, and now again art false to King Henry, so that, like the fish Sepia, thou troublest all the waters wherein thou livest. Thou knowest that in open Parliament I became surety and pledge for thy allegiance, both in body and goods: and can neither thy duty nor my desert restrain thee from seeking my destruction? In faith, but I will rather help forward thine.' With that he commanded his horses to be made ready, and presently took his journey towards Windsor, where the King then lay.

Hayward 1599

The Duke of Aumerle had no time either to consult with his friends, or to consider with himself what was best to be done: but taking advice upon the sudden, he mounted likewise on horseback, and posted towards Windsor another way. It was no need to force him forward; his youthful blood, and his sudden danger, were instead of two wings, to keep his horse in Pegasus pace: so that he came to Windsor, and was alighted at the castle, before his stiff aged Father could come near. Then he entered the gates, and caused them to be surely locked, and took the keys into his own hands, pretending some secret cause for which he would deliver them unto the King. When he came in presence, he kneeled down and humbly craved of the King mercy and forgiveness. The King demanded, for what offence? Then with a confused voice, and sad countenance, casting down his eyes as altogether abashed, partly with fear of his danger, and partly with shame of his discredit, he declared unto the King all the manner of the conspiracy. The King seemed neither rashly to believe, nor negligently to distrust the Duke's report; neither stood it with policy to entertain the discovery with any hard and violent usage: therefore with gracious speeches he comforted the Duke, and 'If this be true,' said he, 'we pardon you: if it be feigned, at your extreme peril be it.'

By this time the Duke of York was rapping at the Castle gates, and being admitted to the King's presence, he delivered to him the indenture of confederacy, which he had

Hayward 1599

taken from his **son. When the King** had read **it, and was** thereby persuaded of the **truth of** the matter, he was not a little disquieted in mind, complaining of the inconstant disposition of those men, whom **neither** cruelty (he said) could make firm **to King** Richard, **nor** clemency to him; but upon dislike of every present government, **they** were desirous of any change. So being possessed with deeper thoughts than **to** gaze upon games, he laid his journey aside, **and** determined **to** attend at Windsor what course his enemies would **take,** and which way **they** would set forward: knowing right **well that in** civil tumults, an advised patience, and opportunity well taken, **are the** only weapons of advantage; and that it is a special point of wisdom **to** make benefit of the enemy's folly. In the **meantime he** directed his letters to the Earl of Northumberland **his High** Constable, and to the Earl of Cumberland his **High** Marshal, and to others his most assured friends, concerning these **sudden** and unexpected accidents.

The confederates all this **time hearing** nothing **of** the Duke of Aumerle, and seeing **no preparation** for the King's coming, were out of doubt **that** their treason was betrayed. And now, considering that once before they had been pardoned, the guilt of **this** their rebellion excluded them from all hope of further mercy: whereupon they became desperate, and **so** resolved to prosecute that by open arms wherein their privy practices had failed. And first they apparelled Magdalen (a man very like to King Richard both in stature and countenance, and **of** years not disagreeable) in princely attire; and gave forth that he was King Richard, and that either by favour or negligence of his keepers, he was escaped out of prison, and desired the faith and aid of his loving subjects. Then they determined to dispatch messengers to Charles, King of France, to desire his help and assistance on the behalf of his son-in-law, if need should require.

The common people, which commonly are soon changeable,

and on the sudden as prone to pity as they were before Hayward
excessively cruel, most earnestly wished the enlargement of 1599
King Richard, and earnestly wishing, did easily believe it;
in which imaginary conceit, being otherwise men of no deep
search, the presence of Magdalen most strongly confirmed
them. And so, either upon ignorance of truth, or delight
in trouble, they joined themselves in great troops to the
Lords, desiring nothing more than to be the means whereby
King Richard should be restored, as in a manner resuming
their first affections and humours towards him. Then the
Lords of this association, with great force, but with greater
fame, as the manner is of matters unknown, advanced
forward in battle array towards Windsor, against King
Henry, as against an enemy of the common state; having in
their company above forty thousand armed men. The
King, upon intelligence of their approach, secretly, with a
few horse, the next Sunday night after New Year's day,
departed from Windsor to the Tower of London, and the
same night, before it was day, the confederates came to the
Castle of Windsor; where, missing their expected prey,
they stood doubtful and divided in opinions which way to
bend their course. Some advised them with all speed to
follow the King to London, and not to leave him any leave
and liberty to unite an army against them; that winter was
no let but in idle and peaceable times; that in civil dissen-
sions nothing is more safe than speed, and greater advantage
always groweth by dispatching than deferring; that whilst
some were in fear, some in doubt, and some ignorant, the
City, yea, the realm, might easily be possessed; and that
many armies, whose fury at the first rush could not be resisted,
by delays did wear out and waste to nothing. Others, who
would seem to be considerate and wise, but in very deed
were no better than dastards, persuaded rather to set
King Richard first at liberty; for if their counterfeiting
should be discovered before they possessed themselves of

Hayward
1599

his person, the people **undoubtedly** would fall from them, **to** the certain confusion of them **all.** Hereupon they gave **over** the pursuit, **and** retired to Colebrook, and there delayed out the time of doing in deliberating, being neither courageously quick, nor considerately **staid, but** faintly and fearfully shrinking **back**; and when they **once** began to relent, they decreased every day more and **more both** in power and **in hope.**

King Henry, the next morning after he was come **to the Tower, sent to the Mayor** of the City to put soldiers **in arms for his** assistance, who presently presented unto him three thousand archers, **and three** thousand bill men, besides those that were appointed for **defence of the** City. The King spent upon him many good **speeches,** and liberally loaded **him** with promises and thanks; **and** soon after he issued out of London with twenty **thousand tall men, and** came to Hounslow Heath, abiding there, and, **as it were,** daring his enemies to join issue in the field: contemning their disorderly multitude as a vain terror of **names** without forces. But the confederates, either for fear of the King's power or for distrust of their own, or else lingering, perhaps, **after** some succour out of France, refused the encounter; and doubtful it is whether they showed greater courage in setting up the **danger, or cowardice in declining it** when it was presented **unto them.**

Sir John Hayward.

THE PASSAGE OF THE ALPS

Holland
1600

ANNIBALL being departed from Druentia, marched for the most through the champion countries, and came in peace and quietly to the foot **of the** Alps, for any trouble from the peasants that there inhabited. And albeit **he had** some knowledge of the Alps before by report (which **useth** to make things **that** are uncertain much more than in deed and truth they are), yet seeing now near at hand the height of those hills, and the snows, entermingled along with the sky; the rude and misshapen houses set upon rocks; the cattle, sheep, oxen, and horses, singed with cold; the people with long shagged hair, and without any trimming, both living and lifeless creatures, even parched stiff and stark with frost; and all things else more strange and ill-favoured than can be spoken: then began his soldiers to fear afresh. So soon as they advanced forward, and began to march up the first cliffs, there appeared over their heads the mountain people, who had seized the hills: who, if they had kept the secret and hidden valleys, and suddenly all at once charged upon them, they would have made a foul slaughter of them, and put them to flight. Then Anniball commandeth the ensigns to stand still, and sent certain Gauls afore, as espials; by whom he understood that there was no passage that way: whereupon he pitched his camp amongst those craggy and steep rough places upon as large a plain and valley as he could find. Then by the same Gauls (who much differed not in tongue and manners from the other, and had entermingled themselves in talk with mountaineers) he understood that they kept the passage but in the daytime, and slipt away in the night, every one to his own harbour.

So at the break of day he mounted those steep hills, as if he would openly in the daytime march through the straits. Thus having spent the day in making semblance and shew of one thing, and intending another, he encamped himself strongly where he had rested and stayed: and so soon as he perceived that the mountain people were departed from the steep hills and kept not so strait watch and ward; after that he had made shew of fires, more than for the number of those that remained behind; and left with the Cavalry all the bag and baggage, with the greatest part of the footmen: himself in person took unto

Holland him the nimblest, most active, and valiant soldiers lightly ap-
1600 pointed, and with all **speed passed** through the straits aforesaid, and encamped on the **very** hills which the enemies before held and beset. Then in the morning betime his camp dislodged: and the army behind began to march and set forward. By which time the mountaineers, **at** the ordinary signal given, came forth out of their castles and forts, and **met at the** usual place of their accustomed guards; **but** then **all at** once they might see some of the enemies **over** their heads, **to** have gained their own fortress, and **others** also marching in the way. **Both** which objects at one time presented to their eye, made them blank and to stand still **in a** muse a good **while.** But **afterwards,** when they saw Anniball **his** army distressed **in the** straits, **and** in great **trouble and** disorder **among themselves** in the march, by reason especially the horses **were so** affrighted, supposing that the least fear and terror **(besides)** that they could procure would be enough for their enemies' overthrow and confusion, **they** crossed **the rocks** overthwart, and (as they were accustomed and used **to** them) ran to and fro, up and down through the blind **and** unhaunted byways.

But then, verily, the Carthaginians were much encumbered, as well **by** their enemies as also by the disadvantage of the place, and more ado **there was among** them (whiles every one strived avie who should first escape the danger) than with the **enemy.** There **was** nothing that disordered and troubled the **army in the** march so much **as their own** horses, which (by reason of the dissonant and divers cries, that the echoes between the woods and valleys redoubled) were affrighted; and also if any of them chanced to be stricken, galled, or wounded, they kept such wincing and flinging about them, that they overthrew and made great havoc of men, and **of all** sorts of carriage. Besides, the press was so great, and the straits of both sides so steep and craggy, that **many a** man was thrown down headlong a mighty height: yea, and some of them armed: and the sumpter horses and beasts for carriage, especially, tumbled down amain with their load, as if a house or castle had come down with a mischief. Which, although it were terrible to behold, yet Anniball for a while stood still, and kept his own men together, for fear of increasing this disorder and affright. But after that he saw his army disbanded and marching in disarray, and that it was to no purpose to lead his army safe through the straits, if he lost the carriages: for fear hereof he ran down from the higher ground, and albeit, with the violence of his charge, he discomforted the enemy, yet he increased the trouble and fear of his own people.

Holland 1600

But that was soon appeased in a very moment, after the ways and passages were once cleared, by reason of the mountaineers that were fled; so that within a while the whole host passed through, not only at ease and leisure, but also in a manner without any noise at all. This done, he seized upon a castle, which was the chief strength of that country, with other villages lying about it; and for three days' space he victualled and maintained his whole army with the cattle of his prisoners. And for that he was now neither molested with the mountaineers, who were at the first discomfited, nor greatly encumbered with the difficulties of the ways, in those three days he rid a good deal of ground, and journeyed a great way into the country; until at the length he came to another coast well peopled (for such mountain and hilly quarters) where he had like to have been overtaken, not by open force, but even in his own professed cunning: first, by a subtle practice, and after by a secret ambush. Certain ancient men, the rulers and governors of the castles, repaired unto Anniball as Orators, saying, that they having been taught and made wise by the profitable example of other men's harms, made choice rather to try the amity than prove the force of the Carthaginians; and therefore were willing to do his commandment, and be at his devotion: requesting him to take at their hand victuals and guides for their journey, yea, and hostages also for better assurance of promises to be performed. Anniball neither overhastily and rashly believing them, nor yet churlishly distrusting and refusing their offer, lest being rejected and cast off, they might become open and professed enemies, gave them good language, and a courteous answer, received the hostages whom they gave, accepted victuals which they had brought with them to maintain his army by the way, and followed their guides, but so, as his army was not disarrayed in their march, as if he had been amongst his friends, and in a peaceable country.

First went in the **vauntguard the** elephants **and the** horsemen; himself marched after with the flower and strength of his footmen, looking all about him with an heedful eye. So soon as he was entered a narrow passage, which of the one side lay under a steep hill that commanded them aloft, the **barbarous** people rose out of their ambush from all parts at once, both before **and** behind, and charged **upon** him both afar off and near at hand; yea and rolled **down** mighty huge stones upon them as they marched. But the greatest number came behind upon their backs: against whom he turned and made head with the power of his footmen, and without all peradventure (if the tail both of his army had not been strong and well fortified) they must **need** have received in that lane and straits an exceeding great overthrow. And even then, as it was, they came to **an** extremity of danger, and in manner fell into a present mischief. For whiles Anniball made long stay, and doubted whether he should engage the regiment of footmen within the straits, for that he had not left any succours in the rear-guard to back the footmen, like as himself was a defence **to** the horsemen; the mountaineers **came** overthwart and flanked them; and breaking through the files of the battle, beset the way, and crossed upon him. So that Anniball took up his lodging for one night, without his carriages and horsemen. The morrow after, whenas the barbarous people ran between them more coldly than before, he joined his forces together, and passed the strait, not without great damage and loss; but with more hurt of the sumpter horses than of men. After this, the mountaineers (fewer in number, and in robbing wise rather than in warlike sort) ran in heaps, one while upon the vaward, other while upon the rearward, as any one of them could either get the vantage of ground, or by going one while afore, and by staying another while behind, win and catch any occasion and opportunity.

Holland 1600

The elephants, as they were driven with great leisure, because through these narrow straits they were ready ever and anon to run on their noses: so what way soever they went, they kept the army safe and sure from the enemies; who being not used unto them, durst not once come near. The ninth day he won the very tops of Alps, through by-lanes and blind cranks: after he had wandered many times out of the way, either through the deceitfulness of their guides, or for that, when they durst not trust them, they adventured rashly themselves upon the valleys, and guessed the way at adventure, and went by aim. Two days abode he encamped upon the tops thereof, and the soldiers wearied with travel and fight rested that time; certain also of the sumpter horses (which had slipt aside from the rocks) by following the tracks of the army as it marched, came to the camp. When they were thus overtoiled and wearied with these tedious travails, the snow that fell (for now the star Vergilie was set and gone down out of the horizon) increased their fear exceedingly. Now whenas at the break of day the ensigns were set forward, and the army marched slowly through the thick and deep snow; and that their appeared in the countenance of them all slothfulness and desperation: Anniball advanced before the

Holland
1600

standards and **commanded** his soldiers to stay upon a certain high hill (from whence they **had a** goodly prospect and might see a great way all **about** them), and there shewed unto them Italy, and the goodly champain fields about the Po, which lie hard under the foot **of the** Alpine mountains: saying, that even then they mounted the **walls, not** only of Italy, but also of the City of Rome; **as for all** besides (saith he) will be plain and easy to be travelled: **and after one** or **two** battles at the most, ye shall have at your command **the very Castle and** head City of all Italy.

Then began the army **to** march forward; and as **yet** the enemies verily themselves adventured nothing at all **but** some petty robberies **by** stealth, as opportunity and **occasion** served. Howbeit **they had** much more difficult travelling down **the hill than in the** climbing and getting up; for that most of the **avenues to the Alps** from Italy side, as they be shorter, so **they are more** upright: for all the way in a manner was steep, narrow, and slippery, **so as** neither they could hold themselves from sliding, nor if any tripped and stumbled never **so** little, could they possibly (they staggered so) recover themselves and keep sure footing, but one fell upon another, as well horse as man. After this they came to a much narrower rock, with crags **and rags** so steep downright, that hardly a nimble soldier without his armour and baggage (do what he could **to take** hold with hands upon the twigs and plants that thereabout grew forth) was able to creep down. This place being before naturally of itself steep and pendant with a downfall, now was choked and dammed up with a new fall of earth, which left a bank behind it of a wonderful and monstrous height. There the horsemen stood still as if they had been come to their way's end; and when Anniball marvelled much what the matter might be that stayed them so as they marched not on, **word** was brought him that the rock was unaccessible and unpassable.

Whereupon he went himself in person to view the place, and then he saw indeed without all doubt that although he had fetched a compass about, yet he had gained nought thereby, but conducted his army to pass through wilds, and such places as before had never been beaten and trodden. And verily, that (of all other) was such, as it was impossible to pass through. For whereas there lay old snow untouched and not trodden on, and over it other snow newly fallen, of a small depth; in this soft and tender snow, and the same not very deep, their feet as they went easily took hold; but that snow, being once with the gait of so many people and beasts upon it fretted and thawed, they were fain to go upon the bare ice underneath, and in the slabbery snow-broth, as it relented and melted about their heels. There they had foul ado and much struggling, for that they could not tread sure upon the slippery ice; and again, going as they did (down hill), their feet sooner failed them; and when they had helped themselves once in getting up, either with hands or knees, if they chanced to fall again, when those their props and stays deceived them, there were no twigs nor roots about whereon a man might take hold and rest or stay himself, either by hand or foot. And, therefore, all that the poor garrons[1] and beasts could do was to tumble and wallow only upon the slippery and glassy ice, and the molten, slabbie snow. Otherwhiles, also, they perished as they went in the deep snow, whilst it was yet soft and tender; for when they were once slidden and fallen, with flinging out their heels, and beating with their hoofs more forcibly for to take hold, they brake the ice through, so as most of them, as if they had been caught fast and fettered, stuck still in the deep, hard-frozen, and congealed ice.

At last, whenas both man and beast were wearied and overtoiled, and all to no purpose, they encamped upon the top of a hill, having with very much ado cleansed the place

Holland 1600

[1] Geldings.

Holland
1600

aforehand for that purpose: such a deal of snow there was to be digged, fayed,[1] and thrown out. This done, the soldiers were brought to break that rock, through which was their only way; and against the time that it was to be hewed through, they felled and overthrew many huge trees that grew thereabout, and made a mighty heap and pile of wood: the wind served fitly for the time to kindle a fire, and then they set all a-burning. Now, when the rock was on fire and red-hot, they poured thereon strong vinegar for to calcine for to dissolve it. Whenas the rock was thus baked (as it were) with fire, they digged into it, and opened it with pickaxes, and made the descent gentle and easy by means of moderate windings and turnings: so as not only the horses and other beasts, but even the elephants, also, might be able to go down. Four days he spent about the levelling of this rock: and the beasts were almost pined and lost for hunger. For the hill tops for the most are bare of grass, and look what fog[2] and forage there was, the snow over-hilled it. The dales and lower grounds have some little banks lying to the sun, and rivers withal near unto the woods, yea, and places more meet and beseeming for men to inhabit. There were labouring beasts put out to grass and pasture, and the soldiers that were wearied with making the ways had three days allowed to rest in.

Philemon Holland.

THE MOST CHRISTIAN KING

Danett
1601

AMONG men famous for devotion, he sent into Calabria for one Friar Robert, whom he called the Holy Man, because of his holy life, and in whose honour the King that now is caused a church to be built at Plessis du Parc, in place

[1] Cleaned out.   Green fodder.

of the chapel near to Plessis, at the bridge foot. This hermit being twelve years of age entered into a rock, where he remained till he was forty-three years old, or thereabout, to wit, even till this present that the King sent for him by one of the stewards of his house, whom the Prince of Tarente, the King of Naples' son, accompanied thither. For the said hermit would not depart thence, without permission both of the Pope and of his Prince; which was great wisdom in so simple a man. He builded in the place where he lived two churches, and never ate, since the time he entered into this strait kind of life, either fish, flesh, eggs, any kind of white-meat, or of fat. I never saw in my time a man of so holy life, nor by whose mouth the Holy Ghost seemed rather to speak; for he never had been scholar, but was utterly unlearned; true it is, that his Italian tongue caused somewhat the greater admiration of him. This hermit passed through Naples, being honoured and received, as if he had been a great Legate sent from the See Apostolic, both by the King and by his children; with whom he communed of the affairs of the court, as if he had been a courtier all the days of his life. From thence he went to Rome, where he was visited by all the Cardinals, and had audience given him thrice of the Pope, communing with him alone; and sitting each time hard by him in a goodly chair three or four hours together, which was great honour to so simple a person. His answers were so wise that all men wondered at them; so far forth that our Holy Father gave him leave to erect a new order, called the Hermits of St. Francis. From thence he came to the King, who honoured him as if he had been the Pope himself, falling down before him, and desiring him to prolong his life; whereunto he answered as a wise man should. I have often heard him talk with the King that now is, in presence of all the nobility of the realm, and that within these two months, and sure he seemed by his words to be inspired with the Holy Ghost; otherwise he could never have

Danett
1601

communed of such matters as he did. He is yet living and may change either to better or worse; wherefore I will speak no further of him. Some mocked at his hermit's coming, whom they called the Holy Man; but they knew not the deep cogitations of this wise King, neither had seen the occasions that moved him to send for him.

The King lay in his Castle of Plessis, accompanied with few besides the archers of his Guard, and troubled with suspicions. Notwithstanding, he had given good order for this inconvenience, for he left none of those whom he suspected either in the town or country, but made his archers to cause them to depart, and to convey them away. No man debated any matter with him, unless it were of some great importance that concerned himself: he seemed rather a dead corpse than a living creature, for he was leaner than a man would believe: he apparelled himself sumptuously, yea, more sumptuously than in all his life before; for he wore no gown but of crimson satin, furred with good martens; he gave gifts to whom it pleased him without any suit; for no man durst move any suit to him, nor debate any matter with him. He punished faults sharply, to the end he might be feared, and not lose his authority, as himself told me. He changed officers, cassed[1] companies of men of arms, diminished pensions, or took them clean away; and told me but a few days before his death that he passed away the time in making and marring of men. To be short, he caused himself to be more spoken of within his realm than ever was any King, and all for fear lest men should think him dead. For, as I said, few saw him; but when they heard of his doings, all men stood in fear of him, so far forth, that they hardly believed him to be sick. Out of the realm he had men in all places, as, for example in England he had some to feed King Edward still with hope of his daughter's marriage, and he paid truly both him and his servants all that was due unto them. Out of Spain he received

---

[1] Broke, *i.e.* disbanded.

goodly words and fair promises of perfect friendship and amity, and great presents from all places. He made a good horse or a good mule to be bought for him whatsoever it cost; but this he did not in this realm, but in some strange country, to persuade men that he was in health. Dogs he sent for round about, into Spain for a kind of Spanish greyhound, called in French *Allans*; into Britain for little beagles, grey-hounds, and spaniels, which he paid dear for; into Valence for little rugged dogs which he made to be bought above the owner's own price. Into Sicily he sent for good mules, especially to some officer of the country, for the which he paid double the value; to Naples for horses, and for divers strange beasts into divers countries, as into Barbary for a kind of little lions, no greater than little foxes, which he called Adites; into Denmark and Sweden for two kinds of strange beasts, one of the which were called Helles, being of shape like a hart, and of the greatness of a buff, with horns short and thick; the other Rengiers, being of the bigness and colour of a buck, save that their horns be much greater: for each of the which two beasts he gave to the merchants that sold them 4500 guildons. But when all these strange things were brought him he made no account of them, no, very seldom spake with those that brought them. To be short, he did so many such like strange things, that he was more feared now both of his neighbours and subjects than ever before, which was his only desire, for to that end did he all this. . . .

He discoursed continually of some matter or other, and that very gravely, and his disease endured from Monday till Saturday night. Wherefore I will now make comparison between the troubles and sorrows he caused others to suffer, and those he suffered himself before his death, because I trust they have carried him into Paradise, and been part of his Purgatory. For notwithstanding that they were not so grievous, neither endured so long, as those which he caused

Danett
1601

Danett
1601

divers others to suffer, yet because his vocation in this **world** was higher than theirs, by **means** whereof he had never been contraried, but so well obeyed, that he seemed a Prince able to have governed all Europe: this little trouble that he endured contrary **to** his accustomed nature was to him a great torment. He hoped ever **in this** good hermit that was at Plessis, whom he caused to come **to** him out of Calabria, and continually sent to him: saying, that if it pleased **him he** could prolong his life. For notwithstanding all these commandments given to those whom he sent to the Dauphin, his son, yet came his spirits again to him, in such sort **that** he was in hope to **recover**; and if it had so happened, he **would** easily have disparkled the assembly sent to this new King. But because of **the vain** hope he had in this hermit, a Doctor of Divinity and certain others thought good to advertise him that his only hope must be **in** the mercy of God; and they devised that Master James Cothier, his Physician, in whom he had reposed his whole confidence, and to whom he gave monthly ten thousand crowns in hope he would prolong his life, should be present when this speech should be used to him. This was Master Oliver, his barber's device, to the end he might wholly think upon his conscience, and leave all his other imaginations conceived of this holy man, and of the said Master James, his Physician. But even like as he advanced the said Master Oliver and others too suddenly, without any desert, **to a** higher estate than was fit for them; even so they took **upon them** boldly to do such a message to so great a Prince otherwise than became them, not using **that** reverence and humility that was to be used in **such a** case, and such as they should have used, whom he had brought up of a long time, and lately commanded out **of his** presence for the suspicions conceived of them.

And again, like **as** unto two great personages whom he had put to death **in his time** (to wit, the Duke of Nemours **and the** Earl of **Saint** Paul: for one **of** the which he repented him at his death, and for the other not), he had sent a sharp message of death by commissioners appointed thereunto; who briefly pronounced their sentence unto them, and forthwith gave them confessors, and but a very short space to dispose of their consciences: even so the abovenamed signified his death unto him rudely and in few words, saying: 'Sir, it is reason we do our duties, hope no more in this holy man, nor any other thing, for sure you are but dead; therefore think upon your conscience, for your hour is come'; and every one of them said somewhat briefly to him to that effect. But he answered: 'I trust God will help me; and, peradventure, I am not so sick as you suppose.' What a sharp corrosive was it to him to hear these news and this cruel sentence! For never man feared death more than he, nor sought so many ways to avoid it as he did. Moreover, in all his lifetime he had given commandment to all his servants, as well myself as others, that when we should see him in danger of death, we should only move him to confess himself and dispose of his conscience, not sounding in his ear this dreadful word *Death*, knowing that he should not be able patiently to hear that cruel sentence; notwithstanding, he endured both that and divers other punishments till the very hour of death more patiently than ever I saw any man. To this son, whom he called King, he sent many messages, and confessed himself very devoutly, and said divers prayers answerable to the Sacraments he received, which also himself demanded. He spake as heartily as if he had not been sick, and talked of all matters touching the King his son's estate; and among other things gave commandment that the Lord of Cordes should not depart from his son by the space of half a year after his death; and further, that he should be entreated to attempt nothing against Calais, nor elsewhere; saying, that notwithstanding he had devised these enterprises for the King's profit and the benefit of the realm: yet were they

Danett 1601

Danett
1601

very dangerous, especially that of Calais, for fear of moving the Englishmen thereby to war. Further, he willed especially that after his death the realm should rest in peace the space of five or six years, a matter which he would never yield unto during his life, though very needful; for notwithstanding it were great and large, yet was it in poor and miserable estate, especially because of the passing to and fro of the men of arms, who continually removed from one country to another. He gave order, also, that no quarrel should be picked in Britaine, but that Duke Francis should be suffered to live in quiet, and not be put in any doubt or fear of war, neither yet any other neighbour bordering upon the realm, to the end the King and the realm might rest in peace till the King were of years to dispose thereof at his own pleasure.

Thus you see how indiscreetly his death was signified to him, which I have rehearsed because I began to make a comparison between those evils which he had caused divers of his subjects to suffer and those himself suffered before his death, to the end you may perceive that, notwithstanding they were not so grievous nor so long (as I have said), yet were they grievous to him considering his nature, which demanded obedience, and had been better obeyed than any Prince in his time; so that one half word contrarying his mind was to him a grievous punishment. Five or six days before his death he had all men in suspicion, especially all that were worthy of credit and authority, yea, he grew jealous of his own son, and caused him to be straitly guarded, neither did any man see him or speak with him but by his commandment; at the length he began to stand in doubt also of his daughter, and of his son-in-law, now Duke of Bourbon, and would needs know what men entered into Plessis with them, and in the end brake off an assembly that the Duke of Bourbon, his son-in-law, held there by his commandment. Moreover, at the same time that his said son-in-law and the Earl of Dunois (returning from the convoy of the embassage that came to Amboise to the marriage of the King, his son, and the Queen) entered into the Castle of Plessis with a great band of men: the King, who caused the gates to be straitly kept, being in the gallery that looked into the court of the said Castle, caused one of the Captains of his Guard to come to him, whom they commanded to feel, as he talked with the said Noblemen's servants, whether they ware any brigandines under their cloaks, not making show as though he came purposely for that intent. Hereby you may perceive if he caused divers others to live in fear and suspicion under him, whether he were paid now with the like himself; for of whom could he be assured, mistrusting his son, his daughter, and his son-in-law? Wherefore thus much I will say not only of him, but of all other Princes that desire to be feared, that they never feel the revenge thereof till their age, and then their penance is to fear all men.

What great grief think you was it to this poor King to be troubled with these passions? He had a Physician called Master James Cothier, to whom he gave in five months 54,000 crowns, after the rate of 10,000 the month, and 4000 over, besides the Bishopric of Amiens for his nephew, and other offices and lands for him and his friends. The said Physician used him so roughly, that a man would not give his servant so sharp language as he gave the King; and yet the King so much feared him, that he durst not command him out of his presence; for notwithstanding that he complained to divers of him, yet durst he not change him as he did all his other servants, because this Physician once said thus boldly to him: 'I know that one day you will command me away as you do all your other servants, but you shall not live eight days after,' binding it with a great oath. Which words put the King in such fear, that ever after he flattered him, and bestowed gifts upon him, which was a marvellous Purgatory to him in this world, considering of how many Noblemen and gentlemen he had been obeyed.

Danett
1601

Danett
1601

Moreover, he **had caused divers** cruel prisons to be made; as, for example, cages, being eight feet square, and one foot more than a man's height, some **of iron,** and some of wood plated with iron both within and without, with horrible iron works. He that first devised them was the Bishop of Verdun, who incontinent was himself put into the first that was made, where he remained fourteen **years.** Many have cursed him for his device, and among others myself, for I lay in one of them, under the King that now reigneth, the space of eight months. He had also caused certain Almains to make terrible heavy irons **to** lay men in, among the which there **was** a fetter to put on their feet very hard to be opened, **like** to a carcan, with a weighty chain, and a great iron ball **at the end** thereof, **heavy beyond** all measure. These irons were called the King's Nets. Notwithstanding, I have seen divers gentlemen lie **in** them as prisoners, who came forth afterward with great honour, and were advanced by him to high estates: as, for example, a son of the Lord of Grutuze, in Flanders, taken prisoner in the wars, whom the King afterward richly married, and made one of his Chamber and Seneschal of Anjou, and gave him charge of a hundred lances; and, in like manner, the Lord of Piennes and the Lord of Vergy, taken prisoners also in the wars, who both had charge of men of arms under the King and other goodly offices, and were of the Privy Chamber either to him or his son. The like happened also to the Lord of Richbourg, the Constable's brother, and to one Roquebertin of the country of Cathelony, being likewise taken prisoners in the wars, whom he afterward highly advanced, with divers others of divers countries too long to rehearse.

But now to return **to** the matter. As in his time these divers and sundry cruel prisons were devised, even so **he** before his death lay in the like, yea, in much crueller prison than any of them, and was in greater fear than they **that** stood in **fear** of him, which I account as a

great grace towards him, and as part of his Purgatory, and Danett
rehearse it only to show that every man, of what estate or 1601
condition soever he be, is punished either secretly or openly,
especially those that punish others. Further, the King a
little before his death enclosed his **Castle of Plessis** with a
grate of iron bars, and at the four corners of the said Castle
caused four strong watch-houses of iron to be built. The
said grate was made directly over against the Castle wall
round about the Castle, on the outer side of the ditch, which
was very steep. He caused also to be masoned into the wall
a great number of iron spears, each of them having divers
heads set close together. Moreover, he appointed ten cross-
bow-men to be continually in the said ditches, and to lie in
the four iron houses built in the bottom of the said ditches,
and gave them commandment to shoot at every man that
approached near to the gate, before the gate opened. He
knew well that this fortification was to no purpose against
a great force or an army, but that he doubted not: his only
fear was that certain Noblemen of his realm, having intelligence in the Castle, would attempt to enter it in the night,
partly by love and partly by force, and take the government
upon them, and make him live as a man bereft of his wits,
and unworthy to rule. The Castle gate never opened before
eight of the clock in the morning, neither was the drawbridge let down till that hour, and then entered his officers;
and the Captains of his Guard placed the ordinary warders,
and appointed archers to the watch, both at the gate and
within the court, as if it had been a frontier town straitly
kept. Neither entered any man without the King's commandment but by the wicket, save the stewards of his house,
and such like officers that went not to him. Is it possible,
then, to hold a King (I mean using him like a Prince) in a
straiter prison than he held himself? The cages wherein
he held others were about eight feet square, and he, being
so great a Prince, had but a little court in the Castle to walk

Danett
1601

in, yea, and seldom came he into that; for usually he kept himself in the gallery, from whence he never stirred but when he went to mass, at which time he passed through the chambers, and not through the court.

Think you that he was not in fear as well as others, seeing he locked himself in after this sort, kept himself thus close, stood in such fear of his children and nearest kinsmen, and changed and removed his servants from day to day, whom he had brought up and whose good estate depended wholly upon him, in such sort that he durst trust none of them, but bound himself in these strange chains and bands? The place, I confess, was larger than a common prison, so was his estate greater than a common prisoner's. But a man will say, peradventure, that other Princes have been more suspicious than he, whereunto I agree; but none, sure, in our time, neither any so wise as he, nor that had so good subjects as he had; and as touching them, peradventure they were cruel tyrants, but he never punished any without desert. All this above written I have rehearsed, not so much to publish the suspicions of the King our Master, as partly to prove that the patient enduring of these passions, being equal with those he had caused others to endure, and of this sickness being sharp and troublesome to him, and the which he feared greatly before he fell into it, is to be accounted as a punishment God gave him in this world, to ease him in the world to come; and partly to give an example to those that shall come after him, to have some more compassion on their people than he had, and to be less rigorous in punishing than he was. Notwithstanding, for my part I am not able to accuse him, neither saw I ever a better Prince; for though himself pressed his subjects, yet would he suffer none other so to do, friend or foe.

After all these fears, sorrows, and suspicions, God (according to His accustomed goodness) wrought a miracle upon him, healing him both in soul and body: for He took him out of this miserable world, being perfect of sense, understanding, and memory, having received all his Sacraments without all grief to man's judgment, and talking continually even within a *Pater noster* while of his death; so that he gave order for his funeral, and named those that should accompany his body to the grave; saying ever, that he trusted to die on no day but Saturday, and that our Lady, in whom he had ever put his confidence, and always devoutly served, had purchased him this grace; and sure so it happened, for he ended his life upon Saturday, the 30th of August, in the year 1483, at eight of the clock at night, in the said Castle of Plessis, where he fell sick the Monday before. His soul, I trust, is with God, and resteth in His blessed Realm of Paradise.

Danett
1601

Thomas Danett.

JULIUS CAESAR

HIS pleasures could never make him lose one minute of an hour, nor turn one step from the occasions, that might any way further his advancement. This passion did so soveraignly oversway all others, and possessed his mind with so uncontrolled an authority, that she carried him whither she list. Truly I am grieved, when in other things I consider this man's greatness, and the wondrous parts that were in him; so great sufficiency in all manner of knowledge and learning, as there is almost no science wherein he hath not written. He was so good an orator, that divers have preferred his eloquence before Cicero's; and himself (in mine opinion) in that faculty thought himself nothing short of him. And his two *Anti-Catos* were especially written to overbalance the eloquence which Cicero had employed in his *Cato*. And for all other matters;

Florio
1603

Florio
1603

was ever mind so vigilant, so active, and so patient of labour as his? And doubtless, it was also embellished with sundry rare seeds of virtue. I mean lively, natural, and not counterfeits. He was exceeding sober, and so homely in his feeding, that Oppius reporteth: how upon a time, through a certain Cook's negligence, his meat being dressed with a kind of medicinable Oil instead of Olive-oil, and so brought to the board, although he found it, yet he fed heartily of it, only because he would not shame his Host: another time he caused his Baker to be whipped, because he had served him with other than common household bread. Cato himself was wont to say of him, that he was the first sober man had addressed himself to the ruin of his country. And whereas the same Cato called him one day drunkard, it happened in this manner. Being both together in the Senate House, where Catiline's conspiracy was much spoken of, wherein Caesar was greatly suspected to have a hand; a note was by a friend of his brought, and in very secret sort delivered him, which Cato perceiving, supposing it might be something that the Conspirators advertised him of, instantly summoned him to show it, which Caesar, to avoid a greater suspicion, refused not: it was by chance an amorous letter, which Servilia, Cato's sister, writ to him: Cato having read it, threw it at him, saying: 'Hold it again, thou drunkard.' I say it was rather a word of disdain and anger, than an express reproach of this vice, as often we nickname those that anger us with the first nicknames of reproaches that come into our mouth, though merely impertinent to those with whom we fall out. Considering that the vice wherewith Cato charged him hath near coherency unto that wherein he had surprised Caesar: for Venus and Bacchus (as the vulgar Proverb saith) agree well together, but with me Venus is much more blithe and gamesome, being accompanied with sobriety.

The examples of his mildness and clemency, toward such

as had offended him, are infinite: I mean, besides those
he showed during the Civil Wars, which (as by his own
writings may plainly appear) he used to blandish and allure
his enemies, to make them fear his future domination and
victories the less. But if any shall say, those examples are
not of validity to witness his genuine and natural affability,
we may lawfully answer, that at least they show us a
wonderful confidence and greatness of courage to have been
in him. It hath often befallen him, to send whole armies
back again to his enemies, after he had vanquished them,
without deigning to bind them so much as with an oath, if
not to favour, at least not to bear arms against him. He
hath three or four times taken some of Pompey's chief
Captains prisoners, and as often set them at liberty again.
Pompey declared all such as would not follow and accompany
him in his wars, to be his enemies; and he caused those to
be proclaimed as friends, who either would not stir at all, or
not effectually arm themselves against him. To such of his
Captains as fled from him to procure other conditions, he
sent them their weapons, their horses, and all other furniture.
The Cities he had taken, by main force, he freed to follow
what faction they would, giving them no other garrison than
the memory of his clemency and mildness. In the day of
his great battle of Pharsalia, he expressly inhibited, that
unless they were driven to unavoidable extremity, no man
should lay hands upon any Roman citizen. In my judgment
these are very hazardous parts, and it is no wonder, if in
the Civil War's tumultuous broils we have now on foot those
that fight for the ancient laws and state of their country, as
he did, do not follow and imitate the example. They are
extraordinary means, and which only belongs to Caesar's
fortune, and to his admirable foresight, successfully to direct,
and happily to conduct them. When I consider the in-
comparable greatness and invaluable worth of his mind, I
excuse Victory, in that she could not well give him over, in

Florio
1603

Florio 1603

this most unjust and **unnatural cause.** But to return to **his** clemency; **we** have divers **genuine and** lively examples, even in the time of his all-swaying government, when all things were reduced into **his** hands, **and** he needed no longer to dissemble. Caius Memmius had written certain detracting and railing Orations against **him, which he** at full **and most sharply had** answered; nevertheless, **he** shortly **after helped** to make him consul. Caius Calvus, who had composed divers most injurious Epigrams against him, **having** employed sundry **of his** friends to be reconciled **to him** again, Caesar descended **to write** first unto him. And our good Catullus, **who under the name of** Mumurra had **so rudely** and bitterly **railed** against him, **at** last coming to **excuse** himself, Caesar **that very night** made him to sup at his own table. Having **been advertised** how some were over lavish in railing against him, **all he** did was but in a publike oration to declare how he was advertised of it. His enemies **he** feared less than **he hated them.** Certain conspiracies and conventicles **were made** against his life, which being discovered unto him, he was contented by an edict to publish, how he was throughly informed of them, and never prosecuted the Authors. Touching the respect he ever bare unto his friends: Caius Oppius travelling with him, **and** falling very sick, having but one chamber, he resigned **the same** unto him, and himself was contented to lie all night **abroad and upon the** bare ground. Concerning his justice, he caused a servant of his, whom he exceedingly loved, to be executed, forsomuch as he had lain with the wife of a Roman Knight, although no man sued or complained **of** him. Never was **man** that showed more moderation in his victory, **or** more **resolution** in his adverse fortune. But **all** these noble inclinations, rich **gifts,** worthy qualities, were altered, smothered, **and** eclipsed by this furious passion of Ambition, by which he suffered himself to be so far misled, **that** it may be well affirmed she only ruled the Stern of all his actions. Of a liberal man, she made him a common thief, that so he might the better supply his profusion and prodigality; and made him utter that vile and most injurious speech: that if the wickedest and most pernicious men of the world had for his service and furtherance been faithful unto him, he would to the utmost of his power have cherished and preferred them, as well as if they had been the honestest. It so besotted, and as it were made him drunk with so extreme vanity, that in the presence of all his fellow-citizens he durst vaunt himself, to have made that great and far-spread Roman Commonwealth a shapeless and bodiless name; and pronounce that his Sentences or Answers should thenceforward serve as Laws: and sitting to receive the whole body of the Senate coming toward him, and suffer himself to be adored: and in his presence divine honours to be done him. To conclude, this only vice (in mine opinion) lost and overthrew in him the fairest natural and richest ingenuity that ever was, and hath made his memory abhominable to all honest minds, insomuch as by the ruin of his country, and subversion of the mightiest state and most flourishing Commonwealth that ever the world shall see, he went about to procure his glory.

John Florio.

Florio
1603

TAMERLANE

NOW the Prince of Ciarcan had divided his forces into two parts, and given commandment to the first, that as soon as they perceived the enemies to pursue the hundred horse that so disorderly of purpose fled, they should receive them, and so retire all together. He in the meantime with the rest of his power stood close in a valley, near to a wood side, unseen at all. Where having suffered two thousand of the Enemies' Horse (the vantcurriers of the Turks' army) to

Knolles
1603

Knolles
1603

pass by him, he **following them in the tail, charged** them home, the other which before retired now turning upon them also; so that the Turks seeing themselves thus beset, and hardly laid unto both before and behind, **as** men discouraged fled; in which flight most of them were **slain,** and the rest taken Prisoners. This was the first encounter betwixt the Turks and the Parthians; all the Prisoners there taken were by the Prince as a present sent to Tamerlane, **and** among the rest the **Bassa of** Natolia who led these troops; **of whom** Tamerlane earnestly demanded what caused Bajazet so little to esteem of him, as to show so great contempt of his army, which he **should find strong** enough to abate his pride. Whereunto the Bassa answered, that **his** Lord was the Sun **upon** Earth, which **could not endure any** equal; and that he rather was astonished to see, **how he from** so far **had** enterprised so dangerous a journey, to hinder **the** fortune of his lord, in whose favour the Heavens (as he said) did bend themselves to further his greatness, and unto whom all the world subjected itself; and that he committed great folly in going about to resist the same. Unto which so proud a speech Tamerlane replied, that he was sent from Heaven to punish **his** rashness, and to teach him, that the proud are hated of God, **whose promise is to** pluck down the mighty and **raise up** the lowly. 'As for thyself' (said he) 'thou hast already **felt** (although **I pity** thy mishap) what the valour of my Parthian Horse is against thy Turkish; and thy Master I have already caused to raise his siege of Constantinople and to look to his own **things** here in Asia.' Furthermore, Tamerlane changing his speech demanded, if his Master did come resolved to bid him battle? 'Assure yourself' (said he) 'there is nothing he more desireth; and would to God I might acknowledge **your** greatness in giving me leave to assist my Lord at that battle.' 'Good leave have thou' (said Tamerlane); 'go thy ways and tell thy Lord that thou hast seen me, and that **he** shall in the battle find me on horseback, where he shall see a green ensign displayed.' The Bassa, thanking him, swore that next unto his Lord he vowed unto him his service. And so returning, declared unto Bajazet how that he had seen Tamerlane, and truly reported unto him all that he had willed him to say; not forgetting over all, to publish his courtesy and bounty; who besides that he had frankly set him at liberty, had also given him a very fair horse well furnished, although he well knew he was to serve against himself. Whereunto Bajazet answered no more, but that he would shortly make trial of him, and that he well hoped before the march were ended, to make him acknowledge his own folly.

Knolles 1603

The next day the two Armies drew near together, and encamped within a league the one of the other; where all the night long you might have heard such noise of horses, as that it seemed the Heavens were full of voices, the air did so resound, and every man thought the night long, to come to the trial of his valour, and the gaining of his desires. The Scythians (a people no less greedy than needy) talked of nothing but the spoil; the proud Parthians, of their honour; and the poor Christians, of their deliverance, all to be gained by the next day's victory; every man during the night time speaking according to his own humour. All which Tamerlane walking this night up and down in his camp heard, and much rejoiced to see the hope that his soldiers had already in general conceived of the victory. Who after the second watch returning unto his pavilion, and there casting himself upon a carpet, had thought to have slept a while; but his cares not suffering him so to do, he then, as his manner was, called for a book, wherein was contained the lives of his Fathers and Ancestors, and of other valiant Worthies, the which he used ordinarily to read, as he then did; not as therewith vainly to deceive the time, but to make use thereof, by the imitation of that which was by them worthily done, and declining of such

Knolles
1603

dangers as they by their **rashness** or oversight fell into. And afterwards having a **little slum**bered, he commanded **Axalla** to be sent for, who forthwith **came** unto him, **with divers** other great Lords and Captains, **the** chief Commanders **of** his Army; with whom after he **had a** while consulted of the order of the battle, he mounted **on horseback** himself, and **sent** every one of them to their own charges, **to put** the same **in readiness.** At which very instant he **received news** that **the Enemy** marched forward and came to take his ground **for the battle;** whose order of march Tamerlane was **desirous to see, that** so accordingly he might marshal his own. And having caused **three thousand Horsemen** to advance forward, **with** charge to begin the **skirmish, himself** followed after **to lodge every** part of his forces **in such places as** he had foreseen to be **fittest for his advantage.**

Now, seeing the Janizaries march **in a square** battle in **the** midst, and upon the two fronts **two great** squadrons of Horsemen, which seemed to **be** thirty thousand Horse, and another **which** advanced and covered the battalion of **the** Janizaries, **he** thought this their order **to be very** good, and hard to be broken; and thereupon turning himself to Axalla, **who was** near unto him, said: 'I had thought this day **to have** fought on **foot, but I see** that it behoveth me **now to** fight on horseback, to **give** courage unto my Soldiers, **to open** the great battalion of our Enemies. And my will **is, that** my **men** come forward unto me as soon as they may, for I will advance forward with an hundred thousand Footmen, fifty thousand upon each of my two wings, **and** in the midst of them forty thousand of my best Horsemen. My pleasure is, that after they have tried the force of these men, that they come unto my avantguard, of whom I will dispose, and fifty thousand Horse more **in** three bodies, **whom** thou shalt command; which I will assist with eighty thousand Horse, wherein shall be mine **own** Person, having **an** hundred thousand Footmen behind me, who shall march in two squadrons; and for my rearward I appoint forty thousand Horse and fifty thousand Footmen, who shall not march but to my aid. And I will make choice of ten thousand of my best Horse, whom I will send into every place where I shall think needful within my army, for to impart my commands.' Over the first forty thousand Horse the Prince Ciarcan commanded; over the foremost Footmen was the Lord Synopes, a Genoese, kinsman to Axalla, and his lieutenant over the Footmen, a captain of great estimation; the Prince Axalla's own charge consisted of five squadrons of Horsemen. Bajazet his army, being also both fair and great, came bravely still on forward towards their enemies, who stirred not one whit from the place they had taken for the battle, except certain light Horsemen, Scythians, Parthians, and Muscovites, who sent out as loose men, hotly skirmished betwixt the two armies. Now was Tamerlane by an espy advertised that Bajazet, having before given order for the disposing of his army, was on foot in the midst of thirty thousand Janizaries, his principal men of war and greatest strength, wherein he meant that day to fight, and in whom he had reposed his greatest hope. His battle of Horse was very fair, amounting to the number of an hundred and forty thousand Horse, all old soldiers. The Sultan of Egypt having also sent unto his aid thirty thousand Mamalukes, all very good Horsemen, with thirty thousand Foot. So that his army, marching all in one front, in form of an half-moon (but not so well knit together as was Tamerlane's, whose squadrons directly followed one another), seemed almost as great as his; and so with infinite numbers of most horrible outcries still advanced forward; Tamerlane his soldiers all the while standing fast, with great silence.

There was not possible to be seen a more furious charge, than was by the Turks given upon the Prince of Ciarcan, who had commandment not to fight before the Enemy came unto him; neither could have been chosen a fairer plain, and

Knolles
1603

Knolles
1603

where the skilful choice **of the** place was of less advantage for the one or the other; but **that** Tamerlane had the river on the left hand of his army serving him to some small advantage. Now this young Prince of Ciarcan, with his forty thousand Horse, was in this first **encounter** almost wholly overthrown; yet having fought right valiantly**, and** entered even into the midst of the Janizaries **(where the** Person of Bajazet was), putting them in disorder, **was himself** there slain. **About which** time Axalla set upon them **with** the avantguard, **but** not with like danger; for having overthrown one of the Enemy's wings, and cut it all to pieces, and **his** Footmen coming **to join with him,** as they had been com**manded,** he faced the **battalion of** the Janizaries, who right **valiantly** behaved **themselves for the** safety of their Prince. **This hard** fight continued **one hour, and yet** you could not **have seen any** scattered, **but the one still** resolutely fighting against the other. You might there have **seen the** Horsemen like mountains rush together, and infinite numbers of men die, cry, lament, and threaten all at **one** instant. Tamerlane had patience all this while to see the event of **this** so mortal a fight; but perceiving his men at length to give ground, he sent **ten thousand** of his Horse to join again with the ten thousand **appointed** for the **rearward,** and commanded them to assist **him at** such time **as he** should have need of them, and at **the very** same time charged himself, and made them to give him room, causing the Footmen to charge also, over whom the Prince of Thanais commanded, who gave a furious onset upon the battalion **of** the Janizaries, wherein was yet the Person of Bajazet, **who** had sustained a great burden.

Now Bajazet had in his army a great number of mercenary **Tartars,** called Destenses, with many thousands of other soldiers taken up in **the** countries of the poor exiled Mahometan Princes; in whose just quarrel, and the Greek Emperor's, Tamerlane had chiefly undertaken that war; these Tartarians and other soldiers, seeing some their friends, and othersome their natural and loving Princes in the army of Tamerlane, stricken with the terror of disloyalty, and abhorring the cruelty of the proud Tyrant, in the heat of the battle revolted from Bajazet to their own Princes; which their revolt much weakened Bajazet's forces. Who nevertheless, with his own men of war, especially the Janizaries, and the help of the Christian soldiers brought to his aid from Servia and other places of Europe, with great courage maintained the fight; but the multitude, and not true valour, prevailed; for, as much as might be done by valiant and courageous men, was by the Janizaries and the rest performed both for the preservation of the Person of their Prince, and the gaining of the victory. But in the end, the Horsemen with whom Tamerlane himself was, giving a fresh charge, and his avantguard wholly knit again unto him, reinforcing the charge, he with much ado obtained the victory.

Bajazet himself wounded, and now mounted on horseback, thinking to have escaped by flight, fell into the hands of Axalla; unto whom he yielded himself, thinking it had been Tamerlane; who for a space knew him not, but took him for some other great commander of the Turks. Musa (surnamed Zelebi, or the Noble) one of Bajazet his sons, with divers others of Bajazet his great captains, were there taken also; and amongst the rest, George, the Despot of Servia, who notwithstanding this misfortune had that day gained unto himself the reputation of a great and worthy Captain; insomuch that Tamerlane, even in the very heat of the battle, marvelling to see him and the Servians, with the other Christians which he had brought to the aid of Bajazet, so valiantly to fight, said unto some of the Captains that were near unto him: 'See how courageously yonder religious fight;' supposing them by their strange attire to have been some of the Turks' superstitous votaries. But being now taken, and afterwards brought to Tamerlane, he was by him courteously welcomed; but yet withal reproved, for that he had fought for Bajazet against him, who

Knolles
1603

Knolles 1603 — was come in favour of the Christian Emperor, and the other poor oppressed princes, such as the Despot himself was. Who thereunto boldly answered, that indeed it was not according to his duty, but according to the prosperity of Bajazet, unto whom it seemed that all the World did bend, and that his own safety had caused him, though against his will, to take part with him. Whereupon Tamerlane held him excused; and so without more ado gave him leave at his own pleasure to depart.

Bajazet also himself being afterwards brought unto Tamerlane as a prisoner, and by him courteously entertained, never showed any token of submission at all, but according to his proud nature, without respect of his present state, presumptuously answered him unto whatsoever he demanded. Wherewith Tamerlane moved, told him, that it was now in his power to make him to lose his life. Whereunto he answered no more, but, 'Do it'; for that that loss should be his greatest happiness. Tamerlane afterwards demanding of him what made him so proud as to enterprise to bring into his subjection so noble a Prince as was the Greek Emperor, he answered: 'Even the same thing that hath moved thee to invade me, namely, the desire of glory and sovereignty.' 'But wherefore, then' (said Tamerlane), 'dost thou use so great cruelty towards them thou hast overcome, without respect of age or sex?' 'That did I' (said he) 'to give the greater terror unto my Enemies.' 'And what wouldst thou have done with me' (said Tamerlane) 'had it been my fortune to have fallen into thy hands, as thou art now in mine?' 'I would' (said Bajazet) 'have enclosed thee in a cage of iron, and so in triumph have carried thee up and down my Kingdom.' 'Even so' (said Tamerlane) 'shalt thou be served.' And so causing him to be taken out of his presence, turning unto his followers, said: 'Behold a proud and cruel man, he deserveth to be chastised accordingly, and to be made an example unto all the proud and cruel of the world, of the just wrath of

God against them. I acknowledge that God hath this day delivered into my hands a great Enemy, to whom we must therefore give thanks.' Which he performed the same day; for the battle was won at four of the clock, and there was yet five hours of daylight. The next day Tamerlane commanded the dead to be buried; where among the rest they found the body of the Prince of Ciarcan, dead in the midst of the Janizaries, where he lay enclosed with their dead bodies, in token he died not unrevenged; whose untimely death Tamerlane for all that greatly lamented, for he was his Kinsman, and like enough one day to have done great service. Whose dead body Tamerlane caused to be embalmed, and with two thousand Horse (and divers of the Turks prisoners chained and tied together) to be conveyed to Samercand, until his coming thither. All the other dead bodies were, with all honour that might be, buried at Sennas.

Knolles
1603

This great and bloody battle, fought in the year of our Lord 1397, not far from the Mount Stella (where sometime the great King Mithridates was by Pompey the Great in a great battle overthrown), was fought from seven o'clock in the morning, until four in the afternoon; Victory all that while, as it were with doubtful wings, hovering over both armies, as uncertain where to light; until at length the fortune of Tamerlane prevailed. Whose wisdom, next unto God, gave that day's victory unto his soldiers; for that the politic tiring of the strong forces of Bajazet was the safeguard of his own; whereas if he had gone unto the battle in one front, assuredly the multitude finding such strong resistance had put itself into confusion, whereas this successive manner of aiding of his men made them all unto him profitable. The number of them that were in this battle slain is of divers diversely reported; the Turks themselves reporting, that Bajazet there lost the noble Mustapha, his son, with two hundred thousand of his men, and Tamerlane not many fewer; and some other speaking of a far less number, as that there should

Knolles 1603

be slain of the Turks about threescore thousand, and of Tamerlane's army not past twenty thousand. But leaving the certainty of the number unto the credit of the reporters, like enough it is, that the slaughter was exceeding great in so long a fight, betwixt two such armies as never before (as I suppose) met in field together.

By this one day's event is plainly to be seen the uncertainty of worldly things, and what small assurance even the greatest have in them. Behold, Bajazet the Terror of the World, and, as he thought, superior to fortune, in an instant with his state in one battle overthrown into the bottom of misery and despair; and that at such time as he thought least, even in the midst of his greatest strength. It was three days (as they report) before he could be pacified, but as a desperate man still seeking after death, and calling for it; neither did Tamerlane, after he had once spoken with him, at all afterwards courteously use him, but as of a proud man caused small account to be made of him; and to manifest that he knew how to punish the haughty, made him to be shackled in fetters and chains of gold, and so to be shut up in an iron cage made like a grate, in such sort as that he might on every side be seen; and so carried him up and down as he passed through Asia, to be of his own people scorned and derided. And to his further disgrace, upon festival days used him for a footstool to tread upon when he mounted to horse, and at other times scornfully fed him like a dog with crumbs fallen from his table. A rare example of the uncertainty of worldly honour, that he unto whose ambitious mind Asia and Europe, two great parts of the world, were too little, should be now carried up and down cooped up in a little iron cage, like some perilous wild beast. All which Tamerlane did not so much for hatred to the man as to manifest the just judgment of God against the arrogant folly of the proud. It is reported that Tamerlane being requested by one of his noblemen that might be bold to speak unto him, to remit some part of his severity against the person of so great a Prince, answered, that he did not use that rigor against him as a King, but rather did punish him as a proud ambitious Tyrant, polluted with the blood of his own brother.

Richard Knolles.

Knolles
1603

TWO CHARACTERS

I

THE PATIENT MAN

THE patient man is made of a metal, not so hard as flexible. His shoulders are large; fit for a load of injuries: which he bears, not out of baseness and cowardliness, because he dare not revenge; but out of Christian fortitude, because he may not: he hath so conquered himself, that wrongs cannot conquer him; and herein alone finds, that victory consists in yielding. He is above nature, while he seems below himself. The vilest creature knows how to turn again; but, to command himself not to resist, being urged, is more than heroical. His constructions are ever full of charity and favour: either this wrong was not done, or not with intent of wrong; or, if that, upon mis-information; or, if none of these, rashness, though a fault, shall serve for an excuse. Himself craves the offender's pardon, before his confession; and a slight answer contents, where the offended desires to forgive. He is God's best witness: and, when he stands before the bar for truth, his tongue is calmly free, his forehead firm; and, he, with erect and settled countenance, hears his unjust sentence, and rejoices in it. The gaolers, that attend him, are to him his pages of honour; his dungeon, the lower part of the vault of heaven; his rack or wheel, the stairs of his ascent to glory: he challengeth his executioners; and encounters the fiercest pains, with

Hall
1608

strength of resolution; and, while he suffers, the beholders pity him, the tormentors complain of weariness, and both of them wonder. No anguish can master him; whether by violence or by lingering. He accounts expectation no punishment; and can abide to have his hopes adjourned, till a new day. Good laws serve for his protection, not for his revenge; and his own power, to avoid indignities, not to return them. His hopes are so strong, that they can insult over the greatest discouragements; and his apprehensions so deep, that, when he hath once fastened, he sooner leaveth his life than his hold. Neither time nor perverseness can make him cast off his charitable endeavours, and despair of prevailing; but, in spite of all crosses and all denials, he redoubleth his beneficial offers of love. He trieth the sea, after many shipwrecks; and beats still at that door, which he never saw opened. Contrariety of events doth but exercise, not dismay him; and, when crosses afflict him, he sees a divine hand invisibly striking with these sensible scourges: against which he dares not rebel, not murmur. Hence, all things befall him alike; and he goes with the same mind to the shambles and to the fold. His recreations are calm and gentle; and not more full of relaxation than void of fury. This man only can turn necessity into virtue, and put evil to good use. He is the surest friend; the latest and easiest enemy; the greatest conqueror; and so much more happy than others, by how much he could abide to be more miserable.

II

THE SLOTHFUL MAN

HE is a religious man, and wears the time in his cloister; and, as the cloak of his doing nothing, pleads contemplation: yet is he no whit the leaner for his thoughts; no whit learneder. He takes no less care how to spend

time than others how to gain by the expense; and, when Hall
business importunes him, is more troubled to forethink what 1608
he must do than another to effect it. Summer is out of his
favour for nothing but long days, that make no haste to their
even. He loves still to have the sun witness of his rising;
and lies long, more for lothness to dress him than will to
sleep: and, after some stretching and yawning, calls for
dinner, unwashed; which having digested with a sleep in
his chair, he walks forth to the bench in the market-place,
and looks for companions: whomsoever he meets, he stays
with idle questions and lingering discourse: how the days
are lengthened; how kindly the weather is; how false the
clock; how forward the spring; and ends ever with 'What
shall we do?' It pleases him no less to hinder others than
not to work himself. When all the people are gone from
church, he is left sleeping in his seat alone. He enters
bonds; and forfeits them by forgetting the day: and asks
his neighbour, when his own field was fallowed, whether the
next piece of ground belong not to himself. His care is
either none or too late: when winter is come, after some
sharp visitations, he looks on his pile of wood, and asks how
much was cropped the last spring. Necessity drives him to
every action; and what he cannot avoid, he will yet defer.
Every change troubles him, although to the better; and his
dullness counterfeits a kind of contentment. When he is
warned on a jury, he would rather pay the mulct than
appear. All but that which nature will not permit, he
doth by a deputy: and counts it troublesome to do nothing;
but, to do anything, yet more. He is witty in nothing but
framing excuses to sit still; which, if the occasion yield not,
he coineth with ease. There is no work, that is not either
dangerous or thankless; and whereof he foresees not the
inconvenience and gainlessness, before he enters: which if
it be verified in event, his next idleness hath found a reason
to patronise it. He would rather freeze, than fetch wood:

Hall
1608

and chooses rather to steal, than work; to beg, **than take pains to steal**; and, in many things, to want, than beg. **He** is so loath to leave his neighbour's fire, that he is fain to walk home in the dark; and, if he be not looked to, wears out the night in the chimney-corner; **or,** if not that, lies down in his clothes to save two labours. **He** eats and prays himself asleep; and dreams of no other torment, but work. This man is a standing pool; and cannot choose but gather **corruption: he is** descried, amongst a thousand neighbours, **by a** dry and nasty hand, that stills savours of the sheet; a beard uncut, uncombed; an eye and an ear yellow with their excretions; a coat shaken on, ragged, unbrushed; **by** linen and face striving **whether** shall excell in uncleanliness. For body, he hath a swollen leg, a dusky and swinish eye, a **blown cheek, a** drawling tongue, a heavy foot, and is nothing **but a colder** earth moulded with standing water: to conclude, **is a** man in nothing, but **in** speech and shape.

Joseph Hall, Bishop of Norwich.

CHARACTER OF A GALLANT

Dekker
1609

FIRST, **having** diligently enquired out an Ordinary of the largest reckoning, whither **most** of your courtly gallants do resort, let it be your use to repair thither some half hour after eleven; for then you shall find **most** of your fashionmongers planted in the room waiting for meat. Ride thither upon your galloway-nag, or your Spanish jennet, a swift ambling pace, **in your** hose, and doublet (gilt rapier and poniard bestowed **in their** places), **and** your French lackey carrying your cloak, and running before you; or rather in a coach, for that will both **hide** you from the basilisk eyes of your creditors, and outrun a whole kennel of bitter-mouthed sergeants.

Being arrived in the room, salute not any but those of

your acquaintance: walk up and down by the rest as scornfully and as carelessly as a gentleman-usher: select some friend (having first thrown off your cloak) to walk up and down the room with you, let him be suited, if you can, worse by far than yourself, he will be a foil to you: and this will be a means to publish your clothes better than Paul's, a Tennis-court, or a Play-house: discourse as loud as you can, no matter to what purpose if you but make a noise, and laugh in fashion, and have a good sour face to promise quarrelling, you shall be much observed.

If you be a soldier, talk how often you have been in action: as the Portingale voyage, Cales voyage, the Island voyage, besides some eight or nine employments in Ireland and the Low Countries: then you may discourse how honourably your Grave used you; observe that you call your Grave Maurice, your Grave: How often you have drunk with Count such a one, and such a Count, on your knees to your Grave's health: and let it be your virtue to give place neither to Saint Kynock, nor to any Dutchman whatsoever in the Seventeen Provinces, for that soldier's complement[1] of drinking. And if you perceive that the untravelled company about you take this down well, ply them with more such stuff, as how you have interpreted between the French King and a great Lord of Barbary, when they have been drinking healths together, and that will be an excellent occasion to publish your languages, if you have them: if not, get some fragments of French, or small parcels of Italian, to fling about the table: but beware how you speak any Latin there: your Ordinary most commonly hath no more to do with Latin than a desperate town of garrison hath.

If you be a courtier, discourse of the obtaining of suits: of your mistress's favours, etc. Make inquiry, if any gentleman at board have any suit, to get which he would use the good means of a great man's interest with the King: and

Dekker
1609

[1] Accomplishment.

Dekker 1609

withal (if you **have not so much** grace left **in you** as to blush) that you are (thanks **to your** stars) in mighty credit, though in your own conscience **you** know, and are guilty to yourself, that you dare **not (but** only upon the privileges of handsome clothes) presume **to peep** into the presence. Demand if there be any gentleman **(whom any** there is acquainted with) that is troubled with **two** offices; or any **vicar** with two church-livings; which will politely insinuate, **that your inquiry** after them is because **you have** good **means to obtain** them; yea and rather than your tongue should not **be heard in the** room, but that you should sit (like an **ass) with your finger** in your mouth, and speak nothing: **discourse how often this** Lady hath sent her coach **for** you; and **how** often **you have sweat** in the tennis-court with that great **Lord: for indeed** the sweating together in France (I mean the society **of tennis) is a** great argument of most dear affection, **even** between noblemen **and** peasants.

If you be a poet, and come into **the** Ordinary (though it can **be no** great glory to be an Ordinary poet) order yourself thus. Observe no man, doff not cap to that gentleman to-day **at** dinner, to whom, not **two** nights since, you were beholden for a supper; **but, after a** turn **or two in** the room, take occasion (pulling out your gloves) to have some epigram, or satire, or sonnet fastened in one of them, that may (as it were vomitingly to you) offer itself to the Gentlemen; they will presently desire it: but, without much conjuration from them, and **a pretty kind of** counterfeit lothness in yourself, do not read it; and though it be none of your own, swear you made it. Marry, **if you** chance to get into your hands **any** witty thing **of another** man's, that is somewhat better. I would counsel you then, if demand be made who composed it, you may say: 'Faith, **a** learned gentlemen, **a very** worthy **friend.'** And this seeming to lay it on another man will be counted either modesty in you, or a sign that you are not ambitious of praise, **or** else that you dare not take it upon you for fear of the sharpness it carries with it. Besides, it will add much to your fame to let your tongue walk faster than your teeth, though you be never so hungry, and, rather than you should sit like a dumb coxcomb, to repeat by heart either some verses of your own or of any other man's, stretching even very good lines upon the rack of the censure: though it be against all law, honesty, or conscience, it may chance save you the price of your Ordinary, and beget you other suppliments. Marry, I would further intreat our poet to be in league with the Mistress of the Ordinary, because from her (upon condition that he will but rhyme Knights and young Gentlemen to her house, and maintain the table in good fooling) he may easily make up his mouth at her cost, gratis.

Thus much for particular men. But in general let all that are in *Ordinary*-pay, march after the sound of these directions. Before the meat come smoking to the board, our gallant must draw out his tobacco-box, the ladle for the cold snuff into the nostril, the tongs and prining-iron: all which artillery may be of gold or silver (if he can reach to the price of it), it will be a reasonable useful pawn at all times, when the current of his money falls out to run low. And here you must observe to know in what state tobacco is in town better than the merchants, and to discourse of the apothecaries where it is to be sold and to be able to speak of their wines, as readily as the apothecary himself reading the barbarous hand of a doctor: then let him show his several tricks in taking it, as the Whiff, the Ring, etc. For these are complements that gain Gentlemen no mean respect, and for which indeed they are more worthily noted, I ensure you, than for any skill that they have in learning.

When you are set down to dinner, you must eat as impudently as can be (for that is most gentleman-like): when your Knight is upon his stewed mutton, be presently, though you be but a Captain, in the bosom of your goose: and when

Dekker
1609

your Justice of Peace is knuckle-deep in goose, you may, without disparagement to your blood, though you have a Lady to your mother, fall very manfully to your woodcocks. . . .

After dinner, every man as his business leads him: some to dice, . . . some to plays, some to take up friends in the Court, some to take up money in the City, some to lend testers in Paul's, others to borrow crowns upon the Exchange: and thus, as the people is said to be a beast of many heads (yet all those heads like Hydra's) ever growing, . . . so, in an Ordinary, you shall find the variety of a whole Kingdom in a few apes of the Kingdom.

You must not swear in your dicing: for that argues a violent impatience to depart from your money, and in time will betray a man's need. Take heed of it. No! whether you be at primero or hazard, you shall sit as patiently (though you lose a whole half-year's exhibition) as a disarmed gentleman does when he's in the unmerciful fingers of Serjeants. Marry, I will allow you to sweat privately, and tear six or seven score pair[1] of cards, be the damnation of some dozen or twenty bale of dice, and forswear play a thousand times in an hour, but not swear. Dice yourself into your shirt: and, if you have a beard that your friend will lend but an angel upon, shave it off, and pawn that, rather than to go home blind[2] to your lodging. Further, it is to be remembered, he that is a great gamester may be trusted for a quarter's board at all times, and apparel provided, if need be.

At your twelvepenny Ordinary, you may give any Justice of Peace, or young Knight (if he sit but one degree towards the equinoctial of the saltseller) leave to pay for the wine; and he shall not refuse it, though it be a week before the receiving of his quarter's rent, which is a time albeit of good hope, yet of present necessity.

Thomas Dekker.

[1] Packs. [2] Penniless.

THREE CHARACTERS

I

A WORTHY COMMANDER IN THE WARS

IS one that accounts learning the nourishment of military virtue, and lays that as his first foundation. He never bloudies his sword but in heat of battle; and had rather save one of his own soldiers than kill ten of his enemies. He accounts it an idle, vainglorious, and suspected bounty to be full of good words; his rewarding, therefore, of the deserver arrives so timely, that his liberality can never be said to be gouty-handed. He holds it next his creed, that no coward can be an honest man, and dare die in it. He doth not think his body yields a more spreading shadow after a victory than before; and when he looks upon his enemy's dead body, 'tis with a kind of noble heaviness, not insultation; he is so honourably merciful to women in surprisal, that only makes him an excellent courtier. He knows the hazard of battles, not the pomp of ceremonies, are soldiers' best theatres, and strives to gain reputation, not by the multitude, but by the greatness of his actions. He is the first in giving the charge, and the last in retiring his foot. Equal toil he endures with the common soldier: from his example they all take fire, as one torch lights many. He understands in war there is no mean to err twice; the first, and least fault being sufficient to ruin an army: faults, therefore, he pardons none; they that are presidents of disorder, or mutiny, repair it by being examples of his justice. Besiege him never so strictly, so long as the air is not cut from him, his heart faints not. He hath learned so well to make use of a victory, as to get it, and in pursuing his enemy like a whirlwind carries all afore him; being assured, if ever a man would benefit himself upon his foe, then is the time, when they have lost force, wisdom,

Overbury
1616

Overbury 1616

courage, and reputation. **The goodness of his cause is the** special motive to his valour; **never** is he known to slight the weakest enemy that comes **armed** against him in the hand of justice. **Hasty** and **overmuch heat he** accounts the stepdame **to** all great actions, that will **not** suffer them to thrive: if **he** cannot overcome his enemy **by** force, he **does** it by time. If ever he shake hands with **war, he can** die more calmly than most courtiers, for his continual dangers have **been, as it** were, so many meditations of death; he thinks not out of his own calling when he accounts life a continual warfare, and his prayers then best become him when armed *cap-à-pie*. He utters them like the great Hebrew general, **on** horseback. **He casts a** smiling contempt upon calumny, **it meets** him as if **glass** should encounter adamant. He thinks war is **never to be** given **o'er,** but on one of these three conditions: an assured peace, absolute victory, or an honest death. Lastly, when peace folds **him** up, his silver head should lean near **the golden sceptre, and die in** his prince's bosom.

II

A TINKER

Is **a movable: for** he hath no abiding place. By his motion **he** gathers heat, thence his choleric nature. He seems to be very devout, for his life is a continual pilgrimage, and sometimes in humility goes barefoot, thereon making necessity a virtue. His house is as ancient as Tubal Cain's, and so is [he] a runagate by antiquity: yet he proves himself a gallant, for he carries all his wealth upon his back; or a philosopher, for he bears all his substance about him. From his art was music first invented, and therefore is he always furnished with a song: to which his hammer keeping tune, proves that he was the first founder of the kettle-drum. Note, that where the best ale is, there stands his music most upon crotchets. The companion of his travels is some foul, sunburnt quean, that since the terrible Statute recanted gipsyism, and is turned pedleress. So marches he all over England with his bag and baggage. His conversation is unreprovable; for he is ever mending. He observes truly the statutes, and therefore he can rather steal than beg, in which he is unremovably constant in spite of whips or imprisonment: and a so strong enemy to idleness, that in mending one hole he had rather make three than want work, and when he hath done he throws the wallet of his faults behind him. He embraceth naturally ancient custom, conversing in open fields and lowly cottages. If he visit cities or towns, 'tis but to deal upon the imperfections of our weaker vessels. His tongue is very voluble, which with canting proves him a linguist. He is entertained in every place, but enters no further than the door, to avoid suspicion. Some would take him to be a coward; but believe it, he is a lad of mettle, his valour is commonly three or four yards long, fastened to a pike in the end for flying off. He is very provident, for he will fight but with one at once, and then also he had rather submit than be counted obstinate. To conclude, if he 'scape Tyburn and Banbury he dies a beggar.

Overbury 1616

III

A FAIR AND HAPPY MILK-MAID

Is a country wench, that is so far from making herself beautiful by art, that one look of hers is able to put all face-physic out of countenance. She knows a fair look is but a dumb orator to commend virtue, therefore minds it not. All her excellencies stand in her so silently, as if they had stolen upon her without her knowledge. The lining of her apparel (which is herself) is far better than outsides of tissue: for though she be not arrayed in the spoil of the

Overbury 1616

silk-worm, she is decked in innocency, a far better wearing. She doth not, with lying long abed, spoil both her complexion and conditions; nature hath taught her too immoderate sleep is rust to the soul: she rises, therefore, with chanticleer, her dame's cock, and at night makes the lamb her curfew. In milking a cow, and straining the teats through her fingers, it seems that so sweet a milk-press makes the milk the whiter or sweeter; for never came almond glove or aromatic ointment on her palm to taint it. The golden ears of corn fall and kiss her feet when she reaps them, as if they wish to be bound and led prisoners by the same hand that felled them. Her breath is her own which scents all the year long of June, like a new made haycock. She makes her hand hard with labour, and her heart soft with pity: and when winter evenings fall early (sitting at her merry wheel) she sings a defiance to the giddy wheel of fortune. She doth all things with so sweet a grace, it seems ignorance will not suffer her to do ill, being her mind is to do well. She bestows her year's wages at next fair; and in choosing her garments, counts no bravery in the world like decency. The garden and bee-hive are all her physic and chirurgery, and she lives the longer for it. She dares go alone and unfold sheep in the night, and fears no manner of ill, because she means none: yet to say truth, she is never alone, for she is still accompanied with old songs, honest thoughts, and prayers, but short ones; yet they have their efficacy, in that they are not palled with ensuing idle cogitations. Lastly, her dreams are so chaste that she dare tell them; only a Friday's dream is all her superstition: that she conceals for fear of anger. Thus lives she, and all her care is she may die in the spring-time, to have store of flowers stuck upon her winding-sheet.

Sir Thomas Overbury.

THE DELIGHTFUL PASSAGE OF THE PUPPET-PLAY

HERE Tyrians and Trojans were all silent, I mean all the spectators of the motion [1] had their ears hanged upon the interpreter's mouth, that should declare the wonders. By and by there was a great sound of kettle-drums and trumpets, and a volley of great-shot within the motion, which passing away briefly, the boy began to raise his voice and to say: 'This true history, which is here represented to you, is taken word for word out of the French Chronicles and the Spanish Romants, which are in everybody's mouth, and sung by boys up and down the streets. It treats of the liberty that Signor Don Gayferos gave to Melisendra, his wife, that was imprisoned by the Moors in Spain, in the city of Sansuenna, which was then so called, and now Saragosa; and look you there how Don Gayferos is playing at tables according to the song:

Shelton
1620

> "Now Don Gayferos at Tables doth play,
> Unmindful of Melisendra away."

And that personage that peeps out there with a crown on his head and a sceptre in his hand is the Emperor Charlemaine, the supposed father of the said Melisendra, who, grieved with the sloth and neglect of his son-in-law, comes to chide him: and mark with what vehemency and earnestness he rates him, as if he meant to give him half-a-dozen cons [2] with his sceptre. Some authors there be that say he did, and sound ones too; and after he had told him many things concerning the danger of his reputation, if he did not free his spouse, 'twas said he told him "I have said enough; look to it." Look ye, Sir, again, how the Emperor turns his

[1] Puppet show.   [2] Raps.

Shelton
1620

back, and **in what case he leaves** Don Gayferos, **who,** all enraged, flings the tables and **the** tablemen from him, and hastily calls for his armour, **and** borrows his cousin-german Roldan his sword Durindana, **who** offers him his company in this difficult enterprise. But **the valorous** enraged knight would not accept it, saying, that **he is** sufficient to free his spouse, though she were put in the deep centre of the earth : and now **he** goes to arm himself for his journey.

'Now turn your eyes to yonder tower that appears, for you must suppose it is one of the towers of the Castle of Saragosa, **which** is now called the Aliaferia, and that lady that appears **in** the window, clad **in a Moorish** habit, is the peerless **Melisendra,** that many a time looks towards France, thinking **on Paris** and her spouse, the **only comforts** in her imprisonment. Behold, also, a strange **accident** now that happens, perhaps never the like seen! **See** you not **that** Moor that comes fair and softly, with his finger **in** his mouth, behind Melisendra? Look what a smack he gives **her** in the midst of her lips, and how suddenly she begins to spit and to wipe **them** with her white smock sleeve, and how she laments, and **for very** anguish despiteously roots up her fair hairs, as if they **were to** blame for this wickedness. Mark you, also, that grave **Moor** that stands **in** that open gallery, it is Marsilius, King **of** Sansuenna, who, when he saw the Moor's sauciness, although he were **a** kinsman and a great favourite of his, he commanded him straight to be apprehended, and to have two hundred stripes given him, and to be carried through the chief streets of the city with minstrels before and rods of justice behind. And look ye how the sentence **is** put in execution, before the fault be scarce committed; for your Moors use not (as we do) any legal proceeding.'
'Child, child' (cried Don Quixote aloud), 'on with your story in a direct line, and fall not into your crooks and your transversals, for to verify **a** thing I tell you there had need **be a** legal proceeding.' Then Master Peter, too, said from

THE DELIGHTFUL PASSAGE OF THE PUPPET-PLAY 263

within: 'Boy, fall not you to your flourishes, but do as that Shelton
gentleman commands you, which is the best course. Sing 1620
you your plain-song, and meddle not with the treble, lest
the strings break.' 'I will, master' (said the boy), and proceeded, saying:

'He that you see there' (quoth he) 'on horseback, clad in
a Gascoigne cloak, is Don Gayferos himself, to whom his wife
(now revenged on the Moor for his boldness) shows herself
from the battlements of the castle, taking him to be some
passenger with whom she passed all the discourse mentioned
in the Romant, that says:

> "Friend, if toward France you go,
> Ask if Gayferos be there or no."

The rest I omit, for all prolixity is irksome; 'tis sufficient
that you see there how Don Gayferos discovers himself, and
by Melisendra's jocund behaviour we may imagine she knows
him, and the rather because now we see she lets herself
down from a bay-window to ride away behind her good
spouse; but alas, unhappy creature, one of the skirts of her
kirtle hath caught upon one of the iron bars of the window,
and she hovers in the air without possibility of coming to
the ground; but see how pitiful heaven relieves her in her
greatest necessity! for Don Gayferos comes, and, without
any care of her rich kirtle, lays hold of it, and forcibly brings
her down with him, and at one hoist sets her astride upon his
horse's crupper, and commands her to sit fast and clasp her
arms about him that she fall not; for Melisendra was not
used to that kind of riding. Look you how the horse by
its neighing shows that he is proud with the burden of his
valiant master and fair mistress. Look how they turn their
backs to the city, and merrily take their way toward Paris.
Peace be with you, O peerless couple of true lovers! Safely
may you arrive at your desired country, without fortune's
hindering your prosperous voyage! May your friends and

Shelton 1620

kindred see you enjoy the rest of your years (as many as Nestor's) peaceably!'

Here Master Peter cried out aloud again, saying: 'Plainness, good boy, do not you soar so high, this affectation is scurvy.' The interpreter answered nothing but went on saying: 'There wanted not some idle spectators that pry into everything, who saw the going down of Melisendra, and gave Marsilius notice of it, who straight commanded to sound an alarm; and now behold how fast the city even sinks again with the noise of bells that sound in the high towers of the Mesquits.'[1]

'There you are out, boy' (said Don Quixote), ' and Master Peter is very improper in his bells; for amongst Moors you have no bells, but kettledrums and a kind of shawms that be like our waits; so that your sounding of bells in Sansuenna is a most idle foppery.' 'Stand not upon trifles, Signor Don Quixote' (said Master Peter), 'and so strictly upon everything, for we shall not know how to please you. Have you not a thousand comedies ordinarily represented as full of incongruities and absurdities, and yet they run their career happily, and are heard not only with applause, but great admiration also? On boy, say on, and so I fill my purse, let there be as many improprieties as motes in the sun.' 'You are in the right' (quoth Don Quixote), and the boy proceeded:

'Look what a company of gallant knights go out of the city in pursuit of the Catholic lovers, how many trumpets sound, how many shawms play, how many drums and kettles make a noise. I fear me they will overtake them, and bring them back both bound to the same horse's tail, which would be a horrible spectacle.'

Don Quixote, seeing and hearing such a deal of Moorism, and such a coil, he thought fit to succour those that fled. So, standing up, with a loud voice, he cried out: 'I will never consent while I live that in my presence such an outrage as

[1] 'Moorish Churches.'

this be offered to so valiant and to so amorous a bold knight as Don Gayferos. Stay, you base scoundrels, do not you follow or persecute him: if you do you must first wage war with me.' So doing and speaking, he unsheathed his sword, and at one frisk he got to the motion, and with an unseen, posting fury he began to rain strokes upon the Puppetish Moorism, overthrowing some and beheading others, maiming this and cutting in pieces that; and amongst many other blows he fetched one so downright that, had not Master Peter tumbled and squatted down, he had clipped his mazzard as easily as if it had been made of march-pane. Master Peter cried out, saying: 'Hold, Signor Don Quixote, hold; and know that these you hurl down, destroy, and kill are not real Moors, but shapes made of pasteboard: look you, look you now (wretch that I am), he spoils all, and undoes me.' But, for all this, Don Quixote still multiplied his slashes, doubling and redoubling his blows as thick as hops.

Shelton
1620

And in a word, in less than two credos, he cast down the whole motion (all the tackling first cut to fitters, and all the puppets). King Marsilius was sore wounded, and the Emperor Charlemaine his head and crown were parted in two places; the Senate and Auditors were all in a hurry; and the ape got up to the top of the house, and so out of the window; the Scholar was frighted; the Page clean dastarded; and even Sancho himself was in a terrible perplexity, for (as he swore after the storm was past) he never saw his master so outrageous.

The general ruin of the motion thus performed, Don Quixote began to be somewhat pacified, and said: 'Now would I have all those here at this instant before me that believe not how profitable knights-errant are to the world; and had not I been now present what (I marvel) would have become of Signor Don Gayferos and the fair Melisendra? I warrant, ere this, those dogs would have overtaken, and showed them some foul play: when all is done, long live knight-errantry above all things living in the world!'

Shelton 1620

'Long live it, in **God's name**' (said Master **Peter** again, with a pitiful voice), 'and **may I die** since I live **to** be so unhappy as to say with **King** Don Rodrigo, yesterday I was Lord of all Spain, but to-day have not a battlement I can call mine. . . . It is **not** yet half an hour, scarce half **a** minute, **that I** was master **of** kings and emperors, had my stables, coffers, and bags full of horses and treasure; but now I am desolate, dejected, and poor; and, to add more affliction, without my ape, that before I can catch him again **I am like to sweat for** it, and all through the inconsiderate furies of **this Sir** Knight, who is said to protect the **fatherless, to rectify wrongs,** and to do other charitable works, **but** to me only this his **generous** intention hath been defective, I thank God **for it.** In fine, it could be none but the Knight of the Sorrowful Countenance that discountenanced me and mine.' Sancho grew **compassionate to** hear Master Peter's lamentation, and said: 'Weep not nor grieve, Master Peter, for thou breakest my heart; and let me tell thee that my master Don Quixote is so scrupulous and Catholical a Christian that if he fall into the reckoning that he hath done thee any wrong, he knows how, and will satisfy it with much advantage.' 'If' (said Master Peter) 'Don Quixote would but pay me for some **part of the pieces that** he hath spoiled I should be contented, **and his** worship might not be troubled in conscience; for he that keeps that that is another man's against the owner's will, and restores it not, can hardly be saved.'

'That's true' (quoth **Don** Quixote), 'but hitherto, Master Peter, I know not whether I have detained ought of yours.' 'No? not?' said Master Peter: 'why these poor relics that lie upon **the** hard and barren earth, who scattered and annihilated them but the invincible force of that powerful arm? **and** whose were those bodies but mine? and with whom did I maintain myself but with them?' 'Well, I now' (said Don Quixote) 'verily believe what **I** have done often, that the **enchanters** that persecute me do nothing but put shapes, really as they are before my eyes, and by and by truck and change them at their pleasures. Verily, my masters, you that hear me, I tell you all that here passed seemed to me to be really so, and immediately that that Melisendra was Melisendra; Don Gayferos, Don Gayferos; and Marsilius, Marsilius; and Charlemaine, Charlemaine. And this was it that stirred up my choler; and, to accomplish my profession of knight-errant, my meaning was to succour those that fled, and to this good purpose I did all that you have seen: which, if it fell out unluckily, 'twas no fault of mine, but of my wicked persecutors; yet for all this error (though it proceeded from no malice of mine) I myself will condemn myself in the charge; let Master Peter see what he will have for the spoiled pieces, and I will pay it all in present current coin of Castile.'

Master Peter made him a lowleg, saying: 'I could expect no less from the unheard of christianity of the most valorous Don Quixote de la Mancha, the true succourer and bulwark of all those that be in need and necessity, or wandering vagamunds; and now let the Venter[1] and the Grand Sancho be arbitrators, and price-setters between your worship and me, and let them say what every torn piece was worth.' The Venter and Sancho both agreed; and by and by Master Peter reached up Marsilius, King of Saragosa, headless, and said: 'You see how impossible it is for this Prince to return to his first being, and therefore, saving your better judgments, I think fit to have for him two shillings and threepence.'

'On then,' quoth Don Quixote. 'Then for this' (quoth Master Peter) 'that is parted from head to foot' (taking the Emperor Charlemaine up), 'I think two shillings and sevenpence halfpenny is little enough.' 'Not very little,' quoth Sancho. 'Nor much,' said the Venter; 'but moderate the bargain, and let him have half-a-crown.' 'Let him have his full asking' (said Don Quixote); 'for, for such a mishap as

Shelton 1620

[1] Sp. *Ventero*=innkeeper.

Shelton 1620

this, we'll ne'er stand upon **three** halfpence more or less, and make an end quickly, Master Peter, for it is near supper-time, and I have certain suspicions that I shall eat.' 'For this puppet,' said Master Peter, 'without a nose and an eye wanting, of the fair Melisendra, I **ask** but in justice fourteenpence halfpenny.'

'Now the Devil's in it' (said Don Quixote), '**if** Melisendra be not now in France, or upon the borders at least, with her husband, for the horse they rid on to my seeming rather flew **than ran**; and therefore sell me not a cat for a coney, presenting me here, Melisendra, noseless, when she, if the **time require it, is** wantonly solacing with her husband **in** France. God give each man **his own,** Master Peter, let us have plain dealing; and so proceed.' Master Peter, that saw **Don** Quixote **in a wrong vein, and that** he returned to his old theme, thought yet he should **not escape** him, and so replied: 'Indeed this should not be Melisendra, now I think on't, but some one of the damsels **that served her, so** that fivepence for her will content me.'

Thus he went on pricing of other torn puppets, which the arbitrating judges moderated to the satisfaction of both parties, and the whole prices of all were twenty-one shillings and elevenpence, which, when Sancho had disbursed, Master Peter demanded, over and above, twelvepence for his labour to look for the ape. 'Give it him, Sancho' (said Don Quixote), 'not to catch his ape but a monkey,[1] and I would give five pounds for **a** reward to anybody that would certainly tell me that the Lady Melisendra and Don Gayferos were safely arrived in France among their own people.' 'None can better tell than my ape' (said Master Peter), 'though the Devil himself will scarce catch him; **yet I** imagine making much of him and hunger will force him to seek me to-night, and by morning we shall come **together.**'

[1] As we say 'to catch a fox.'

Well, to conclude, the storm of the motion passed and all supped merrily, and like good fellows, at Don Quixote's charge, who was liberal in extremity. Before day, the fellow with the lances and halberts was gone, and somewhat after the Scholar and the Page came to take leave of Don Quixote, the one to return homeward, and the other to prosecute his intended voyage, and, for a relief, Don Quixote gave him six shillings. Master Peter would have no more to do with him, for he knew him too well. So he got up before the sun, and, gathering the relics of the motion together, and his ape, he betook him to his adventures. The Venter, that knew not Don Quixote, wondered as much at his liberality as his madness. I conclude Sancho payed him honestly by his master's order, and, taking leave about eight of the clock, they left the vente,[1] and went on their way, where we must leave them.

Thomas Shelton.

Shelton 1620

THE PROVING OF ALIPIUS

ALIPIUS (having not forsaken that course of the world, which his parents had inculcated so often to him) went before me to Rome, that he might study the laws; where he was, with an incredible appetite, carried away to see the gladiators fight. For when first he was averse and did detest such spectacles as those, certain friends and fellows of his in study, meeting casually one day after dinner, and conducting him with a familiar kind of violence to the amphitheatre (at such time as those tragical and dismal pastimes were presented to the people), he of himself did vehemently resist and refuse to go; yet being forced, he said thus: 'If you drag my body thither, and place it there, shall you therefore be able to make me apply my mind, and open mine eyes

Mathew 1620

---

[1] Sp. *Venta* = inn.

to those spectacles? No; but I will be absent even while I am present; and so will I conquer both them and you.' Whereupon yet they were not the less desirous to lead him on, perhaps out of a kind of curiosity to know whether or no he could be as good as his word.

As soon as they were arrived and placed, that whole world was swelling and even boiling again with those most vast and unnatural entertainments. He, shutting the windows of his eyes, forbade his mind to mingle itself with that mischief; and I would to God he had also stopped his ears! For by occasion of a certain fatal blow which was given, and by a strong cry of the whole people, which rung so loud about him (being overcome by curiosity, and, as it were, resolved that whatsoever it were he would overcome that also, and despise it even after he had seen it), he opened his eyes, and was stricken with a deeper wound in his soul than the other was in his body; and he fell more miserably than the man whom he desired to behold. For upon that fall it was that the cry was made, which entered into his ears and opened his eyes, that there might be a way whereby he also should be wounded and defeated at the heart.

He was at that time a man rather of a bold than of a valiant mind; and so much the weaker he was, for that he presumed upon himself, who ought to have confided only in Thee. For as soon as he beheld that blood, he withal drunk down a kind of savageness of mind, and turned not his head aside, but fastened his sight upon it, and swallowed up the very Furies themselves, and knew not of it; and he was enamoured with the wickedness of those combats, and made drunk with a delight in blood. He was now no more the man that came thither, but he grew to be even one of that common people to which he went, and an entire companion of those that led him. What shall I say more? He beheld them, he cried out for company, he was inflamed with the pleasure of it; and he carried home from thence such a measure of madness as provoked him to return, not only now with them by whom he was formerly debauched, but more earnestly than they, and so far as to be seducing of others. But yet even from thence Thou drewest him with a most powerful and merciful hand, and Thou taughtest him that he was to confide in Thee and not in himself. But this was done long after.

But this was laid up in his memory for his recovery afterward; as also when he studied at Carthage under me, and walking at noon-day in the market-place (considering that which he was to recite, according to the custom of scholars), thou sufferedst him to be apprehended as a thief by the officers of the place. Nor didst Thou, as I think, permit it for any other reason, O our God, but for that he, who was afterward to prove so great a man, might early begin to learn that one man was not easily to condemn another with temerarious cruelty, of whose cause he was juridically to take knowledge. He was walking then alone before the tribunal, with his tables and style in his hand; when behold, a certain young scholar, who was indeed a thief, carrying secretly a hatchet, did enter, without being observed by him, into certain grates of lead which overlooked Silver Street, and he began to cut the lead. But the noise of the hatchet being heard, the silversmiths who dwelt below began to mutter; and sent forth to apprehend whom they should chance to find. And as soon as he overheard their talk he fled away, leaving the instrument behind him, as fearing lest with it, and by it, he might be taken.

But Alipius, who perceived him not as he went in, heard him as he came out; and saw him speedily depart away. And being desirous to understand the cause, went into the place, and finding the hatchet, he paused a while and wondered at it. When behold! they that were sent found him alone with the instrument in his hand, by the noise whereof they were stirred up. They stay him, they draw

Mathew
1620

him along; **and** having **gathered** together the next dwellers of the market-place, they congratulated with themselves for taking such a notorious thief; **and** from thence they were carrying him towards the justice.

Hitherto he was in need to be instructed; but then, O **Lord,** Thou didst instantly come **to the succour of** his innocency, whereof Thou only wert the **witness.** And when he was to be led either to the prison or place **of** punishment, there encountered them a certain architect **who** had the chief care of public buildings. They were particularly glad to meet him, who was often wont to have advertisement of such things as were stolen out **of** the market-place; as **if he** perhaps might **know by whom** this particular offence had **been committed.** But **this** man had often seen Alipius in the house of a certain **senator whom he** used to court, and instantly knowing him, **he took him by the** hand and separated him from that **confusion of people.** And inquiring after **the** cause of that so great mischance, he understood what **had** been done, and willed all them who were there, in rage and tumult, to go along with him; and so they went to the house of that young man who had committed the fact. Now **there was** a boy standing at the door, and he was so young **as that** (being without **fear of** doing his master any hurt thereby) he disclosed **the** whole matter freely, for he was a kind of a foot-boy that followed him to the market; whom afterwards, as soon as Alipius remembered, he intimated so much to the architect. And he showed the hatchet to the boy, asking **him** whose it was, who instantly answered, 'Ours'; then, also, being examined, he confessed the rest. **And** so was this crime removed from Alipius to that house; **and** the multitude being confounded for having already begun to triumph over this man (who futurely was to become a dispenser of Thy word, and an examiner **of** many causes in Thy Church), he departed with increase **of** experience and knowledge.

Sir Tobie Mathew.

A WONDER FOR WISE MEN

THIS King (to speak of him in terms equal to his deserving) was one of the best sort of wonders: a wonder for wise men. He had parts (both in his virtues and his fortune) not so fit for a commonplace as for observation. Certainly he was religious, both in his affection and observance. But as he could see clear (for those times) through superstition; so he would be blinded now and then by human policy. He advanced church-men. He was tender in the privilege of sanctuaries, though they wrought him much mischief. He built and endowed many religious foundations, besides his memorable hospital of the Savoy: and yet was he a great alms-giver in secret; which showed that his works in public were dedicated rather to God's glory than his own. He professed always to love and seek peace; and it was his usual preface in his treaties, that when Christ came into the world peace was sung, and when He went out of the world peace was bequeathed. And this virtue could not proceed out of fear or softness, for he was valiant and active; and therefore no doubt it was truly Christian and moral. Yet he knew the way to peace was not to seem to be desirous to avoid wars. Therefore would he make offers and fames of wars, till he had mended the conditions of peace. It was also much, that one that was so great a lover of peace should be so happy in war. For his arms, either in foreign or civil wars, were never infortunate; neither did he know what a disaster meant. The war of his coming in, and the rebellions of the Earl of Lincoln and the Lord Audley, were ended by victory. The wars of France and Scotland by peaces sought at his hands. That of Brittaine by accident of the Duke's death. The insurrection of the Lord Lovell, and that of Perkin at Exeter and in Kent, by flight of the rebels before they

Bacon
1622

Bacon
1622

came to blows. So that his fortune of arms was still inviolate. The rather sure, for that in the quenching of the commotions of his subjects he ever went in person: sometimes reserving himself to back and second his lieutenants, but ever in action. And yet that was not merely forwardness, but partly distrust of others.

He did much maintain and countenance his laws; which (nevertheless) was no impediment to him to work his will. For it was so handled that neither prerogative nor profit went to diminution. And yet as he would sometimes strain up his laws to his prerogative, so would he also let down his prerogative to his Parliament. For mint and wars and martial discipline (things of absolute power) he would nevertheless bring to Parliament. Justice was well administered in his time, save where the King was party; save also that the Council Table intermeddled too much with *meum* and *tuum*. For it was a very court of justice during his time; especially in the beginning. But in that part both of justice and policy which is the durable part, and cut as it were in brass or marble, which is the making of good laws, he did excel. And with his justice he was also a merciful prince: as in whose time there were but three of the nobility that suffered; the Earl of Warwick; the Lord Chamberlain; and the Lord Audley: though the first two were instead of numbers in the dislike and obloquy of the people. But there were never so great rebellions expiated with so little blood drawn by the hand of justice, as the two rebellions of Blackheath and Exeter. As for the severity used upon those which were taken in Kent, it was but upon a scum of people. His pardons went ever both before and after his sword. But then he had withal a strange kind of interchanging of large and inexpected pardons with severe executions: which (his wisdom considered) could not be imputed to any inconstancy or inequality; but either to some reason which we do not now know, or to a principle he had set unto himself, that he would vary, and try both ways in turn. But the less blood he drew the more he took of treasure: and as some construed it, he was the more sparing in the one that he might be the more pressing in the other; for both would have been intolerable. Of nature assuredly he coveted to accumulate treasure; and was a little poor in admiring riches. The people (into whom there is infused for the preservation of monarchies a natural desire to discharge their princes, though it be with the unjust charge of their counsellors and ministers) did impute this unto Cardinal Morton and Sir Reignold Bray; who as it after appeared (as counsellors of ancient authority with him) did so second his humours, as nevertheless they did temper them. Whereas Empson and Dudley that followed, being persons that had no reputation with him otherwise than by the servile following of his bent, did not give way only (as the first did) but shape him way to those extremities, for which himself was touched with remorse at his death; and which his successor renounced, and sought to purge.

Bacon
1622

This excess of his had at that time many glosses and interpretations. Some thought the continual rebellions wherewith he had been vexed had made him grow to hate his people: some thought it was done to pull down their stomachs and to keep them low: some, for that he would leave his son a golden fleece: some suspected he had some high design upon foreign parts. But those perhaps shall come nearest the truth that fetch not their reasons so far off; but rather impute it to nature, age, peace, and a mind fixed upon no other ambition or pursuit: whereunto I should add, that having every day occasion to take notice of the necessities and shifts for money of other great princes abroad, it did the better by comparison set off to him the felicity of full coffers. As to his expending of treasure, he never spared charge which his affairs required: and in his buildings was magnificent; but his rewards were very limited. So that his

Bacon
1622

liberality was rather upon his own state and memory than upon the deserts of others. He was of an high mind, and loved his own will and his own way; as one that revered himself, and would reign indeed. Had he been a private man he would have been termed proud: but in a wise prince, it was but keeping of distance; which indeed he did towards all; not admitting any near or full approach either to his power or to his secrets. For he was governed by none. His Queen (notwithstanding she had presented him with divers children; and with a crown also, though he would not acknowledge it) could do nothing with him. His mother he reverenced much, heard little. For any person agreeable to him for society (such as was Hastings to King Edward the Fourth, or Charles Brandon after to King Henry the Eighth), he had none; except we should account for such persons Foxe and Bray and Empson, because they were so much with him. But it was but as the instrument is much with the workman. He had nothing in him of vainglory, but yet kept state and majesty to the height; being sensible that majesty maketh the people bow, but vain-glory boweth to them.

To his confederates abroad he was constant and just; but not open. But rather such was his inquiry and such his closeness, as they stood in the light towards him, and he stood in the dark to them; yet without strangeness, but with a semblance of mutual communication of affairs. As for little envies or emulations upon foreign princes (which are frequent with many Kings), he had never any; but went substantially to his own business. Certain it is, that though his reputation was great at home, yet it was greater abroad. For foreigners that could not see the passages of affairs, but made their judgments upon the issues of them, noted that he was ever in strife and ever aloft. It grew also from the airs which the princes and states abroad received from their ambassadors and agents here; which were attending the court in great number; whom he did not only content with courtesy, reward, and privateness; but (upon such conferences as passed with them) put them in admiration to find his universal insight into the affairs of the world: which though he did suck chiefly from themselves, yet that which he had gathered from them all seemed admirable to every one. So that they did write ever to their superiors in high terms concerning his wisdom and art of rule. Nay, when they were returned, they did commonly maintain intelligence with him; such a dexterity he had to impropriate to himself all foreign instruments.

He was careful and liberal to obtain good intelligence from all parts abroad; wherein he did not only use his interest in the liegers here, and his pensioners which he had both in the court of Rome and other the courts of Christendom, but the industry and vigilancy of his own ambassadors in foreign parts. For which purpose his instructions were ever extreme curious and articulate; and in them more articles touching inquisition than touching negotiation: requiring likewise from his ambassadors an answer, in particular distinct articles, respectively to his questions.

As for his secret spials which he did employ both at home and abroad, by them to discover what practices and conspiracies were against him; surely his case required it; he had such moles perpetually working and casting to undermine him. Neither can it be reprehended; for if spials be lawful against lawful enemies, much more against conspirators and traitors. But indeed to give them credence by oaths or curses, that cannot be well maintained; for those are too holy vestments for a disguise. Yet surely there was this further good in his employing of these flies[1] and familiars; that as the use of them was cause that many conspiracies were revealed, so the fame and suspicion of them kept (no doubt) many conspiracies from being attempted.

Bacon 1622

[1] Familiar and menial spirits.

Bacon
1622

Towards his Queen he was nothing uxorious; nor scarce indulgent; but companiable and respective, and without jealousy. Towards his children he was full of paternal affection, careful of their education, aspiring to their high advancement, regular to see that they should not want of any due honour and respect; but not greatly willing to cast any popular lustre upon them.

To his Council he did refer much, and sat oft in person; knowing it to be the way to assist his power and inform his judgment: in which respect also he was fairly patient of liberty both of advice and of vote, till himself were declared. He kept a strait hand on his nobility, and chose rather to advance clergymen and lawyers, which were more obsequious to him, but had less interest in the people; which made for his absoluteness, but not for his safety. Insomuch as I am persuaded it was one of the causes of his troublesome reign. For that his nobles, though they were loyal and obedient, yet did not co-operate with him, but let every man go his own way. He was not afraid of an able man, as Lewis the Eleventh was. But contrariwise he was served by the ablest men that then were to be found; without which his affairs could not have prospered as they did. For war, Bedford, Oxford, Surrey, Dawbeny, Brooke, Poynings. For other affairs, Morton, Foxe, Bray, the Prior of Lanthony, Warham, Urswick, Hussey, Frowick, and others. Neither did he care how cunning they were that he did employ: for he thought himself to have the master-reach. And as he chose well, so he held them up well. For it is a strange thing, that though he were a dark prince, and infinitely suspicious, and his times full of secret conspiracies and troubles; yet in twenty-four years' reign he never put down or discomposed Councillor or near servant, save only Stanley the Lord Chamberlain. As for the disposition of his subjects in general towards him, it stood thus with him; that of the three affections which naturally tie the hearts of the subjects

to their sovereign,—love, fear, and reverence—he had the
last in height; the second in good measure; and so little of
the first, as he was beholding to the other two.

He was a Prince, sad, serious, and full of thoughts and
secret observations; and full of notes and memorials of his
own hand, especially touching persons; as whom to employ,
whom to reward, whom to inquire of, whom to beware of,
what were the dependencies, what were the factions, and
the like; keeping (as it were) a journal of his thoughts.
There is to this day a merry tale: that his monkey (set on
as it was thought by one of his Chamber) tore his principal
note-book all to pieces, when by chance it lay forth: whereat the Court which liked not those pensive accounts was
almost tickled with sport.

He was indeed full of apprehensions and suspicions. But
as he did easily take them, so he did easily check them and
master them; whereby they were not dangerous, but
troubled himself more than others. It is true, his thoughts
were so many, as they could not well always stand together;
but that which did good one way, did hurt another. Neither
did he at some times weigh them aright in their proportions.
Certainly that rumour which did him so much mischief
(that the Duke of York should be saved and alive) was (at
the first) of his own nourishing, because he would have more
reason not to reign in the right of his wife. He was affable,
and both well and fair spoken; and would use strange
sweetness and blandishments of words, where he desired
to effect or persuade anything that he took to heart. He
was rather studious than learned; reading most books that
were of any worth, in the French tongue. Yet he understood the Latin, as appeareth in that Cardinal Hadrian and
others, who could very well have written French, did use to
write to him in Latin.

For his pleasures, there is no news of them. And yet by
his instructions to Marsin and Stile touching the Queen of

Bacon
1622

Bacon
1622

Naples, it seemeth he could interrogate well touching beauty. He did by pleasures as great princes do by banquets, come and look **a** little upon them, **and** turn away. For never prince **was** more wholly given **to his** affairs, nor in them more of himself: insomuch as in triumphs of jousts and tourneys and balls and masques (which they then called disguises) he **was** rather a princely and gentle **spectator** than seemed much to be delighted.

    No doubt, in him as in all men (and most of all in Kings) **his fortune** wrought upon his nature, and his nature upon his **fortune. He** attained to the crown, not only from a private **fortune,** which might endow **him** with moderation; but also from the fortune of **an** exiled man, **which** had quickened in **him all seeds of observation and industry.** And his times being rather prosperous **than** calm, had raised **his** confidence **by** success, but almost marred **his** nature by troubles. His **wisdom,** by often evading from perils, was turned rather into a dexterity to deliver himself from dangers when they pressed him, than into **a** providence **to prevent and remove** them afar off. And even **in nature, the** sight **of his** mind was like **some** sights of **eyes;** rather strong **at hand** than to carry **afar** off. For his **wit** increased upon the occasion; and so much **the more** if the occasion were sharpened by danger. Again, **whether it** were the shortness of his foresight, or the strength **of his** will, **or the** dazzling of his suspicions, or what **it was; certain it is** that the perpetual troubles of his fortunes **(there** being **no** more matter out of which they grew) could not have **been** without some great defects and **main** errors in his nature, customs, and proceedings, which **he had** enough **to** do **to save and** help with a thousand little industries and watches. **But those** do best appear in the **story** itself. Yet **take him** with all his defects, if a man **should** compare him **with the** Kings his concurrents in France and Spain, he shall **find him** more politic than Lewis the Twelfth **of** France, **and** more entire and sincere than Ferdinando of Spain. But if you shall change Lewis the Twelfth for Lewis the Eleventh, who lived a little before, then the consort is more perfect. For that Lewis the Eleventh, Ferdinando, and Henry may be esteemed for the *tres magi* of Kings of those ages. To conclude, if this King did no greater matters, it was long of himself; for what he minded he compassed.

Bacon 1622

He was a comely personage, a little above just stature, well and straight limbed, but slender. His countenance was reverend, and a little like a churchman: and as it was not strange or dark, so neither was it winning or pleasing, but as the face of one well disposed. But it was to the disadvantage of the painter, for it was best when he spake.

His worth may bear a tale or two, that may put upon him somewhat that may seem divine. When the Lady Margaret his mother had divers great suitors for marriage, she dreamed one night that one in the likeness of a bishop in pontifical habit did tender her Edmund, Earl of Richmond (the King's father), for her husband. Neither had she ever any child but the King, though she had three husbands. One day when King Henry the Sixth (whose innocency gave him holiness) was washing his hands at a great feast, and cast his eye upon King Henry, then a young youth, he said: 'This is the lad that shall possess quietly that that we now strive for.' But that that was truly divine in him, was that he had the fortune of a true Christian as well as of a great King, in living exercised and dying repentant. So as he had an happy warfare in both conflicts, both of sin and the cross.

He was born at Pembroke Castle, and lieth buried at Westminster, in one of the stateliest and daintiest monuments of Europe, both for the chapel and for the sepulchre. So that he dwelleth more richly dead, in the monument of his tomb, than he did alive in Richmond or any of his palaces. I could wish he did the like in this monument of his fame.

Francis Bacon, Viscount St. Alban.

STEPS IN HIS SICKNESS

MEDITATION I

Donne
1624

VARIABLE, and therefore miserable condition of man; this minute I was well, and am ill, this minute. I am surprised with a sudden change, and alteration to worse, and can impute it to no cause, nor call it by any name. We study health, and we deliberate upon our meats, and drink, and air, and exercises, and we hew, and we polish every stone that goes to that building; and so our health is a long and a regular work; but in a minute a cannon batters all; overthrows all; diminishes all: a sickness unprevented for all our diligence, unsuspected for all our curiosity; nay, undeserved, if we consider only disorder, summons us, destroys us in an instant. O miserable condition of man! which was not imprinted by God, who as He is immortal Himself, had put a coal, a beam of immortality into us, which we might have blown into a flame, but blew it out by our first sin; we beggared ourselves by hearkening after false riches, and infatuated ourselves by hearkening after false knowledge. So that now, we do not only die, but die upon the rack, die by the torment of sickness; nor that only, but are preafflicted, superafflicted with these jealousies and suspicions, and apprehensions of sickness, before we can call it a sickness: we are not sure we are ill; one hand asks the other by the pulse, and our eye asks our own urine how we do. O multiplied misery! we die, and cannot enjoy death, because we die in this torment of sickness; we are tormented with sickness, and cannot stay till the torment come, but preapprehensions and presages prophesy those torments, which induce that death before either come; and our dissolution is conceived in these first changes, quickened in the sickness itself, and born in death, which bears date from these first changes. Is this the honour which man hath by being a little world, that he hath these earthquakes in himself, sudden shakings, these lightnings, sudden flashes; these thunders, sudden noises; these eclipses, sudden effuscations, and darkening of his senses; these blazing stars, sudden fiery exhalations; these rivers of blood, sudden red waters? Is he a world to himself only therefore, that he hath enough in himself, not only to destroy and execute himself, but to presage that execution upon himself? to assist the sickness, to antedate the sickness, to make the sickness the more irremediable by sad apprehensions, and as if he would make a fire the more vehement, by sprinkling water upon the coals, so to wrap a hot fever in cold melancholy, lest the fever alone should not destroy fast enough without this contribution, nor perfect the work (which is destruction) except we joined an artificial sickness of our own melancholy, to our natural, our unnatural fever? O perplexed discomposition! O riddling distemper! O miserable condition of man!

MEDITATION II

The heavens are not the less constant, because they move continually, because they move continually one and the same way. The earth is not the more constant, because it lies still continually, because continually it changes and melts in all the parts thereof. Man, who is the noblest part of the earth, melts so away as if he were a statue, not of earth, but of snow. We see his own envy melts him, he grows lean with that; he will say, another's beauty melts him; but he feels that a fever doth not melt him like snow, but pour him out like lead, like iron, like brass melted in a furnace; it doth not only melt him, but calcine him, reduce him to atoms, and to ashes, not to water, but to lime. And how quickly? Sooner than thou canst receive an answer, sooner than thou canst conceive the question; earth is the centre of **my body, heaven is the centre of my** soul: these two are the natural places **of** these two; but those **go** not to these two in an equal pace: my body falls down without pushing, my soul does not go **up** without pulling: ascension is my soul's pace and measure, but precipitation my body's: and even angels, whose home is heaven, and who are winged too, yet **had** a ladder to go to heaven **by** steps. The sun **which** goes **so many** miles in a minute, **the stars** of the firmament which go so very many more, go not so **fast, as my body** to the earth. In the same instant that I **feel** the first attempt of **the** disease, **I** feel the victory; in the twinkling **of** an eye, I can **scarce see**; instantly the taste is insipid and **fatuous**; instantly the **appetite** is dull and desireless; instantly **the knees are sinking and** strengthless; and in an instant sleep, which **is the** picture, **the copy** of death, is taken away, that the original, death itself, may succeed, and that so I might have death **to the life.** It was part of Adam's punishment: *In the* **sweat** *of* **thy brows** *thou shalt eat thy bread*: **it** is multiplied **to** me, **I have** earned bread **in** the sweat of **my** brows, in the labour **of my calling, and I** have **it; and** I sweat again, and again, **from the brow to** the sole of the foot, but I eat no bread, I taste no sustenance: miserable distribution of mankind, where one-half lacks meat, and the other stomach.

MEDITATION III

We attribute but one privilege and advantage to man's body, above other moving creatures: that he is not as others, grovelling, but of an erect, of an upright form, naturally built, and disposed **to the** contemplation of heaven. Indeed it is a thankful form, and recompenses that soul, **which gives** it, with carrying that soul so many foot higher **towards** heaven. Other creatures look to the earth; and even that is no unfit object, no unfit contemplation for man;

for thither he must come; but because man is not to stay there, as other creatures are, man in his natural form is carried to the contemplation of that place, which is his home, heaven. This is man's prerogative: but what state hath he in this dignity? A fever can fillip him down, a fever can depose him; a fever can bring that head, which yesterday carried a crown of gold, five foot towards a crown of glory, as low as his own foot, to-day. When God came to breathe into man the breath of life, He found him flat upon the ground; when He comes to withdraw that breath from him again, He prepares him to it, by laying him flat upon his bed. Scarce any prison so close, that affords not the prisoner two or three steps. The anchorites that barked themselves up in hollow trees, and immured themselves in hollow walls; that perverse man, that barrelled himself in a tub, all could stand, or sit, and enjoy some change of posture. A sickbed is a grave, and all that the patient says there is but a varying of his own epitaph. Every night's bed is a type of the grave; at night we tell our servants at what hour we will rise; here we cannot tell ourselves, at what day, what week, what month. Here the head lies as low as the foot; the head of the people, as low as they whom those feet trod upon; and that hand that signed pardons, is too weak to beg his own, if he might have it for lifting up that hand: strange fetters to the feet, strange manacles to the hands, when the feet and hands are bound so much the faster, by how much the cords are slacker; so much the less able to do their offices, by how much more the sinews and ligaments are the looser. In the grave I may speak through the stones, in the voice of my friends, in the accents of those words, which their love may afford my memory; here I am mine own ghost, and rather affright my beholders, than instruct them; they conceive the worst of me now, and yet fear worse; they give me for dead now, and yet wonder how I do, when they wake at midnight, and ask

Donne
1624

how I do to-morrow. Miserable, and (though common to all) inhuman posture, **where I** must practise my lying in the grave, **by** lying still, and not practise my resurrection, by rising any more.

MEDITATION IV

IT **is too** little to call man a little world : except God, man **is a** diminutive to nothing. Man consists of more pieces, more parts, than the world ; than the world doth, nay, than **the** world is. And **if** those pieces were extended and stretched out in **man, as** they are in the world, man would be the giant, and the **world the dwarf,** the world but the map, and the **man the world.** If all the veins in our bodies were extended to rivers, **and all the sinews** to veins of **mines,** and all the muscles, that lie upon one another, **to** hills, and all the bones to quarries **of stones,** and all the other pieces to the proportion of those which correspond to them **in** the world, the air would be too little for this **orb of man to** move in, the firmament would be but enough for this star ; **for,** as the whole world has nothing, to which something in man doth not answer, so hath man many pieces, of which the whole world hath no representation. Enlarge this meditation upon this great world, man, so far, as to consider **the** immensity of the creatures this world produces : our creatures are our thoughts, creatures that are born giants ; that reach **from** east to west, from earth **to** heaven, that do not **only** bestride all the sea and land, but span the sun and firmament at once ; my thoughts reach all, comprehend all. Inexplicable mystery : **I** their creator am in a close prison, in a sick bed, anywhere, and any one of my creatures, my thoughts, is with the sun, and beyond the sun, overtakes the sun, and overgoes the sun in one pace, one step, everywhere. And then as the other world produces **serpents, and vipers,** malignant and venomous creatures, and worms, and caterpillars, that endeavour to devour that world produces them, and monsters compiled and complicated of diverse parents and kinds, so this world, ourselves, produces all these in us, in producing diseases and sicknesses of all those sorts: venomous and infectious diseases, feeding and consuming diseases, and manifold and entangled diseases made up of many several ones. And can the other world name so many venomous, so many consuming, so many monstrous creatures, as we can diseases of all those kinds? O miserable abundance, O beggarly riches! How much do we lack of having remedies for every disease, when as yet we have not names for them? But we have a Hercules against these giants, these monsters; that is, the physician: he musters up all the forces of the other world to succour this; all nature to relieve man. We have the physician, but we are not the physician. Here we shrink in our proportion, sink in our dignity, in respect of very mean creatures, who are physicians to themselves. The hart that is pursued and wounded, they say, knows an herb which, being eaten, throws off the arrow: a strange kind of vomit. The dog that pursues it, though he be subject to sickness, even proverbially, knows his grass that recovers him. And it may be true, that the drugger is as near to man as to other creatures; it may be that obvious and present simples, easy to be had, would cure him; but the apothecary is not so near him, nor the physician so near him, as they two are to other creatures; man hath not that innate instinct to apply those natural medicines to his present danger as those inferior creatures have; he is not his own apothecary, his own physician, as they are. Call back, therefore, thy meditations again, and bring it down: What is become of man's great extent and proportion, when himself shrinks himself, and consumes himself to an handful of dust? What is become of his soaring thoughts, his compassing thoughts, when himself brings himself to the ignorance, to the thoughtlessness

Donne
1624

Donne 1624 — of the grave? **His diseases are** his own, but the physician not; he hath them **at** home, but he must send for the physician.

John Donne, Dean of St. Paul's.

TWO PILGRIMS

I

THE DEATH OF JOHN DAVYS

Mitchelbourne 1625

HERE **as I** stood for Patane, about the 27th of December, I met with **a** junk of the Japons, which had been pirating **along** the coast of China and Camboia. Their Pilot being **dead, with** ignorance and foul weather they had cast away their **ship on the** sholds of the great island Borneo; and to enter **into** the country of Borneo they durst not: for the Japons are not suffered to land in any port in India with weapons, being accounted a people so desperate **and** daring, that they are feared in all places where they come. These people, their ship being **splitted,** with their shallops entered this junk, wherein I met them, which was of Patane, and killed all **the** people save one old Pilot. This junk was laden with rice, which when they had possessed and furnished with such furniture, necessaries, and arms as they saved out of their sunken ship, they shaped their course for Japan; but the badness of their junk, contrary winds, and unseasonableness of the year forced them **to** leeward, which was the cause of mine unlucky meeting them.

After I had hailed them, and made them come to leeward, sending my boat aboard them, I found them by their men and furniture very unproportionable for such a ship as they were **in,** which was a junk not above seventy **tons in** burthen, and they were ninety men, and most of them in too gallant **a** habit for sailors, and such an equality of behaviour among them that they seemed all fellows; yet one among them there was that they called Captain, but gave him little respect. I caused them to come to an anchor, and upon further examination I found their lading to be only rice, and for the most part spilt with wet, for their ship was leak both under and above water. Upon questioning with them, I understood them to be men of war, that had pillaged on the coast of China and Camboia, and, as I said before, had cast away their ship on the sholds of Bornea. Here we rode at anchor under a small island, near to the Isle of Bintam, two days entertaining them with good usage, not taking anything from them, thinking to have gathered by their knowledge the place and passage of certain ships, on the coast of China to have made my voyage. But these rogues, being desperate in winds and fortunes, being hopeless in that paltry junk ever to return to their country, resolved with themselves either to gain my ship or to lose their lives. And upon mutual courtesies with gifts and feastings between us, sometimes five-and-twenty or six-and-twenty of their chiefest came aboard: whereof I would not suffer above six to have weapons. There was never the like number of our men aboard their junk. I willed Captain John Davis in the morning to possess himself of their weapons, and to put the company before mast, and to leave some guard on their weapons, while they searched in the rice, doubting that by searching and finding that which would dislike them they might suddenly set upon my men, and put them to the sword: as the sequel proved.

Captain Davis, being beguiled with their humble semblance, would not possess himself of their weapons, though I sent twice of purpose from my ship to will him to do it. They passed all the day, my men searching in the rice, and they looking on. At the sun-setting, after long search and nothing found, save a little storax and benjamin, they seeing opportunity, and talking to the

Mitchelbourne
1625

Mitchelbourne 1625

rest of the company which were in my ship, being near to their junk, they resolved, at a watch-word between them, to set upon us resolutely in both ships. This being concluded, they suddenly killed and drove overboard all my men that were in their ship; and those which were aboard my ship sallied out of my cabin, where they were put, with such weapons as they had, finding certain targets in my cabin, and other things that they used as weapons. Myself being aloft on the deck, knowing what was likely to follow, leapt into the waist, where, with the boatswains, carpenter, and some few more, we kept them under the half-deck. At their first coming forth of the cabin, they met Captain Davis coming out of the gunroom, whom they pulled into the cabin, and giving him six or seven mortal wounds, they thrust him out of the cabin before them. His wounds were so mortal, that he died as soon as he came into the waist. They pressed so fiercely to come to us, as we receiving them on our pikes, they would gather on our pikes with their hands to reach us with their swords. It was near half an hour before we could stone them back into the cabin: in which time we had killed three or four of their leaders. After they were driven into the cabin, they fought with us at the least four hours before we could suppress them, often firing the cabin, burning the bedding, and much other stuff that was there. And had we not with two demy-culverins, from under the half-deck, beaten down the bulk-head and the pump of the ship, we could not have suppressed them from burning the ship. This ordnance being charged with crossbars, bullets, and case-shot, and bent close to the bulk-head, so violently marred therewith boards and splinters, that it left but one of them standing of two-and-twenty. Their legs, arms, and bodies were so torn, as it was strange to see how the shot had massacred them. In all this conflict they never would desire their lives, though they were hopeless to escape, such was the desperateness of these Japonians.

Only one leapt overboard, which afterward swam to our ship again, and asked for grace ; we took him in, and asked him what was their purpose ? He told us, that they meant to take our ship, and to cut all our throats. He would say no more, but desired that he might be cut in pieces.

Mitchelbourne
1625

II

AN ORDEAL BY FIRE

THE seven-and-twentieth, all night being very tempestuous, fearful thunder and lightning, and abundance of rain, we had under our house, in a room for that purpose, some small store of steel betel-boxes, and such like; where also lay two men, appointed by Captain Bonner to watch the house, the boat being left behind them ashore. That night John Cocket (*alias* Tucker), a youth, who had long lived at Surat, and he also lodged there: about midnight came thieves to open the door, which one within perceiving, with crying out feared them away. Two hours after they returned, and one of them, putting in his arm, was struck at with a sword, but missed, fled away the second time; and they within made the door so fast as they could (which was but hurdles). About four in the morning, coming again, and opening the door, one went in, taking some brass betel-boxes, our men being all fast asleep; and in returning, rubbed against Tucker's legs, who, starting up, caught hold of him and cried: 'A thief, I have him;' which scarce pronounced, with a pitiful accent, cried out again: 'O! he is gone, and hath stabbed me with his creeze:' which was so suddenly done, as those who lay by him had not time to rescue him. There was at that time aloft the surgeon of the *Dragon*, etc., who presently ran down with a light, but too late; the villain having with a knife given him two wounds, one whereof to the heart, who, without speaking

Hore
1625

Hore 1625

more words than 'Lord have mercy upon me,' presently died.

We in vain searched each bush and place about our house, and I went to call the Cowals (or waiters), who every night till this kept watch in a balley[1] within twenty paces of our house; missing whom, I went instantly to the Pongolo Cowalla's house, and calling him, asked him, where was the watch? He said at the balley, which I denying, he affirmed to have charged one that night. Then I told him we had a man slain, and willed him to search narrowly if any suspicious person could be apprehended; he forthwith went and acquainted the King therewith, who presently came down with the Chief thereabouts, saw the dead body, and affirmed he would do what might be to find the murderer. Master Nichols charged the Cowals to be actors or authors hereof, and required to have them all sent for, and one after another to touch the corpse, whereto the King gave order. And when each one had taken him by the hand, and no cause to suspect any appeared, Master Nichols demanded if there were no more Cowals; it was answered, no more save one, who was sick, and kept his bed. Him the King commanded to be sent for, whose very looks and demeanour condemned him, in the opinion of all, to be the villain sought for. The King commanded to take the dead man by the hand, which with extreme quaking, and many distracted gestures and answers, he did, but would not hold it any time. Master Nichols urged this to be the man, and required justice. The King caused him to be bound, and professed in his conscience that was the man who killed him, but that he must be tried by their law also, whereto the fellow assented.

And while preparation was made thereto, we sent word to Captain Bonner, who came ashore to see the event hereof: presently after whose coming, a fire was made, and an iron pan with a gallon of oil set thereon, which leisurely boiled

[1] [?]

till it came to such a degree of heat, that a green leaf but dipped therein was sodden and shivered. The prisoner then called, and persisting in denial of the fact, was, in testimony of his innocency, to take out of the said oil a small ball of brass, little bigger than a musket-shot, with his naked hand; and that if any burning or scalding appeared thereon, he was contented to die, which he addressed himself to perform. Stripping up his sleeve above the elbow, and taking a kind of protestation, desiring that as he was clear thereof, so he might prosper in this act; [he] dipped his hand to the wrist in the burning oil, took out the ball, held it fast, and crying, '*Olla Basar*,' or 'Great is the Lord,' tossed it up, caught it again, and then cast it on the ground, showing his hand unto all that would, which had no more sign of hurt than if he had experimented the same in cold water—the devil, it seems, being loth at that time to lose his credit. The fellow was instantly released, and within an hour after returned in his holiday apparel, and none so lusty as he, though but a little before he had been sick, and so weak, as he was fain to be brought upon men's shoulders to his trial. And this was all the justice we could have for our murdered man, though in all likelihood, and their judgments also, he was the actor.

Hore 1625

Purchas his Pilgrims.

SOME UNIVERSITY CHARACTERS

I.

AN OLD COLLEGE BUTLER

IS none of the worst Students in the house, for he keeps the set hours at his book more duly than any. His authority is great over men's good names, which he charges many times with shrewd aspersions, which they hardly wipe

Earle 1628

Earle
1628

off without payment. His Box and Counters prove him to be a man of reckoning; yet he is stricter in his accounts than a Usurer, and delivers not a farthing without writing. He doubles the pain of *Gallobelgicus*, for his books go out once a quarter, and they are much in the same nature, brief notes and sums of affairs, and are out of request as soon. His comings in are like a Tailor's, from the shreds of bread, the chippings, and remnants of the broken crust; excepting his vails[1] from the barrel, which poor folks buy for their hogs, but drink themselves. He divides a halfpenny loaf with more subtlety than Kekerman, and subdivides the *a primo ortum* so nicely, that a stomach of great capacity can hardly apprehend it. He is a very sober man, considering his manifold temptations of drink and strangers, and if he be overseen, 'tis within his own liberties, and no man ought to take exceptions. He is never so well pleased with his place as when a gentleman is beholding to him for showing him the Buttery, whom he greets with a cup of single beer and sliced manchet, and tells him 'tis the fashion of the College. He domineers over Freshmen when they first come to the Hatch, and puzzles them with strange language of Cues and Cees, and some broken Latin which he has learnt at his Bin. His faculty's extraordinary is the warming of a pair of Cards, and telling out a dozen of Counters for Post and Pair, and no man is more methodical in these businesses. Thus he spends his age, till the tap of it is run out, and then a fresh one is set abroach.

II

A DOWNRIGHT SCHOLAR

Is one that has much learning in the Ore, unwrought and untried, which time and experience fashions and refines. He is good metal in the inside, though rough and unscoured

[1] Profits.

without, and therefore hated of the Courtier, that is quite contrary. The time has got a vein of making him ridiculous, and men laugh at him by tradition, and no unlucky absurdity but is put upon his profession, and done like a scholar. But his fault is only this, that his mind is somewhat much taken up with his mind, and his thoughts not loaden with any carriage besides. He has not put on the quaint garb of the age, which is now become a man's Total. He has not humbled his meditations to the industry of Compliment, nor afflicted his brain in an elaborate leg. His body is not set upon nice Pins, to be turning and flexible for every motion, but his scrape is homely, and his nod worse. He cannot kiss his hand and cry Madam, nor talk idly enough to bear her company. His smacking of a Gentlewoman is somewhat too savoury, and he mistakes her nose for her lip. A very Woodcock would puzzle him in carving, and he wants the logick of a Capon. He has not the glib faculty of sliding over a tale, but his words come squeamishly out of his mouth, and the laughter commonly before the jest. He names this word College too often, and his discourse beats too much on the University. The perplexity of mannerliness will not let him feed, and he is sharp set at an argument when he should cut his meat. He is discarded for a gamester at all games but one-and-thirty, and at tables he reaches not beyond doublets. His fingers are not long and drawn out to handle a Fiddle, but his fist is clenched with the habit of disputing. He ascends a horse somewhat sinisterly, though not on the left side, and they both go jogging in grief together. He is exceedingly censured by the Inns a Court men for that heinous Vice, being out of fashion. He cannot speak to a Dog in his own Dialect, and understands Greek better than the language of a Falconer. He has been used to a dark room and dark Clothes, and his eyes dazzle at a Sattin Doublet. The Hermitage of his Study has made him somewhat uncouth in the world, and men make him worse by staring on him.

Earle
1628

Earle
1628

Thus is he silly and ridiculous, and it continues with him for some quarter of a year, out of the University. But practise him a little in men, and brush him o'er with good company, and he shall outbalance those glisterers as much as a solid substance does a feather, or Gold Gold-lace.

III

A MERE YOUNG GENTLEMAN OF THE UNIVERSITY

Is one that comes there to wear a gown and to say hereafter he has been at the University. His Father sent him thither because he heard there were the best Fencing and Dancing Schools; from these he has his Education, from his Tutor the oversight. The first element of his Knowledge is to be shown the Colleges and initiated in a Tavern by the way, which hereafter he will learn of himself. The two marks of his Seniority is the bare Velvet of his gown and his proficiency at Tennis, where, when he can once play a Set, he is a Freshman no more. His Study has commonly handsome Shelves, his Books neat Silk strings, which he shows to his Father's man, and is loath to untie or take down for fear of misplacing. Upon foul days for recreation he retires thither, and looks over the pretty book his Tutor reads to him, which is commonly some short history, or a piece of *Euphormio*; for which his Tutor gives him Money to spend next day. His main loitering is at the Library, where he studies Arms and books of Honour, and turns a Gentleman-Critick in pedigrees. Of all things, he endures not to be mistaken for a Scholar, and hates a black suit though it be of Sattin. His companion is ordinarily some stale fellow, that has been notorious for an Ingle[1] to gold hatbands, whom he admires at first, afterward scorns. If he have spirit or wit, he may light of better company, and may learn some flashes of wit which may do

[1] A parasite.

him Knight's service in the Country hereafter. But he is now gone to the Inns of Court, where he studies to forget what he learned before, his acquaintance and the fashion.

Earle
1628

IV

AN UNIVERSITY DUN

Is a Gentleman's follower cheaply purchased, for his own money has hired him. He is an inferior Creditor of some ten shillings or downwards, contracted for Horse-hire, or perchance for drink, too weak to be put in Suit, and he arrests your modesty. He is now very expensive of his time, for he will wait upon your Stairs a whole Afternoon, and dance attendance with more patience than a Gentleman-Usher. He is a sore beleaguerer of Chambers, and assaults them sometimes with furious knocks; yet finds strong resistance commonly, and is kept out. He is a great complainer of Scholars' loitering, for he is sure never to find them within, and yet he is the chief cause many times that makes them study. He grumbles at the ingratitude of men, that shun him for his kindness, but indeed it is his own fault, for he is too great an upbraider. No man puts them more to their brain than he; and by shifting him off they learn to shift in the world. Some choose their rooms a purpose to avoid his surprisals, and think the best commodity in them his Prospect. He is like a rejected acquaintance, hunts those that care not for his company, and he knows it well enough, and yet will not keep away. The sole place to supply him is the Buttery, where he takes grievous use upon your Name, and he is one much wrought with good Beer and Rhetorick. He is a man of most unfortunate voyages, and no Gallant walks the street to less purpose.

John Earle, Bishop of Salisbury.

AN UNEQUAL COMBAT

Digby
1629

FOR after Theagenes had **embarked** himself to follow on his intended journey, a favourable wind in a short time brought him to Alexandria; **whither he sent a servant** one day before **him to** provide him a **convenient house near** the Ambassador's, and other necessaries; and the **next** day came thither himself, and **the** first thing he did was to go kiss the hand of his kinsman Aristobulus, who received him with all **the** demonstration **of joy** and honour that might be, and caused **him to stay supper** with **him;** after which he sent **his** son Leodivius, with **many of his** servants and torches, to accompany him **to** his **lodging,** which was not far off. But the night **had** slided **so insensibly** away while they were in **their** pleasing conversation, **it being the** nature of long absence **of** dear friends to **cause at their** first encounter much greediness of enjoying **each** other, **that when** they came out of the house they found **the streets quiet and** no living creature stirring in them; **and the moon,** which was then **near** the full, shining out **a clear light** upon them, so that **the** coolness and solitude **was** the greatest sign that it was not **noonday.**

Wherefore **they caused** the lights and other servants to stay there, **who then** could serve but for vain magnificence, and Theagenes **sent** his servants to his lodging before, while he, **and** Leodivius, and another gentleman, that Leodivius took with **him to** accompany him, that he might **not** return all **alone** to his father's house, came softly **after,** sucking **in the** fresh air, and pleasing themselves **in the** coolness of **the** night which succeeded a hot day, it **being** then in the beginning of the summer: but as they **were** entertaining themselves in some gentle discourse, a **rare** voice, accompanied with a sweet instrument, called **their ears** to silent attention, while with their eyes they

AN UNEQUAL COMBAT

sought to inform themselves where the person was that sung, when they saw a gentlewoman in a loose and night habit, that stood in an open window supported like a gallery with bars of iron, with a lute in her hand, which with excellent skill she made to keep time with her divine voice, and that issued out of as fair a body, by what they could judge at that light; only there seemed to sit so much sadness upon her beautiful face, that one might judge she herself took little pleasure in her own soul-ravishing harmony.

The three spectators remained attentive to this fair sight and sweet music, Leodivius only knowing who she was, who coming a little nearer towards the window, fifteen men all armed, as the moon shining upon their bucklers and coats of mail did make evident, rushed out upon him with much violence, and with their drawn swords made so many furious blows and thrusts at him, that if his better genius had not defended him it had been impossible that he could have outlived that minute; but he, nothing at all dismayed, drew his sword, and struck the foremost of them such a blow upon the head, that if it had not been armed with a good cap of steel, certainly he should have received no more cumber from that man; yet the weight of it was such that it made the Egyptian run reeling backwards two or three steps, and the blade, not able to sustain such a force, broke in many pieces, so that nothing but the hilts remained in Leodivius's hand; who seeing himself thus disarmed, suddenly recollected his spirits, and using short discourse within himself, resolved, as being his best, to run to his father's house to call for assistance to bring off in safety his kinsman and his other friend, whose false sword served him in the same manner as Leodivius's had done, as though they had conspired to betray their masters in their greatest need. Here one might see differing effects from like causes, for a like resolute valour without astonishment that caused Leodivius to run discreetly away

Digby
1629

AN UNEQUAL COMBAT

Digby 1629

for succour, **caused him to stand** still in the place **where** his sword broke, defending **his** enemies' blows with **the** piece that remained in his **hand,** as being ashamed **to** leave Theagenes **in the** midst of **so** many that strived to take his life from **him:** but he **was soon out of danger** by all their pressing beyond him, **whom** they **saw** disarmed, to come to Theagenes, who had interposed himself between **Leodivius and** them that followed him; of which the master **of all these bravos was** one, **so that the rest** seeing him **engaged in a fierce** battle, they **all came to assist** him. Theagenes then **found** himself in **great perplexity,** for having retired to a **narrow place of the** street, that he might **keep** his assailants all in front **before him,** the overhanging pentises **took away the light of the** moon, and his enemies having at the **top of their bucklers** artificial lanterns whose light was cast only **forwards by their being** made with an **iron plate on** that **side towards the holders, so that** their bodies remained in **darkness, had** not only the advantage of seeing him when he could not see them, but also **dazzled** and offended his eyes with the many near lights, which **made** him mistake those objects that **dimly he** discerned. The **number** of his **enemies, and** the **disparity** of the weapons, **might** have given him just **cause to seek the** saving of his **life** rather **by the** swiftness **of his** legs than by an obstinate **defence;** but he, that did not value it **at** so high a rate as **to think that** it could warrant such an action, resolved rather to die in the midst of his enemies, than to **do** anything that might be interpreted to proceed from fear: **with** which resolution he made good the place he stood **in, and** whensoever any **of them** were too **bold** in coming near him, he entertained **them** with such **rude** welcomes, that **they** had little encouragement to make **a** second return.

After Theagenes had remained some time thus beating down their swords and wounding many **of** them, and showing wonderful effects of **a** settled and not transported valour,

and that their beginning to slack their fury in pressing upon
him gave a little freedom to his thoughts, all his spirits being
before united in his heart and hands, he considered how it
must certainly be some mistake that made him to be thus
treated by men that he knew not, and to whom he was sure
he in his particular could have given no offence, being but
that day arrived at Alexandria from very remote parts;
wherefore he spoke to them in the best manner he could, to
make himself understood in a tongue that he was not well
master of, and asked what moved them to use him so discourteously that was a stranger there, and was not guilty of
having injured any of them; to which words of his, one that
seemed to be of the best quality among them, by a cassock
embroidered with gold which he wore over his jack of mail,
answered him with much fury in this manner: Villain,
thou liest, thou hast done me wrong which cannot be satisfied
with less than thy life; and by thy example let the rest of
thy lascivious countrymen learn to shun those gentlewomen
where other men have interest, as they would do houses
infected with the plague, or the thunder that executeth
God's vengeance.' These words put all patience out of
Theagenes's breast, so that now he dispensed his blows
rather with fury than art; but his hand was so exercised
in the perfectest rules of true art, that without his endeavours or taking notice, it never failed of making exactly
regulated motions, which had such force imparted to them
by a just anger, that few of them were made in vain.

But at length his enemies, that had bought with much
of their blood the knowledge of his power and strength,
attempted to do that behind him, which they durst not to his
face; for some of them running down a little lane that was
near the place where they fought, made a circuit and came to
assault Theagenes behind, which he perceived by a blow upon
his shoulders: but it seemed that the fearful giver of it was
so apprehensive lest Theagenes should turn about, that his

quaking hand laid it **on so softly** that it did him **no** hurt, but served to warn him of **the** danger he was in. He then perceiving himself thus beset **on** every side, summoned all his spirits to serve him at **this** his so great necessity, and choosing **to cut his** way through the thickest of them, that so it might appear that he wrought his own liberty in despite of their strongest oppositions, did make a **quick thrust at** him **that** was nearest before him, which **entering** within his weapons before he was aware that he **had occasion to** ward it, Theagenes accompanied it with the whole weight **of** his body, running on so violently, as the other's jack not giving **way,** and his sword not yielding, he bore him down, and running **over** him made him serve for a bridge to cross the kennel. **He** being **thus acquit of their** beseiging him, began to retire himself with **a settled pace** towards the Ambassador's house, but in **such a manner,** that though his feet carried him one way his **face** looked another, and his hands sent forwards many bloody messages of his angry spirit; but **one** of them pressed so eagerly and unwarily upon him, that as he lifted **up** his sword **to** make a blow at Theagenes, he avoided it with a gentle **motion** of his body, and gave him such a strong reverse upon **the head, that** finding it disarmed, for he **had lost** his iron **cap** with much stirring in the scuffle, it divided **it in two** parts, and his brains flew into his neighbour's face; upon whom Theagenes turned, having thus rid himself of his fiercest enemy, and stepping in with his left leg, made himself master of his sword, and with his own did **run** him into the belly under his jack, so that he fell down, **witnessing** with a deep groan that his life was at her last **minute.** The other Egyptians by that knew him to be their **master,** for whose quarrel only they all fought, so that they left Theagenes, and **all of** them attended to succour their wounded lord; but all **too** late, for without ever speaking, he gave up his ghost in their arms; while by this means Theagenes, who received **but** little hurt, had **time to** walk leisurely to the Ambassador's house, from whence, upon the alarm that Leodivius gave, many were coming to his rescue with such arms as, hastily, they could recover; the cause of whose coming so late, for he met them half way, was, that it was long before Leodivius, though he knocked and called aloud, could get the gates open; for all in the house were gone to take their rest.

Digby 1629

Sir Kenelm Digby.

THREE CHARACTERS

I

A MISTRESS

IS the fairest treasure the avarice of Love can covet; and the only white at which he shoots his arrows, nor while his aim is noble can he ever hit upon repentance. She is chaste, for the devil enters the Idol and gives the Oracle, when wantonness possesseth beauty and wit maintains it lawful. She is as fair as Nature intended her, helped perhaps to a more pleasing grace by the sweetness of education, not by the sleight of Art. She is young, for a woman past the delicacy of her spring may well move by virtue to respect, never by beauty to affection. She is innocent even from the knowledge of sin, for vice is too strong to be wrestled with, and gives her frailty the foil. She is not proud, though the amorous youth interpret her modesty to that fence; but in her virtue wears so much Majesty lust dares not rebel, nor though masqued, under the pretence of love, capitulate with her. She entertains not every parley offered, although the Articles pretended to her advantage; advice and her own fears restrain her, and woman never owed ruin to too much caution. She glories not in the plurality of servants, a multitude of adorers heaven can only challenge, and it is impiety in her weakness to desire superstition from many. She is deaf to the whispers of love, and even on the marriage

Habington 1635

Habington 1635

hour can break off, without the least suspicion of scandal, to the former liberty of her carriage. She avoids a too near conversation with man, and, like the Parthian, overcomes by flight. Her language is not copious but apposite, and she had rather suffer the reproach of being dull company, than have the title of Witty with that of Bold and Wanton. In her carriage she is sober, and thinks her youth expresseth life enough without the giddy motion, fashion of late hath taken up. She danceth to the best applause but doats not on the vanity of it, nor licenseth an irregular meeting to vaunt the levity of her skill. She sings, but not perpetually, for she knows, silence in woman is the most persuading oratory. She never arrived to so much familiarity with man as to know the diminutive of his name, and call him by it; and she can show a competent favour: without yielding her hand to his grip. She never understood the language of a kiss, but at salutation, nor dares the Courtier use so much of his practised impudence as to offer the rape of it from her: because chastity hath writ it unlawful, and her behaviour proclaims it unwelcome. She is never sad, and yet not jiggish; her conscience is clear from guilt, and that secures her from sorrow. She is not passionately in love with poetry, because it softens the heart too much to love; but she likes the harmony in the Composition; and the brave examples of virtue celebrated by it she proposeth to her imitation. She is not vain in the history of her gay kindred or acquaintance; since virtue is often tenant to a cottage, and familiarity with greatness (if worth be not transcendant above the title) is but a glorious servitude, fools only are willing to suffer. She is not ambitious to be praised, and yet values death beneath infamy. And I'll conclude (though the next synod of Ladies condemn this character as an heresy brought by a Precisian) that only she who hath as great a share in virtue as in beauty, deserves a noble love to serve her, and a free Poesie to speak her.

II

A WIFE

Is the sweetest part in the harmony of our being. To the love of which, as the charms of Nature inchant us, so the law of grace by special privilege invites us. Without her, Man, if piety not restrain him, is the creator of sin; or, if an innated cold render him not only the business of the present age, the murderer of posterity. She is so religious that every day crowns her a martyr, and her zeal neither rebellious nor uncivil. She is so true a friend, her Husband may to her communicate even his ambitions, and if success crown not expectation, remain nevertheless uncondemned. She is colleague with him in the Empire of prosperity; and a safe retiring place when adversity exiles him from the World. She is so chaste, she never understood the language lust speaks in, nor with a smile applauds it, although there appear wit in the Metaphore. She is fair only to win on his affections, nor would she be Mistress of the most eloquent beauty, if there were danger, that might persuade the passionate auditory to the least irregular thought. She is noble by a long descent, but her memory is so evil a herald, she never boasts the story of her Ancestors. She is so moderately rich, that the defect of portion doth neither bring penury to his estate, nor the superfluity license her to Riot. She is liberal, and yet owes not ruin to vanity, but knows Charity to be the soul of goodness, and Virtue without reward often prone to be her own destroyer. She is much at home, and when she visits 'tis for mutual commerce, not for intelligence. She can go to Court and return no passionate doater on bravery; and when she hath seen the gay things muster up themselves there she considers them as Cobwebs the Spider vanity hath spun. She is so general in her acquaintance, that she is familiar with all whom fame speaks virtuous; but thinks there can be no friendship but with one; and there-

Habing-
ton
1635

fore had she neither friend nor private servant. She so squares her passion to her Husband's fortunes, that in the Country she lives without a froward Melancholy, in the Town without a fantastic Pride. She is so temperate she never read the modern policy of glorious forfeits; since she finds Nature is no Epicure if Art provoke her not by curiosity. She is inquisitive only of new ways to please him, and her wit sails by no other compass than that of his direction. She looks upon him as Conjurors upon the Circle, beyond which there is nothing but Death and Hell; and in him she believes paradise circumscrib'd. His virtues are her wonder and imitation; and his errors, her credulity thinks no more fraility than makes him descend to the title of Man. In a word, she so lives that she may die; and leave no cloud upon her Memory, but have her character nobly mentioned: while the bad Wife is flattered into infamy, and buys pleasure at too dear a rate if she only pays for it Repentance.

III

A FRIEND

Is a man. For the free and open discovery of thoughts to woman cannot pass without an over licentious familiarity, or a justly occasioned suspicion; and friendship can neither stand with vice or infamy. He is virtuous, for Love begot in sin is a mishapen monster, and seldom outlives his birth. He is noble, and inherits the virtues of all his progenitors; though happily unskilful to blazon his paternal coat; so little should nobility serve for story, but when it encourageth to action. He is so valiant, Fear could never be listened to when she whispered danger; and yet fights not unless religion confirms the quarrel lawful. He submits his actions to the government of virtue, not to the wild decrees of popular opinion; and when his conscience is fully satisfied, he cares not how mistake and ignorance interpret him. He

hath so much fortitude he can forgive an injury; and when
he hath overthrown his opposer, not insult upon his weakness. He is an absolute governor, no destroyer, of his
passions, which he employs to the noble increase of virtue.
He is wise, for who hopes to reap a harvest from the sands
may expect the perfect offices of friendship from a fool.
He hath by a liberal education been softened to civility; for
that rugged honesty some rude men possess, is an undigested
Chaos; which may contain the seeds of goodness, but it
wants form and order.

Habington
1635

He is no flatterer; but when he finds his friend any way
imperfect, he freely but gently informs him; nor yet shall
some few errors cancel the bond of friendship; because he
remembers no endeavours can raise man above his frailty.
He is as slow to enter into that title, as he is to forsake it;
a monstrous vice must disobliege, because an extraordinary
virtue did first unite; and when he parts, he doth it without
a duel. He is neither effeminate, nor a common courtier;
the first is so passionate a doater upon himself, he cannot
spare love enough to be justly named friendship: the latter
hath his love so diffusive among the beauties, that man is
not considerable. He is not accustomed to any sordid way
of gain, for who is any way mechanick will sell his friend
upon more profitable terms. He is bountiful, and thinks no
treasure of fortune equal to the preservation of him he loves;
yet not so lavish as to buy friendship and perhaps afterward
find himself overseen in the purchase. He is not exceptious,
for jealousy proceeds from weakness, and his virtues quit
him from suspicions. He freely gives advice, but so little
peremptory is his opinion that he ingeniously submits it to
an abler judgment. He is open in expression of his thoughts
and easeth his melancholy by enlarging it; and no Sanctuary
preserves so safely, as he his friend afflicted. He makes use
of no engines of his friendship to extort a secret; but if
committed to his charge his heart receives it, and that and

it come both to light together. In life he is the most amiable object to the soul, in death the most deplorable.

William Habington.

Habington 1635

A BOUT WITH THE ADVERSARY

Blair 1636

HAVING declared how gracious the Lord hath been toward me, and that people he sent me to, I shall next show how the murderer Satan, visibly appearing to a wicked man, stirred him up to stab me, and how mercifully I was delivered therefrom. I was spending a day in family humiliation, and was come to the mid-day, when one comes to the gate and knocks. Now I had given order beforehand that if any knocked at the gate that day, none should open but myself. When I opened, I saw two men standing without; the one whereof (being a rich man) was chief constable of that paroch, the other was a tenant of his. Their errand was to shew me that the tenant had a bairn to be baptized (for I baptized none till first I conferred with the father, and exhorted and instructed him as need required). When I had spoken what I thought necessary, and was ready to turn into my house, the constable, dismissing the other, told me he had something to say to me in private. I looking upon him, saw his eyes like the eyes of a cat in the night, did presently conceive that he had a mischief in his heart; yet I resolved not to refuse what he desired, but I keeped a watchful eye upon him, and stayed at some distance; and being near to the door of the church, I went in and invited him to follow me. As soon as he entered within the doors, he fell a trembling, and I a wondering. His trembling continuing and growing without any speech, I approached to him and invited him to a seat, wherein he could hardly sit. The great trembling was like to throw him out of the seat; I laid my arm about him, and asked him what ailed him; but for a time he could speak none.

At last his shaking ceased, and he began to speak, telling me that for a long time the Devil had appeared to him: first, at Glasgow he bought a horse from him, receiving a sixpence in earnest, and that in the end he offered to him a great purse full of silver to be his, making no mention of the horse; he said that he blessed himself, and so the buyer with the silver and gold that was poured out upon the table vanished. But some days thereafter he appeared to him at his own house, naming him by his name, and said to him, 'Ye are mine, for I arled[1] you with a sixpence, which yet ye have.' Then said he, 'I asked his name, and he answered, "They call me Nickel Downus"' (I supposed that he repeated evil, that he should have said Nihil Damus). Being thus molested with these and many other apparitions of the Devil, he said he left Scotland; but being come to Ireland, he did often likewise appear to him: 'And now of late he still commands me to kill and slay; and often,' says he, 'my whinger hath been drawn and kept under my cloak to obey his commands, but still something holds my hand that I cannot strike.' But then I asked him whom he was bidden kill? He answered: 'Any that comes in my way; but

"The better they be,
The better service to me,
Or else I shall kill thee."'

When he uttered these words, he fell again a trembling, and was stopped in his speaking, looking lamentably at me, designing me to be the person he aimed at; then he fell a crying and lamenting.

I showed him the horribleness of his ignorance and drunkenness; he made many promises of reformation, which were not well keeped; for within a fortnight he went to an ale-house to crave the price of his malt, and, sitting there long at drink, as he was going homeward, the Devil appeared to him, and challenged him for opening to me

[1] Hanselled.

Blair
1636

what had passed betwixt them secretly, and followed him to the house, pulling his cap off his head and his band from about his neck, saying to him: 'On Hallow-night I shall have thee, soul and body, in despite of the minister and of all that will do for thee.' The man being exceedingly terrified, sent presently for me, and told me, as is here formerly set down, being driven to his bed by this terror. When I came, his wife told me with what amazement he entered the house bare-headed, and his band rent, saying he had hardly escaped. He entreated me, for Christ's sake, to be with him that night wherein Satan had threatened to carry him away. I instructed him the best I could, and praying with him, promised to be with him that night, providing he would fly to Christ for refuge, and not to me, who was but a weak and wretched creature. I intended to have spent the day before that night wherein I was to be with him, as I had done that day when he first came to me, and thought to have killed me; but when the day came I had no mind of my resolution till it was near night, and being in great doubt what to do, I went to my chamber in great heaviness. I durst not break or slight my promise, and how durst I go, being so unprepared for so pitched a conflict?

Being thus humbled before the Lord, I was encouraged to go, trusting to His gracious goodness, who is the preserver of men against the wiles and violences of Satan; and so coming about daylight going, I called to one man of that village who was under the reputation of a godly man, and an elder of the congregation. To him I imparted the whole matter, desiring him to convene the people of that village, and tell them no more but that I would stay that night in the house of the sick man with them. I began with prayer, and thereafter expounded the doctrine of Christ's tentations, closing with a prayer, and singing of a psalm; and after that did the like on another passage of Scripture; and after that another, still intermixing prayer and singing, till toward the morning.

All this time my chair being close by the sick man's bedside, when I uttered anything which he did not understand, with his hand he laid hold on my arm, requesting me to say that better. I hearkened to him, and laboured to do so. In the morning he took great courage to himself, defying Satan and all his works.

Thereafter he recovered, behaving himself better, and was charitable to the poor; but I was never satisfied with him, he continuing still ignorant. In the end he sickened, and therein seemed very penitent. The last time I saw him, I asked at him: whether Satan had ever appeared to him after that night wherein I continued with him? He answered, 'Never,' taking the Lord witness thereof; and shortly thereafter died.

Rev. Robert Blair.

A STRATAGEM

HIS Majesty being earnestly importuned by his Scottish subjects to have the assistance of some of his ships to redress the spoils committed by the pirates on their coast, out of care to them, and honour to himself, he dispatched Sir William Monson and Sir Francis Howard in great haste upon that service, commanding such victuals and other things as they stood in need of to be sent after them.

They departed from Margate Road the 14th May, and arrived at Leith in Scotland on the 23d of the same; thence he immediately went to Edinburgh, and presented himself to the Lords of that Realm, acquainting them with the cause of his coming, and the charge he had from his Majesty to defend that coast from pirates; and therefore desired to be informed by their Lordships concerning their strength, their number, and their place of abode. He desired to be furnished with able pilots; for his Majesty's ships were of greater burden and value than usually had been employed on those

Monson
1636

coasts; and besides, that **the** navigation to the northward of that place **was** not frequented **by** our nation, and therefore unknown **to us.** It pleased **their** Lordships **to** recommend the care **thereof to** the Trinity House of Leith, expressly commanding them to appoint the ablest pilots that could be chosen amongst **them.** This command of theirs was accordingly obeyed, and their pilots repaired aboard the next morning. Sir William immediately set sail, leaving instructions for his **victuals to** follow him to the Island of Orkney; which the Lords **of** Scotland took into their provident care, and performed it accordingly.

The first of **June** Sir William **arrived** at Sinclair Castle, **the** house **of the Earl** of Caithness, the utmost promontory of **Great Britain. Here he found neither the** number nor the **danger of pirates so terrible as report made** them; from **twenty they** were **vanished to two, and both** of them men **of base** condition; the **one of them not long** before my **boatswain's** mate in the **narrow seas; the other of** as mean quality **and** rank, and **first** made a seaman **by** Sir William. Neither can this man be properly called a pirate; for being amongst them, and misliking their damnable courses, he, with three others, left their society, and in an English barque they had **taken,** stole from them, and put himself into the hands of the **Earl** of Caithness, where I found both him and **the** bark, which I brought away with me. The day before I **came** to Caithness I was disappointed of meeting the boatswain's mate, the pirate, Clarke by name, who had been ashore with the Earl and friendly entertained, because his **house** and tenants lay open to his spoil. That day there **arrived** a Scottish barque from the Frith, which gave an **account** of Sir William's coming to Leith with an intent **to** pursue such pirates as he could hear of. This news made Clarke quit that coast and fly into **the** island, where he refreshed himself amongst the fishermen.

But **Sir** William being **now** out of hope of him, and out of doubt of any others thereabout, **stayed not at Caithness, but the same night** passed to the Island of Orkney, **where he** found more **civil, kind,** and friendly usage, than could be expected from such kind of creatures in show. **Here he left** Sir Francis Howard for guard of the coast and **prosecuted** his intention against Clarke, **not sparing any place to seek him** in where there was a possibility to find him. **After** some time spent at sea, he **put into the Island of Shetland,** and from thence **to those of** Hebrides, where he designed Sir Francis Howard should **meet** him. The brutishness and uncivility of those people of the Hebrides exceeds the savages of America; and it may be well said of them that education is a second nature; for there cannot **be greater difference** betwixt day and night than **betwixt the conversation of** those of Orkney and those of the Hebrides.

Being out of hopes of meeting with Clarke, **Sir William** directed his course for Broad Haven **in Ireland, a harbour** frequented by pirates, in respect of the security thereof, and the remoteness, **few** knowing it, and the relief such people find by a gentleman there dwelling, who spared not his own daughters **to bid them welcome.** The danger Sir William **ran into was great, and worse to think, that two ships of His** Majesty's of that consequence should be hazarded on so slender an occasion, as the pursuit of so few petit[1] pirates. Betwixt **those** islands and Ireland he met with so great a storm **and ground-seas, that** it were fit only for a poet to describe. Of four vessels he had in company, one was swallowed up in the seas; the other three were separated, and saw **one** another no more till they met in England. When the seas had spent their fury the storm began to abate, and the 28th he arrived at Broad **Haven,** a place unknown to any one in his ship but the pirate he had taken **from** the Earl of Caithness, as you have heard, of whom he made use to execute this stratagem.

Monson
1636

[1] Petty.

A STRATAGEM

Monson 1636

Being now come to the well-head of all pirates, and desirous to be fully informed of the condition of those people of Broad Haven, as soon as he came to an anchor he made choice of such persons of his company as formerly had been pirates, to give the less suspicion of his purpose. These men he sent in his boat to the gentlemen of that place, and took upon him to be a pirate, and the name of Captain Manwaring. The man he trusted in this service extolled the wealth he had on board him; his royal disposition and liberality to those that showed him courtesy. This hope of wealth and reward set their hearts on fire. He used the commendations and names of sundry pirates, their acquaintance; and feigned messages to the women from their sweethearts, who he made believe had sent them tokens, which he had on board for them. The silly women conceived so great a joy at it, that it took away all suspicion of deceit. The gentleman of that place, like a wily fox, absented himself, and left his wife and hackney daughters to entertain the new welcome guests, till he beheld the coast clear. And when he saw his time, he returned; and to make his credit and reputation seem the greater with Captain Manwaring, expressed the favours he had done to sundry pirates, though it was to his eminent peril, which he did not esteem, if he might do Captain Manwaring any service. So much he was devoted to his person when he heard the report of his wealth; and to endear him the more he promised to send two gentlemen of trust the next morning on board him, to give him the better assurance of his fidelity; and in the meantime, because he should not be unfurnished of victuals, he directed him to send his men ashore armed, and in a warlike manner, that it might appear their cattle were taken by violence, which he would appoint in a place with their ears slit, to be distinguished from other beasts.

The messenger being fully satisfied, and having executed

A STRATAGEM

his stratagem, returned aboard that night. At the dawning of the day the play began, for that was the hour appointed for the wolf to seek his prey; and Captain Chester, with fifty armed men, in a disorderly manner, like pirates, went on shore, and acted so much as was agreed on; and the cattle being killed, he was, in a secret manner, invited to the house of the gentleman; but at his entreaty was to make it appear publicly that he came not by invitation, but of his own accord. Here he was welcomed and friendly entertained by the daughters, whose desire was to hear of their sweethearts and to receive their tokens; but all in general coveted to see Captain Manwaring, who they confidently believed would enrich them all. The gentleman, Mr. Cormack by name, was punctual in all his undertaking, and the two ambassadors he promised came aboard and delivered a friendly (though in a rude manner, like their country) message of their love, and assurance of their service to Captain Manwaring. Their message ended, Sir William wished them to observe and consider whether they thought that ship and company to be pirates? for they could well judge of pirates because of their familiarity and acquaintance with them? It was a folly to dissemble any longer; for though they would, yet they could not betray Sir William's design; and therefore in as rough and rude a manner as they delivered their message, he told them how they had transgressed, and the next thing they were to expect was death; and commanded them to be put in irons, in dark and several places, being careful to permit neither boat nor man to go ashore until his own landing.

The time approached Sir William promised to visit them; and for his greater honour they had drawn down four or five hundred people to attend on the shore side: which he perceiving, and seeming to be jealous of their number, pretended to be shy of going ashore, for fear of treachery. But if oaths, vows, or any kind of protestations would serve him he had them; **and when they saw** him thus convinced **of** their sincerity, and that he put himself upon them, three **of** their principal men run up **to the** arm-pits **in** water, striving **who** should have the credit to carry him **ashore.** One of these three was an Englishman, **a** late tradesman in London, **and** attended the arrival of pirates. The second had been **a** schoolmaster, **and a man** attended **like another** Apollo amongst **these rude** people. The **third a** merchant of Galloway, but his **chiefest** trade was to **buy** and sell with pirates. These **three** gallants, like gentleman-ushers, **conducted** Sir William to Mr. Cormack's house, and the meaner **sort** followed with acclamations of joy. At his landing **happy was he to whom he** would lend his ear. Falling into discourse, one **told him they knew** his friends, and though his name had not discovered it, yet his face did shew him to **be a** Manwaring. **In short, they made** him believe he might command them and their country, **and that no man** was ever so welcome as Captain Manwaring.

Entering into the house of Mr. Cormack, his three hackney daughters rose to entertain him, and conducted him to the hall newly strewed with rushes, as the richest decking their abilities or the meanness **of the place** could afford. In the corner **was a** harper, who played merrily, to make his welcome the greater. After some discourse, and several questions asked by **the** three daughters concerning their acquaintance and friends; **but above all, being** desirous to handle the tokens promised, and laughing and jeering at their two messengers aboard, who they did not suspect were detained prisoners, **but** drinking and frolicking in the ship, as the use was upon the arrival of pirates. After these passages the women **offered** to dance, **one** chose Sir William, which he excused, but gave free liberty **for** the rest of his company. The Englishman was so pleasant and merry that he seemed to **have new** life infused into him: he told Sir William the heavens did foresee he was born to serve him and to relieve him; he shewed him a pass, procured upon false pretences from the Sheriff of that county, authorising him to travel from place to place to make inquisition of his goods, which he falsely pretended he was robbed of at sea; he laughed at the cheat he had put upon the Sheriff in getting his pass, and urged the advantage that might be made of it in sending to and fro in the country without suspicion. He proffered Sir William the service of ten mariners of his acquaintance, that lay lurking thereabouts, expecting the coming in of men-of-war, which sea-faring men he had power to command. His antic behaviour was enough to to put the melancholiest man in good humour; sometimes he played the part of a commanding Sheriff; then he acted his own, with many witty passages how he deceived the Sheriff. Sir William embraced his offer of ten mariners, with a promise of reward, and caused him to write effectually for them, as may appear by this that follows:—

'Honest brother Dick, and the rest, we are all made men; for valiant Captain Manwaring, and all his gallant crew are arrived in this place. Make haste; for he flourisheth in wealth, and is most kind to all men. Farewell; and once again make haste.'

This letter being writ and the pass enclosed in it, Sir William took it into his own hand, offering to hire a messenger to carry it; but night drawing on, which required his return on board, and having drawn from the country all the secret he desired, he caused the harp to cease playing and commanded silence, because he was to speak. He told them that hitherto they had played their part, and he had no part in the comedy; but though his was last, and might be termed the epilogue, yet it would prove more tragical than theirs. He put them out of doubt that he was no pirate, but a scourge to such, and was sent from His Majesty to discover, suppress, and punish them and their abettors, whom His Majesty did not think worthy the name of subjects; he told them that he had received sufficient information of the protection given to pirates in that harbour, and by Cormack; and that he could find no better expedient to confirm what had been told him, than by taking upon him the habit of a pirate, and one of their associates; and that they had made themselves guilty in the law, without further accusations: and now there remained nothing but to proceed to their execution, by virtue of his commission; and to that purpose, he had brought a gallows ready framed, which he caused to be set up, meaning to begin the mournful dance with the two men they thought had been merry dancing aboard the ship. He told the Englishman, he should be the next, because his offence did surpass the rest, being an Englishman, who should be a pattern of good life to those people we have sought to reduce to civility, since we first possessed that country; and seeing man naturally is rather up to follow evil example than good, he should be hanged for example. He told the schoolmaster he was a fit tutor for the children of the devil, and that he had apt scholars to follow his damnable instructions; and that as the members are governed by the head, the way to make his members sound was to shorten him by the head, and therefore willed him to admonish his scholars from the top of the gallows, which should be a pulpit prepared for him. He asked the merchant, whether he imagined there could be thieves if there were no receivers? And as the contriver and plotter of evil is worse than he that executes it, so is the abettor and a receiver to be condemned before the thief. He told him that pirates could no more live by their occupation were it not for buyers, than a poor labourer work without wages; that the offence in a merchant was more heinous than in another man, because his trade must be maintained and upheld by peace; his time he told him was not long, and wished him to make his account with God, that he might be found a good merchant and factor to him though he had been a malefactor to the law.

Monson 1636

Here was seen the mutability of the world; their mirth was turned into mourning, and their dancing into lamenting, each bewailing and repenting, as is the custom of offenders. The night calling Sir William away he appointed their guard to a boat, and left the carpenter ashore to finish the gallows, which was done by morning, and the prisoners ready to receive their doom; but being sued to by the whole country, with a promise never to connive again at pirates, after four and twenty hours fright in irons, he pardoned them. The Englishman was banished, not only from the coast, but from the sea-side throughout Ireland; and a copy of his pass sent to the Sheriff, with advice to be more cautious for the future in granting his safe conduct.

Sir William Monson.

A COVENANTING ARMY

OUR ready obedience being perceived, behold our unhappy party makes a new onset. They persuade the King to proclaim, in our borders, towards the former proclamation of our treason, and the offer of pardon, and their master's lands, to these who would desert us. This was done at Duns with a strong convoy of English horse. The like was intended at Kelso; but there Monro, Fleming, and Erskine, presenting themselves in battle array, did make Holland, with some thousand foot and horse, with their show alone, to retire in haste in a shameful disorder. It is thought Holland's commission was to cut off all he met in opposition

Baillie 1639

Baillie
1639

to him; but his soldiers that **day** were a great deal more nimble in their legs nor arms, except their cavaliers, whose right arms were no less weary **in** whipping, than their heels in jadding[1] their horses. We are informed that to repair that disgrace Holland was commanded to return with far more forces to execute his former commission: whereupon our **General** raises his camp from Dunglass, advertises his troops at Kelso to march towards him; both of them that night meet together **at** Duns, and there they set down on the head of that fair Law.[2] We found that advantage was made of our obedience, and a course **yet again,** without **respect to** promises, to be taken for our wreck. So we returned **to our** former resolution of present fighting, and **sent** posts athort all the country to haste on our friends for that end. . . .

This our march did much affray the English camp; Duns Law was in their sight within six or seven miles, for they lay **in** pavilions some two miles above Berwick, **on** the other side of Tweed, in a fair plain **along the** river. **The** King himself, beholding us through **a** prospect,[3] did conjecture us to be sixteen **or** eighteen thousand men; **we were** indeed above twelve **thousand; but at** once **we were** above twenty. **We might have** doubled that number, but we had **none there from the one** full half of Scotland; not a man beyond **Tay; few** from Lothian, Fife, Edinburgh, March, for they were waiting on the ships, or employed in carriages; the South behoved to observe the Border about Carlisle; and the West the Irish shore: albeit that was needless, for all that were either in the ships, or on the South border, or might be spared from Ireland, were called quickly to the royal standard; and when all were together, their number was thought did not exceed in horse and foot, English, Scots, Irish, sixteen thousand men, and these not of the stoutest; for it was constantly reported that one night a

[1] Goading. [2] Hill. [3] Glass.

false alarm being in our camp, when our drums began to beat and our matches on the hill to shine through the darkness, there arose such a fray[1] in the English camp that very many did betake them to their heels, expecting from us a present invasion; yea, had not our wise and valorous Prince, with his General Arundel, done diligence to encourage, and to find out the groundless vanity of the fray, there had been a greater flight than with honour could have been gotten stayed.

Baillie
1639

It would have done you good to have cast your eyes athort our brave and rich Hill, as oft as I did, with great contentment and joy, for I (quoth the wren) was there among the rest, being chosen preacher by the gentlemen of our shire, who came late with my Lord of Eglinton. I furnished to half a dozen of good fellows muskets and pikes, and to my boy, a broadsword. I carried myself, as the fashion was, a sword, and a couple of Dutch pistols at my saddle; but I promise, for the offence of no man, except a robber in the way; for it was our part alone to pray and preach for the encouragement of our countrymen, which I did to my power most cheerfully. Our Hill was garnished on the top towards the south and east with our mounted cannon, well near to the number of forty, great and small. Our regiments lay on the sides of the hill, almost round about: the place was not a mile in circle, a pretty round rising in a declivity, without steepness, to the height of a bowshot; on the top somewhat plain; about a quarter of mile in length, and as much in breadth, as I remember, capable of tents for forty thousand men. The Crowners[2] lay in canvas lodges, high and wide; their Captains about them in lesser ones; the soldiers about all in huts of timber covered with divott or straw. Our Crowners for the most part were noblemen: Rothes, Lindsay, Sinclair, had among them two full regiments at least from Fife; Balcarras, a horse troop; Loudoun, Mont-

[1] Panic.   [2] Commandants of Counties; here used for Colonels.

gomerie, Erskine, Boyd, **Fleming**, Kirkcudbright, **Yester,** Dalhousie, Eglinton, Cassillis, **and others,** either with **whole or half regiments.** Montrose's regiment **was** above fifteen hundred men in the Castle of Edinburgh: himself was expected. . . . Argyll **was sent** for to the treaty of peace; for without him none would mint[1] **to treat: he** came and set up his tent on the Hill, but few of his people with him. **It was** thought meet that he and his should lie about Stirling, in the heart of **the country, to be always** ready in subsidies for unexpected **accidents; to be a** terror to our neutralists, or but **masked friends;** to make all, without din, march **forward,** lest his uncanny trewsmen[2] should light on **to** call them up in their rear; always to have an eye what either the North, **or the ships, or** the West, or our staill[3] host should mister[4] **of help. It** was thought **the country** of England was more afraid for the barbariety of his Highlanders than of any other terror: those of the English that came to visit our camp did gaze much with admiration upon those souple fellows, with their plaids, targes, and dorlachs.[5] **There were** some companies **of** them under Captain Buchanan, **and** others **in** Erskine's regiment. Our Captains [were], for the most part, barons or gentlemen of good note; our Lieutenants, almost all soldiers who had served over sea in good charges; every company had, flying **at the** Captain's tent door, a brave new colour, stamped with **the** Scottish Arms, and this ditton, FOR CHRIST'S CROWN AND COVENANT, in golden letters. Our General had a brave royal tent; but it was not set up; his constant guard was some hundreds of our lawyers, musketeers, under Durie and Hope's command, all the way standing in good arms, with cocked matches, before his gate, well apparelled. He lay at the foot of the Hill in the Castle, with Baillie, his serjeant-major, or lieutenant-general. That place was destinate **for** Almond, in whose wisdom and valour

---

[1] Try. [2] **Men** in trews. [3] Campaigning.
[4] Need. [5] Daggers: also wallets.

we had but too much confidence; yet in the time of our most need, the grievousness of his gravel, or the pretence of it, made him go to France to be cut : always when he came there it was found that he needed not incision, so he passed to his charge in Holland where to us he was as dead in all our dangers.

Baillie
1639

The councils of war were keeped daily in the Castle; the ecclesiastic meetings in Rothes's large tent. The General, with Baillie, came nightly for the setting of the [watch] on their horses. Our soldiers were all lusty and full of courage; the most of them stout young ploughmen; great cheerfulness in the face of all : the only difficulty was to get them dollars or two the man for their voyage from home, and the time they entered in pay; for among our yeomen, money at any time, let be then, used to be very scarce ; but once having entered on the common pay, their sixpence-a-day, they were galliard. None of our gentlemen was anything worse of lying some weeks together in their cloak and boots on the ground, or standing all night in arms in the greatest storm. Whiles,[1] through storm of weather and neglect of the commissaries, our bread would be too long in coming, which made some of the Eastland soldiers half-mutinous; but at once order being taken for our victuals from Edinburgh, East Lothian, and the country about us, we were answered better than we could have been at home. Our meanest soldiers were always served in wheat-bread, and a groat would have gotten them a lamb-leg, which was a dainty world to the most of them. There had been an extraordinary crop in that country the former year, beside abundance which still was stolen away to the English camp for great prices; we would have feared no inlake[2] for little money in some months to come. March and Tevidale are the best mixed and most plentiful shires both for grass and corn, for fleshes and bread, in all our land. We were much obliged to the

[1] Sometimes.   [2] Necessity.

Baillie 1639

town of Edinburgh for money; Harry Rollock, by his sermons, moved them to shake out their purses; the garners of non-covenanters, especially of James Maxwell and my Lord Winton, gave us plenty of wheat. One of our ordinances was to seize on the rents of non-covenanters, for we thought it but reasonable, fra[1] they sided with those who put our lifes and our lands for ever to seal,[2] for the defence of our church and country, to employ for that cause (wherein their enteresse was as great as ours, if they would be Scottish men) a part of their rent for one year; but for all that, few of them did incur any loss by that our decreit,[3] for the peace prevented the execution.

Our soldiers grew in experience of arms, in courage, in favour daily; every one encouraged another; the sight of the nobles and their beloved pastors daily raised their hearts; the good sermons and prayers, morning and even, under the roof of heaven, to which their drums did call them for bells; the remonstrances very frequent of the goodness of their cause, of their conduct hitherto by a hand clearly divine; also Lesley his skill and fortune made them all so resolute for battle as could be wished. We were afraid that emulation among our nobles might have done harm when they should be met in the fields; but such was the wisdom and authority of that old, little, crooked soldier that all, with an incredible submission, from the beginning to the end, gave over themselves to be guided by him as if he had been Great Solyman. Certainly the obedience of our nobles to that man's advice was as great as their forbears wont to be to their King's commands: yet that was the man's understanding of our Scots humours, that gave out, not only to the nobles, but to very mean gentlemen, his directions in a very homely and simple form, as if they had been but the advices of their neighbour and companion; for, as he rightly observed, a difference would be used in commanding soldiers of fortune

[1] Seeing that.   [2] Sale (?)   [3] Sentence.

A COVENANTING ARMY

and of soldier volunteers, of which kind the most part of our camp did stand. He keeped daily in the Castle of Duns an honourable table for the nobles and strangers with himself, for gentleman waiters thereafter, at a long side table. I had the honour, by accident, one day to be his chaplain at table, on his left hand; the fare was as became a General in time of war: not so curious by far as Arundel's to our nobles; but you know that the English sumptuosity, both in war and peace, is despised by all their neighbours. It seems our General's table was on his own charge; for, so far as yet I know, neither he, nor any noble or gentlemen of considerable rent, got anything for their charge. Well I know that Eglinton, our Crowner, entertained all the gentlemen of note that were with him at his own table, all the time of our abode; and his son, Montgomerie, keeped with him very oft the chief officers of his regiments: for this was a voyage wherein we were glad to bestow our lives, let be our estates.

Had you lent your ear in the morning, or especially at even, and heard in the tents the sound of some singing psalms, some praying, and some reading scripture, you would have been refreshed: true, there was swearing, and cursing, and brawling in some quarters, whereat we were grieved; but we hoped, if our camp had been a little settled, to have gotten some way for these misorders; for all of any fashion did regrait, and all did promise to contribute their best endeavours for helping all abuses. For myself, I never found my mind in better temper than it was all that time fra[1] I came from home, till my head was again homeward; for I was as a man who had taken my leave from the world, and was resolved to die in that service without return. I found the favour of God shining upon me, and a sweet, meek, humble, yet strong and vehement spirit leading me all along; but I was no sooner on my way westward, after the conclusion of peace, than my old security returned.

Rev. Principal Baillie.

Baillie
1639

[1] After.

CAREY'S RAID

Carey 1639

WHEN I was warden of the East March, I had to do but with the opposite March, which Sir Robert Car had; but here I had to do with the East, Middle, and West Marches of Scotland. I had very good justice with Sir Robert Car, and the Laird of Fenhest, that had charge over the east part of the Middle March; but the west part, which was Liddisdale and the West March, kept me a great while in cumber. The first thing they did was the taking of Hartwesell, and carrying away of prisoners and all their goods. I sent to seek for justice for so great a wrong. The opposite officer sent me word: it was not in his power, for that they were all fugitives, and not answerable to the King's laws. I acquainted the King of Scots with his answer. He signified to me that it was true, and that if I could take my own revenge without hurting his honest subjects, he would be glad of it. I took no long time to resolve what to do, but sent some two hundred horse to the place where the principal outliers lived, and took and brought away all the goods they had. The outlaws themselves were in strongholds, and could no way be got hold of. But one of the chief of them, being of more courage than the rest, got to horse and came pricking after them, crying out and asking: What he was that durst avow that mighty work? One of the company came to him with a spear and ran him through the body, leaving his spear broke in him, of which wound he died. The goods were divided to poor men from whom they were taken before.

This act so irritated the outlaws that they vowed cruel revenge; and that before the next winter was ended they would leave the whole country waste, that there should be none to resist them. His name was Sim of the Cat-hill that was killed (an Armstrong), and it was a Ridley of Hartwesell that killed him. They presently took a resolution to be revenged on that town. Thither they came, and set many houses of the town on fire, and took away all their goods; and as they were running up and down the streets with lights in their hands to set more houses on fire, there was one other of the Ridleys that was in a strong stone house that made a shot out amongst them, and it was his good hap to kill an Armstrong, one of the sons of the chiefest outlaw. The death of this young man wrought so deep an impression amongst them, as many vows were made, that before the end of next winter, they would lay the whole Border waste. This (the murder) was done about the end of May. The chief of all these outlaws was old Sim of Whittram. He had five or six sons, as able men as the Borders had. This old man and his sons had not so few as two hundred at their commands, that were ever ready to ride with them to all actions at their beck.

The high parts of the March towards Scotland were put in a mighty fear, and the chief of them, for themselves and the rest, petitioned to me, and did assure me, that unless I did take some course with them by the end of that summer, there was none of the inhabitants durst, or would, stay in their dwellings the next winter, but they would fly the country, and leave their houses and lands to the fury of the outlaws. Upon this complaint I called the gentlemen of the country together, and acquainted them with the misery that the highest parts of the March towards Scotland were likely to endure, if there were not timely prevention to avoid it, and desired them to give me their best advice what course were fit to be taken. They all shewed themselves willing to give me their best counsels, and most of them were of opinion, that I was not well advised to refuse the hundred horse that my Lord Euers had; and that now my best way was speedily to acquaint the Queen and Council with the necessity of having more soldiers, and that there

Carey
1639

could not be less than a hundred horse sent down for the defence of the country, besides the forty that I had already in pay, and that there was nothing but force of soldiers could keep them in awe: and to let the Council plainly understand that the March, of themselves, were not able to subsist, whenever the winter and long nights came in, unless present cure and remedy were provided for them.

I desired them to advise better of it, and to see if they could find out any other means to prevent their mischievous intentions, without putting the Queen or country to any further charge. They all resolved there was no second means. Then I told them my intention what I meant to do, which was: 'That myself, with my two deputies, and the forty horse that I was allowed, would, with what speed we could, make ourselves ready to go up to the wastes, and there we would entrench ourselves, and lie as near as we could to the outlaws; and, if there were any brave spirits among them that would go with us, they should be very welcome, and fare and lie as well as myself: and I did not doubt before the summer ended to do something that should abate the pride of these outlaws.' Those that were unwilling to hazard themselves liked not this motion. They said, that in so doing, I might keep the country in quiet the time I lay there; but, when the winter approached, I could stay there no longer, and that was the thieves' time to do all their mischief. But there were divers young gentlemen that offered to go with me, some with three, some with four horses, and to stay with me so long as I would there continue. I took a list of all those that offered to go with me, and found that, with myself, my officers, the gentlemen, and our servants, we should be about two hundred good men and horse; a competent number, as I thought, for such a service.

The day and place was appointed for our meeting in the wastes, and, by the help of the foot[1] of Liddisdale and

---

[1] Garrisons.

Risdale, we had soon built a pretty fort, and within it we had all cabins made to lie in, and every one brought beds or mattresses to lie on. There we stayed from the midst of June till almost the end of August. We were between fifty or sixty gentlemen, besides their servants, and my horsemen; so that we were not so few as two hundred horse. We wanted no provision for ourselves nor our horses, for the country people were well paid for anything they brought us; so that we had a good market every day before our fort, to buy what we lacked.

The chief outlaws, at our coming, fled their houses where they dwelt, and betook themselves to a large and great forest (with all their goods), which was called the Tarras. It was of that strength, and so surrounded with bogs and marsh grounds, and thick bushes and shrubs, as they feared not the force nor power of England nor Scotland so long as they were there. They sent me word that I was like the first puff of a haggis, hottest at the first, and bade me stay there as long as the weather would give me leave. They would stay in the Tarras-wood till I was weary of lying in the waste; and when I had had my time, and they no whit the worse, they would play their parts, which should keep me waking the next winter. Those gentleman of the country that came not with me were of the same mind; for they knew (or thought at least) that my force was not sufficient to withstand the fury of the outlaws.

The time I stayed at the fort I was not idle, but cast, by all means I could, how to take them in the great strength they were in. I found a means to send a hundred and fifty horsemen into Scotland (conveyed by a muffled[1] man, not known to any of the company) thirty miles within Scotland; and the business was so carried that none in the country took any alarm at this passage. They were quietly brought to the backside of the Tarras, to Scotland-ward. There they divided

[1] Disguised.

Carey
1639

themselves into three parts, and took up three passages which the outlaws made themselves secure of, if from England side they should at any time be put at. They had their scouts on the tops of hills on the English side, to give them warning if at any time any power of men should come to surprise them. The three ambushes were safely laid without being discovered, and, about four o'clock in the morning, there were three hundred horse and a thousand foot that came directly to the place where the scouts lay. They gave the alarm; our men broke down as fast as they could into the wood. The outlaws thought themselves safe, assuring themselves at any time to escape; but they were so strongly set upon on the English side as they were forced to leave their goods and to betake themselves to their passages towards Scotland. There was presently five taken of the principal of them. The rest, seeing themselves, as they thought, betrayed, retired into the thick woods and bogs that our men durst not follow them for fear of losing themselves. The principal of the five that were taken were two of the eldest sons of Sim of Whittram. These five they brought to me to the fort, and a number of goods, both of sheep and kine, which satisfied most part of the country that they had stolen them from.

The five that were taken were of great worth and value amongst them: insomuch, that for their liberty, I should have what conditions I should demand or desire. First, all English prisoners were set at liberty. Then had I themselves, and most part of the gentlemen of the Scottish side so strictly bound in bonds, to enter to me, in fifteen days warning, any offender, that they durst not, for their lives, break any covenant that I made with them; and so, upon these conditions, I set them at liberty, and was never after troubled with these kind of people. Thus God blessed me in bringing this great trouble to so quiet an end. We broke up our fort, and every man retired to his own house.

After God had put an end to this troublesome business I rested in quiet the rest of the summer, and the next winter after; and had leisure, by little and little, to purge the March of inbred thieves: and God so blessed me, that I failed not in any of my undertakings, but did effect what I went for, which did so astonish all the malefactors as they were afraid to offend; so that the March rested very quiet from the invasion of the foreign, and from the petty stealths of the thieves that lived amongst ourselves.

Carey 1639

Robert Carey, Earl of Monmouth.

A NIGHT'S ADVENTURES

THE night was somewhat dark and dusky, and the hour eleven, and having gone through two or three streets, and seeing himself all alone, and that he had nobody with whom to talk and converse, Don Juan resolved with himself to return home, and putting it in execution, passing through a street which had a walking place built upon pillars of marble, he might hear from a certain door that some did whist unto him with a soft and low voice.

Mabbe 1640

The darkness of the night, which was made the more by means of that close walk, would not let him guess and conjecture whence that whisting directly came. Whereupon he stood still a while, attentively listening whence it should come; and whilst he was thus busied, he might see a door half-way open itself. He drew near thereunto, and might hear a low voice which spake thus: 'Is it Fabio?' Don Juan answered: 'Yes.' 'Then take this' (replied they within), 'and have a care to have it safely kept, and return hither presently again, for it much importeth us.' Don Juan puts forth his hand and felt a bulk, he knew not what, and, thinking to take it with one of his hands, he found that he had need to use **both, and they had** scarce put it **into** his hands but they shut the door upon him and **left** him. And he went his way and found himself in the street **with** his hands full, but knew not what burthen he bare. But within a little while after he heard **a babe** begin to cry, which it should **seem had been** but newly **born.** Whereat **Don Juan remained amazed** and suspensive, not knowing what he should do, or what **course** to take in this strange **case. For** to return back to the door, and call there unto them, he considered with himself that he might **run some danger for the babe's sake, having personated** another man to whom it was intended, and in **leaving it there at the door, the babe might have its life hazarded. And to carry it home to his** own house, he **had** not any one there that could **give it the** teat and **those other** helps **that** were needful, **nor did he** know in all **the** city anybody whither he might carry it. But sithence that they had said unto him that he should see it safe and return again presently, **he** determined to carry it to his own house, and **to leave it in the power** and custody of a woman **that served** them, and **to return** forthwith **to** see whether **or no** they had any further need of his **service,** since that he plainly perceived that they had taken **him for** another, **and that** it was **a mere** mistake in giving the babe unto him.

In conclusion, **without** making any further discourses, he came home with it **to his** house, whenas Don Antonio was not there. He entered **into one of** the rooms next at hand, and called his woman-servant unto him, and caused her to unswathe the babe, **and** found **it** to be one of the fairest creatures that ever they had seen. The clothes wherein it was lapt told that it came of rich and noble parents. When the woman had unswathed and opened it, they saw that it **was a** man child. Then said Don Juan to his woman: 'We must needs get one to **give** this child suck; but first of all, I would have you take away these rich mantles, and lay them

aside in some safe place, and to put and wrap it in others
more mean and humble. And without making it known
that I brought it hither, you shall carry it to the house of
some one midwife or other, for such kind of women are
never commonly unprovided of necessary remedy in such
like necessities; you shall take money along with you,
wherewith she may remain satisfied and contented, and you
shall give it such parents as you yourself shall think fit, for
the better covering of the truth of my bringing it hither.'
His woman made answer, all should be done as he had
ordered it.

Mabbe
1640

This business was no sooner put into so good a way, but
that Don Juan with all the haste he could returned to see
whether they would whist once more unto him; but a
little before that he came to the said house where they had
called unto him, he might hear a great clashing of swords,
as if many had been together by the ears slashing one
another. He stood listening a while, but could not hear any
one word pass between them. This hammering of iron was
in the dark, save only that by the light of those sparks
which the stones, wounded by their swords, raised, he had a
glimpse that there were many that had set upon one, and
he was confirmed in this truth by hearing that one say: 'O
traitors, though ye be many and I but a single man, yet
shall not your overmatching me in number make you prevail
in your purpose.' Which Don Juan hearing and seeing,
transported by his valiant heart, at two leaps he made into
the side of him that was assaulted, and taking his sword in
one hand and his buckler which he brought along with him
in the other, he said unto him that defended himself, in the
Italian tongue, that he might not be known to be a Spaniard:
'Fear you nothing, sir, for such succour is now come to you
as shall not fail you till his life fail. Bestir yourself, and set
yourself roundly to them; for traitors, though they be many,
are able to do but little' To these words replied one of the

adverse part: 'Thou liest in thy throat, for here is no traitor; but for the recovering of a man's lost honour it is lawful to take this or any other advantage whatsoever.'

There passed no more words between them, because the haste which they made to offend and wound their enemies would not give them leave to talk, who were (to Don Juan seeming) some six of them. They did press so hard upon his companion, that at two home-thrusts which they made at him at once full in his breast, they laid him flat on the ground. Don Juan thought that they had killed him, and with strange nimbleness and valour he bestirred **him**, and set upon them **all, whom** he made to give ground by the force of **a** shower which he rained down upon them of blows and thrusts. But all his diligence had **not been** able for to offend them and defend himself, if good fortune had not offered him her aid, by causing the neighbours thereabouts in that street to **open** their windows and come forth with lights, and to call out aloud to the Justice. Which they of the contrary part perceiving forsook the street, and turning their **backs went** their way.

Now, by this time, he that was fallen **had** got up again, for those stoccados and thrusts that were made at him lighted on a **privy coat which** he had, that was as hard and impenetrable as if it had been a rock of diamonds. Don Juan in **this** fray had let fall his hat, and seeking for it, instead of his own, lighted by chance on another, which he clapped on his head without looking whether it were his own or no. His fellow that was fallen came unto him and said: 'Sir, whosoever you be, I confess that I am indebted to you for **my** life, the which, with all that my estate besides can **reach** unto, I will spend in your service. Let me intreat **you to** do me a favour to tell me who you are, and what is **your** name, to the end that I may know to whom I owe so much, that I may manifest my thankfulness.' Whereunto replied Don Juan: '**I** will not (sir), seeing myself now disinterested, be discourteous with you. To comply, therefore, with your desire, and to fulfil your pleasure, I shall only tell that I am a gentleman, a Spaniard, and a student in this University; if the knowing of my name may any whit import you, I shall tell it you. But if, happily, you shall be pleased in any other thing to make use of my service, I would then (sir) have you know that my name is Don Juan de Gamboa.' 'You have done me a great favour herein,' replied he that was fallen. 'But I (Señor Don Juan de Gamboa) will not tell you who I am, nor my name, because I am willing you should rather know it from another than myself, and I will take care that both shall be made known unto you.' Don Juan had but a little before asked of him whether or no he had not received some hurt, because he saw that they had given him two great stoccados; whereunto he answered, that the goodness of his privy coat, next under God, had defended him, but that yet, notwithstanding, his enemies had made an end of him, if he had not stuck so close unto him.

By this time there came towards them a company of people more in number than those they had before to do withal; whereupon Don Juan said: 'If these be those our enemies, stand (sir) upon your guard, and behave yourself like yourself.' 'I believe' (replied the other) 'that they are not enemies, but friends, which make towards us.' And it was so indeed; for they that came were in all eight persons, who compassed him round that was fallen, and whispered some few words in his ear, but they were so soft and so secret, that Don Juan could not hear them. The party defended turned presently aside from them to Don Juan, and said unto him: 'Had not these my friends come in unto me, I would by no means (Señor Don Juan) have left you till you had finished this your well-begun work by setting me in some place of safety. But now, with all the indearingness that I can, I shall intreat you that you

Mabbe
1640

Mabbe 1640 will leave me, for it much importeth me that you yield to my request.' Having said **this, he** put his hand to his head, and found that he was **without a** hat, and, turning himself to those that came to him, he spake unto them to give him a hat, for his own was in fighting fallen from **him.** He had scarce spoke the word but that Don Juan put that which he had found upon his head. He that fell felt it with his hand, and, returning it to Don Juan, said unto **him**: 'That hat is none of mine. As you love me (Don Juan), take it, and carry it away with you as a trophy of this skirmish, **and** keep it well, for I believe it is known.'

They gave him another hat, and Don Juan, **for to** comply with that which he had intreated of him, interchanging some other but short compliments, he left him, not knowing who **he** was, and came home **to his own** house, without offering to go to that door where they **had given** him the babe, because he perceived that all the whole street was up, being awakened out of their sleep, and in a kind of tumult and uproar by reason of this quarrel.

James Mabbe (Don Diego Puede-Ser).

TWO FAVOURITES

I

LEICESTER

Naunton 1641 IT will be out of doubt, that my Lord of Leicester was one of the first whom she [Elizabeth] made Master of the Horse. He was the youngest son then living of the Duke of Northumberland, beheaded *primo Mariæ*; and his father was **that** Dudley which **our** histories couple with Empson; and **both** so much infamed for the Caterpillars of the Commonwealth during the reign **of** Henry the Seventh. He being **of a** noble extract, was executed the first year of Henry the

Eight: but not thereby [made] so extinct but that he left a plentiful estate, and such a son, who, as the vulgar speaks it, could live without the teat. For out of the ashes of his father's infamy he rose to be a Duke, and as high as subjection could permit or sovereignty endure; and though he could not find out any appellation to assume the Crown in his own person, yet he projected, and very nearly effected it for his son Gilbert, by inter-marriage with the Lady Jane Grey, and so by that way to bring it about into his loins. Observations, which, though they lie behind us, and seem impertinent to the text, yet are they not much extravagant: for they must lead, and show us how the after-passages were brought about with the dependances, and on the hinges of a collateral workmanship.

And truly, it may amaze a well-settled judgment to look back into those times, and to consider how this Duke could attain to such a pitch of greatness; his father dying in ignominy and at the gallows, his estate confiscate, and that for peeling and polling, by the clamour and crucifige of the people. But when we better think upon it, we find that he was given up but as a sacrifice to please the people, not for any offence committed against the person of the King; so that upon the matter he was a martyr of the Prerogative, and the King in honour could do no less than give back to his son the privileges of his blood, with the acquirings of his father's profession: for he was a lawyer, and of the King's Councils at Law, before he became *ex interioribus consiliis*, where, besides the licking of his own fingers, he got the King a mass of riches, and that not with the hazard, but the loss of his fame and life for the King's father's sake. Certain it is that his son was left rich in purse and brain, which are good foundations, and full to ambition; and it may be supposed, he was on all occasions well heard of the King, as a person of mark and compassion in his eye. But I find not that he did put up for advancement during Henry the Eight's

Naunton 1641

time, although a vast aspirer and provident storer. It seems he thought the King's reign was given to the falling sickness: but espying his time fitting, and the sovereignty in the hands of a pupil Prince, he thought he might as well then put up for it as the best. For having then possession of blood, and a purse, with a head-piece of a vast extent, he soon got honour, and no sooner there, but he began to side it with the best, even with the Protector, and in conclusion got his and his brother's heads; still aspiring, till he expired, in the loss of his own. So that posterity may by reading the father and grandfather make judgment of the son; for we shall find that this Robert (whose original we have now traced, the better to present him) was inheritor of the genius and craft of his father. . . .

We take him now as he was admitted into the Court, and the Queen's favour, where he was not to seek to play his part well, and dexterously. But his play was chiefly at the fore-game; not that he was a learner at the latter, but he loved not the after-wit, for they report (and I think not untruly) that he was seldom behind hand with his gamesters, and that they always went away with the loss. He was a very goodly person, and singular well-featured, and all his youth well-favoured, and of a sweet aspect, but high-fore-headed, which, as I should take it, was of discommendation: but towards his latter end (which, with old men, was but a middle age) he grew high-coloured and red-faced. So that the Queen in this, had much of her father, for (excepting some of her kindred, and some few that had handsome wits in crooked bodies) she always took personage in the way of her election; for the people hath it to this day in proverb, King Harry loved a man. [He] being thus in her grace, she called to mind the sufferings of his ancestors, both in her father's and sister's reigns, and restored his and his brother's blood, creating Ambrose, the elder, Earl of Warwick, and himself Earl of Leicester, etc. And he was *ex primitiis*, or of her first choice; for he rested not there, but long enjoyed her favour: and therewith much that he listed, till Time and Emulation (the companions of great ones) had resolved on his period, and to cover him at his setting in a cloud at Cornbury: not by so violent a death, and by the fatal sentence of judicature, as that of his father and grandfather was, but, as it is suggested, by that poison which he had prepared for others, wherein they report him a rare artist. I am not bound to give credit to all vulgar relations, or to the libels of the times, which are commonly forced, and falsified suitable to the moods and humours of men in passion and discontent. But that which leads me to think him no good man is, amongst others of known truth, that [matter] of my Lord of Essex death in Ireland, and the marriage of his Lady yet living: which I forbear to press, in regard that he is long since dead, and others living whom it may concern.

Naunton 1641

To take him in the observations of his letters and writings (which should best set him off), for such as fell into my hands, I never yet saw a style or phrase more seeming religious, and fuller of the streams of devotion; and were they not sincere, I doubt much of his well-being; and I may fear he was too well seen in the aphorisms and principles of Nicholas the Florentine, and in the reaches of Caesar Borgia. Hitherto I have touched him in his courtship; I conclude him in his lance. He was sent Governor by the Queen to the United States of Holland; where we read not of his wonders; for they say that he had more of Mercury than of Mars; and that his device might have been, without prejudice to the Great Caesar, *Veni, vidi, redii.*

II

RALEIGH

SIR WALTER RAWLEIGH was one, that (it seems) fortune had picked out of purpose, of whom to make an example, or to use as her tennis-ball, thereby to shew what she could do; for she tossed him up of nothing, and to and fro to greatness, and from thence down to little more than to that wherein she found him, (a bare gentleman). Not that he was less, for he was well descended, and of good alliance, but poor in his beginnings: and for my Lord of Oxford's jest of him (the Jack, and an upstart), we all know it savours more of emulation and his humour than of truth; and it is a certain note of the times, that the Queen in her choice never took into her favour a mere new man or a mechanic, as Comines observes of Lewis the Eleventh of France, who did serve himself with persons of unknown parents; such as was Oliver the Barber, whom he created Earl of Dunoyes, and made him *ex secretis consiliis*, and alone in his favour and familiarity.

His approaches to the University and Inns of Court were the grounds of his improvement; but they were rather excursions than sieges or settings down, for he stayed not long in a place; and being the youngest brother, and the house diminished in patrimony, he foresaw his own destiny; that he was first to roll (through want and disability to subsist otherways) before he could come to a repose, and, as the stone doth by long lying, gather moss. He first exposed himself to the land service of Ireland, a militia which then did not yield him food and raiment, (for it was ever very poor): nor had he patience to stay there, though shortly after he came thither again under the command of my Lord Grey, but with his own colours flying in the field, having in his interim cast a new chance, both in the Low-Countries, and in a voyage to sea. And if ever man drew virtue out of necessity, it was he: therewith was he the great example of industry; and though he might then have taken that of the Merchant to himself, *Per mare, per terras, currit mercator ad Indos,* he might also have said, and truly with the Philosopher, *Omnia mea mecum porto.* For it was a long time before he could brag of more than he carried at his back; and when he got on the winning side, it was his commendations, that he took pains for it, and underwent many various adventures for his after-perfection, and before he came into the publike note of the world. And that it may appear how he came up (*per ardua*) *Per varios casus, per tot discrimina rerum*, not pulled up by chance, or by any gentle admittance of Fortune, I will briefly describe his native parts, and those of his own acquiring, which were the hopes of his rising.

He had in the outward man a good presence, in a handsome and well compacted person, a strong natural wit, and a better judgment, with a bold and plausible tongue, whereby he could set out his parts to the best advantage; and to these he had the adjuncts of some general learning, which by diligence he enforced to a great augmentation, and perfection. For he was an indefatigable reader, whether by sea or land, and none of the least observers both of men and the times. And I am confident, that among the second causes of his growth, that variance between him, and my Lord Grey, in his descent into Ireland, was a principal; for it drew them both over the Council Table, there to plead their cause. Where what advantage he had in the cause I know not, but he had much better in the telling of his tale; and so much, that the Queen and the Lords took no slight mark of the man and his parts; for from thence he came to be known, and to have access to the Queen and the Lords: and then we are not to doubt how such a man would comply, and learn the way of progression. And whether Leicester had then cast in a good word for him to the Queen, which would have done no harm, I do not determine. But true it is, he had gotten the Queen's ear at a trice, and she began to be taken with his elocution, and loved to hear his reasons to her demands: and the truth is, she took him for a kind of Oracle, which nettled them all. Yea, those that he relied on began to take his sudden favour as an alarum, and to be

Naunton 1641 — sensible of their own supplantation, **and to** project his, which made him shortly after sing, *Fortune my Foe*, etc. So that, finding his favour declining, and falling into a recess, **he** undertook a new peregrination, to **leave** that *terra infirma* of the Court for **that** of the Wars, and by declining himself, and by absence, **to** expel his and the passion of his enemies: which in Court was a strange device of recovery, but that he knew **there** was some ill office done him, that he durst not attempt to mind any other **ways, than** by going **aside**; thereby **to** teach envy a new **way of** forgetfulness, **and** not so much as to think of him.

Howsoever, he had it always in mind never to forget himself; and his device **took so well,** that at his return he came in (as rams do, by going backward) with the greater strength, and so continued to her last, great **in** her grace and Captain of the Guard, where I must leave him; but with this observation: that though he gained much at the Court, yet he took it not out of the Exchequer, or merely out of the Queen's purse, but by his wit, and the help of the Prerogative. **For** the Queen **was** never profuse in the delivering out of her **treasure,** but payed many, and **most** of her servants part in money and the rest with grace, which, as the case stood, was taken for good payment, leaving **the arrear of** recompence due to their merit **to her great** successor, who paid them all with advantage.

Sir Robert Naunton.

DISCOVERIES

I

DE SHAKESPEARE NOSTRAT.

Jonson 1641 — I REMEMBER the players have **often** mentioned it as an honour to Shakespeare, that in his writing (what**soever he** penned) he never blotted out a line. My answer hath been: 'Would he had blotted a thousand,' which they thought a malevolent speech. I had not told posterity this, but for their ignorance, who chose that circumstance to commend their friend by, wherein he most faulted; and to justify mine own candour: for I loved the man, and do honour his memory, on this side idolatry, as much as any. He was, indeed, honest, and of an open and free nature; had an excellent phantasy, brave notions, and gentle expressions; wherein he flowed with that facility that sometimes it was necessary he should be stopped: *Sufflaminandus erat*, as Augustus said of Haterius. His wit was in his own power, would the rule of it had been so too. Many times he fell into those things, could not escape laughter: as when he said in the person of Caesar, one speaking to him, 'Caesar, thou dost me wrong.' He replied, 'Caesar did never wrong but with just cause,' and such like, which were ridiculous. But he redeemed his vices with his virtues. There was ever more in him to be praised than to be pardoned.

II

DOMINUS VERULAMIUS

I have known many excellent men that would speak suddenly, to the admiration of their hearers; who upon study and premeditation have been forsaken by their own wits, and no way answered their fame: their eloquence was greater than their reading; and the things they uttered, better than those they knew: their fortune deserved better of them than their care. For men of present spirits, and of greater wits than study, do please more in the things they invent than in those they bring. And I have heard some of them compelled to speak, out of necessity, that have so infinitely exceeded themselves, as it was better both for them and their auditory that they were so surprised, not

Jonson 1641

prepared. Nor was it safe **then to cross** them, for their adversary, their anger made them more eloquent. Yet these men I could **not** but love and admire, that they returned to their studies. **They left not** diligence (as many do) when their rashness prospered; **for** diligence **is a** great aid, even to an indifferent wit; when we are not contented with the examples **of our own** age, but would know the face of the former. **Indeed, the** more we confer with, **the** more we profit **by, if** the persons be chosen.

One, though he be excellent, **and the chief, is not to be** imitated alone: **for no** imitator ever **grew** up to his author; likeness is **always on this** side truth. Yet there happened in my **time one noble** speaker, who was full of gravity in his speaking. His language (where he could spare or pass by a jest) was nobly censorious. No man ever spake **more** neatly, more pressly, **more** weightily, or suffered less emptiness, less idleness, in what he uttered. No member of his speech, but consisted of **his own** graces. **His** hearers could not cough, or look aside from him, without **loss.** He commanded where he spoke; **and had** his judges angry **and** pleased **at** his devotion. **No man** had their affections more in his **power,** The fear of every man that **heard him was,** lest he should make an end.

Cicero **is** said to be the **only** wit that the people of Rome had equalled **to** their empire. *Ingenium par imperio.* We have had many, and **in** their several ages (to take in but the former *seculum*) Sir **Thomas** More, the elder Wyatt, Henry Earl of Surrey, Chaloner, Smith, Elyot, Bishop Gardiner, were **for** their times admirable; and the more because they began eloquence with us. **Sir** Nicholas Bacon **was** singular, and almost alone, in the beginning of Queen Elizabeth's time. **Sir** Philip Sidney, and **Mr.** Hooker (in different matters) **grew** great masters of wit and language, and in whom all vigour of invention **and** strength of judgment met. The Earl of Essex, noble and high: and Sir Walter Raleigh, not to be contemned, either for judgment or style. Sir Henry Savile, grave, and truly lettered; Sir Edwin Sandys, excellent in both; Lord Egerton, the Chancellor, a grave and great orator, and best when he was provoked. But his learned and able (though unfortunate) successor is he who hath filled up all numbers, and performed that in our tongue, which may be compared, or preferred, either to insolent Greece or haughty Rome. In short, within his view, and about his times, were all the wits born, that could honour a language or help study. Now things daily fall, wits grow downward, and eloquence grows backward: so that he may be named, and stand as the mark and $\dot{\alpha}\kappa\mu\dot{\eta}$ of our language.

I have ever observed it to have been the office of a wise patriot, among the greatest affairs of the state, to take care of the commonwealth of learning. For schools, they are the seminaries of state, and nothing is worthier the study of a statesman than that part of the republic which we call the advancement of letters. Witness the case of Julius Caesar, who, in the heat of the Civil War, writ his books of Analogy, and dedicated them to Tully. This made the late Lord St. Alban entitle his work *Novum Organum*, which though by the most of superficial men, who cannot get beyond the title of nominals, it is not penetrated nor understood, it really openeth all defects of learning whatsoever, and is a book *Qui longum noto scriptore proroget aevum.*

My conceit of his person was never increased toward him by his place, or honours: but I have and do reverence him, for the greatness that was only proper to himself, in that he seemed to me, ever by his work, one of the greatest men, and most worthy of admiration, that had been in many ages. In his adversity I ever prayed that God would give him strength; for greatness he could not want. Neither could I condole in a word or syllable for him, as knowing no accident could do harm to virtue, but rather help to make it manifest.

III

THE TRUE ARTIFICER

Jonson 1641

IT cannot but come to pass, that these men who cunningly seek to do more than enough may sometimes happen on something that is good and great; but very seldom: and when it comes, it doth not recompense the rest of their ill. For their jests, and their sentences (which they only and ambitiously seek for) stick out, and are more eminent, because all is sordid and vile about them; as lights are more discerned in a thick darkness than a faint shadow. Now because they speak all they can (however unfitly) they are thought to have the greater copy:[1] where the learned use ever election and a mean; they look back to what they intended at first, and make all an evened and proportioned body. The true artificer will not run away from nature, as he were afraid of her; or depart from life and the likeness of truth; but speak to the capacity of his hearers. And though his language differ from the vulgar somewhat, it shall not fly from all humanity, with the Tamer-lanes and Tamerchams of the late age, which had nothing in them but the scenical strutting, and furious vociferation, to warrant them to the ignorant gapers. He knows it is his only art, so to carry it as none but artificers perceive it. In the meantime, perhaps, he is called barren, dull, a poor writer, and by what contumelious word can come in their cheeks, by these men, who without labour, judgment, knowledge, and almost sense, are received or preferred before him. He gratulates them, and their fortune. Another age, or juster men, will acknowledge the virtues of his studies, his wisdom in dividing, his subtlety in arguing, with what strength he doth inspire his readers, with what sweetness he strokes them; in inveighing, what sharpness; in jest what urbanity he uses:

[1] Abundance.

how he doth weigh in men's affections: how invade and break in upon them; and makes their minds like the things he writes. Then in his elocution to behold what word is proper, which hath ornaments, which height, what is beautifully translated, where figures are fit, which gentle, which strong, to show the composition manly: and how he hath avoided faint, obscure, obscene, sordid, humble, improper, or effeminate phrase; which is not only praised of the most, but commended (which is worse) especially for that it is naught.

Jonson 1641

Ben Jonson.

SIR FRANCIS DRAKE

FRANCIS DRAKE was born nigh South Tavistock in Devonshire, and brought up in Kent; God dividing the honour betwixt two counties, that the one might have his birth, and the other his education. His father, being a minister, fled into Kent for fear of the Six Articles, wherein the sting of popery still remained in England, though the teeth thereof were knocked out, and the Pope's supremacy abolished. Coming into Kent, he bound his son Francis apprentice to the master of a small bark, which traded into France and Zealand, where he underwent a hard service; and pains with patience in his youth did knit the joints of his soul, and made them more solid and compacted. His master dying unmarried, in reward of his industry, bequeathed his bark unto him for a legacy.

Fuller 1642

For some time he continued his master's profession. But the narrow seas were a prison for so large a spirit, born for greater undertakings. He soon grew weary of his bark, which would scarce go alone, but as it crept along by the shore; wherefore, selling it, he unfortunately, in 1567, ventured most of his estate with Captain John Hawkins into the West Indies, whose goods were taken by the

Fuller
1642

Spaniards at St. John de Ulva, and he himself scarce escaped with life. The King of Spain being so tender in those parts, that the least touch doth wound him, and so jealous of the West Indies, his wife, that willingly he would have none look upon her, and therefore used them with the greater severity.

Drake was persuaded by the minister of his ship that he might lawfully recover in value of the King of Spain, and repair his losses upon him anywhere else. The case was clear in sea-divinity, and few are such infidels as not to believe doctrines which make for their own profit. Whereupon Drake, though a poor private man, hereafter undertook to revenge himself on so mighty a monarch; who, as not contented that the sun riseth and setteth in his dominions, may seem to desire to make all his own where he shineth. And now let us see how a dwarf, standing on the mount of God's providence, may prove an overmatch for a giant.

After two or three several voyages to gain intelligence in the West Indies, and some prizes taken, at last he effectually set forward from Plymouth with two ships, the one of seventy, the other twenty-five tons, and seventy-three men and boys in both. He made with all speed and secrecy to Nombre de Dios, as loth to put the town to too much charge, which he knew they would willingly bestow, in providing beforehand for his entertainment; which city was then the granary of the West Indies, wherein the golden harvest brought from Panama was hoarded up till it could be conveyed into Spain. They came hard aboard the shore, and lay quiet all night, intending to attempt the town in the dawning of the day.

But he was forced to alter his resolution, and assault it sooner; for he heard his men muttering amongst themselves of the strength and greatness of the town, and when men's heads are once fly-blown with buzzes of suspicion, the vermin multiply instantly, and one jealously begets another. Wherefore he raised them from their nests before they had hatched their fears, and, to put away those conceits, he persuaded them it was day-dawning when the moon rose, and instantly set on the town, and won it, being unwalled. In the market-place the Spaniards saluted them with a volley of shot; Drake returned their greeting with a flight of arrows, the best and ancient English compliment, which drove their enemies away. Here Drake received a dangerous wound, though he valiantly concealed it a long time, knowing if his heart stooped, his men's would fall, and loth to leave off the action, wherein if so bright an opportunity once setteth it seldom riseth again. But at length his men forced him to return to his ship, that his wound might be dressed, and this unhappy accident defeated the whole design. Thus victory sometimes slips through their fingers, who have caught it in their hands.

Fuller
1642

But his valour would not let him give over the project as long as there was either life or warmth in it. And therefore having received intelligence from the negroes, called Symerons,[1] of many mules' lading of gold and silver, which was to be brought from Panama, he, leaving competent numbers to man his ships, went on land with the rest, and bestowed himself in the woods by the way as they were to pass, and so intercepted and carried away an infinite mass of gold. As for the silver, which was not portable over the mountains, they digged holes in the ground and hid it therein.

There want not those who love to beat down the price of every honourable action, though they themselves never mean to be chapmen. These cry up Drake's fortune herein, to cry down his valour: as if this his performance were nothing, wherein a golden opportunity ran his head, with his long forelock, into Drake's hands beyond expectation. But certainly his resolution and unconquerable patience deserved

[1] Cimaroon Indians

much praise, to adventure **on such** a design, which had in it just no more probability **than** what was enough to keep it from being impossible: **yet** I admire not so much at all the treasure he took, as **at the rich** and **deep** mine of God's providence.

Having **now full** freighted himself with wealth, and burnt **at the House of** Crosses above two hundred thousand pounds worth **of** Spanish merchandise, he returned with honour and safety **into** England, and some years after undertook that his famous voyage **about** the world, most accurately described by our English authors: and yet a word or two thereof will not be amiss. Setting **forward** from Plymouth, he bore up for Cape **Verd**, where, near **to the** island of **St.** Jago, he took prisoner Nuno da Silva, an experienced Spanish pilot, whose direction he used in the coasts of Brazil and Magellan Straits, and after**wards safely** landed him at Guatulco **in** New Spain. Hence they took their course to the Island of Brava, and hereabouts they met with those tempestuous winds, whose only praise is that they continue not an hour, in which time they change all the points of the compass. Here they had great plenty of rain, **poured, not as in other places, as** it were out of sieves, but as **out of spouts**, so that a butt of water falls down in a place: **which**, notwithstanding, is but a courteous injury in that hot climate far from land, and where otherwise fresh water cannot **be provided**. Then, cutting the line, they saw the face of **that heaven** which earth hideth from us, but therein only three **stars of** the first greatness; the rest few **and** small compared **to** our hemisphere, as if God, on purpose, had set up the best and biggest candles in that room wherein **his** civilest guests are entertained.

Sailing the south **of** Brazil, he afterwards passed the Magellan Straits, and then entered *Mare Pacificum*, [and] came **to the** southernmost land at the height of $55\frac{1}{2}°$ latitude; thence **directing** his course northward, he pillaged many Spanish **towns, and** took rich **prizes of** high value in the kingdoms of

Chili, Peru, and New Spain. Then bending eastwards, he coasted China and the Moluccas, where, by the King of Terrenate, a true gentleman pagan, he was most honourably entertained. The King told them they and he were all of one religion in this respect, that they believed not in gods made of stocks and stones as did the Portuguese. He furnished them also with all necessaries that they wanted.

Fuller
1642

On the 9th of January following (1579), his ship, having a large wind and a smooth sea, ran aground on a dangerous shoal, and struck twice on it, knocking twice at the door of death, which no doubt had opened the third time. Here they stuck from eight o'clock at night till four the next afternoon, having ground too much, and yet too little to land on, and water too much, and yet too little to sail in. Had God, who, as the wise man saith (Prov. xxx. 4), 'holdeth the winds in His fist,' but opened His little finger, and let out the smallest blast, they had undoubtedly been cast away, but there blew not any wind all the while. Then they conceiving aright that the best way to lighten the ship was first to ease it of the burden of their sins by true repentance, humbled themselves by fasting under the hand of God. Afterwards they received the communion, dining on Christ in the sacrament, expecting no other than to sup with Him in heaven. Then they cast out of their ship six great pieces of ordnance, threw overboard as much wealth as would break the heart of a miser to think on it, with much sugar, and packs of spices, making a caudle of the sea round about. Then they betook themselves to their prayers, the best lever at such a dead lift indeed, and it pleased God that the wind, formerly their mortal enemy, became their friend, which, changing from the starboard to the larboard of the ship, and rising by degrees, cleared them off to the sea again, for which they returned unfeigned thanks to Almighty God.

By the Cape of Good Hope and west of Africa he returned

Fuller
1642

safe into England, and landed **at** Plymouth, being almost the first of those that made a thorough light through the world, having in his whole voyage, though a **curious** searcher after the time, lost **one** day through the **variation** of several climates. He feasted the Queen in his ship **at** Dartford, who knighted him for his service : yet it grieved him not a little, that some prime courtiers refused the gold he offered them, **as gotten by** piracy. Some of them would have been loth to **have been** told that they had *aurum tholosanum* in their own **purses.** Some **think** that they did **it** to show that their **envious** pride **was** above their covetousness, who of **set** purpose did blur **the** fair copy of his **performance,** because **they would not take** pains to write after **it.**

I pass by his next West Indian voyage (1585), wherein he took the cities of St. Jago, St. Domingo, Carthagena, and St. Augustine in Florida: as **also his service** performed in 1588, wherein he, with many others, helped to the waning of that half-moon[1] which sought to govern all the motion of our sea. I haste to his last voyage in 1595.

Queen Elizabeth, perceiving that **the** only way **to** make the Spaniard a cripple **for ever was to cut** his sinews of war in the **West** Indies, furnished Sir Francis Drake and Sir John Hawkins with six of her own ships, besides twenty-one ships and **barks** of their **own** providing, containing in all 2500 men and boys, **for some** service on America. But, **alas!** this voyage **was** marred before begun. For so great preparations being **too** big for a cover, the King of Spain knew of it, and sent **a** caraval of adviso to the West Indies; so that they had intelligence three weeks before the fleet set forth of England, either to fortify or remove their treasure; whereas in other of Drake's voyages not two of his **own** men knew whither he went; and managing such a design is like carrying a mine in war: if it hath any vent, **all is** spoiled. Besides, **Drake** and Hawkins, being in joint

[1] The Armada.

commission, hindered each other. The latter took himself to be inferior rather in success than skill; and the action was unlike to prosper, when neither would follow, and both could not handsomely go abreast. It vexed old Hawkins that his counsel was not followed, in present sailing to America, but that they spent time in vain in assaulting the Canaries; and the grief that his advice was slighted, say some, was the cause of his death. Others impute it to the sorrow he took for the taking of his bark called the *Francis*, which five Spanish frigates had intercepted. But when the same heart hath two mortal wounds given it together, it is hard to say which of them killeth.

Fuller
1642

Drake continued his course for Port Rico, and, riding within the road, a shot from the castle entered the steerage of the ship, took away the stool from under him as he sat at supper, wounded Sir Nicholas Clifford and Brute Brown to death. 'Ah, dear Brute,' said Drake, 'I could grieve for thee, but now is no time for me to let down my spirits.' And indeed a soldier's most proper bemoaning a friend's death in war is in revenging it. And sure, as if grief had made the English furious, they soon after fired five Spanish ships of two hundred tons apiece, in despite of the castle.

America is not unfitly resembled to an hour-glass, which hath a narrow neck of land (suppose it the hole where the sand passeth) betwixt the parts thereof, Mexico and Peru. Now, the English had a design to march by land over this isthmus from Port Rico to Panama, where the Spanish treasure was laid up. Sir Thomas Baskervile, general of the land forces, undertook the service with seven hundred and fifty armed men. They marched through deep ways, the Spaniards much annoying them with shot out of the woods. One fort in the passage they assaulted in vain, and heard two others were built to stop them, besides Panama itself. They had so much of this breakfast, they thought they should surfeit of a dinner and supper of the same. No hope of

Fuller
1642

conquest, except with cloying the jaws of death, and thrusting men on the mouth of the cannon. Wherefore, fearing to find the proverb true, that gold may be bought too dear, they returned to their ships. Drake afterwards **fired Nombre de Dios, and many other** petty towns, whose treasure the Spaniards had conveyed away, burning the empty casks, when their precious liquor was run out before, and then prepared for their returning home.

Great was the difference betwixt the Indian cities now from **what they were when** Drake first haunted these coasts. At first the Spaniards here were safe and secure, counting their **treasure sufficient to** defend itself, the remoteness thereof **being the greatest,** almost only, resistance, and **the** fetching of it more than the fighting for it. Whilst the King of Spain guarded the head and heart **of** his dominions in Europe, he left his long legs in America open to blows, till, finding them to smart, being beaten black and blue by the English, he learned to arm them at last, fortifying the most important of them to make them impregnable.

Now began Sir Francis his discontent to feed **upon** him. **He** conceived that expectation, a merciless usurer, **computing each day** since his departure, exacted an interest and **return of honour and** profit proportionable **to his** great pre**parations, and** transcending his former achievements. He saw that all the good which he had done in this voyage consisted in the evil he had done to the Spaniards afar off, whereof he could present but small visible fruits in England. These apprehensions accompanying, if not causing, the disease of the flux wrought his sudden **death.** And sickness **did** not so much untie his clothes, as sorrow did rend at once **the** robe of his mortality asunder. He lived by the sea, died **on** it, and was buried in it. Thus an extempore performance, **scarce** heard to be begun before we hear it is ended, comes **off with** better applause, or miscarries with less disgrace, than a long-studied and openly-premeditated action. Besides, we see how great spirits, having mounted to the highest pitch of performance, afterwards strain and break their credits in striving to go beyond it. Lastly, God oftentimes leaves the brightest men in an eclipse, to show that they do but borrow their lustre from His reflection.

We will not justify all the actions of any man, though of a tamer profession than a sea-captain, in whom civility is often counted preciseness. For the main, we say that this our captain was a religious man towards God and His houses, generally sparing churches where he came, chaste in his life, just in his dealings, true of his word, and merciful to those that were under him, hating nothing so much as idleness. And therefore, lest his soul should rust in peace at spare hours, he brought fresh water to Plymouth. Careful he was for posterity, though men of his profession have as well an ebb of riot as a float of fortune, and providently raised a worshipful family of his kindred. In a word, should those that speak against him fast till they fetch their bread where he did his, they would have a good stomach to eat it.

Rev. Thomas Fuller.

Fuller
1642

THE TRUE GENTLEMAN

WE will consider him in his birth, breeding, and behaviour.

1. *He is extracted from ancient and worshipful parentage.* When a pepin is planted on a pepin stock: the fruit growing thence is called a renate, a most delicious apple, as both by sire and dam well descended. Thus his blood must needs be well purified who is gently born on both sides.

2. *If his birth be not, at least his qualities are generous.* What if he cannot with the Hevenninghams of Suffolk count five-and-twenty knights of his family, or tell sixteen knights

Fuller
1642

successively with the Tilneys of Norfolk, or with the Nauntons show where their ancestors had seven hundred pounds a year before or at the Conquest: yet **he** hath endeavoured by his own deserts to ennoble himself. Thus valour makes him son to Caesar; learning entitles him kinsman to Tully; and piety reports him nephew to godly Constantine. It graceth a gentleman of low descent and high desert, when he will own the meanness of his parentage. **How ridiculous is it when many** men brag that their families **are** more ancient than the moon, which all know are later than the star which some seventy years since shined in Cassiopea! But if he be generously born, see how his parents breed him.

3. *He is not in his youth possessed with the great hopes of his possession.* No flatterer reads constantly in his ears a survey of the lands he is to inherit. This hath made many boys' thoughts swell so great, they could never be **kept** in compass afterwards. Only his parents acquaint him that he is the next undoubted heir to correction, if misbehaving himself; **and he** finds no more favour from his schoolmaster than his schoolmaster finds diligence in him, whose **rod** respects **persons no** more than bullets are **partial** in **a battle.**

4. *At the University he is so studious as if he intended learning for his profession.* **He knows well** that cunning is no burthen to carry, as paying neither porterage by land, nor poundage by sea. Yea, though **to** have land **be** a good first, yet to **have** learning is the surest second, which may stand to it when the other may chance to be taken away.

5. *At the Inns of Court he applies himself to learn the laws of the kingdom.* Object not, why should a gentleman learn law, who, if he needeth **it,** may have it for his money, and if he have never so much of his own, he must but give it away? **For** what a shame **it is** for a man of quality to be ignorant of Solon in our Athens, of Lycurgus in our Sparta! Besides, law will help him to keep his own, and bestead his neighbours. Say not that there be enough who make this their

set practice: for so there are also many masters of defence by their profession; and shall private men therefore learn no skill at their weapons?

As for the hospitality, the apparel, the travelling, the company, the recreations, the marriage of gentlemen, they are described in several of the following chapters. A word or two of his behaviour in the country.

6. *He is courteous and affable to his neighbours.* As the sword of the best-tempered metal is most flexible, so the truly generous are most pliant and courteous in their behaviour to their inferiors.

7. *He delights to see himself and his servants well mounted:* therefore he loveth good horsemanship. Let never any foreign Rabshakeh send that brave to our Jerusalem, offering 'to lend her two thousand horses, if she be able for her part to set riders upon them.' We know how Darius got the Persian empire from the rest of his fellow peers, by the first neighing of his generous steed. It were no harm if in some needless suits of intricate precedency betwixt equal gentlemen, the priority were adjudged to him who keeps a stable of most serviceable horses.

8. *He furnisheth and prepareth himself in peace against time of war;* lest it be too late to learn when his skill is to be used. He approves himself courageous when brought to the trial, as well remembering the custom which is used at the creation of knights of the bath, wherein the king's master-cook cometh forth, and presenteth his great knife to the new-made knights, admonishing them to be faithful and valiant, otherwise he threatens them that that very knife is prepared to cut off their spurs.

9. *If the commission of the peace finds him out, he faithfully discharges it.* I say, finds him out, for a public office is a guest which receives the best usage from them who never invited it. And though he declined the place, the country knew to prize his worth, who would be ignorant of his own.

Fuller
1642

Fuller
1642

He compounds many **petty** differences betwixt his neighbours, which are easier ended in his **own** porch than in Westminster Hall; for many people think if once they have fetched a warrant from a justice, they have given earnest to follow the suit, though otherwise the **matter be** so mean that **the** next night's sleep would have bound both parties **to the peace, and made them as** good **friends** as ever before. Yet,

10. *He connives not at the smothering of punishable faults.* **He hates** that **practice, as** common as dangerous amongst country **people, who, having** received again the goods **which** were stolen from them, partly out **of** foolish pity, and partly **out** of covetousness to save charges in **prosecuting** the law, **let** the thief escape unpunished. Thus whilst private losses **are** repaired, the **wounds** to the commonwealth, in the breach **of** the laws, are left uncured; and thus petty larceners are encouraged into felons, **and afterwards are** hanged for pounds, because never whipped for pence, who, if they had felt the chord, had never been brought to the halter.

11. *If chosen a member of Parliament, he is willing to do his country service.* If he be no rhetorician to raise affections **(yea, Mercury was a greater** speaker than Jupiter himself), **he counts it great wisdom to be** the good manager of yea and **nay.** The slow pace of his judgment is recompensed by the swift following of his affections, when his judgment is once soundly informed. **And** here we leave him in consultation, wishing him, **with the rest of** his honourable society, all happy success.

Rev. Thomas Fuller.

A VISION OF ENGLAND

Milton
1644

NOW once again **by all** concurrence **of** signs, and by **the** general instinct of holy and devout men, as they daily and solemnly express their thoughts, God is decreeing

A VISION OF ENGLAND

to begin some new and great period in His Church, even to the reforming of reformation itself; what does He then but reveal Himself to His servants, and as His manner is, first to His Englishmen? I say, as His manner is, first to us, though we mark not the method of His counsels, and are unworthy. Behold now this vast city, a city of refuge, the mansion-house of liberty, encompassed and surrounded with His protection; the shop of war hath not there more anvils and hammers working, to fashion out the plates and instruments of armed justice in defence of beleaguered truth, than there be pens and heads there, sitting by their studious lamps, musing, searching, revolving new notions and ideas wherewith to present, as with their homage and their fealty, the approaching reformation: others as fast reading, trying all things, assenting to the force of reason and convincement.

Milton 1644

What could a man require more from a nation so pliant and so prone to seek after knowledge? What wants there to such a towardly and pregnant soil, but wise and faithful labourers, to make a knowing people, a nation of prophets, of sages, and of worthies? We reckon more than five months yet to harvest; there need not be five weeks, had we but eyes to lift up, the fields are white already. Where there is much desire to learn, there of necessity will be much arguing, much writing, many opinions; for opinion in good men is but knowledge in the making. Under these fantastic terrors of sect and schism, we wrong the earnest and zealous thirst after knowledge and understanding, which God hath stirred up in this city. What some lament of, we rather should rejoice at, should rather praise this pious forwardness among men, to reassume the ill-deputed care of their religion into their own hands again. A little generous prudence, a little forbearance of one another, and some grain of charity might win all these diligences to join and unite into one general and brotherly search after truth; could we but forego this prelatical tradition of crowding free

Milton
1644

consciences and Christian liberties into canons and precepts of men. I doubt not, if **some great and** worthy stranger should come among us, **wise** to discern the mould **and** temper of **a** people, and how **to** govern **it,** observing the high hopes and aims, the diligent alacrity of our extended thoughts and reasonings in the pursuance of truth and **freedom, but** that he would cry out as Pyrrhus did, admiring **the Roman** docility and courage : 'If such were my Epirots, **I would** not despair the greatest design **that** could **be** attempted to make a church or kingdom happy.'

Yet these are the men cried out against for schismatics **and** sectaries, as if, while the temple of the Lord was **building, some** cutting, **some** squaring the marble, others hewing the cedars, there should be a sort of irrational men, who could not consider **there** must be many schisms and many dissections made **in the** quarry and in the timber ere **the** house of God can be built. And when **every** stone is laid artfully together, it cannot be united into a continuity, **it can but** be contiguous in this world : neither can every piece **of** the building **be** of **one form ; nay,** rather the perfection **consists in this, that out of** many moderate varieties **and** brotherly dissimilitudes that **are** not vastly disproportional, arises the goodly and the graceful symmetry that commends **the whole pile** and structure.

Let us therefore **be** more considerate builders, more wise in spiritual **architecture, when** great reformation is expected. For now the time seems come, wherein Moses, the great prophet, may sit in heaven rejoicing to see that memorable and glorious wish of **his** fulfilled, when not only our seventy elders, but all the Lord's people, are become prophets. No marvel then though some men, and some good men too, perhaps, but young in goodness, as Joshua then was, envy them. They fret, **and** out of their own weakness are in agony, lest these divisions and subdivisions will undo us. The adversary **again** applauds, and waits the hour : when they have branched themselves out, saith he, small enough into parties and partitions, then will be our time. Fool! he sees not the firm root, out of which we all grow, though into branches; nor will beware, until he see our small divided maniples cutting through at every angle of his ill-united and unwieldy brigade. And that we are to hope better of all these supposed sects and schisms, and that we shall not need that solicitude, honest, perhaps, though over-timorous, of them that vex in this behalf, but shall laugh in the end at those malicious applauders of our differences, I have these reasons to persuade me.

Milton
1644

First, when a city shall be as it were besieged and blocked about, her navigable river infested, inroads and incursions round, defiance and battle oft rumoured to be marching up, even to her walls and suburb trenches; that then the people, or the greater part, more than at other times, wholly taken up with the study of highest and most important matters to be reformed, should be disputing, reasoning, reading, inventing, discoursing, even to a rarity and admiration, things not before discoursed or written of, argues first a singular good will, contentedness, and confidence in your prudent foresight and safe government, Lords and Commons; and from thence derives itself to a gallant bravery and well-grounded contempt of their enemies, as if there were no small number of as great spirits among us, as his was who, when Rome was nigh besieged by Hannibal, being in the city, bought that piece of ground at no cheap rate whereon Hannibal himself encamped his own regiment.

Next, it is a lively and cheerful presage of our happy success and victory. For as in a body when the blood is fresh, the spirits pure and vigorous, not only to vital, but to rational faculties, and those in the acutest and the pertest operations of wit and subtlety, it argues in what good plight and constitution the body is; so when the cheerfulness of the people is so sprightly up, as that it has not only where-

Milton
1644

with to guard well its own freedom and safety, but to spare, and to bestow upon the solidest and sublimest points of controversy and new invention, it betokens us not degenerated, nor drooping to a fatal decay, by casting off the old and wrinkled skin of corruption to outlive these pangs, and wax young again, entering the glorious ways of truth and prosperous virtue, destined to become great and honourable in these latter ages. Methinks I see in my mind a noble and puissant nation rousing herself like a strong man after sleep, and shaking her invincible locks: methinks I see her as an eagle mewing her mighty youth, and kindling her undazzled eyes at the full midday beam; purging and unscaling her long-abused sight at the fountain itself of heavenly radiance; while the whole noise of timorous and flocking birds, with those also that love the twilight, flutter about, amazed at what she means, and in their envious gabble would prognosticate a year of sects and schisms.

John Milton.

A KING OF FRANCE

Howel
1645

FRANCE, as all Christendom besides (for there was then a truce twixt Spain and the Hollander), was in a profound peace, and had continued so twenty years together, when Henry the Fourth fell upon some great martial design, the bottom whereof is not known to this day; and being rich (for he had heap'd up in the Bastile a mount of gold that was as high as a lance), he levy'd a huge army of 40,000 men, whence came the song, *The King of France with Forty Thousand Men*; and upon a sudden he put this army in perfect equipage, and some say he invited our Prince Henry to come unto him to be a sharer in his exploits. But going one afternoon to the Bastile, to see his treasure and ammunition, his coach stopp'd suddenly, by reason of some

A KING OF FRANCE

Howel 1645

colliers' and other carts that were in that narrow street; whereupon one Ravillac, a Lay-Jesuit (who had a whole twelve-month watch'd an opportunity to do the act), put his foot boldly upon one of the wheels of the coach, and with a long knife stretch'd himself over their shoulders who were in the boot of the coach, and reach'd the King at the end, and stabb'd him right in the left side to the heart, and pulling out the fatal steel, he doubled his thrust; the King with a ruthful voice cry'd out, '*Je suis blessé*' (I am hurt), and suddenly the blood issued out at his mouth. The regicide villain was apprehended, and command given that no violence should be offer'd him, that he might be reserved for the Law, and some exquisite torture.

The Queen grew half distracted hereupon, who had been crown'd Queen of France the day before in great triumph; but a few days after she had something to countervail, if not to overmatch, her sorrow: for according to Saint Lewis's law she was made Queen-Regent of France during the King's minority, who was then but about ten years of age.

Many consultations were held how to punish Ravillac, and there was some Italian Physicians that undertook to prescribe a torment that should last a constant torment for three days; but he scap'd only with this. His body was pull'd between four horses, that one might hear his bones crack, and after the dislocation, they were set again, and so he was carry'd in a cart, standing half naked, with a torch in that hand which had committed the murder: and in the place where the act was done, it was cut off, and a gauntlet of hot oil was clap'd upon the stump, to stanch the blood, whereat he gave a doleful shriek. Then was he brought upon a stage, where a new pair of boots was provided for him, half filled with boiling oil, then his body was pincer'd, and hot oil pour'd into the holes. In all the extremity of this torture he scarce shew'd any sense of pain; but when the gauntlet was clap'd upon his arm to stanch

Howel 1645

the flux at that time of reeking **blood, gave a** shriek only. **He** bore up against all these torments about three hours before he died: all the confession that could be drawn from him was, *That he thought he had done* **God** *good Service to take away that King which would have embroiled all Christendom in an endless* **War.**

A fatal thing it **was,** that France should have three of her **Kings** come to such violent deaths in **so short** a revolution **of time.** Henry the Second, running at tilt with Monsieur Montgomery, was kill'd by a splinter of a lance that pierc'd his eye; Henry the Third, not long after, was kill'd by a young Friar, who, in lieu of a letter which he pretended to have for him, pull'd **out of his** long sleeve a knife, and thrust him into the bottom of the belly . . . and so dispatch'd him; but **that regicide was** hack'd to pieces in the **place** by the Nobles. The same destiny attended this King by Ravillac, which is become now a common name of reproach and infamy in France.

Never was King so much lamented as this; there are a world not only **of his pictures, but** statues up and down France, and there**'s scarce** a market-town but hath **him** erected in the market-place **or** over some gate, not upon sign-posts, **as** our Henry the Eight; and by a publick Act of Parliament which was confirm'd in the Consistory at Rome, **he** was entitled Henry the Great, and so plac'd in the Temple of Immortality. A notable Prince he was, and of an admirable temper of body and mind. He had a graceful facetious way to gain both love and awe; he would be never transported beyond himself with choler, but he would pass by anything with some reparty, some witty strain, wherein he was excellent. I will instance in a few which were told me from a good hand.

One day he was charg'd by the Duke of Bouillon to have changed his religion, he answer'd: 'No, cousin, I have chang'd no Religion, but an Opinion'; and the Cardinal of

Perron being by, he enjoin'd him to write a treatise for his vindication. The Cardinal was long about the work, and when the King ask'd from time to time where his book was, he would still answer him: 'That he expected some manuscripts from Rome before he could finish it.' It happen'd, that one day the King took the Cardinal along with him to look on his workmen, and new-buildings at the Louvre; and passing by one corner which had been a long time begun, but left unfinish'd, the King ask'd the Chief Mason why that corner was not all this while perfected? 'Sir, it is because I want some choice stones.' 'No, no,' said the King, looking upon the Cardinal, 'it is because thou wantest manuscripts from Rome.' . . . Another time, when at the siege of Amiens, he having sent for the Count of Soissons (who had 100,000 franks a year pension from the Crown) to assist him in those wars, and that the Count excus'd himself by reason of his years and poverty, having exhausted himself in the former wars, and all that he could do now was to pray for his Majesty, which he would do heartily. This answer being brought to the King, he reply'd: 'Will my cousin, the Count of Soissons, do nothing else but pray for me? Tell him that Prayer without Fasting is not available; therefore I will make my cousin fast also from his pension of 100,000 per An.'

He was once troubled with a fit of the gout; and the Spanish Ambassador coming then to visit him, and saying he was sorry to see his Majesty so lame; he answer'd: 'As lame as I am, if there were occasion, your Master the King of Spain should no sooner have his foot in the stirrup but he should find me on horseback.'

By these few you may guess at the genius of this sprightfull Prince: I could make many more instances, but then I should exceed the bounds of a letter. When I am in Spain you shall hear further from me; and if you can think on anything wherein I may serve you, believe it, Sir, that any

Howel 1645

Employment from you, shall be welcome to—your most obliged Servant,

James Howel.

LUTHER AT WORMS

ON Tuesday in the Passion week, (said Luther), I was cited by the herald to appear at the Diet; he brought with him a safe-conduct from the Emperor and many other Princes, but the safe-conduct was soon broken, even the next day (Wednesday), at Worms, where I was condemned, and my books burned. Now, when I came to Erfurt, I received intelligence that I was cast and condemned at Worms, yea, and that in all cities and places thereabout it was published and spread abroad; insomuch that the herald asked me whether I meant to go to Worms or no? Although I was somewhat astonished at the news, yet I answered the herald, and said: 'Although in Worms there were as many devils as there are tiles on the houses, yet, God willing, I will go thither.'

When I came to Oppenheim, in the Palatinate, not far from Worms, Bucer came unto me, and dissuaded me from entering into the town; for, said he, Sglapion, the Emperor's confessor, had been with him, and had entreated him to warn me not to go thither, for I should be burned; but rather that I should go to a gentleman there near at hand, Francis Von Sickingen, and remain with him, who willingly would receive and entertain me. This plot the wicked wretches (said Luther) had devised against me, to the end I should not appear; for if I had contracted the time, and stayed away three days, then my safe-conduct had been expired, and then they would have locked the town-gates, and without hearing I should have been condemned and made away. But I went on in all simplicity, and when I saw the city, I wrote presently to Spalatine, and gave him notice of my coming, and desired to know where I should be lodged. Then they all wondered at my coming, which was so far from their expectation; for they verily thought I would have stayed away, as scared through their threatenings. There were two worthy gentlemen (John Von Hirschfeld and St. John Schott), who received me by the Prince Elector's command, and brought me to their lodging.

Bell 1646

No Prince came unto me, but only Earls and gentlemen, who earnestly looked upon me, and who had exhibited four hundred articles to his Imperial Majesty against those of the spirituality, and desired a redress and a removing of those their grievances, otherwise they themselves should be constrained to remedy the same; from all which grievances they are now delivered through the Gospel, which I (God be praised) have brought again to light. The Pope at that time wrote to the Emperor, that he should not perform the safe-conduct; for which end all the Bishops also pressed the Emperor; but the Princes and States of the Empire would not consent thereunto: for they alleged that a great tumult thereupon would arise. I received of them a great deal of courtesy, insomuch that the Papists were more afraid of me than I was of them. For the Landgrave of Hesse (being then but a young Prince) desired that I might be heard, and he said openly unto me, 'Sir, is your cause just and upright, then I beseech God to assist you.' Now being in Worms, I wrote to Sglapion, and desired him to make a step unto me, but he would not. Then being called, I appeared in the Senate House before the Council and State of the whole Empire, where the Emperor and the Princes Electors in person were assembled.

Then Dr. Eck (the Bishop of Trier's fiscal) began, and said unto me: 'Martin, thou art called hither to give answer whether thou acknowledgest these writings to be thy books or no?' (The books lay on a table which he showed unto

Bell
1646

me.) I answered and said: 'I believe they be mine.' But Hierome Schurfe presently thereupon said: 'Let the titles of them be read.' Now when the same were read, then I said: 'Yea, they are mine.' Then he said: 'Will you revoke them?' I answered and said: 'Most gracious Lord and Emperor, some of my books are books of controversies, wherein I touch my adversaries: some, on the contrary, are books of doctrine; the same I neither can nor will revoke. But if in case I have in my books of controversies been too violent against any man, then I am content therein to be better directed, and for that end I desire respite of time.' Then they gave me one day and one night. The next day I was cited by the Bishops and others, who were appointed to deal with me touching my revocation. Then I said: 'God's Word is not my word, therefore I know not how to give it away; but in whatsoever is therein, besides the same, I will show obedience.' Then Marquis Joachim said unto me: 'Sir Martin, so far as I understand, you are content to be instructed, excepting only what may concern the Holy Writ.' I said, 'Yea'; then they pressed me to refer the cause to His Imperial Majesty. I said I durst not presume so to do. Then they said: 'Do you not think that we are also Christians, who with all care and diligence would finish and end such causes? You ought to put so much trust and confidence in us, that we would conclude uprightly.' To that I answered and said: 'I dare not trust you so far, that you should conclude against yourselves, who even now have cast and condemned me, being under safe-conduct; yet, nevertheless, that ye may see what I will do, I will yield up into your hands my safe-conduct, and do with me what ye please.' Then all the Princes said: 'Truly, he offereth enough, if not too much.' Afterwards they said: 'Yield unto us yet in some articles.' I said: 'In God's name, such articles as concern not the Holy Scriptures I will not stand against.' Presently hereupon, two Bishops went to the Emperor, and showed him that I had revoked. Then the Emperor sent another Bishop unto me, to know if I had referred the cause to him, and to the Empire; I said, I had neither done it, nor intended so to do.

In this sort, (said Luther), did I alone resist so many, insomuch that my Doctor, and divers others of my friends, were much offended and vexed by reason of my constancy; yea, some of them said, if I had referred the articles to their consideration, they would have yielded, and given way to those articles which in the council at Costnitz had been condemned. Then came Cocleus upon me, and said: 'Sir Martin, if you will yield up your safe-conduct, then I will enter into dispute with you.' I, for my part, (said Luther), in my simplicity, would have accepted thereof. But Hieronimus Schurfe earnestly entreated me not to do the same, and in derision and scorn answered Cocleus and said: 'O brave offer, if a man were so foolish as to entertain it!'

Then came a Doctor unto me, belonging to the Marquis of Baden, essaying, with a strain of high-carried words, to move me, admonished me, and said: 'Truly, Sir Martin, you are bound to do much, and to yield for the sake of fraternal love, and to the end that peace and tranquillity among the people may be preserved, lest tumults and insurrections should be occasioned and raised. Besides, it were also greatly befitting you to show obedience to the Imperial Majesty, and diligently to beware of causing offences in the world; therefore I would advise you to revoke.' Whereupon (said Luther), I said: 'For the sake of brotherly love and amity I could and would do much, so far as it were not against the faith and honour of Christ.' When all these had made their vain assaults, then the Chancellor of Trier said unto me: 'Martin Luther, you are disobedient to the Imperial Majesty; therefore you have leave and licence to depart again with your safe-conduct.' In this sort I again departed from Worms with a great deal of gentleness and courtesy, to

Bell
1646

Bell
1646

the wondering of the whole Christian world, insomuch that the Papists wished they **had left me at home.**

Captain Henry Bell.

A PRIVATE BRAWL

Herbert
1648

I HAD not been long in London, when a violent burning fever seized upon me, which brought me almost to my death, though at last I did by slow degrees recover my health. Being thus upon my amendment, **the** Lord Lisle, afterwards **Earl of Leicester, sent me** word that Sir John Ayres intended to kill me **in my bed, and** wished me keep a guard upon my chamber and person. **The same** advertisement was confirmed by Lucy, Countess **of Bedford, and the** Lady Hoby shortly after. Hereupon I thought **fit** to entreat Sir William Herbert, now Lord Powis, to go **to Sir John** Ayres, and tell him that I marvelled much at the information given me by these great persons, and that I could not imagine **any** sufficient ground hereof; howbeit, if he had anything to say to me in a fair and noble way, I would give him the meeting **as soon as I** had got strength enough to stand upon my legs. **Sir William** hereupon brought me so ambiguous and doubtful **an** answer from him, that whatsoever he meant, he would **not** declare yet his intention, which was really, as I found afterwards, to kill me any way that he could. . . . Finding no means thus to surprise me, he sent me a letter to this effect: that he desired to meet me somewhere, and that it might so fall out as I might return quietly again. To this I replied, that if he desired to fight with me upon equal terms, I should upon assurance of the field and fair play give him meeting when he did any way specify the cause, and that I did not think fit to come to him upon any other terms, having been sufficiently informed of his plots to assassinate me.

After this, finding he could take no advantage against me, then, in a treacherous way, he resolved to assassinate me in this manner: hearing I was to come to Whitehall on horseback, with two lackeys only, he attended my coming back in a place called Scotland Yard, at the hither end of Whitehall, as you come to it from the Strand, hiding himself here with four men armed on purpose to kill me.

I took horse at Whitehall Gate, and passing by that place, he being armed with a sword and dagger, without giving me so much as the least warning, ran at me furiously, but instead of me, wounded my horse in the brisket, as far as his sword could enter for the bone. My horse hereupon starting aside, he ran him again in the shoulder, which, though it made the horse more timorous, yet gave me time to draw my sword. His men thereupon encompassed me, and wounded my horse in three places more; this made my horse kick and fling in that manner, as his men durst not come near me; which advantage I took to strike at Sir John Ayres with all my force, but he warded the blow both with his sword and dagger; instead of doing him harm, I broke my sword within a foot of the hilt. Hereupon some passenger that knew me, and observing my horse bleeding in so many places, and so many men assaulting me, and my sword broken, cried to me several times, 'Ride away, ride away;' but I, scorning a base flight upon what terms soever, instead thereof, alighted as well as I could from my horse.

I had no sooner put one foot upon the ground, but Sir John Ayres, pursuing me, made at my horse again, which the horse perceiving, pressed on me on the side I alighted, in that manner that he threw me down, so that I remained flat upon the ground, only one foot hanging in the stirrup, with that piece of a sword in my right hand. Sir John Ayres hereupon ran about the horse, and was thrusting his sword into me, when I, finding myself in this danger, did with both my arms reaching at his legs, pull them towards me, till he

Herbert 1648

fell down backwards **on his** head. One of my footmen hereupon, who was a little Shropshire boy, freed my foot out of the stirrup; the other, which was **a** great fellow, having run away as soon as he saw the first assault. This gave **me** time to get upon my legs, and to put myself in the best **posture** I could with that poor remnant of a weapon.

Sir John Ayres by this time likewise was got up, standing betwixt me and some part of Whitehall, with two men on each side of him, and his brother behind him, with at least twenty or thirty persons of his friends, or attendants of the Earl of Suffolk. Observing thus a body of men standing in opposition against me, though to speak truly I saw no swords drawn **but** by Sir John Ayres and his men, I ran violently against Sir John **Ayres**; but he knowing my sword had no **point,** held his sword and dagger over his head, as believing I could strike rather than thrust; which I no sooner perceived but I put a home thrust to the middle of his breast, that I threw him down with so much force, that his head fell first to the ground, and his heels upwards. His men hereupon assaulted me; when one, Mr. Mansel, a Glamorganshire gentleman, finding so many set against me alone, closed with one of them; a Scotch gentleman, also closing with another, took him off also. All I could well do to those two which remained was to ward their thrusts, which I did with that resolution, that I got ground upon them.

Sir John Ayres **was** now got up a third time, when I, making towards him with the intention to close, thinking that there was otherwise no safety for me, put by a thrust of his with my left hand, and so coming within him, received a stab with his dagger on my right side, which ran down my ribs **as** far as my hip, which I feeling, did with my right elbow force his hand, together with the hilt of the dagger, so near the upper part of my right side, that I made him leave hold. The dagger now sticking in me, Sir Henry Cary, afterwards **Lord** of Falkland, and Lord Deputy of Ireland, finding the dagger thus in my body, snatched it out. This while I, being closed with Sir John Ayres, hurt him on the head, and threw him down a third time, when, kneeling on the ground, and bestriding him, I struck at him as hard as I could with my piece of a sword, and wounded him in four several places, and did almost cut off his left hand. His two men this while struck at me; but it pleased God even miraculously to defend me; for when I lifted up my sword to strike at Sir John Ayres, I bore off their blows half a dozen times. His friends, now finding him in this danger, took him by the head and shoulders, and drew him from betwixt my legs, and carried him along with them through Whitehall, at the stairs whereof he took boat. Sir Herbert Croft (as he told me afterwards) met him upon the water, vomiting all the way, which I believe was caused by the violence of the first thrust I gave him. His servants, brother, and friends being now retired also, I remained master of the place and his weapons; having first wrested his dagger from him, and afterwards struck his sword out of his hand.

This being done, I retired to a friend's house in the Strand, where I sent for a surgeon, who, searching my wound on the right side, and finding it not to be mortal, cured me in the space of some ten days, during which time I received many noble visits and messages from some of the best in the kingdom. Being now fully recovered of my hurts, I desired Sir Robert Harley to go to Sir John Ayres, and tell him, that though I thought he had not so much honour left in him that I could be any way ambitious to get it, yet that I desired to see him in the field with his sword in his hand. The answer that he sent me was, that . . . he would kill me with a musket out of a window.

Lord Herbert of Cherbury.

Herbert
1648

FLODDEN FIELD

Drummond
1649

WHILEST the King stayed at Linlithgow, attending the gathering of his army, now ready to set forward, and full of cares and perplexity, in the Church of St. Michael [he] heard evensong (as then it was called). While he was at his devotion, an ancient man came in, his amber coloured locks hanging down upon his shoulders, his forehead high and inclining to baldness, his garment of **azure colour** somewhat long-girded about him with a towel or table napkin, **of a comely and reverend aspect.** Having enquired for the **King, he** intruded himself into the prease, passing thorow till he came to him; with a clownish simplicity, leaning over the Canon's **seat where the** King sat : 'Sir,' (said he), 'I am sent hither to intreat you for this time to delay your expedition, and to proceed no farther in your intended journey : for if you do, ye shall not prosper in your enterprise, nor any of your followers. I am farther charged to warn you, **if** ye be so refractory as to go forward, not to use the acquaintance, company, or counsel of women, as ye tender your honour, life, **and** estate.' After **this** warning he withdrew himself back again **into the** prease; when service was ended, the King enquired earnestly for him, but he could nowhere be found, neither could any of the standers by (of whom diverse did narrowly observe him, meaning afterwards to **have** discoursed further with him) feel or perceive how, when, **or** where he passed from them: having as it were vanished in their hands.

After his army had mustered in the Borough-moor of Edinburgh (a field then spacious and delightful by the shades of many stately and aged oaks), about the midst of the night there **is a** Proclamation heard at the Market Cross of the **town,** summoning **a great** many Burgesses, Gentlemen, **Barons,** Noblemen **to** appear within forty days before the tribunal of one Plot-cock;[1] the Provost of the town in his timber gallery having heard his own name cited, cried out that he declined that Judicatory, and appealed to the mercy of God Almighty.

Drummond 1649

Nothing was the King moved with those advertisements, thinking them scenic pieces acted by those who hated the French and favoured the English faction; being so boldly and to the life personated that they appalled and stroke with fear ordinary and vulgar judgments, as tragi-comedies of Spirits. The Earl of Angus dissuaded him from that expedition, and many of the most reverend Churchmen, but the Angel which most conjured him was Margaret, his Queen, who at that time was with child: her tears and prayers shook the strongest beams of his resolutions. She had acquainted him with the visions and affrightments of her sleep; that her chains and armlets appeared to be turned into pearls; she had seen him fall from a great precipice; she had lost one of her eyes. When he had answered these were but dreams, arising from the many thoughts and cares of the day: 'But it is no dream' (saith she) 'that ye have but one son, and him a weakling; if otherwise than well happen unto you, what a lamentable day will that be, when ye shall leave behind you, to so tender and weak a successor, under the government of a woman, for inheritance, a miserable and bloody war? It is no dream that ye are to fight a mighty people, now turned insolent by their riches at home and power abroad: that your Nobility are indigent ye know, and may be bribed to leave you in your greatest danger. What a folly, what a blindness is it to make this war yours, and to quench the fire in your neighbour's house of France, to kindle and burn up your own in Scotland! Ye have no such reason to assist the French, as ye have to keep your promises to England, and enjoy a peace at home. Though the English should make a conquest of France, will they take

[1] The Devil.

Drummond 1649

your Crown, or disinherit **their own race?** This is even as the left hand would cut off the right! Should the letters **of** the Queen of France, (a woman twice married (the first half in adultery, the last **almost** incest) whom **ye** did never nor shall ever see) prove more powerful with you, **than** the cries of your little **son, and** mine, than the tears, complaints, curses of the orphans and widows which ye are to make? If ye will go, suffer me to accompany you; it may be my countrymen prove more kind towards me than they will to you; and for my sake yield unto a peace. I hear the Queen my sister will be with the army in her husband's absence; if we shall meet, who knows what God by our means may bring to **pass?**'

The king answered all her complaints with a speedy march which he made over the Tweed: not staying till the whole **forces came to** him, which were arising and prepared. The twenty-two of August coming into England, he encamped near the Water of Twisel in Northumberland, where at Twisel-haugh he made an Act, that if any man were slain or hurt to death by the English, during the time of his abode in England, his heirs should have his ward, relief and marriage. Norham, Wark, Foord, Eatel, are taken and cast down. Amidst this hostility the Lady Foord (a noble captive) was brought **in** a pity-pleading manner, with her daughter (a maid of excellent beauty) **to** the camp. Not without the Earl of Surrey's direction, as many supposed, for they have a **vigorous** Prince and his son (though natural, by the gifts of nature and education above many lawful) to try the magic of their eloquence and beauty upon. The King delighting in their company, not only hearkeneth to the discourse of the mother, but giveth way **to** her counsel: which was, if she should **be** dismissed, to send him true and certain intelligence of what **the** English would attempt, taking her way to their camp; but in effect proved the winning of time to the Earl **of** Surrey, **and** the losing of occasion to him. Her few days' stay bred in him a kind of carelessness, sloth, procrastination and delay, a neglect and as it were a forgetfulness of his army and business: eighteen days' tarrying in England, in a territory not very fertile, had consumed much provision, the soldiers began to want necessaries, a number in the night by blind paths returned to their own country. In a short time only the Noblemen and their Vassals attended the King. These request him not to spend more time on that barren soil, but to turn their forces against Berwick, which town was of more importance than all the hamlets and poor villages of Northumberland, neither was it impregnable or difficult to be taken, the town and castle being no ways provided and furnished to endure a siege. The Courtiers move the King to continue the beleaguering of Berwick till their coming back: which would be an easy conquest, Northumberland once forraged,[1] in absence of the bravest of the English then in France.

Drummond 1649

Whilest the army languished, and the King spent time at Foord, the Earl of Surrey directeth an Herald to his camp, requiring him either to leave off the invasion of his master's country and turn back, giving satisfaction for wrongs committed, or that he would appoint a day and place wherein all differences might be ended by the sword. This challenge being advised in Council, most voices were that they should return home, and not with so small number as remained endanger the state of the whole kingdom, enough being already achieved for fame, and too much for their friendship with France; why should a few soldiers, and these already tired out by forcing of strengths, throwing down castles, be hazarded against such multitudes of the English, supplied lately, and increased with fresh auxiliaries? Thomas Howard, Admiral, a son of the Earl of Surrey, having newly brought with him to Newcastle, out of the army lying in France, five thousand men and one thousand tall seamen. If they should

[1] Forayed.

Drummond
1649

return home, the English army could not but disband, and not conveniently this year be gathered again, consisting of men levied from far and distant places. Again, if they should be engaged to come to a battle; their own country, being fields to them well known, would prove more commodious and secure to fight upon than English ground, besides the opportunity of furnishing and providing the camp with all necessaries at less charges. The French Embassador and others of his faction remonstrate to the King, what a shameful retreat he would make, if at the desire of the enemy he returned, and without the hazard of a battle, being so near unto him; that by fighting in England, he kept his own country unforraged; and consumed the provision of his enemy which at last would weaken his forces. That for contentment to both armies, Islay, a Scottish Herald, should return with Rouge-Cross, the English, and condescend upon a day, promising them the meantime tarrying and abode till the righteousness of the cause were decided in a battle.

The set and appointed day by the Heralds, in which the two armies should have joined, being come, and the English not appearing, nor any from them, the Nobility again resort to the King; show how by the flight of the enemy matters were prolonged from one day to another: the English forces daily increasing, whilest the Scottish wear away and waxed fewer; that flight should be opposed to flight; the day designed by the Heralds not being kept, it would be no reproach to them to turn home without battle, or if retiring, to fight upon their own gronnd. If this counsel pleased him not, but that he would there give them battle, the next was to study all advantages for victory, either by stratagem, or the odds and furtherance of the place of fight; where the Cheviot Hills decline towards the plainer fields arising behind them with high tops with best ordnance should be fortified; the Water of Till running deep and foordless upon the right hand, and but passable at the Bridge, the first companies of the enemy being passed, before they could be relieved and succoured by their followers, the Bridge by the artillery should be beaten down, and the army charged when they began to pass the water.

Drummond 1649

The King, impatient of counsel, answered: though their number encreased to as many more as they were, he with that remainder of his army would fight them. That advantages were to be imbraced according to the occasion of the fight without tedious deliberation: if any man was afraid he might, if he pleased, return home. A strange resolution in a Prince, who imagined every man in his army to have the same strength, courage, boldness, and resolution with himself! This answer astonished the Nobility, and since they could not persuade him to a fair retreat, but that he will fight, and that without the advantage of the Bridge, being inferior in number to the English (for they were reckoned by the scouts six and twenty thousand), they fortify themselves according to the commodity of the hill where they lay encamped with a resolution not to suffer the King to hazard his person in the battle. If victory should incline to them, their gains were but small and glory less, extending but over some few of the Nobility, and a small parcel of the body of the State of England, a number of yeomen and pressed horsemen, the flower of the Kingdom being in France. But if they were overthrown, their loss would prove uncomparable, yea, unspeakable, a martial young King either killed, taken, or put to flight; wherefore they think it fitting, not necessary, the King be pleased, with so many as either chance or election might separate with him, to be a spectator of the fortune of the day. To this the King replied, he neither wanted ability to discharge the part of a Soldier, nor wisdom to command as a General, and to outlive so many valiant countrymen would be more terrible to him than death itself. When forced to give way for his personal presence in the field, they appoint some to be arrayed in

Drummond 1649

like furniture of arms and a like guard as the King. Shadows to personate him in sundry quarters of the field, that the enemy should not set one man as their chief mark to invade, from whose death the victory and conclusion of the war might depend: and if the King should fall, the army should not lose courage, nor be brought to believe he were lost, so long as they saw a General with his coignoscance and guard present and near them to be a witness of their valour and achievements, as not long before at the battle of Fornou in Italy had been practised by the French to their King Charles the Eight.

By this time the Earl of Surrey, with the power of the North of England, was come within three miles of the place where the Scottish army was encamped; and, perceiving he could not but with great disadvantage fight them, he sendeth an Herald requiring the King to come forth of his strength to some indifferent ground, where he would be ready to encounter him. The King being forward to condescend to this request, the Lords cried out: it was madness to accept of opportunity of fighting from his enemies, and to set all at a main chance according to their appointment, it being their advantage to prolong time, and trifle with him, in whose camp there was already scarcity of victuals, which ere long might put him to such a stand, that he should not know well what to do. Neither was it likely he could be furnished from the inner parts of the country, by reason of the cumbersome ways for carriage to pass, after the falling of so great and continued rains, and the softening of the ground. That by sitting still, and committing nothing to fortune, he might have his enemy at his pleasure; if they dared assail him, at their perils be it. He lacked nothing but patience to be victorious.

The Scots keeping their trenches, the Earl essayeth to draw them out, and the ninth of September removing his camp, marcheth towards the same Hill of Flodden where they lay encamped; his vanguard with the cannon passeth the Water of Till at Twisel Bridge, the rearward going over at Mylnfoord. King James seeing them pass the waters, imagineth they meant to win a hill between his camp and them. To prevent which (setting fire to the cabanes raised of boughs of trees and reeds) he removeth to another hill, before the English could observe his motion, the smoke darkening the air between the two armies. Whilest the Scottish army was removing, the English advance to the foot of Flodden Hill, by which they have double advantage : the Scottish ordinance could not much annoy them, they marching upwards and under the level thereof; again, by their shot they might easily gall their enemies as they came downwards upon them.

The fatal hour of the battle approaching, the English draw up in good order six and twenty thousand men (some write thirty) in two battles, any of which was equal in number to the whole Scottish army. Thomas Lord Howard, Admiral, had the vant-guard, of which Sir Edmond Howard, his brother, led one of the wings, and Sir Marmaduke Constable the other; the Lords Dacres and Clifford, with Sir Edward Stanley, kept the rear: the Earl of Surrey, with Latymer Scroop [and] Sir Stephen Bull, kept the main battle. The Scots by their fewness of number not being able to order many battaillons, marshal themselves in four, three of which should enter in fight and the fourth attend for supply. The King kept the middle or main; Alexander Gordon, Earl of Huntley, had the right wing of the van; the Earls of Crawford and Montrose led the other, and some have recorded the Lord Hume. The third army was guided by Matthew, Earl of Lennox, and the Earl of Argyle, where was Mackenney and Macklean, with the fierceness of the Highlanders. Adam Hepburn, Earl of Bothwell, with his friends and the flower of the Gentry of Lothian, kept off for sudden dispatches and chances of the battle.

Drummond 1649

Drummond 1649

The Earl of Huntley, making down the hill where they encamped near the foot of **Branx** Town, encountereth that wing of the **English host which was led by** Sir Edmond Howard, which, after a furious and long fight **he** put to flight, and so **eagerly pursued** the advantage, that Sir Edmond had either **been** killed or taken, if he had **not** been rescued by Bastard **Hieron and the** Lord Dacres. **The** battaillon which the **Earls Lennox** and Argyle led (being **Highlandmen**) encouraged with this first glance of victory, loosing their ranks, abandoning all order (for ought that the French Ambassador, **La** Motte, by signs, threatenings, clamours, could do to them), break furiously upon the enemy, **and** invade him in **the** face, **of whom** they are **not only** valiantly received, **but by** Sir Edward Stanley's **traversing the hill enclosed, cut** down at their backs, and [laid] **prostrate. The middle** ward which **the King** led, with which **now the Earl of** Bothwel with the **power of** Lothian was joined, fought **it out** courageously, **body against** body, and sword **to sword.** Numbers upon either side falling, till darkness, and the black shadows of the night, forced as it were **by consent of both a retreat:** neither **of them** understanding **the fortune of the** day, and **unto whom victory appertained.**

Many **brave Scots did here** fall, esteemed to above five thousand, **of the noblest and** worthiest families **of** the kingdom: who **chose rather** to die than **outlive** their friends **and** compatriots. The King's natural son, Alexander Arch-**Bishop** of St. Andrews, the Bishop of the Isles, the Abbots **of** Inchjefray and Kill-Winny; the Earls of Crawford, Morton, **Argyle,** Lennox, Arrel, Cathness, Bothwel, Athol; the Lords Elphinstoun, Aerskin, Forbes, Ross, Lovet, Saintclare, Maxwell, with his three brothers, Simple, Borthicke; numbers **of** Gentlemen, Balgowny, Blacka-Towre, Borchard, Sir Alexander Seatoun, Mackenny, with Macklean, George, Master of Angus, and Sir William Dowglas of Glenbervy, with some **two hundred** Gentlemen of their name and Vassals were here slain. The English left few less upon the place, but most part of them being of the common sort of soldiers, and men of no great mark, compared with so many Nobles killed and a King lost, the number was not esteemed nor the loss thought anything of. . . .

Drummond 1649

This fight began September 9, about four of the clock after noon, and continued three hours, the year 1513. About the dawning of the next morning the Lord Dacres, with his horse troops, taking a view of the field, and seeing the brazen ordnance of the Scots not transported, with most part of the fallen bodies not rifled, sendeth speedy advertisement to the Howards and the pensive army; inviting all to the setting up of trophies, spoil, and transporting of their great ordnance to Berwick, amongst which were seven culverins of like size and making, called the Seven Sisters.

Divers diversely report of the fortune of the King; we without affirming anything for certain, shall only set down what Fame hath published: a false witness often of human accidents, and which many times by malignant brains is forged, and by more malignant ears received and believed. The English hold that he was killed in this battle; the Scots, that many in like arms with the like guards were killed, every one of which was held for the King. Amongst others, Alexander Lord Elphinstoun, his favourite, who had married Elizabeth Barley, one of the Dames of Honour of Queen Margaret. He was a man not unlike to the King in face and stature, and representing him in arms in the field, with the valiantest and most courageous of the army fought it out, and acting heroically his part, as a King was killed, heaps of slaughtered bodies environing his. In the search where the fight was, the number, tallness, furniture of the dead bodies being observed, their faces and wounds viewed, his body, as if it breathed yet majesty, was amidst the others selected, acknowledged for his Master's, brought to Berwick and embalmed. That it was not the body of the King, the

Drummond 1649

girdle of iron which he **ever wore,** and then was not found about him, gave some, though not certain, testimony.

Some have recorded that, the fortune of the day inclining to the English, four tall men mounted upon lusty horses, wearing upon the points of their lances, for coignoscances, streamers of straw, mounting the King on a sorrel hackney, conveyed him far from the place of fight, and that he was seen beyond the Tweed, between Kelso and Dunce. After which what became of him was uncertain. Many hold **he** was killed in the Castle of Hume, either by the intelligence between the English and the Lord Hume's kindred, or out of fear (for they were **at the** slaughter of the King's father and the most violent in that fight), or of hopes of great fortunes, which **would follow** innovations and the confusion of the State, being **men who** lived best in a troubled Commonwealth and upon the Borders. One Carr a follower of the Lord Hume's, that same night the battle was fought, thrust the Abbot of Kelso out of his Abbacy: which he never durst attempt the King being alive. Another, David Carbreath, in the time of John the Governor, vaunted that however John wronged the Humes, he was one of six who had abated the insolence of King James, and brought him to know he was a Mortal. To these is added, that the Governor John, not long hereafter, cut off the heads of the Lord Hume and his brother without any known great cause.

The common people (ever more addicted to superstition **than** verity) believed he was living, and had passed over the seas, and according to his promise visited the Holy Sepulchre in Palestine. There, for his other offences and the bearing of arms against his father, in prayers and penance he spent the remainder of his tedious days.

William Drummond of Hawthornden.

BIBLIOGRAPHY

A CHARACTER OF IRISHMEN

FROM the version of *Polychronicon Ranulphi Higden Monachi Cestrensis* (Bk. I. c. 34), edited for the Master of the Rolls by Churchill Babington (1865), after a manuscript in St. John's College Library, Cambridge, only a few years later in date than Trevisa's translation (1387).

THE COURT OF THE GREAT CHAN

Chapter 22 of *The Voiage and travaile of Sir John Maundeville, Kt. . . . Which treateth of the Way to Hierusalem; and of Marvayles of Inde, With other Ilands and countryes.* 'Now (1725) published entire from an original MS. in the Cotton Library.'

THE BATTLE OF ST. ALBANS

No. 239 of *The Paston Letters*, as reprinted by Mr. James Gairdner (London 1875). It first appeared in Vol. xx. of the *Archaeologia* (p. 519 et seq.), to which it was communicated in 1822 by Mr. Bayley, Keeper of the Records in the Tower. For the *Letters* themselves, two volumes were printed for the first time in 1787, from autographs in the possession of their editor, Mr. Fenn, of East Dereham; two more appeared in 1789; a fifth, left ready at Fenn's death, was published by Mr. Serjeant Frere in 1823. The MSS. of the first two, presented to George III., have disappeared, as have those of the two next: only the fifth remaining in MS. to attest the authenticity of the letters.

THE DOLOROUS SHIRT

From the Second Book of *The Volume entituled and Named* The Recuyell of the Hystoryes of Troye, *composed and drawen oute of dyverce bookes of Latyn into Frensshe by the right venerable persone and worshipful man* Raoul le Feure *preest and chapelayn unto the right noble, glorious, and myghty prynce, in his tyme, Phelip, duc of Bourgoyne, etc.* 1464., *And translated and drawn out of Frenssh into Englisshe by* William Caxton, *Mercer of the Cyte of London'* (1471). Our text is that of the Kelmscott edition (1893).

HOW THE MONK SAW HEAVEN

Chapters lv. and lvi., with part of Chapter lvii., of *The Revelation of the Monk of Evesham*: written (Mr. Arber thinks) not later than 1196; abridged, under date of that year, in Roger de Wendover's *Flowers of History*; and printed (c. 1482) by William de Machlinia, to whom, as responsible for the existing text, its authorship is here, for convenience's sake, assigned. Our text is that of Mr. Arber's reprint (1869) from the unique copy in the British Museum. The full title is *A meruelous reuelacion that was schewyd of almighty god by Sent Nycholas to a monk of Euyshamme yn the dayes of kyng Richard the fyrst And the yere of owre lorde, MCLXXXXVI.*

BIBLIOGRAPHY

The Adventure of the Chariot

Book XIX., Chapters 3, 4, and 5, of *Le Morte Darthur*, recreated by Sir Thomas Malory from 'certain books of French,' and printed by William Caxton at London, in 1485. Our text is that of Sir Edward Strachey's edition (1861): itself the result of a collation of the Southey-Upcott edition (1817) with the *editio princeps*.

A Mourning Remembrance

Selected from *A Mornynge Remembrance*, the funeral sermon 'compyled by the Reverent Fader in God, Johan Fisher, Bysshop of Rochester,' in honour of Margaret, Countess of Richmond, mother of Henry VII., and delivered in 1505. Printed by Wynkyn de Worde in 1509, and reprinted in 1708 by Thomas Baker, whose text is ours.

A Pageant

Number 953 of *The Paston Letters* (Gairdner, 1875) addressed (17th January 1506) by William Makefyrr to Darcy and Alyngton.

The Killing of Lord Hastings

From *The History of King Richard the Third* (*unfinished*), *written by* Master Thomas More *then one of the undersherriffs of London: about the yeare of our Lorde*, 1513. First printed in the Chronicles of Hardyng (1543) and Hall (1550); included in the folio edition of the *Works* of Sir Thomas More (1557); and reprinted *verbatim* (1883) by Dr. Lumby, whose text we follow.

Wat Tyler's Ending

From Vol. I. Chapter ccclxxxiv. of **Sir John** Froissart's *Cronycles of Englande, Fraunse, Spayne, Portugall, Scotlande, Bretaine, Flaunders, and other places adioynynge*: 'Translated out of French into our maternall Englisshe tongue, by John Bouchier, knyghte, Lord Berners: At the commandement of our most hyghe redouted soveraygne lorde Kynge Henry the VIII., Kynge of Englande, Fraunce, and Irelande, defender of the faith: and of the church of Englande and also of Irelande in earth the supreme heade.' Our text is modernised from that of the edition, in two volumes quarto, of 1812: itself a reprint of the *editio princeps* produced by Pynson in 1523-1525.

The Conquest of Britain

From the version by John Tiptoft, Earl of Worcester, of Caesar's *Commentaryes* (1530): 'Newly translated owte of laten in to Englyshe as much as concernyth thys realm of England sometyme callyd Bretayne: which is the eldest hystoryes of all other that can be found that ever wrote of thys realm of England.' It has never been reprinted. Our text is that of the copy in the King's Library.

The Image of Detraction

Excerpted from Book III. Chapter xxix. of *The Boke named The Governor devised by* Sir Thomas Elyot, Knyght (London 1531). Our text is that of Mr. H. H. S. Croft's edition of 1880.

BIBLIOGRAPHY

THE CROWNING OF ANN BOLEYN.

Addressed the 25th day of June, 1533, to Archdeacon Hawkyns; included among the Harleian MSS.; here reprinted from *The Remains of Thomas Cranmer, D.D.*, collected and arranged (London, 1833) by the Rev. Henry Jenkyns, M.A.

A ROMAN VICTORY

The Seventeenth Chapter of the Sixth Book of *The History and Croniklis of Scotland*, translated (1530-33) from the *Scotorum Historiae* (1528) of Hector Boece by John Bellenden, Archdean of Moray and Canon of Ross, and printed at Edinburgh (c. 1536), by 'Thomas Davidson, a Northlande man, born on the Water of Dee,' presently (1540) Royal Printer. Our text is modernised from that of the edition prepared by Lord Dundrennan, for W. & C. Tait, and printed by them at Edinburgh in 1821.

SEEING THE WIND

Excerpted from *Toxophilus* (1545): the text being edited from that of Mr. Arber's reprint (1868).

A CHARACTER OF LONDON

Excerpted from *A Notable Sermon of ye reverende father*, MAISTER HUGH LATIMER, *which he preached in ye Shrouds at paules churche in London on the xviii daye of Januarye. The yere of oure Lorde M.D. XLVIII:* in which year it was also published in the shape of a small black-letter quarto.

RALPH HYTHLODAYE

From *a Fruteful and pleasaunt Worke of the beste state of a publique Weale, and of the newe Yle called Utopia: written in Latine*, by Syr Thomas More, *knyght, and translated into Englyshe* by Raphe Robinson, *Citizein and Goldsmith of London*. Printed at London in 1551. Our text is that of Mr. Arber's reprint (1869) of the second edition (1556).

WOLSEY'S ARREST

From *The Life of Thomas Wolsey Cardinal Archbishop of York*, written (c. 1557) by George Cavendish, and printed, more or less incorrectly, in 1641. Our text is based on the edition issued from the Kelmscott Press in 1893, which is presented as a verbal and literal reproduction of the author's manuscript.

TWO BISHOPS

From John Foxe's *Actes and Monuments of these Latter and Perillous Dayes Touching Matters of the Church:* 'Wherein are comprehended and described the Great Persecutions and Horrible Troubles that have been wrought and practised by the Romishe Prelates, speciallye in this Realme of England and Scotlande from the year of Our Lorde a thousande unto the tyme nowe present. Gathered together and collected according to the true copies and wrytinges certificatorie as wel of the parties themselves that suffered, as also out of the Bishops Registers, which war the doers therof, by John Foxe.' 'Imprinted (1563) at London, by John Day, dwelling over Aldersgate. Cum privilegio Regie Magistatis.' Our text is that of the Townsend-Cattley edition of 1837-1842.

BIBLIOGRAPHY

A Pretty Theft

From Book IV., Chapters 19 and 20 of *The Golden Asse*, translated from the Latin of Apuleius by William Adlington. The first edition appeared in 1566; there were half-a-dozen in some seventy years; the present text is that of the edition of 1639.

An Old Man's Misadventure

From *A Caveat or Warning for Common Cursitors, vulgarly called Vagabonds*, written by Thomas Harman Esquire and printed (for William Griffith) at London, 1566-7. No copy of this first edition is known to exist: our text is modernised from the reprint, by Dr. Furnivall and Mr. Edward Viles, of the third (1667) after collation with the second and fourth of 1567 and **1573**.

An Escape

From *The Cronicles of Scotland*, by Robert Lindsay of Pitscottie. Our text is that of the edition prepared by [Sir] John Graham Dalyell, from the existing manuscripts, and published at Edinburgh, in two volumes, in 1814.

The Killing of David Beaton

From the First Book (1494-1558) of the *History of the Reformatioun of Religioun within the Realme of Scotland: Conteanyng the Maner and by What Persons the Light of Christis Evangell Hath Been Manifested unto this Realme, after that Horrible and Universall Defectioun from the Trewth which Hes Cume by the Meanes of that Romane Antichrist*. Written in 1566 —(so the late David Laing opined)—by John Knox. Printed at London, in 1586-87, by Vautrollier, and seized by order ere the impression was complete: at London in 1644, with many interpolations and falsifications, by David Buchanan; and correctly at Edinburgh in 1732 under the supervision of the Rev. Matthew Crawfurd. Our **text** is modernised from the edition prepared by the late David Laing **for** the Bannatyne Club (Edinburgh, 1846), from a manuscript of 1566, written (it is held) at Knox's dictation and annotated and corrected in Knox's own hand. The passage is given under date of Knox's death.

A Scot Abroad

From the *Autobiography and Diary*, 1556-1601, of the Rev. James Melvill (1556-1614), 'Minister of Kilrenny in Fife, and Professor of Theology in the University of St. Andrews:' first printed at Edinburgh, for the Wodrow Society, in 1842, under the care of Robert Pitcairn, F.S.A. Scot. The original of the sketch was the author's uncle, Andrew Melville (1545-1622), some time Principal of the Universities of Glasgow and St. Andrews, and finally Professor of Theology at Sedan. He returning to Edinburgh, from a student's round in France and Switzerland, 'a lyttle befor Lambes,' in 1574, the story of his *Wanderjahre* is included under that heading by the diarist.

Agincourt

From *The Chronicles of England, Scotland, and Ireland:* 'First Collected **and** Published (1577) by Raphaell Hollinshed, William Harrison, and Others:

BIBLIOGRAPHY

Now newlie augmented and continued (with manifold matters of singular note and worthie memorie) to the year 1586, by John Hooker *alias* Vowell, Gent, and others.' Save for the proper names, whose spelling is Hollinshed's own, our text is modernised from that of the edition of 1807 (London): printed, the Publishers declare, 'with the utmost Fidelity, from the best preceding Edition' with the Author's own Orthography, and with his Marginal Notes.'

THE YOUNG ALEXANDER

THE BANISHING OF CORIOLANUS

From the *Lives of the Noble Grecians and Romans*. . . . *Translated out of Plutarch's Greek into French by James Amiot*. . . . and *out of French into Englishe by Sir Thomas North*, London, 1579. Our text is that of the folio of 1657.

ENGLAND

Excerpted from *Euphues* Glasse *for Europe*, a chapter in, or appendix to, *Euphues and his England*. Our text is that of Mr. Arber's reprint (1868) from the *editio princeps* of 1580.

HOW WE CAME TO THE TOWN OF HOCHELAGA

From *A Short and Briefe Narration of the two Navigations and Discoveries of the North-weast partes called Newe France: First translated out of French into Italian by that famous learned man Gio. Bapt. Ramutius, and now turned into English by John Florio*: 'Worthy the Reading of all Venturers, Travellers, and Discoverers. Anno Domini 1580.'

A CORONATION

Excerpted from *The most solemne and magnificent coronation of Pheodor Ivanovich, Emperour of Russia*, etc., *the tenth of June, in the yeere* 1584: Seene and observed by Master Jerom Horsey, gentleman and servant to her Majesty, a man of great travell and long experience in those parts: wherewith is also joyned the course of his journey overland from Mosco to Emden.' Included by Richard Hakluyt in the first volume of his very famous *Principall Navigations, Voiages, and Discoueries of the English Nation*, London, 1599-1600. Our text is that of the edition of 1809-1811.

A FALSE WITCH

Book VII., Chapter i., of *The Discovery of Witchcraft; wherein the leud dealing of Witches and Witchmongers is notably detected, the Knaverie of Conjurers, the impiety of Inchantors, the folly of Soothsayers*. . . . London, 1584. Our text is that of Dr. Nicholson's reprint (1886).

THE FIRST LANDING IN VIRGINIA

From *The First Voyage made to the Coasts of America with two barks, wherein were Captaines M. Philip Amadas, and M. Arthur Barlowe, who discovered part of the country now called Virginia*, Anno 1584: 'Written by one of the said Captaines, and sent to Sir Walter Ralegh, Knight, at whose charge and direction the said Voyage was set forth.' First printed in Hakluyt's third volume (London, 1600). Our text is that of the reprint of 1809-11.

AN AFFAIR OF HONOUR

From Chapter vi. of *The Life of the Renowned Sir Philip Sidney*. . . . 'Written by Sir Fulke Grevile, Lord Brook, a Servant to Queen Elizabeth, and his Companion and Friend.' Printed after the text of the *editio princeps* (1652) but set here in the year of Sidney's death.

THE LAST FIGHT OF 'THE REVENGE'

From *A Report of the Truth of the fight about the Isles of Azores this last summer, betwixt* The Revenge, *One of Her Maiestie's Shippes and an Armada of the King of Spain :* Written some few weeks after the event by Sir Walter Raleigh and published the same year (1591) by William Ponsonby. Our text is based on that of Mr. Arber's reprint (1871).

GLORIANA

From the *Memoirs of His Own Life*: written some time before 1607, when the author died, by Sir James Melville, of Halbill, and for the first time accurately printed for the Bannatyne Club (Edinburgh 1827) from what is held to be the Author's own manuscript.

JOHN DAVYS THE NAVIGATOR

Excerpted from *The last Voyage of the worshipfull M. Thomas Candish, Esquire, intended for the South Sea, the Philippines and the coast of China, with 3 tall ships and two barks*: 'Written by M. John Jane, a man of good observation, imployed in the same and many other voyages.' Cavendish set out on this most disastrous expedition in 1591 ; but this story of Davys's part in it, the work of his supercargo, could not have been written till after 1593, under which date it is here presented. It first appeared in Hakluyt's fourth volume, and is here reprinted from the edition of 1809-1811. Authorities (it is to be noted) spell the Navigator's name with a *y* to distinguish him from a contemporary seaman, John Davis of Limehouse.

THE DIVINE ARETINE

From *The Unfortunate Traveller, or the Life of Jack Wilton*, 1594. Our text is modernised from the edition 'printed and issued by Charles Whittingham & Co., at the Chiswick Press, MDCCCXCII.'

DISCOVERING GUIANA

From *The Discouerie of the Large, Rich, and Beautiful Empire of Guiana, with a Relation of the Great and Golden City of Manoa (which the Spaniards call El Dorado) And the provinces of Emeria, Arromaia, Amapaia, and other countries with their riuers adioyning: Performed in the yeare* 1595 *by Sir W. Ralegh, Knight, Captaine of Her Maiestie's Guard, Ld. Warden of the Stanneries, and her Highnesse Lieutenant Generall of the Countie of Cornewall.*' Our text is that of the *editio princeps*: 'Imprinted at London by Robert Robinson, 1596.'

BIBLIOGRAPHY

THE MEN IN BUCKRAM

From Act ii., Scene 4, of *The History of Henry the Fourth; With the Battell at Shrewsburie, between the King and Lord Henry Percy, surnamed Henrie Hotspur of the North; with the Humoures conceits of Sir John Falstaffe.* 'At London, printed by P. S. for Andrew Wise, dwelling in Paules Churchyard at the sign of the Angell.' Our text is that presented by Mr. Aldis Wright in Vol. iv. of *The Works of William Shakespeare* (London, 1891), itself a revised version of that of the First Folio (1623).

A PLOT AGAINST THE THRONE

From *The First Part of the Life and Raigne of Henrie IIII, extending to the end of the first yeare of his Raigne*. Written by Sir John Hayward; published in 1599; and reprinted in 1642, which edition is here followed.

THE PASSAGE OF THE ALPS

From Book XXI. of Philemon Holland's translation of Livy's *Romane Historie*, London, 1600. Our text is that of the *editio princeps*.

JULIUS CAESAR

Excerpted from 'The Historie of Spurina,' Book II. Chapter 33, of the *Essaies Written in French by Michael Lord of Montaigne*: 'Done into English according to the Last French Edition, by John Florio, Reader of the Italian Tongue unto the Soveraigne Maiestie of Anna, Queen of England, Scotland, France, and Ireland, etc., and one of the gentlemen of her Royale Priuie Chamber.' Printed in 1603. Our text is that of the edition of 1632.

THE MOST CHRISTIAN KING

From Book VI., Chapters 8 and 12, of *The Historie of Philip de Commines, Knight, Lord of Argenton*. *Translated by* Thomas Danett, London, 1601.

TAMERLANE

Excerpted from *The Generall Historie of the Turkes from the first beginning of that Nation to the rising of the Othoman Familie* ... by Richard Knolles, London, 1603. Our text is that of the Sixth Edition, London, 1689.

TWO CHARACTERS

No. VI. of the 'Characterisms of Virtues,' and No. VIII. of the 'Characterisms of Vices,' contained in the *Characters of Virtues and Vices. In Two Books* (1608). Written by Joseph Hall, D.D., successively Bishop of Exeter and Norwich. Our text is that of the edition of Hall's *Works*, in Ten Volumes, prepared by Josiah Pratt, and published at London in 1808.

A COMPLETE GALLANT

From Chapter V. of *The Gull's Hornbook*, written by Thomas Dekker, and 'Imprinted at London for R.S., 1609.' Our text is that of Mr. Saintsbury's reprint in *Elizabethan and Jacobean Pamphlets* ('Pocket Library'), 1892.

THREE CHARACTERS

Selected from the set of 'Characters,' or 'Wittie Descriptions of the Properties of Sundry Persons,' issued (1616) with the Ninth Impression of Sir Thomas Overbury's 'poem,' *A Wife*. The first edition of that work, dated 1614, appeared a few months after Overbury's death in the September of 1613; to the second, also of 1614, there were added 'many wittie characters'—twenty-one, to speak by the card—'written by himself and other learned Gentlemen, his friends'; still more were included in subsequent editions, till in the ninth, the original of Dr. Rimbault's (1856), from which our text is modernised, the list is full eighty strong. Overbury's part in the work is, therefore, impossible to determine. But the authorship of our second excerpt, 'A Tinker' (Sixth Edition, 1615), with that of two others, 'An Apparitor' and 'An Almanack Maker,' was claimed by one J. Cocke.

THE PROVING OF ALIPIUS

Book VI., Chapters 8 and 9, of *The Confessiones of the Incompareble Doctour, S. Augustine*: Translated by Sir Tobie Mathew, and printed at London in 1620.

A WONDER FOR WISE MEN

From *The Historie of the Raigne of King Henry the Seventh*: 'Written (1621) by the Right Honourable Francis Lord Verulam, Viscount St. Alban,' and 'Printed' (at London) 'by W. Staresby, for Matthew Lownes and William Barret, 1622.' Our text is that set forth in the Sixth Volume of Spedding's edition of the *Works of Francis Bacon* (London, 1858).

STEPS IN HIS SICKNESS

Meditations, I., II., III., and IV., in *Devotions upon Emergent Occasions, and Several Steps in my Sickness, Digested into* (1) *Meditations upon our Human Conditions*; (2) *Expostulations and Debatements with God*; (3) *Prayers upon the several occasions to Him*: by John Donne, Dean of St. Paul's: London, 1624. Our text is that of Dean Alford's edition, London, 1839.

TWO PILGRIMS

I. From *The Second Voyage of John Davis with Sir Edward Michelbourne, Knight, into the East Indies, in the* Tigre, *a ship of two hundred and forty tonnes, with a pinnace called the* Tigre's Whelpe. Printed (1625) in Part I., Book 3, of *Purchas his Pilgrims*. II. From William Hore's *Discourse of his Voyage in the* Dragon *and Expedition from Surat to Achen*. Printed in Part I., Book 5, of the same collection. These adventures, dated severally 1605, and 1619, are grouped under a common date, which is that of the publication of Purchas his book.

SOME UNIVERSITY CHARACTERS.

From the first edition, 1628, of *Microcosmographie, or, A Peece of the World Discovered in Essayes and Characters*: Attributed (1624) to John Earle, M.A., Fellow of Merton College, Oxford, afterwards Dean of Westminster, 1660, Bishop of Worcester, 1662, and Bishop of Salisbury, 1663. Our text is that of Mr. Arber's reprint (1862).

BIBLIOGRAPHY 393

AN UNEQUAL COMBAT

From *The Private Memoirs of Sir Kenelm Digby: Gentleman of the Bedchamber to King Charles the First:* Written by Himself. The MS., which Digby entitled *Loose Fantasies*, was first edited in 1827 by Sir Harris Nicholas. The characters are pseudonymous: Theagenes being Sir Kenelm himself, while Leodivius is probably the son of the Countess of Bristol by her first husband, Sir John Dive, and Alexandria is certainly Madrid. The passage is quoted under date of 1629, at which year the record ceases.

THREE CHARACTERS

From the Second Edition (1635) of William Habington's *Castara*. Our text is that of Mr. Arber's reprint (1870) of the edition of 1640.

A BOUT WITH THE ADVERSARY

From the *Memoirs* of the Rev. Robert Blair (1593-1666), printed—not in their integrity—in 1754, and republished by the Wodrow Society in 1848. The passage is quoted by Sharpe, pp. 114-116, in his edition of Law's *Memorials* (Edinburgh, 1818).

A STRATAGEM

From Book III. of *Naval Tracts*, written by Sir William Monson (1569-1636), first published in Churchill's *Voyages and Travels*. Our text is that of the Third Edition (iii. 225-228): 'Printed by assignment from Messrs. Churchill for Henry Lintot and John Osborn, at the Golden Bull in Paternoster Row,' London, 1745. The extract is printed under date of Monson's death.

A COVENANTING ARMY

From Vol. I. of the *Letters and Journals* of Robert Baillie (1602-1661), Principal (1661) of the University of Glasgow. Edited by David Laing for the Bannatyne Club, and printed at Edinburgh for Robert Ogle in 1841.

'CAREY'S RAID'

From the *Memoirs of Robert Carey, Earl of Monmouth* (1559-1639), *written by Himself*. Published (1759) at London, 'from the original MS.,' with a Preface and Notes by the Earl of Orrery and Corke. Reprinted for Archibald Constable and John Murray at Edinburgh in 1808, with annotations by Walter Scott, who remarks that in his time the feat of arms depicted in our excerpt was still remembered in Liddisdale as 'Carey's Raid.' The extract is given under date of Carey's death.

A NIGHT'S ADVENTURES

From Book II., 'The Lady Cornelia,' one of the *Exemplarie Novells*, of Miguel de Cervantes Saavedra; 'Turned into English by Don Diego Puede-Ser.' London, 1640.

BIBLIOGRAPHY

TWO FAVOURITES

From the *Fragmenta Regalia* of Sir Robert Naunton (*d.* 1635) Knight, 'One of His Majesty's most Honourable Privy Council, and Master of the Court of Wards and Liveries.' Written (Mr. Arber thinks) about 1630, and first printed in 1641, under which date it is here presented. Our text is edited from that of Mr. Arber's reprint (1870) of the edition of 1653.

DISCOVERIES

Selected and arranged from Ben Jonson's *Timber, or Discoveries made upon Men and Matter, As they have Flowed out of his Daily Readings; or Had their Reflux to His Peculiar Notion of the Times*. 'Written,' says Gifford, 'for the most part subsequently to 1630,' and first printed in the folio of 1641. Our text is that presented in the Ninth Volume of Gifford's edition, London, 1816.

SIR FRANCIS DRAKE—THE TRUE GENTLEMAN

From Thomas Fuller's *Holy and Profane State*, 1642. Reprinted from Pickering's edition, 1846.

A VISION OF ENGLAND

From *Areopagitica: A Speech for the Liberty of Unlicensed Printing. To the Parliament of England*: London, 1644.

A KING OF FRANCE

Excerpted from Book I., Section I, Letter xviii., of the *Epistolae Ho-Elianae, Familiar Letters, Domestic and Foreign*, of 'James Howell, Esq.; One of the Clerks of his late Majesty's most Honourable Privy Council.' The letter, which is addressed 'To Sir James Crofts, from Paris,' is dated 12 May 1620; but, whether written then or not, it was published as late as 1645, under which year it is here presented. Our text is revised from that of Mr. Jacobs's reprint of 1891-3.

LUTHER AT WORMS

From the *Familiar Discourses of Dr. Martin Luther at his Table*: Translated from the High German (1646) by Captain Henry Bell. The text is that of the edition of 1791.

A PRIVATE BRAWL

From the *Autobiography* written by Edward Lord Herbert of Cherbury (1582-3-1648), somewhere after 1642, and printed at Strawberry Hill by Horace Walpole in 1764. Given under date of Herbert's death, from Mr. Sidney Lee's edition, 1886.

BIBLIOGRAPHY

THE BATTLE OF FLODDEN

From *The History of Scotland from the year* 1423 *until the year* 1542. *Containing the Lives and Reigns of James the I., the II., the III., the IV., the V. With several Memorials of State during the Reigns of James VI. and Charles I. By* **William Drummond of Hawthornden.** Published in 1656, with a Prefatory Introduction by Mr. Hall of Gray's Inn. 'Printed by Henry Hills for Rich. Tomlins and himself, and are to be sold at their house near Py-Corner.' The passage is given under date of Drummond's death.

Edinburgh : T. and A. CONSTABLE
Printers to Her Majesty

A LIST OF NEW BOOKS AND ANNOUNCEMENTS OF METHUEN AND COMPANY PUBLISHERS : LONDON 36 ESSEX STREET W.C.

CONTENTS

	PAGE
FORTHCOMING BOOKS,	2
POETRY,	13
GENERAL LITERATURE,	15
THEOLOGY,	17
LEADERS OF RELIGION,	18
WORKS BY S. BARING GOULD,	19
FICTION,	21
NOVEL SERIES,	24
BOOKS FOR BOYS AND GIRLS,	25
THE PEACOCK LIBRARY,	26
UNIVERSITY EXTENSION SERIES,	26
SOCIAL QUESTIONS OF TO-DAY,	28
CLASSICAL TRANSLATIONS,	29
COMMERCIAL SERIES,	29
WORKS BY A. M. M. STEDMAN, M.A.,	30
SCHOOL EXAMINATION SERIES,	32
PRIMARY CLASSICS,	32

OCTOBER 1894

OCTOBER 1894.

MESSRS. METHUEN'S ANNOUNCEMENTS

Poetry

Rudyard Kipling. BALLADS. By RUDYARD KIPLING. *Crown 8vo. Buckram.* 6s. [*May* 1895.

The announcement of a new volume of poetry from Mr. Kipling will excite wide interest. The exceptional success of 'Barrack-Room Ballads,' with which this volume will be uniform, justifies the hope that the new book too will obtain a wide popularity.

Henley. ENGLISH LYRICS. Selected and Edited by W. E. HENLEY. *Crown 8vo. Buckram.* 6s.
  Also 30 copies on hand-made paper. *Demy 8vo.* £1, 1s.
  Also 15 copies on Japanese paper. *Demy 8vo.* £2, 2s.

Few announcements will be more welcome to lovers of English verse than the one that Mr. Henley is bringing together into one book the finest lyrics in our language. Robust and original the book will certainly be, and it will be produced with the same care that made 'Lyra Heroica' delightful to the hand and eye.

"Q" THE GOLDEN POMP: A Procession of English Lyrics from Surrey to Shirley, arranged by A. T. QUILLER COUCH. *Crown 8vo. Buckram.* 6s.
  Also 40 copies on hand-made paper. *Demy 8vo.* £1, 1s.
  Also 15 copies on Japanese paper. *Demy 8vo.* £2, 2s.

Mr. Quiller Couch's taste and sympathy mark him out as a born anthologist, and out of the wealth of Elizabethan poetry he has made a book of great attraction.

Beeching. LYRA SACRA: An Anthology of Sacred Verse. Edited by H. C. BEECHING, M.A. *Crown 8vo.* **Buckram.** 6s.
  Also 25 copies on hand-made paper. 21s.

This book will appeal to a wide public. Few languages are richer in serious verse than the English, and the Editor has had some difficulty in confining his material within his limits.

Yeats. AN ANTHOLOGY OF IRISH VERSE. Edited by W. B. YEATS. *Crown 8vo.* 3s. 6d.

Illustrated Books

Baring Gould. A BOOK OF FAIRY TALES retold by S. BARING GOULD. With numerous illustrations and initial letters by ARTHUR J. GASKIN. *Crown 8vo.* 6s.

    Also 75 copies on hand-made paper. *Demy 8vo.* £1, 1s.
    Also 20 copies on Japanese paper. *Demy 8vo.* £2, 2s.

Few living writers have been more loving students of fairy and folk lore than Mr. Baring Gould, who in this book returns to the field in which he won his spurs. This volume consists of the old stories which have been dear to generations of children, and they are fully illustrated by Mr. Gaskin, whose exquisite designs for Andersen's Tales won him last year an enviable reputation.

Baring Gould. A BOOK OF NURSERY SONGS AND RHYMES. Edited by S. BARING GOULD, and illustrated by the Students of the Birmingham Art School. *Crown 8vo.* 6s.

    Also 50 copies on hand-made paper. *4to.* 21s.

A collection of old nursery songs and rhymes, including a number which are little known. The book contains some charming illustrations by the Birmingham students under the superintendence of Mr. Gaskin, and Mr. Baring Gould has added numerous notes.

Beeching. A BOOK OF CHRISTMAS VERSE. Edited by H. C. BEECHING, M.A., and Illustrated by WALTER CRANE. *Crown 8vo.* 6s.

    Also 75 copies on hand-made paper. *Demy 8vo.* £1, 1s.
    Also 20 copies on Japanese paper. *Demy 8vo.* £2, 2s.

A collection of the best verse inspired by the birth of Christ from the Middle Ages to the present day. Mr. Walter Crane has designed some beautiful illustrations. A distinction of the book is the large number of poems it contains by modern authors, a few of which are here printed for the first time.

Jane Barlow. THE BATTLE OF THE FROGS AND MICE, translated by JANE BARLOW, Author of 'Irish Idylls,' and pictured by F. D. BEDFORD. *Small 4to.* 6s. *net.*

    Also 50 copies on hand-made paper. *4to.* 21s. *net.*

This is a new version of a famous old fable. Miss Barlow, whose brilliant volume of 'Irish Idylls' has gained her a wide reputation, has told the story in spirited flowing verse, and Mr. Bedford's numerous illustrations and ornaments are as spirited as the verse they picture. The book will be one of the most beautiful and original books possible.

Devotional Books

With full-page Illustrations.

THE IMITATION OF CHRIST. By THOMAS À KEMPIS. With an Introduction by ARCHDEACON FARRAR. Illustrated by C. M. GERE. *Fcap. 8vo.* 5s.

    Also 50 copies on hand-made paper. 15s.

THE CHRISTIAN YEAR. By JOHN KEBLE. With an Introduction and Notes by W. LOCK, M.A., Sub-Warden of Keble College, Author of 'The Life of John Keble.' Illustrated by R. ANNING BELL. *Fcap. 8vo.* 5s.

    Also 50 copies on hand-made paper. 15s.

> These two volumes will be charming editions of two famous books, finely illustrated and printed in black and red. The scholarly introductions will give them an added value, and they will be beautiful to the eye, and of convenient size.

General Literature

Gibbon. THE DECLINE AND FALL OF THE ROMAN EMPIRE. By EDWARD GIBBON. A New Edition, edited with Notes and Appendices and Maps by J. B. BURY, M.A., Fellow of Trinity College, Dublin. *In seven volumes. Crown 8vo.*

> The time seems to have arrived for a new edition of Gibbon's great work—furnished with such notes and appendices as may bring it up to the standard of recent historical research. Edited by a scholar who has made this period his special study, and issued in a convenient form and at a moderate price, this edition should fill an obvious void.

Flinders Petrie. A HISTORY OF EGYPT, FROM THE EARLIEST TIMES TO THE HYKSOS. By W. M. FLINDERS PETRIE, D.C.L., Professor of Egyptology at University College. *Fully Illustrated. Crown 8vo.* 6s.

> This volume is the first of an illustrated History of Egypt in six volumes, intended both for students and for general reading and reference, and will present a complete record of what is now known, both of dated monuments and of events, from the prehistoric age down to modern times. For the earlier periods every trace of the various kings will be noticed, and all historical questions will be fully discussed. The volumes will cover the following periods:—
>
>   I. Prehistoric to Hyksos times. By Prof. Flinders Petrie. II. xviiith to xxth Dynasties. III. xxist to xxxth Dynasties. IV. The Ptolemaic Rule. V. The Roman Rule. VI. The Muhammedan Rule.
>
> The volumes will be issued separately. The first will be ready in the autumn, the Muhammedan volume early next year, and others at intervals of half a year.

Flinders Petrie. EGYPTIAN DECORATIVE ART. By W. M. FLINDERS PETRIE, D.C.L. With 120 Illustrations. *Crown 8vo.* 3s. 6d.

A book which deals with a subject which has never yet been seriously treated.

Flinders Petrie. EGYPTIAN TALES. Edited by W. M. FLINDERS PETRIE. Illustrated by TRISTRAM ELLIS. *Crown 8vo.* 3s. 6d.

A selection of the ancient tales of Egypt, edited from original sources, and of great importance as illustrating the life and society of ancient Egypt.

Southey. ENGLISH SEAMEN (Howard, Clifford, Hawkins, Drake, Cavendish). By ROBERT SOUTHEY. Edited, with an Introduction, by DAVID HANNAY. *Crown 8vo.* 6s.

This is a reprint of some excellent biographies of Elizabethan seamen, written by Southey and never republished. They are practically unknown, and they deserve, and will probably obtain, a wide popularity.

Waldstein. JOHN RUSKIN : a Study. By CHARLES WALDSTEIN, M.A., Fellow of King's College, Cambridge. With a Photogravure Portrait after Professor HERKOMER. *Post 8vo.* 5s.

Also 25 copies on Japanese paper. *Demy 8vo.* 21s.

This is a frank and fair appreciation of Mr. Ruskin's work and influence—literary and social—by an able critic, who has enough admiration to make him sympathetic, and enough discernment to make him impartial.

Henley and Whibley. A BOOK OF ENGLISH PROSE. Collected by W. E. HENLEY and CHARLES WHIBLEY. *Cr. 8vo.* 6s.

Also 40 copies on Dutch paper. 21s. *net.*

Also 15 copies on Japanese paper. 42s. *net.*

A companion book to Mr. Henley's well-known 'Lyra Heroica.' It is believed that no such collection of splendid prose has ever been brought within the compass of one volume. Each piece, whether containing a character-sketch or incident, is complete in itself. The book will be finely printed and bound.

Robbins. THE EARLY LIFE OF WILLIAM EWART GLADSTONE. By A. F. ROBBINS. *With Portraits. Crown 8vo.* 6s.

A full account of the early part of Mr. Gladstone's extraordinary career, based on much research, and containing a good deal of new matter, especially with regard to his school and college days.

Baring Gould. THE DESERTS OF SOUTH CENTRAL FRANCE. By S. BARING GOULD. With numerous Illustrations by F. D. BEDFORD, S. HUTTON, etc. *2 vols. Demy 8vo.* 32s.

This book is the first serious attempt to describe the great barren tableland that extends to the south of Limousin in the Department of Aveyron, Lot, etc., a country of dolomite cliffs, and cañons, and subterranean rivers. The region is full of prehistoric and historic interest, relics of cave-dwellers, of mediæval robbers, and of the English domination and the Hundred Years' War. The book is lavishly illustrated.

Baring Gould. A GARLAND OF COUNTRY SONG: English Folk Songs with their traditional melodies. Collected and arranged by S. BARING GOULD and H. FLEETWOOD SHEPPARD. *Royal 8vo.* 6s.

In collecting West of England airs for 'Songs of the West,' the editors came across a number of songs and airs of considerable merit, which were known throughout England and could not justly be regarded as belonging to Devon and Cornwall. Some fifty of these are now given to the world.

Oliphant. THE FRENCH RIVIERA. By Mrs. OLIPHANT and F. R. OLIPHANT. With Illustrations and Maps. *Crown 8vo.* 6s.

A volume dealing with the French Riviera from Toulon to Mentone. Without falling within the guide-book category, the book will supply some useful practical information, while occupying itself chiefly with descriptive and historical matter. A special feature will be the attention directed to those portions of the Riviera, which, though full of interest and easily accessible from many well-frequented spots, are generally left unvisited by English travellers, such as the Maures Mountains and the St. Tropez district, the country lying between Cannes, Grasse and the Var, and the magnificent valleys behind Nice. There will be several original illustrations.

George. BRITISH BATTLES. By H. B. GEORGE, M.A., Fellow of New College, Oxford. *With numerous Plans. Crown 8vo.* 6s.

This book, by a well-known authority on military history, will be an important contribution to the literature of the subject. All the great battles of English history are fully described, connecting chapters carefully treat of the changes wrought by new discoveries and developments, and the healthy spirit of patriotism is nowhere absent from the pages.

Shedlock. THE PIANOFORTE SONATA: Its Origin and Development. By J. S. SHEDLOCK. *Crown 8vo.* 5s.

This is a practical and not unduly technical account of the Sonata treated historically. It contains several novel features, and an account of various works little known to the English public.

Jenks. ENGLISH LOCAL GOVERNMENT. By E JENKS, M.A., Professor of Law at University College, Liverpool. *Crown 8vo.* 2s. 6d.

A short account of Local Government, historical and explanatory, which will appear very opportunely.

Dixon. A PRIMER OF TENNYSON. By W. M. DIXON, M.A., Professor of English Literature at Mason College. *Fcap. 8vo.* 1s. 6d.

This book consists of (1) a succinct but complete biography of Lord Tennyson; (2) an account of the volumes published by him in chronological order, dealing with the more important poems separately; (3) a concise criticism of Tennyson in his various aspects as lyrist, dramatist, and representative poet of his day; (4) a bibliography. Such a complete book on such a subject, and at such a moderate price, should find a host of readers.

Oscar Browning. THE AGE OF THE CONDOTTIERI: A Short History of Italy from 1409 to 1530. By OSCAR BROWNING, M.A., Fellow of King's College, Cambridge. *Crown 8vo.* 5s.

This book is a continuation of Mr. Browning's 'Guelphs and Ghibellines,' and the two works form a complete account of Italian history from 1250 to 1530.

Layard. RELIGION IN BOYHOOD. Notes on the Religious Training of Boys. With a Preface by J. R. ILLINGWORTH. By E. B. LAYARD, M.A. *18mo.* 1s.

Hutton. THE VACCINATION QUESTION. A Letter to the Right Hon. H. H. ASQUITH, M.P. By A. W. HUTTON, M.A. *Crown 8vo.* 1s.

Leaders of Religion

NEW VOLUMES

Crown 8vo. 3s. 6d.

LANCELOT ANDREWES, Bishop of Winchester. By R. L. OTTLEY, Principal of Pusey House, Oxford, and Fellow of Magdalen. *With Portrait.*

ST. AUGUSTINE of Canterbury. By E. L. CUTTS, D.D. *With a Portrait.*

THOMAS CHALMERS. By Mrs. OLIPHANT. *With a Portrait. Second Edition.*

JOHN KEBLE. By WALTER LOCK, Sub-Warden of Keble College. *With a Portrait. Seventh Edition.*

English Classics

Edited by W. E. HENLEY.

Messrs. Methuen propose to publish, **under** this title, a series of the masterpieces of the English tongue.

The ordinary 'cheap edition' appears to have served its purpose: the public has found out the artist-printer, and is now ready for something better fashioned. This, then, is the moment for the issue of such a series as, while well within the reach of the average buyer, shall be at once an ornament to the shelf of him that **owns, and** a delight to the eye of him that reads.

The series, of which Mr. William Ernest Henley is the general editor, will confine itself to no single period or department of literature. Poetry, fiction, drama, biography, autobiography, letters, essays—in all these fields is the material of many goodly volumes.

The books, which are designed and printed by Messrs. Constable, will be issued in two editions—

(1) A small edition, on the finest Japanese vellum, limited in most cases to 75 copies, demy 8vo, 21s. a volume nett;

(2) The popular edition on laid paper, crown 8vo, buckram, 3s. 6d. a volume.

The first six numbers are:—

THE LIFE AND OPINIONS OF TRISTRAM SHANDY. By LAWRENCE STERNE. With an Introduction by CHARLES WHIBLEY, and a Portrait. 2 vols.

THE WORKS OF WILLIAM CONGREVE. With an Introduction by G. S. STREET, and a Portrait. 2 vols.

THE LIVES OF DONNE, WOTTON, HOOKER, HERBERT, AND SANDERSON. By IZAAK WALTON. With an Introduction by VERNON BLACKBURN, **and a** Portrait.

THE ADVENTURES OF HADJI BABA OF ISPAHAN. By JAMES MORIER. With an Introduction by E. S. BROWNE, M.A.

THE POEMS OF ROBERT BURNS. With an Introduction by W. E. HENLEY, and a Portrait. 2 vols.

THE LIVES OF THE ENGLISH POETS. By SAMUEL JOHNSON, LL.D. With an Introduction by JAMES HEPBURN MILLAR, and a Portrait. 3 vols.

Classical Translations

NEW VOLUMES

Crown 8vo. Finely printed and bound in blue buckram.

LUCIAN—Six Dialogues (Nigrinus, Icaro-Menippus, The Cock, The Ship, The Parasite, The Lover of Falsehood). Translated by S. T. IRWIN, M.A., Assistant Master at Clifton; late Scholar of Exeter College, Oxford. 3s. 6d.

SOPHOCLES—Electra and Ajax. Translated by E. D. A. MORSHEAD, M.A., late Scholar of New College, Oxford; Assistant Master at Winchester. 2s. 6d.

TACITUS—Agricola and Germania. Translated by R. B. TOWNSHEND, late Scholar of Trinity College, Cambridge. 2s. 6d.

CICERO—Select Orations (Pro Milone, Pro Murena, Philippic II., In Catilinam). Translated by H. E. D. BLAKISTON, M.A., Fellow and Tutor of Trinity College, Oxford. 5s.

University Extension Series

NEW VOLUMES. Crown 8vo. 2s. 6d.

THE EARTH. An Introduction to Physiography. By EVAN SMALL, M.A. *Illustrated.*

INSECT LIFE. By F. W. THEOBALD, M.A. *Illustrated.*

Social Questions of To-day

NEW VOLUME. Crown 8vo. 2s. 6d.

WOMEN'S WORK. By LADY DILKE, MISS BULLEY, and MISS WHITLEY.

Cheaper Editions

Baring Gould. THE TRAGEDY OF THE CAESARS: The Emperors of the Julian and Claudian Lines. With numerous Illustrations from Busts, Gems, Cameos, etc. By S. BARING GOULD, Author of 'Mehalah,' etc. *Third Edition. Royal 8vo. 15s.*

'A most splendid and fascinating book on a subject of undying interest. The great feature of the book is the use the author has made of the existing portraits of the Caesars, and the admirable critical subtlety he has exhibited in dealing with this line of research. It is brilliantly written, and the illustrations are supplied on a scale of profuse magnificence.'—*Daily Chronicle.*

Clark Russell. THE LIFE OF ADMIRAL LORD COLLINGWOOD. By W. CLARK RUSSELL, Author of 'The Wreck of the Grosvenor.' With Illustrations by F. BRANGWYN. *Second Edition. 8vo. 6s.*

A most excellent and wholesome book, which we should like to see in the hands of every boy in the country.'—*St. James's Gazette.*

Fiction

Baring Gould. KITTY ALONE. By S. BARING GOULD, Author of 'Mehalah,' 'Cheap Jack Zita,' etc. 3 *vols.* *Crown 8vo.*

A romance of Devon life.

Norris. MATTHEW AUSTIN. By W. E. NORRIS, Author of 'Mdle. de Mersai,' etc. 3 *vols.* *Crown 8vo.*

A story of English social life by the well-known author of 'The Rogue.'

Parker. THE TRAIL OF THE SWORD. By GILBERT PARKER, Author of 'Pierre and his People,' etc. 2 *vols.* *Crown 8vo.*

A historical romance dealing with a stirring period in the history of Canada.

Anthony Hope. THE GOD IN THE CAR. By ANTHONY HOPE, Author of 'A Change of Air,' etc. 2 *vols.* *Crown 8vo.*

A story of modern society by the clever **author of** 'The Prisoner of Zenda.'

Mrs. Watson. THIS MAN'S DOMINION. By the Author of 'A High Little World.' 2 *vols.* *Crown 8vo.*

A story of the conflict between love and religious scruple.

Conan Doyle. ROUND THE RED LAMP. By A. CONAN DOYLE, Author of 'The White Company,' 'The Adventures of Sherlock Holmes,' etc. *Crown 8vo.* 6s.

This volume, by the well-known author of 'The Refugees,' contains the experiences of a general practitioner, round whose 'Red Lamp' cluster many dramas—some sordid, some terrible. The author makes an attempt to draw a few phases of life from the point of view of the man who lives and works behind the lamp.

Barr. IN THE MIDST OF ALARMS. By ROBERT BARR, Author of 'From Whose Bourne,' etc. *Crown 8vo.* 6s.

A story of journalism and Fenians, told with much vigour and humour.

Benson. SUBJECT TO VANITY. By MARGARET BENSON. With numerous Illustrations. *Crown 8vo.* 3s. 6d.

A volume of humorous and sympathetic sketches of animal life and home pets.

X. L. AUT DIABOLUS AUT NIHIL, and Other Stories. By X. L. *Crown 8vo.* 3s. 6d.

A collection of stories of much weird power. The title story appeared some years ago in 'Blackwood's Magazine,' and excited considerable attention. The 'Spectator' spoke of it as 'distinctly original, and in the highest degree imaginative. The conception, if self-generated, is almost as lofty as Milton's.'

Morrison. LIZERUNT, and other East End Idylls. By ARTHUR MORRISON. *Crown 8vo.* 6s.

A volume of sketches of East End life, some of which have appeared in the 'National Observer,' and have been much praised for their truth and strength and pathos.

O'Grady. THE COMING OF CURCULAIN. By STANDISH O'GRADY, Author of 'Finn and his Companions,' etc. Illustrated by MURRAY SMITH. *Crown 8vo.* 3s. 6d.

The story of the boyhood of one of the legendary heroes of Ireland.

New Editions

E. F. Benson. THE RUBICON. By E. F. BENSON, Author of 'Dodo.' *Fourth Edition. Crown 8vo. 6s.*

Mr. Benson's second novel has been, in its two volume form, almost as great a success as his first. The 'Birmingham Post' says it is '*well written, stimulating, unconventional, and, in a word, characteristic*': the 'National Observer' congratulates Mr. Benson upon '*an exceptional achievement*,' and calls the book '*a notable advance on his previous work.*'

Stanley Weyman. UNDER THE RED ROBE. By STANLEY WEYMAN, Author of 'A Gentleman of France.' With Twelve Illustrations by R. Caton Woodville. *Fourth Edition. Crown 8vo. 6s.*

A cheaper edition of a book which won instant popularity. No unfavourable review occurred, and most critics spoke in terms of enthusiastic admiration. The 'Westminster Gazette' called it '*a book of which we have read every word for the sheer pleasure of reading, and which we put down with a pang that we cannot forget it all and start again.*' The 'Daily Chronicle' said that '*every one who reads books at all must read this thrilling romance, from the first page of which to the last the breathless reader is haled along.*' It also called the book '*an inspiration of manliness and courage.*' The 'Globe' called it '*a delightful tale of chivalry and adventure, vivid and dramatic, with a wholesome modesty and reverence for the highest.*'

Baring Gould. THE QUEEN OF LOVE. By S. BARING GOULD, Author of 'Cheap Jack Zita,' etc. *Second Edition. Crown 8vo, 6s.*

'The scenery is admirable and the dramatic incidents most striking.'—*Glasgow Herald.*

'Strong, interesting, and clever.'—*Westminster Gazette.*

'You cannot put it down till you have finished it.'—*Punch.*

'Can be heartily recommended to all who care for cleanly, energetic, and interesting fiction.'—*Sussex Daily News.*

Mrs. Oliphant. THE PRODIGALS. By Mrs. OLIPHANT. *Second Edition. Crown 8vo. 3s. 6d.*

Richard Pryce. WINIFRED MOUNT. By RICHARD PRYCE. *Second Edition. Crown 8vo. 3s. 6d.*

The 'Sussex Daily News' called this book '*a delightful story*,' and said that the writing was '*uniformly bright and graceful.*' The 'Daily Telegraph' said that the author was a '*deft and elegant story-teller*,' and that the book was '*an extremely clever story, utterly untainted by pessimism or vulgarity.*'

Constance Smith. A CUMBERER OF THE GROUND. By CONSTANCE SMITH, Author of 'The Repentance of Paul Wentworth,' etc. *New Edition. Crown 8vo. 3s. 6d.*

School Books

A VOCABULARY OF LATIN IDIOMS AND PHRASES. By A. M. M. STEDMAN, M.A. 18mo. 1s.

STEPS TO GREEK. By A. M. M. STEDMAN, M.A. 18mo. 1s. 6d.

A SHORTER GREEK PRIMER OF ACCIDENCE AND SYNTAX. By A. M. M. STEDMAN, M.A. Crown 8vo. 1s. 6d.

SELECTIONS FROM THE ODYSSEY. With Introduction and Notes. By E. D. STONE, M.A., late Assistant Master at Eton. Fcap. 8vo. 2s.

THE ELEMENTS OF ELECTRICITY AND MAGNETISM. With numerous Illustrations. By R. G. STEEL, M.A., Head Master of the Technical Schools, Northampton. Crown 8vo. 4s. 6d.

THE ENGLISH CITIZEN: HIS RIGHTS AND DUTIES. By H. E. MALDEN, M.A. Crown 8vo. 1s. 6d.
A simple account of the privileges and duties of the English citizen.

INDEX POETARUM LATINORUM. By E. F. BENECKE, M.A. Crown 8vo. 4s. 6d.
A concordance to Latin Lyric Poetry.

Commercial Series

A PRIMER OF BUSINESS. By S. JACKSON, M.A. Crown 8vo. 1s. 6d.

COMMERCIAL ARITHMETIC. By F. G. TAYLOR. Crown 8vo. 1s. 6d.

New and Recent Books

Poetry

Rudyard Kipling. BARRACK-ROOM BALLADS; And Other Verses. By RUDYARD KIPLING. *Seventh Edition.* *Crown 8vo.* 6s.

A Special Presentation Edition, bound in white buckram, with extra gilt ornament. 7s. 6d.

'Mr. Kipling's verse is strong, vivid, full of character. . . . Unmistakable genius rings in every line.'—*Times.*

'The disreputable lingo of Cockayne is henceforth justified before the world; for a man of genius has taken it in hand, and has shown, beyond all cavilling, that in its way it also is a medium for literature. You are grateful, and you say to yourself, half in envy and half in admiration: "Here is a *book*; here, or one is a Dutchman, is one of the books of the year."'—*National Observer.*

'"Barrack-Room Ballads" contains some of the best work that Mr. Kipling has ever done, which is saying a good deal. "Fuzzy-Wuzzy," "Gunga Din," and "Tommy," are, in our opinion, altogether superior to anything of the kind that English literature has hitherto produced.'—*Athenæum.*

'These ballads are as wonderful in their descriptive power as they are vigorous in their dramatic force. There are few ballads in the English language more stirring than "The Ballad of East and West," worthy to stand by the Border ballads of Scott.'—*Spectator.*

'The ballads teem with imagination, they palpitate with emotion. We read them with laughter and tears; the metres throb in our pulses, the cunningly ordered words tingle with life; and if this be not poetry, what is?'—*Pall Mall Gazette.*

Henley. LYRA HEROICA: An Anthology selected from the best English Verse of the 16th, 17th, 18th, and 19th Centuries. By WILLIAM ERNEST HENLEY, Author of 'A Book of Verse,' 'Views and Reviews,' etc. *Crown 8vo. Stamped gilt buckram, gilt top, edges uncut.* 6s.

'Mr. Henley has brought to the task of selection an instinct alike for poetry and for chivalry which seems to us quite wonderfully, and even unerringly, right.'—*Guardian.*

Tomson. A SUMMER NIGHT, AND OTHER POEMS. By GRAHAM R. TOMSON. With Frontispiece by A. TOMSON. *Fcap. 8vo.* 3s. 6d.

An edition on hand-made paper, limited to 50 copies. 10s. 6d. net.

'Mrs. Tomson holds perhaps the very highest rank among poetesses of English birth. This selection will help her reputation.'—*Black and White.*

Ibsen. BRAND. A Drama by HENRIK IBSEN. Translated by WILLIAM WILSON. *Crown 8vo. Second Edition.* 3s. 6d.

> 'The greatest world-poem of the nineteenth century next to "Faust." "Brand" will have an astonishing interest for Englishmen. It is in the same set with "Agamemnon," with "Lear," with the literature that we now instinctively regard as high and holy.'—*Daily Chronicle.*

"Q." GREEN BAYS: Verses and Parodies. By "Q.," Author of 'Dead Man's Rock' etc. *Second Edition. Fcap. 8vo.* 3s. 6d.

> 'The verses display a rare and versatile gift of **parody, great command of metre,** and a very pretty turn of humour.'—*Times.*

"A. G." VERSES TO ORDER. By "A. G." *Cr. 8vo.* 2s. 6d. *net.*

> A small volume of verse by a writer whose initials are well known to Oxford men.
> 'A capital specimen of light academic poetry. These verses are very bright and engaging, easy and sufficiently witty.'—*St. James's Gazette.*

Hosken. VERSES BY THE WAY. BY J. D. HOSKEN. *Crown 8vo.* 5s.

> A small edition on hand-made paper. *Price* 12s. 6d. *net.*

> A Volume of Lyrics and Sonnets by J. D. Hosken, the Postman Poet. Q, the Author of 'The Splendid Spur,' writes a critical and biographical introduction.

Gale. CRICKET SONGS. By NORMAN GALE. *Crown 8vo. Linen.* 2s. 6d.

> Also a limited edition on hand-made paper. *Demy 8vo.* 10s. 6d. *net.*

> 'They are wrung out of the excitement of the moment, and palpitate with the spirit of the game.'—*Star.*
> 'As healthy as they are spirited, and ought to have a great success.'—*Times.*
> 'Simple, manly, and humorous. **Every cricketer should buy the book.**'—*Westminster Gazette.*
> 'Cricket has never known such a singer.'—*Cricket.*

Langbridge. BALLADS OF THE BRAVE: Poems of Chivalry, Enterprise, Courage, and Constancy, from the Earliest Times to the Present Day. Edited, with Notes, by Rev. F. LANGBRIDGE. *Crown 8vo. Buckram* 3s. 6d. **School** Edition, 2s. 6d.

> 'A very happy conception happily carried out. These "Ballads of the Brave" are intended to suit the real tastes of boys, and will suit the taste of the great majority.' —*Spectator.*   'The book is full of splendid things.'—*World.*

General Literature

Collingwood. JOHN RUSKIN: His Life and Work. By W. G. COLLINGWOOD, M.A., late Scholar of University College, Oxford, Author of the 'Art Teaching of John Ruskin,' Editor of Mr. Ruskin's Poems. *2 vols. 8vo. 32s. Second Edition.*

This important work is written by Mr. Collingwood, who has been for some years Mr. Ruskin's private secretary, and who has had unique advantages in obtaining materials for this book from Mr. Ruskin himself and from his friends. It contains a large amount of new matter, and of letters which have never been published, and is, in fact, a full and authoritative biography of Mr. Ruskin. The book contains numerous portraits of Mr. Ruskin, including a coloured one from a water-colour portrait by himself, and also 13 sketches, never before published, by Mr. Ruskin and Mr. Arthur Severn. A bibliography is added.

'No more magnificent volumes have been published for a long time. . . .'—*Times.*

'This most lovingly written and most profoundly interesting book.'—*Daily News.*

'It is long since we have had a biography with such varied delights of substance and of form. Such a book is a pleasure for the day, and a joy for ever.'—*Daily Chronicle.*

'Mr. Ruskin could not well have been more fortunate in his biographer.'—*Globe.*

'A noble monument of a noble subject. One of the most beautiful books about one of the noblest lives of our century.'—*Glasgow Herald.*

Gladstone. THE SPEECHES AND PUBLIC ADDRESSES OF THE RT. HON. W. E. GLADSTONE, M.P. With Notes and Introductions. Edited by A. W. HUTTON, M.A. (Librarian of the Gladstone Library), and H. J. COHEN, M.A. With Portraits. *8vo. Vols. IX. and X. 12s. 6d. each.*

Clark Russell. THE LIFE OF ADMIRAL LORD COLLINGWOOD. By W. CLARK RUSSELL, Author of 'The Wreck of the Grosvenor.' With Illustrations by F. BRANGWYN. *Second Edition. Crown 8vo. 6s.*

'A really good book.'—*Saturday Review.*

'A most excellent and wholesome book, which we should like to see in the hands of every boy in the country.'—*St. James's Gazette.*

Clark. THE COLLEGES OF OXFORD: Their History and their Traditions. By Members of the University. Edited by A. CLARK, M.A., Fellow and Tutor of Lincoln College. *8vo. 12s. 6d.*

'Whether the reader approaches the book as a patriotic member of a college, as an antiquary, or as a student of the organic growth of college foundation, it will amply reward his attention.'—*Times.*

'A delightful book, learned and lively.'—*Academy.*

'A work which will certainly be appealed to for many years as the standard book on the Colleges of Oxford.'—*Athenæum.*

Wells. OXFORD AND OXFORD LIFE. By Members of the University. Edited by J. WELLS, M.A., Fellow and Tutor of Wadham College. *Crown 8vo.* 3s. 6d.

This work contains an account of life at Oxford—intellectual, social, and religious—a careful estimate of necessary expenses, a review of recent changes, a statement of the present position of the University, and chapters on Women's Education, aids to study, and University Extension.

'We congratulate Mr. Wells on the production of a readable and intelligent account of Oxford as it is at the present time, written by persons who are, with hardly an exception, possessed of a close acquaintance with the system and life of the University.'—*Athenæum*.

Perrens. THE HISTORY OF FLORENCE FROM THE TIME OF THE MEDICIS TO THE FALL OF THE REPUBLIC. By **F. T.** PERRENS. Translated by HANNAH LYNCH. *In Three Volumes. Vol. I.* 8vo. 12s. 6d.

This is a translation from the French of the best history of Florence in existence. This volume covers a period of profound interest—political and literary—and is written with great vivacity.

'This is a standard book by an honest and intelligent historian, who has deserved well of his countrymen, and of all who are interested in Italian history.'—*Manchester Guardian*.

Browning. GUELPHS AND GHIBELLINES: A Short History of Mediæval Italy, A.D. 1250-1409. By OSCAR BROWNING, **Fellow** and Tutor of King's College, Cambridge. *Second Edition. Crown 8vo.* 5s.

'A very able book.'—*Westminster Gazette*.
'A vivid picture of mediæval Italy.'—***Standard***.

O'Grady. THE STORY OF IRELAND. By STANDISH O'GRADY, Author of ' Finn and his Companions.' *Cr. 8vo.* 2s. 6d.

'Novel and very fascinating history. Wonderfully alluring.'—*Cork Examiner*.
'Most delightful, most stimulating. Its racy humour, its original imaginings, its perfectly unique history, make it one of the freshest, breeziest volumes.'—*Methodist Times*.
'A survey at once graphic, acute, and quaintly written.'—*Times*.

Dixon. ENGLISH POETRY FROM BLAKE TO BROWNING. By W. M. DIXON, M.A. *Crown 8vo.* 3s. 6d.

A Popular Account of the Poetry of the Century.

'Scholarly in conception, and full of sound and suggestive criticism.'—*Times*.
'The book is remarkable for freshness of thought expressed in graceful language.'—*Manchester Examiner*.

Bowden. THE EXAMPLE OF BUDDHA: Being Quotations from Buddhist Literature for each Day in the Year. Compiled by E. M. BOWDEN. With Preface by Sir EDWIN ARNOLD. *Third Edition.* 16mo. 2s. 6d.

MESSRS. METHUEN'S LIST 17

Flinders Petrie. TELL EL AMARNA. By W. M. FLINDERS PETRIE, D.C.L. With chapters by Professor A. H. SAYCE, D.D.; F. LL. GRIFFITH, F.S.A.; and F. C. J. SPURRELL, F.G.S. With numerous coloured illustrations. *Royal 4to. 20s. net.*

Massee. A MONOGRAPH OF THE MYXOGASTRES. By GEORGE MASSEE. With 12 Coloured Plates. *Royal 8vo. 18s. net.*

'A work much in advance of any book in the language treating of this group of organisms. It is indispensable to every student of the Myxogastres. The coloured plates deserve high praise for their accuracy and execution.'—*Nature.*

Bushill. PROFIT SHARING AND THE LABOUR QUESTION. By T. W. BUSHILL, a Profit Sharing Employer. With an Introduction by SEDLEY TAYLOR, Author of 'Profit Sharing between Capital and Labour.' *Crown 8vo. 2s. 6d.*

John Beever. PRACTICAL FLY-FISHING, Founded on Nature, by JOHN BEEVER, late of the Thwaite House, Coniston. A New Edition, with a Memoir of the Author by W. G. COLLINGWOOD, M.A. Also additional Notes and a chapter on Char-Fishing, by A. and A. R. SEVERN. With a specially designed title-page. *Crown 8vo. 3s. 6d.*

A little book on Fly-Fishing by an old friend of Mr. Ruskin. It has been out of print for some time, and being still much in request, is now issued with a Memoir of the Author by W. G. Collingwood.

Theology

Driver. SERMONS ON SUBJECTS CONNECTED WITH THE OLD TESTAMENT. By S. R. DRIVER, D.D., Canon of Christ Church, Regius Professor of Hebrew in the University of Oxford. *Crown 8vo. 6s.*

'A welcome companion to the author's famous 'Introduction.' No man can read these discourses without feeling that Dr. Driver is fully alive to the deeper teaching of the Old Testament.'—*Guardian.*

Cheyne. FOUNDERS OF OLD TESTAMENT CRITICISM: Biographical, Descriptive, and Critical Studies. By T. K. CHEYNE, D.D., Oriel Professor of the Interpretation of Holy Scripture at Oxford. *Large crown 8vo. 7s. 6d.*

This important book is a historical sketch of O.T. Criticism in the form of biographical studies from the days of Eichhorn to those of Driver and Robertson Smith. It is the only book of its kind in English.

'The volume is one of great interest and value. It displays all the author's well-known ability and learning, and its opportune publication has laid all students of theology, and specially of Bible criticism, under weighty obligation.'—*Scotsman.*

A very learned and instructive work.'—*Times.*

Prior. CAMBRIDGE SERMONS. Edited by C. H. PRIOR, M.A., Fellow and Tutor of Pembroke College. *Crown 8vo.* 6s.

A volume of **sermons** preached before the University **of Cambridge** by various preachers, including the Archbishop of Canterbury and Bishop Westcott.

'A representative collection. Bishop Westcott's is a noble sermon.'—*Guardian.*

'Full of thoughtfulness and dignity.'—*Record.*

Beeching. BRADFIELD SERMONS. Sermons by H. C. BEECHING, M.A., Rector of Yattendon, Berks. With a Preface by CANON SCOTT HOLLAND. *Crown 8vo.* 2s. 6d.

Seven sermons preached before the **boys** of Bradfield College.

James. CURIOSITIES OF CHRISTIAN HISTORY PRIOR TO THE REFORMATION. By CROAKE JAMES, Author of 'Curiosities of Law and Lawyers.' *Crown 8vo.* 7s. 6d.

'This volume contains a great deal of quaint and curious matter, affording some "particulars of the interesting persons, episodes, and events from the Christian's point of view during the first fourteen centuries." Wherever we dip into his pages we find something worth dipping into.'—*John Bull.*

Kaufmann. CHARLES KINGSLEY. By M. KAUFMANN, M.A. *Crown 8vo. Buckram.* 5s.

A biography of Kingsley, especially dealing with his achievements in social reform.

'The author has certainly gone about his work with conscientiousness and industry.'—*Sheffield Daily Telegraph.*

Leaders of Religion

Edited by H. C. BEECHING, M.A. *With Portraits, crown 8vo.*

A series of short biographies of the most prominent leaders of religious life and thought of all ages and countries.

2/6 & 3/6

The following are ready— 2s. 6d.

CARDINAL NEWMAN. By R. H. HUTTON. *Second Edition.*

'Few who read this book will fail to be struck by the wonderful insight it displays into the nature of the Cardinal's genius and the spirit of his life.'—WILFRID WARD, in the *Tablet.*

'Full of knowledge, excellent in method, and **intelligent in criticism.** We regard it as wholly admirable.'—*Academy.*

JOHN WESLEY. By J. H. OVERTON, M.A.

'It is well done: the story is clearly told, proportion is duly observed, and there **is** no lack either of discrimination or of sympathy.'—*Manchester Guardian.*

BISHOP WILBERFORCE. By G. W. DANIEL, M.A.
CARDINAL MANNING. By A. W. HUTTON, M.A.
CHARLES SIMEON. By H. C. G. MOULE, M.A.

3s. 6d.

JOHN KEBLE. By WALTER LOCK, M.A. *Seventh Edition.*
THOMAS CHALMERS. By Mrs. OLIPHANT. *Second Edition.*

Other volumes will be announced in due course.

Works by S. Baring Gould

OLD COUNTRY LIFE. With Sixty-seven Illustrations by W. PARKINSON, F. D. BEDFORD, and F. MASEY. *Large Crown 8vo, cloth super extra, top edge gilt,* 10s. 6d. *Fourth and Cheaper Edition.* 6s.

'"Old Country Life," as healthy wholesome reading, full of breezy life and movement, full of quaint stories vigorously told, will not be excelled by any book to be published throughout the year. Sound, hearty, and English to the core.'—*World.*

HISTORIC ODDITIES AND STRANGE EVENTS. *Third Edition. Crown 8vo.* 6s.

'A collection of exciting and entertaining chapters. The whole volume is delightful reading.'—*Times.*

FREAKS OF FANATICISM. *Third Edition. Crown 8vo.* 6s.

'Mr. Baring Gould has a keen eye for colour and effect, and the subjects he has chosen give ample scope to his descriptive and analytic faculties. A perfectly fascinating book.'—*Scottish Leader.*

SONGS OF THE WEST: Traditional Ballads and Songs of the West of England, with their Traditional Melodies. Collected by S. BARING GOULD, M.A., and H. FLEETWOOD SHEPPARD, M.A. Arranged for Voice and Piano. In 4 Parts (containing 25 Songs each), *Parts I., II., III.,* 3s. *each. Part IV.,* 5s. *In one Vol., French morocco,* 15s.

'A rich and varied collection of humour, pathos, grace, and poetic fancy.'—*Saturday Review.*

YORKSHIRE ODDITIES AND STRANGE EVENTS. *Fourth Edition. Crown 8vo.* 6s.

STRANGE SURVIVALS AND SUPERSTITIONS. With Illustrations. By S. BARING GOULD. *Crown 8vo. Second Edition.* 6s.

A book on such subjects as Foundations, Gables, Holes, Gallows, Raising the Hat, Old Ballads, etc. etc. It traces in a most interesting manner their origin and history.

'We have read Mr. Baring Gould's book from beginning to end. It is full of quaint and various information, and there is not a dull page in it.'—*Notes and Queries.*

THE TRAGEDY OF THE CAESARS: The Emperors of the Julian and Claudian Lines. With numerous Illustrations from Busts, Gems, Cameos, etc. By S. BARING GOULD, Author of 'Mehalah,' etc. *Third Edition. Royal 8vo.* 15s.

'A most splendid and fascinating book on a subject of undying interest. The great feature of the book is the use the author has made of the existing portraits of the Caesars, and the admirable critical subtlety he has exhibited in dealing with this line of research. It is brilliantly written, and the illustrations are supplied on a scale of profuse magnificence.'—*Daily Chronicle.*

'The volumes will in no sense disappoint the general reader. Indeed, in their way, there is nothing in any sense so good in English. . . . Mr. Baring Gould has presented his narrative in such a way as not to make one dull page.'—*Athenæum.*

MR. BARING GOULD'S NOVELS

'To say that a book is by the author of "Mehalah" is to imply that it contains a story cast on strong lines, containing dramatic possibilities, vivid and sympathetic descriptions of Nature, and a wealth of ingenious imagery.'—*Speaker.*

'That whatever Mr. Baring Gould writes is well worth reading, is a conclusion that may be very generally accepted. His views of life are fresh and vigorous, his language pointed and characteristic, the incidents of which he makes use are striking and original, his characters are life-like, and though somewhat exceptional people, are drawn and coloured with artistic force. Add to this that his descriptions of scenes and scenery are painted with the loving eyes and skilled hands of a master of his art, that he is always fresh and never dull, and under such conditions it is no wonder that readers have gained confidence both in his power of amusing and satisfying them, and that year by year his popularity widens.'—*Court Circular.*

SIX SHILLINGS EACH

IN THE ROAR OF THE SEA: A Tale of the Cornish Coast.
MRS. CURGENVEN OF CURGENVEN.
CHEAP JACK ZITA.
THE QUEEN OF LOVE.

THREE SHILLINGS AND SIXPENCE EACH

ARMINELL: A Social Romance.
URITH: A Story of Dartmoor.
MARGERY OF QUETHER, and other Stories.
JACQUETTA, and other Stories.

Fiction

SIX SHILLING NOVELS

Corelli. BARABBAS: A DREAM OF THE WORLD'S TRAGEDY. By MARIE CORELLI, Author of 'A Romance of Two Worlds,' 'Vendetta,' etc. *Eleventh Edition. Crown 8vo. 6s.*

Miss Corelli's new romance has been received with much disapprobation by the secular papers, and with warm welcome by the religious papers. By the former she has been accused of blasphemy and bad taste; 'a gory nightmare'; 'a hideous travesty'; 'grotesque vulgarisation'; 'unworthy of criticism'; 'vulgar redundancy'; 'sickening details'—these are some of the secular flowers of speech. On the other hand, the 'Guardian' praises 'the dignity of its conceptions, the reserve round the Central Figure, the fine imagery of the scene and circumstance, so much that is elevating and devout'; the 'Illustrated Church News' styles the book 'reverent and artistic, broad based on the rock of our common nature, and appealing to what is best in it'; the 'Christian World' says it is written 'by one who has more than conventional reverence, who has tried to tell the story that it may be read again with open and attentive eyes'; the 'Church of England Pulpit' welcomes 'a book which teems with faith without any appearance of irreverence.'

Benson. DODO: A DETAIL OF THE DAY. By E. F. BENSON. *Crown 8vo. Fourteenth Edition. 6s.*

A story of society by a new writer, full of interest and power, which has attracted by its brilliance universal attention. The best critics were cordial in their praise. The 'Guardian' spoke of 'Dodo' as *unusually clever and interesting*; the 'Spectator' called it *a delightfully witty sketch of society*; the 'Speaker' said the dialogue was *a perpetual feast of epigram and paradox*; the 'Athenæum' spoke of the author as *a writer of quite exceptional ability*; the 'Academy' praised his *amazing cleverness*; the 'World' said the book was *brilliantly written*; and half-a-dozen papers declared there was *not a dull page in the book*.

Baring Gould. IN THE ROAR OF THE SEA: A Tale of the Cornish Coast. By S. BARING GOULD. *New Edition. 6s.*

Baring Gould. MRS. CURGENVEN OF CURGENVEN. By S. BARING GOULD. *Third Edition. 6s.*

A story of Devon life. The 'Graphic' speaks of it as *a novel of vigorous humour and sustained power*; the 'Sussex Daily News' says that *the swing of the narrative is splendid*; and the 'Speaker' mentions its *bright imaginative power*.

Baring Gould. CHEAP JACK ZITA. By S. BARING GOULD. *Third Edition. Crown 8vo. 6s.*

A Romance of the Ely Fen District in 1815, which the 'Westminster Gazette' calls 'a powerful drama of human passion'; and the 'National Observer' 'a story worthy the author.'

Baring Gould. THE QUEEN OF LOVE. By S. BARING GOULD. *Second Edition. Crown 8vo. 6s.*

The 'Glasgow Herald' says that 'the scenery is admirable, and the dramatic incidents are most striking.' The 'Westminster Gazette' calls the book 'strong, interesting, and clever.' 'Punch' says that 'you cannot put it down until you have finished it.' 'The Sussex Daily News' says that it 'can be heartily recommended to all who care for cleanly, energetic, and interesting fiction.'

Norris. HIS GRACE. By W. E. NORRIS, Author of 'Mademoiselle de Mersac.' *Third Edition. Crown 8vo.* 6s.

'The characters are delineated by the author with his characteristic skill and vivacity, and the story is told with that ease of manners and Thackerayean insight which give strength of flavour to Mr. Norris's novels No one can depict the Englishwoman of the better classes with more subtlety.'—*Glasgow Herald.*

'Mr. Norris has drawn a really fine character in the Duke of Hurstbourne, at once unconventional and very true to the conventionalities of life, weak and strong in a breath, capable of inane follies and heroic decisions, yet not so definitely portrayed as to relieve a reader of the necessity of study on his own behalf.'—*Athenæum.*

Parker. MRS. FALCHION. By GILBERT PARKER, Author of 'Pierre and His People.' *New Edition.* 6s.

Mr. Parker's second book has received a warm welcome. The 'Athenæum' called it *a splendid study of character*; the 'Pall Mall Gazette' spoke of the writing as *but little behind anything that has been done by any writer of our time*; the 'St. James's' called it *a very striking and admirable novel*; and the 'Westminster Gazette' applied to it **the epithet of** *distinguished*.

Parker. PIERRE AND HIS PEOPLE. By GILBERT PARKER. *Crown 8vo. Buckram.* 6s.

'Stories happily conceived and finely executed. There is strength and genius in Mr. Parker's style.'—*Daily Telegraph.*

Parker. THE TRANSLATION OF A SAVAGE. By GILBERT PARKER, Author of 'Pierre and His People,' 'Mrs. Falchion,' etc. *Crown 8vo.* 5s.

'The plot is original and one difficult to work out; but Mr. Parker has done it with great skill and delicacy. The reader who is not interested in this original, fresh, and well-told tale must be a dull person indeed.'—*Daily Chronicle.*

'A strong and successful piece of workmanship. The portrait of Lali, strong, dignified, and pure, is exceptionally well drawn.'—*Manchester Guardian.*

'A very **pretty and** interesting story, and Mr. Parker tells it with much skill. The **story** is one to be read.'—*St. James's Gazette.*

Anthony Hope. A CHANGE OF AIR: A Novel. By ANTHONY HOPE, Author of 'The Prisoner of Zenda,' etc. *Crown 8vo.* 6s.

A bright story by Mr. Hope, who has, the *Athenæum* says, 'a decided outlook and individuality of his own.'

'A graceful, vivacious comedy, true to human nature. The characters are traced with a masterly hand.'—*Times.*

Pryce. TIME AND THE WOMAN. By RICHARD PRYCE, Author of 'Miss Maxwell's Affections,' 'The Quiet Mrs. Fleming,' etc. New and Cheaper Edition. *Crown 8vo.* 6s.

'Mr. Pryce's work recalls the style of Octave Feuillet, by its clearness, conciseness, its literary reserve.'—*Athenæum.*

Marriott Watson. DIOGENES OF LONDON and other Sketches. By H. B. MARRIOTT WATSON, Author of 'The Web of the Spider.' *Crown 8vo. Buckram. 6s.*

'By all those who delight in the uses of words, who rate the exercise of prose above the exercise of verse, who rejoice in all proofs of its delicacy and its strength, who believe that English prose is chief among the moulds of thought, by these Mr. Marriott Watson's book will be welcomed.'—*National Observer.*

Gilchrist. THE STONE DRAGON. By MURRAY GILCHRIST. *Crown 8vo. Buckram. 6s.*

'The author's faults are atoned for by certain positive and admirable merits. The romances have not their counterpart in modern literature, and to read them is a unique experience.'—*National Observer.*

THREE-AND-SIXPENNY NOVELS

Baring Gould. ARMINELL: A Social Romance. By S. BARING GOULD. *New Edition. Crown 8vo. 3s. 6d.*

Baring Gould. URITH: A Story of Dartmoor. By S. BARING GOULD. *Third Edition. Crown 8vo. 3s. 6d.*

'The author is at his best.'—*Times.*
'He has nearly reached the high water-mark of "Mehalah."'—*National Observer.*

Baring Gould. MARGERY OF QUETHER, and other Stories. By S. BARING GOULD. *Crown 8vo. 3s. 6d.*

Baring Gould. JACQUETTA, and other Stories. By S. BARING GOULD. *Crown 8vo. 3s. 6d.*

Gray. ELSA. A Novel. By E. M'QUEEN GRAY. *Crown 8vo. 3s. 6d.*

'A charming novel. The characters are not only powerful sketches, but minutely and carefully finished portraits.'—*Guardian.*

Pearce. JACO TRELOAR. By J. H. PEARCE, Author of 'Esther Pentreath.' *New Edition. Crown 8vo. 3s. 6d.*

A tragic story of Cornish life by a writer of remarkable power, whose first novel has been highly praised by Mr. Gladstone.
The 'Spectator' speaks of Mr. Pearce as *a writer of exceptional power*; the 'Daily Telegraph' calls the book *powerful and picturesque*; the 'Birmingham Post' asserts that it is *a novel of high quality.*

Edna Lyall. DERRICK VAUGHAN, NOVELIST. By EDNA LYALL, Author of 'Donovan,' etc. *Crown 8vo. 3s. 6d.*

Clark Russell. MY DANISH SWEETHEART. By W. CLARK RUSSELL, Author of 'The Wreck of the Grosvenor,' etc. *Illustrated. Third Edition. Crown 8vo. 3s. 6d.*

Author of 'Vera.' THE DANCE OF THE HOURS. By the Author of 'Vera.' *Crown 8vo.* 3s. 6d.

Esmè Stuart. A WOMAN OF FORTY. By Esmè Stuart, Author of 'Muriel's Marriage,' 'Virginie's Husband,' etc. *New Edition. Crown 8vo.* 3s. 6d.

'The story is well written, and some of the scenes show great dramatic power.'—*Daily Chronicle.*

Fenn. THE STAR GAZERS. By G. Manville Fenn, Author of 'Eli's Children,' etc. *New Edition. Cr. 8vo.* 3s. 6d.

'A stirring romance.'—*Western Morning News.*
'Told with all the dramatic power for which Mr. Fenn is conspicuous.'—*Bradford Observer.*

Dickinson. A VICAR'S WIFE. By Evelyn Dickinson. *Crown 8vo.* 3s. 6d.

Prowse. THE POISON OF ASPS. By R. Orton Prowse. *Crown 8vo.* 3s. 6d.

Grey. THE STORY OF CHRIS. By Rowland Grey. *Crown 8vo.* 5s.

Lynn Linton. THE TRUE HISTORY OF JOSHUA DAVIDSON, Christian and Communist. By E. Lynn Linton. Eleventh Edition. *Post 8vo.* 1s.

HALF-CROWN NOVELS

A Series of Novels by popular Authors, tastefully bound in cloth.

2/6

1. THE PLAN OF CAMPAIGN. By F. Mabel Robinson.
2. DISENCHANTMENT. By F. Mabel Robinson.
3. MR. BUTLER'S WARD. By F. Mabel Robinson.
4. HOVENDEN, V.C. By F. Mabel Robinson.
5. ELI'S CHILDREN. By G. Manville Fenn.
6. A DOUBLE KNOT. By G. Manville **Fenn.**
7. DISARMED. By M. Betham Edwards.
8. A LOST ILLUSION. By Leslie Keith.
9. A MARRIAGE AT SEA. By W. Clark Russell.

10. IN TENT AND BUNGALOW. By the Author of 'Indian Idylls.'
11. MY STEWARDSHIP. By E. M'QUEEN GRAY.
12. A REVEREND GENTLEMAN. By J. M. COBBAN.
13. A DEPLORABLE AFFAIR. By W. E. NORRIS.
14. JACK'S FATHER. By W. E. NORRIS.

Other volumes will be announced in due course.

Books for Boys and Girls

Baring Gould. THE ICELANDER'S SWORD. By S. BARING GOULD, Author of 'Mehalah,' etc. With Twenty-nine Illustrations by J. MOYR SMITH. *Crown 8vo.* 6s.

A stirring story of Iceland, written for boys by the author of 'In the Roar of the Sea.'

Cuthell. TWO LITTLE CHILDREN AND CHING. By EDITH E. CUTHELL. Profusely Illustrated. *Crown 8vo. Cloth, gilt edges.* 3s. 6d.

Another story, with a dog hero, by the author of the very popular 'Only a Guard-Room Dog.'

Blake. TODDLEBEN'S HERO. By M. M. BLAKE, Author of 'The Siege of Norwich Castle.' With 36 Illustrations. *Crown 8vo.* 3s. 6d.

A story of military life for children.

Cuthell. ONLY A GUARD-ROOM DOG. By Mrs. CUTHELL. With 16 Illustrations by W. PARKINSON. *Square Crown 8vo.* 3s. 6d.

'This is a charming story. Tangle was but a little mongrel Skye terrier, but he had a big heart in his little body, and played a hero's part more than once. The book can be warmly recommended.'—*Standard.*

Collingwood. THE DOCTOR OF THE JULIET. By HARRY COLLINGWOOD, Author of 'The Pirate Island,' etc. Illustrated by GORDON BROWNE. *Crown 8vo.* 3s. 6d.

'"The Doctor of the Juliet," well illustrated by Gordon Browne, is one of Harry Collingwood's best efforts.'—*Morning Post.*

Clark Russell. MASTER ROCKAFELLAR'S VOYAGE. By W. CLARK RUSSELL, Author of 'The Wreck of the Grosvenor,' etc. Illustrated by GORDON BROWNE. *Second Edition*, Crown 8vo. 3s. 6d.

'Mr. Clark Russell's story of "Master Rockafellar's Voyage" will be among the favourites of the Christmas books. There is a rattle and "go" all through it, and its illustrations are charming in themselves, and very much above the average in the way in which they are produced.'—*Guardian.*

Manville Fenn. SYD BELTON: Or, The Boy who would not go to Sea. By G. MANVILLE FENN, Author of 'In the King's Name,' etc. Illustrated by GORDON BROWNE. *Crown 8vo.* 3s. 6d.

Who among the young story-reading public will not rejoice at the sight of the old combination, so often proved admirable—a story by Manville Fenn, illustrated by Gordon Browne? The story, too, is one of the good old sort, full of life and vigour, breeziness and fun.'—*Journal of Education.*

The Peacock Library

A Series of Books for Girls by well-known Authors, handsomely bound in blue and silver, and well illustrated. Crown 8vo. 3/6

1. A PINCH OF EXPERIENCE. By L. B. WALFORD.
2. THE RED GRANGE. By Mrs. MOLESWORTH.
3. THE SECRET OF MADAME DE MONLUC. By the Author of 'Mdle Mori.'
4. DUMPS. By Mrs. PARR, Author of 'Adam and Eve.'
5. OUT OF THE FASHION. By L. T. MEADE.
6. A GIRL OF THE PEOPLE. By L. T. MEADE.
7. HEPSY GIPSY. By L. T. MEADE. 2s. 6d.
8. THE HONOURABLE MISS. By L. T. MEADE.
9. MY LAND OF BEULAH. By Mrs. LEITH ADAMS.

University Extension Series

A series of books on historical, literary, and scientific subjects, suitable for extension students and home reading circles. Each volume is complete in itself, and the subjects are treated by competent writers in a broad and philosophic spirit.

Edited by J. E. SYMES, M.A.,
Principal of University College, Nottingham.

Crown 8vo. Price (with some exceptions) 2s. 6d.

The following volumes are ready:—

THE INDUSTRIAL HISTORY OF ENGLAND. By H. DE B. GIBBINS, M.A., late Scholar of Wadham College, Oxon., Cobden Prizeman. *Third Edition.* With Maps and Plans. 3s.

'A compact and clear story of our industrial development. A study of this concise but luminous book cannot fail to give the reader a clear insight into the principal phenomena of our industrial history. The editor and publishers are to be congratulated on this first volume of their venture, and we shall look with expectant interest for the succeeding volumes of the series.'—*University Extension Journal.*

A HISTORY OF ENGLISH POLITICAL ECONOMY. By L. L. PRICE, M.A., Fellow of Oriel College, Oxon.

PROBLEMS OF POVERTY: An Inquiry into the Industrial Conditions of the Poor. By J. A. HOBSON, M.A.

VICTORIAN POETS. By A. SHARP.

THE FRENCH REVOLUTION. By J. E. SYMES, M.A.

PSYCHOLOGY. By F. S. GRANGER, M.A., Lecturer in Philosophy at University College, Nottingham.

THE EVOLUTION OF PLANT LIFE: Lower Forms. By G. MASSEE, Kew Gardens. With Illustrations.

AIR AND WATER. Professor V. B. LEWES, M.A. Illustrated.

THE CHEMISTRY OF LIFE AND HEALTH. By C. W. KIMMINS, M.A. Camb. Illustrated.

THE MECHANICS OF DAILY LIFE. By V. P. SELLS, M.A. Illustrated.

ENGLISH SOCIAL REFORMERS. H. DE B. GIBBINS, M.A.

ENGLISH TRADE AND FINANCE IN THE SEVENTEENTH CENTURY. By W. A. S. HEWINS, B.A.

THE CHEMISTRY OF FIRE. The Elementary Principles of Chemistry. By M. M. PATTISON MUIR, M.A. Illustrated.

A TEXT-BOOK OF AGRICULTURAL BOTANY. By M. C. POTTER, M.A., F.L.S. Illustrated. 3s. 6d.

THE VAULT OF HEAVEN. A Popular Introduction to Astronomy. By R. A. GREGORY. With numerous Illustrations.

METEOROLOGY. The Elements of Weather and Climate. By H. N. DICKSON, F.R.S.E., F.R. Met. Soc. Illustrated.

A MANUAL OF ELECTRICAL SCIENCE. By GEORGE J. BURCH, M.A. With numerous Illustrations. 3s.

Social Questions of To-day

Edited by H. DE B. GIBBINS, M.A.

Crown 8vo. 2s. 6d.

2/6

A series of volumes upon those topics of social, economic, and industrial interest that are at the present moment foremost in the public mind. Each volume of the series is written by an author who is an acknowledged authority upon the subject with which he deals.

The following Volumes of the Series are ready :—

TRADE UNIONISM—NEW AND OLD. By G. HOWELL, M.P., Author of 'The Conflicts of Capital and Labour.' *Second Edition.*

THE CO-OPERATIVE MOVEMENT TO-DAY. By G. J. HOLYOAKE, Author of 'The History of Co-operation.'

MUTUAL THRIFT. By Rev. J. FROME WILKINSON, M.A., Author of 'The Friendly Society Movement.'

PROBLEMS OF POVERTY: An Inquiry into the Industrial Conditions of the Poor. By J. A. HOBSON, M.A.

THE COMMERCE OF NATIONS. By C. F. BASTABLE, M.A., Professor of Economics at Trinity College, Dublin.

THE ALIEN INVASION. By W. H. WILKINS, B.A., Secretary to the Society for Preventing the Immigration of Destitute Aliens.

THE RURAL EXODUS. By P. ANDERSON GRAHAM.

LAND NATIONALIZATION. By HAROLD COX, B.A.

A SHORTER WORKING DAY. By H. DE B. GIBBINS and R. A. HADFIELD, of the Hecla Works, Sheffield.

BACK TO THE LAND: An Inquiry into the Cure for Rural Depopulation. By H. E. MOORE.

TRUSTS, POOLS AND CORNERS: As affecting Commerce and Industry. By J. STEPHEN JEANS, M.R.I., F.S.S.
THE FACTORY SYSTEM. By R. COOKE TAYLOR.
THE STATE AND ITS CHILDREN. By GERTRUDE TUCKWELL.

Classical Translations

Edited by H. F. FOX, M.A., Fellow and Tutor of Brasenose College, Oxford.

Messrs. Methuen propose to issue a New Series of Translations from the Greek and Latin Classics. They have enlisted the services of some of the best Oxford and Cambridge Scholars, and it is their intention that the Series shall be distinguished by literary excellence as well as by scholarly accuracy.

Crown 8vo. Finely printed and bound in blue buckram.

CICERO—De Oratore I. Translated by E. N. P. MOOR, M.A., Assistant Master at Clifton. 3s. 6d.

ÆSCHYLUS—Agamemnon, Chöephoroe, Eumenides. Translated by LEWIS CAMPBELL, LL.D., late Professor of Greek at St. Andrews. 5s.

LUCIAN—Six Dialogues (Nigrinus, Icaro-Menippus, The Cock, The Ship, The Parasite, The Lover of Falsehood). Translated by S. T. IRWIN, M.A., Assistant Master at Clifton; late Scholar of Exeter College, Oxford. 3s. 6d.

SOPHOCLES—Electra and Ajax. Translated by E. D. A. MORSHEAD, M.A., late Scholar of New College, Oxford; Assistant Master at Winchester. 2s. 6d.

TACITUS—Agricola and Germania. Translated by R. B. TOWNSHEND, late Scholar of Trinity College, Cambridge. 2s. 6d.

CICERO—Select Orations (Pro Milone, Pro Murena, Philippic II., In Catilinam). Translated by H. E. D. BLAKISTON, M.A., Fellow and Tutor of Trinity College, Oxford. 5s.

Methuen's Commercial Series

BRITISH COMMERCE AND COLONIES FROM ELIZABETH TO VICTORIA. By H. DE B. GIBBINS, M.A., Author of 'The Industrial History of England,' etc., etc. 2s.

A MANUAL OF FRENCH COMMERCIAL CORRESPONDENCE. By S. E. BALLY, Modern Language Master at the Manchester Grammar School. 2*s.*

COMMERCIAL GEOGRAPHY, with special reference to Trade Routes, New Markets, and Manufacturing Districts. By L. D. LYDE, M.A., of The Academy, Glasgow. 2*s.*

COMMERCIAL EXAMINATION PAPERS. By H. DE B. GIBBINS, M.A. 1*s.* 6*d.*

THE ECONOMICS OF COMMERCE. By H. DE B. GIBBINS, M.A. 1*s.* 6*d.*

A PRIMER OF BUSINESS. By S. JACKSON, M.A. 1*s.* 6*d.*

COMMERCIAL ARITHMETIC. By F. G. TAYLOR, M.A. 1*s.* 6*d.*

Works by A. M. M. Stedman, M.A.

INITIA LATINA : Easy Lessons on Elementary Accidence. *Second Edition. Fcap. 8vo.* 1*s.*

FIRST LATIN LESSONS. *Fourth Edition Crown 8vo.* 2*s.*

FIRST LATIN READER. With Notes adapted to the Shorter Latin Primer and Vocabulary. *Second Edition. Crown 8vo.* 1*s.* 6*d.*

EASY SELECTIONS FROM CAESAR. Part I. The Helvetian War. 18*mo.* 1*s.*

EASY SELECTIONS FROM LIVY. Part I. The Kings of Rome. 18*mo.* 1*s.* 6*d.*

EASY LATIN PASSAGES FOR UNSEEN TRANSLATION. *Third Edition. Fcap. 8vo.* 1*s.* 6*d.*

EXEMPLA LATINA : First Exercises in Latin Accidence. With Vocabulary. *Crown 8vo.* 1*s.*

EASY LATIN EXERCISES ON THE SYNTAX OF THE SHORTER AND REVISED LATIN PRIMER. With Vocabulary. *Fourth Edition. Crown 8vo.* 2*s.* 6*d.* Issued with the consent of Dr. Kennedy.

THE LATIN COMPOUND SENTENCE RULES AND EXERCISES. *Crown 8vo.* 2*s.* With Vocabulary. 2*s.* 6*d.*

NOTANDA QUAEDAM: Miscellaneous Latin Exercises on Common Rules and Idioms. With Vocabulary. *Second Edition. Fcap.* 8*vo.* 1*s.* 6*d.*

LATIN VOCABULARIES FOR REPETITION: Arranged according to Subjects. *Fourth Edition. Fcap.* 8*vo.* 1*s.* 6*d.*

A VOCABULARY OF LATIN IDIOMS AND PHRASES. 18*mo.* 1*s.*

LATIN EXAMINATION PAPERS IN MISCELLANEOUS GRAMMAR AND IDIOMS. *Fourth Edition.*
A KEY, issued to Tutors and Private Students only, to be had on application to the Publishers. *Second Edition. Crown* 8*vo.* 6*s.*

STEPS TO GREEK. 18*mo.* 1*s.* 6*d.*

EASY GREEK PASSAGES FOR UNSEEN TRANSLATION. *Fcap.* 8*vo.* 1*s.* 6*d.*

EASY GREEK EXERCISES ON ELEMENTARY SYNTAX.
[*In preparation.*

GREEK VOCABULARIES FOR REPETITION: Arranged according to Subjects. *Second Edition. Fcap.* 8*vo.* 1*s.* 6*d.*

GREEK TESTAMENT SELECTIONS. For the use of Schools. *Third Edition.* With Introduction, Notes, and Vocabulary. *Fcap.* 8*vo.* 2*s.* 6*d.*

GREEK EXAMINATION PAPERS IN MISCELLANEOUS GRAMMAR AND IDIOMS. *Third Edition.* KEY (issued as above). 6*s.*

STEPS TO FRENCH. 18*mo.* 8*d.*

FIRST FRENCH LESSONS. *Crown* 8*vo.* 1*s.*

EASY FRENCH PASSAGES FOR UNSEEN TRANSLATION. *Second Edition. Fcap.* 8*vo.* 1*s.* 6*d.*

EASY FRENCH EXERCISES ON ELEMENTARY SYNTAX. With Vocabulary. *Crown* 8*vo.* 2*s.* 6*d.*

FRENCH VOCABULARIES FOR REPETITION: Arranged according to Subjects. *Third Edition. Fcap.* 8*vo.* 1*s.*

FRENCH EXAMINATION PAPERS IN MISCELLANEOUS GRAMMAR AND IDIOMS. *Seventh Edition. Crown* 8*vo.* 2*s.* 6*d.* KEY (issued as above). 6*s.*

GENERAL KNOWLEDGE EXAMINATION PAPERS. *Second Edition. Crown* 8*vo.* 2*s.* 6*d.* KEY (issued as above). 7*s.*

School Examination Series

Edited by A. M. M. STEDMAN, M.A. *Crown 8vo.* 2s. 6d.

FRENCH EXAMINATION PAPERS IN MISCELLANEOUS GRAMMAR AND IDIOMS. By A. M. M. STEDMAN, M.A. *Sixth Edition.*

    A KEY, issued to Tutors and Private Students only, to be had on application to the Publishers. *Second Edition. Crown 8vo.* 6s.

LATIN EXAMINATION PAPERS IN MISCELLANEOUS GRAMMAR AND IDIOMS. By A. M. M. STEDMAN, M.A. *Fourth Edition.* KEY (issued as above). 6s.

GREEK EXAMINATION PAPERS IN MISCELLANEOUS GRAMMAR AND IDIOMS. By A. M. M. STEDMAN, M.A. *Third Edition.* KEY (issued as above). 6s.

GERMAN EXAMINATION PAPERS IN MISCELLANEOUS GRAMMAR AND IDIOMS. By R. J. MORICH, Manchester. *Third Edition.* KEY (issued as above). 6s.

HISTORY AND GEOGRAPHY EXAMINATION PAPERS. By C. H. SPENCE, M.A., Clifton College.

SCIENCE EXAMINATION PAPERS. By R. E. STEEL, M.A., F.C.S., Chief Natural Science Master Bradford Grammar School. *In three vols. Part I.*, Chemistry ; *Part II.*, Physics.

GENERAL KNOWLEDGE EXAMINATION PAPERS. By A. M. M. STEDMAN, M.A. *Second Edition.* KEY (issued as above). 7s.

Primary Classics

With Introductions, Notes, and Vocabularies. 18mo. 1s. and 1s. 6d.

FIRST LATIN READER. By A. M. M. STEDMAN, M.A. 1s. 6d.

EASY SELECTIONS FROM CAESAR—THE HELVETIAN WAR. Edited by A. M. M. STEDMAN, M.A. 1s.

EASY SELECTIONS FROM LIVY—THE KINGS OF ROME. Edited by A. M. M. STEDMAN, M.A. 1s. 6d.

EASY SELECTIONS FROM HERODOTUS—THE PERSIAN WARS. Edited by A. G. LIDDELL, M.A. 1s. 6d.